Contents

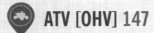

Official Partners:  ABORIGINAL TOURISM ASSOCIATION OF BC our story, your experience ATV/BC BCFROA BCParks BCWF BC WILDLIFE FEDERATION

I

Acknowledgements

backroadmapbooks.com

#106- 1500 Hartley Ave,
Coquitlam, BC, V3K 7A1
Toll Free: 1-877-520-5670
E-mail: info@backroadmapbooks.com

DIRECTORS Russell Mussio, Wesley Mussio
VICE PRESIDENT Chris Taylor
EDITOR-IN-CHIEF Russell Mussio

GIS & CARTOGRAPHY TEAM
MANAGER Andrew Allen
GIS SPECIALISTS Farah Aghdam, Courtney Fry
Dave Mancini
CARTOGRAPHERS Aaron Dixon, Oliver Herz,
Matthew Steblyna, Dale Tober

MARKETING & CREATIVE SERVICES
MANAGER Nazli Faghihi
GRAPHIC DESIGN Elisa Codazzi, Farnaz Faghihi,
Nicole Larsen
CONTENT WRITERS Sean Anderson, Linda Aksomitis,
Leslie Bryant-McLean,
Kaan Eraslan, Trent Ernst,
Fernanda Fukamati, Jay Hoare,
Colin Hughes, Mike Manyk
SALES Basilio Bagnato,
Marshall Mackinder, Chris Taylor
ADMINISTRATION Shaun Filipenko, Jo-ana Maki

COVER PHOTO
LOCATION 83 Mile Creek, Cariboo, BC
PHOTOGRAPHER(S) Michael Wheatley

Library and Archives Canada Cataloguing in Publication

Hoare, Jay, 1981-

Backroad mapbook, Cariboo Chilcotin Coast, B.C.
[cartographic material] / Jay Hoare. -- 4th ed.

Spiral binding. Includes index.

ISBN 978-1-926806-35-8

1. Recreation areas--British Columbia--Cariboo Region--Maps.
2. Recreation areas--British Columbia--Central Coast--Maps.
3. Outdoor recreation--British Columbia--Cariboo Region--Guidebooks.
4. Outdoor recreation--British Columbia--Central Coast--Guidebooks.
5. Cariboo Region (B.C.)--Maps. 6. Central Coast (B.C.)--Maps.
7. Cariboo Region (B.C.)--Guidebooks. 8. Central Coast (B.C.)--Guidebooks.
I. Mussio Ventures Ltd II. Title. III. Title: Cariboo Chilcotin Coast, BC.

G1172.C37E63H63 2012   796.509711'75   C2012-904793-7

Copyright © 2015 Mussio Ventures Ltd.

All materials contained within this Mapbook are the property of the publisher and may not be
reproduced in whole or in part without the expressed written consent of the publishers.
Printed in Canada

Acknowledgements

We want to thank the many, many people who have helped over the years and with this updated edition; notably, the dedicated and talented people at Mussio Ventures Ltd. This is a hat off to the talented research and writing team of Leslie Bryant-Mclean, Lorne Collicutt, Kaan Eraslan, Fernanda Fukamati, Jay Hoare, Colin Hughes and Mike Manyk who spent countless hours digging up new places to visit and recreate at. This coupled with the previous work of Trent Ernst, Brian Harris, Jason Marleau and others before has created a wealth of information only found in this book. We also want to thank the many mappers, graphics, marketing and sales and technical support people in our growing company. Thank you Farah Aghdam, Andrew Allen, Basilio Bagnato, Aaron Dixon, Farnaz Faghihi, Nazli Faghihi, Graeme Fay, Shaun Filipenko, Courtney Fry, Oliver Herz, Nicole Larsen, Marshall Mackinder, Jo-ana Maki, David Mancini, Matthew Steblyna, Chris Taylor, and Dale Tober for putting together the most comprehensive guidebook available for the area many call the final frontier!

As always, we could not have done this edition of the book without the help that was provided to us by various folks who live, work, and play in this area. In particular we would like to thank the Cariboo Chilcotin Coast Tourism Association (CCTA). We also would like to thank Douglas Baker from Tourism Bella Coola, Katie Lemire of BC Parks, John Massier Director Area C Cariboo Regional District in Wells as well as Marie Fournier-Beck and Allison MacDonald from Squamish - Lillooet Regional District.

Thanks also to all of our readers who have provided updates and/or tracks and waypoints in our track sharing program with the Backroad GPS Maps. With so much information being moved to the internet, we find we are not talking to as many people as we used to, but to all those who provide that information, thank you for sharing. Although the names are many, we would like to note a few of the people who have provided more than their fair share of updates. Thanks again Mike Baker, Douglas Erickson, Arnold Grimm, Ryan Klassen, Steve McAbee, Vincent Pigeon and Fred Swirp. If you do find errors or omissions or would just like to see a more accurate trail or road, please send your note or tracks to updates@backroadmapbooks.com.

These maps are a synthesis of a variety of sources, mostly Federal, Provincial and Municipal Government. We would like to express our gratitude to the helpful map providers © Department of Natural Resources Canada. Also, the maps contains information licensed under the Open Government License – British Columbia.

Finally we would like to thank Allison, Devon, Jasper, Nancy, Madison and Penny Mussio for their continued support of the Backroad Mapbook Series. As our family grows, it is becoming more and more challenging to break away from it all to explore our beautiful country.

Sincerely,

Russell & Wesley Mussio

Disclaimer

Backroad Mapbooks does not warrant that the backroads, paddling routes and trails indicated in this Mapbook are passable nor does it claim that the Mapbook is completely accurate. Therefore, please be careful when using this or any source to plan and carry out your outdoor recreation activity.

Please note that traveling on logging roads, river routes and trails is inherently dangerous, and without limiting the generality of the foregoing, you may encounter poor road conditions, unexpected traffic, poor visibility, and low or no road/trail maintenance. Please use extreme caution when traveling logging roads and trails.

Please refer to the Fishing and Hunting Regulations for closures and restrictions. It is your responsibility to know when and where closures and restrictions apply.

Help Us Help You

A comprehensive resource such as Backroad Mapbooks for Cariboo Chilcotin Coast BC could not be put together without a great deal of help and support. Despite our best efforts to ensure that everything is accurate, errors do occur. If you see any errors or omissions, please continue to let us know.   All updates will be posted on our web site.

Please contact us at:

Backroad Mapbooks
#106- 1500 Hartley Ave, Coquitlam, BC, V3K 7A1
P: 604-521-6277 | F: 604-521-6260 | Toll Free 1-877-520-5670
Email: updates@backroadmapbooks.com
Website: www.backroadmapbooks.com

  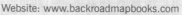

Introduction
Cariboo Chilcotin Coast BC

Welcome to the fourth edition of the Cariboo Chilcotin Coast BC Backroad Mapbook!

We are happy to bring you the most comprehensive guide to one of British Columbia's final frontiers: the Cariboo Chilcotin Coast. This lush region hides swaths of untapped wilderness just waiting to be discovered. From remote forest regions far from any roads, to preserved pieces of land untouched by human development, the area is a veritable playground for the outdoor enthusiast.

Begin your travels along Highway 20, which bisects the rolling plateau of the Chilcotin and provides a lifeline for small communities out west. Branching off the highway, you will find a few main arteries leading past remote parks and lakes and eventually petering out near the mountains or major river crossings. The main highway will take you right through the heart of Tweedsmuir Provincial Park into the central coast region, where rugged terrain and towering, glacial mountains bring the phrase 'Beautiful British Columbia' to life.

Bella Coola, one of the region's major centres, marks the end of Highway 20. The only means of continuing on is by boat or float plane. Before the community of Bella Coola, the continent fragments, splits and ends in a smattering of relatively untouched islands and islets. Few people inhabit the region, with only a handful of small settlements cropping up, including Bella Bella, the largest community at a mere 1,200 people. The Hakai Area boasts a number of fishing lodges nestled amidst the mostly wild and remote archipelago. This area is a paradise for kayakers and boaters, who spend summers exploring the many channels, bays, inlets and islets that make up the rugged west coast.

As you continue, get onto Highway 97 to the east of the Fraser River, where the main centres are linked. Explore 100 Mile House, Williams Lake and Quesnel for their long and rich histories. Take Highway 97 along the famous gold rush trail that birthed a massive economy centuries ago. Visitors still come in search of gold – but the prize sought now is the area's boast-worthy fish. Anglers from across the continent seek out the wild rainbow trout of central BC lakes. The Interlakes Highway (24), will lead you through an angler's haven, with the Bridge and Sheridan lakes and a number of pothole trout hot spots spouting an abundance of fish.

Hikers, mountain bikers, horseback riders and paddlers will find a lifetime worth of trails and routes to discover and play on. The region is home to the world-famous Bowron Lakes Canoe Route, as well as other less busy and equally remote routes. The Cariboo Chilcotin is rich with history, thanks to the historical trade routes that were used for thousands of years.

Your *Cariboo Chilcotin Coast BC Backroad Mapbook* equips you with all you need to explore the vast and bountiful lands of this part of the province. For the armchair traveler, it transports you to remote and wild terrains just waiting for you to visit. So sit back – or get going – and enjoy the ride.

Waterfall at Bowron Lake Provincial Park, BC

BACKROAD HISTORY

The Backroad Mapbook idea came into existence when Wesley and Russell Mussio were out exploring. They had several books and a few maps to try to find their way through the maze of logging roads around southern BC. The brothers were getting very frustrated trying to find their way and eventually gave up. Not to be outdone, the two ambitious brothers started brainstorming. Eventually the Backroad Mapbook idea was born.

They published their first book in January 1994 and it quickly sold out. Rather than simply reprinting it, they listened to the feedback of customers and made several alterations that helped improve the book. This formula of continuing to make the product better continues today and has helped establish the Backroad Mapbook series as the top selling outdoor recreation guidebook series in the country. From the tiny beginnings in that Vancouver apartment with maps strewn all over the walls, to one of the most sought-after outdoor products in the country, the Backroad Mapbook series has truly come a long way.

RESOURCE ROADS ARE PLANNED AND CONSTRUCTED TO DEVELOP AND PROTECT BC'S NATURAL RESOURCES; WHILE PRIMARILY USED BY FORESTRY, AGRICULTURE, MINING, AND OIL AND GAS THEY ALSO PROVIDE ACCESS TO RECREATIONAL OPPORTUNITIES.

WHAT TO EXPECT

Resource roads are gravel or dirt and they may be single lane with sharp turns, soft shoulders, narrow bridges, poor alignment and grades steeper than on highways. Not all hazards will be marked and there might not be protective barriers at dangerous or steep sections; roadside brush may limit visibility.

APPLY THE SAME RULES OF THE ROAD AS USED ON HIGHWAYS

Drive on the right hand side. Wear your seatbelt. Don't drink and drive. Take your license and insurance. Obey the speed limit — unless posted otherwise, it's up to 80 km/hr. but many roads are designed and built for 60 km/hr. or less.

DRIVE ACCORDING TO ROAD CONDITIONS

Travel a speed that allows you to stop within half of your line of sight (other vehicles need room to stop too). If dusty or slippery, slow down so you can react to oncoming traffic, potholes, wildlife, changing road conditions and unexpected hazards; large industrial vehicles can't manoeuver as quickly as passenger vehicles.

FOCUS ON YOUR DRIVING; EXERCISE CAUTION, PATIENCE AND COURTESY

Keep your headlights and taillights on. Industrial drivers are familiar with the road; let them go ahead and give them room to do their job. It might be advantageous for you to follow industrial vehicles, watch for brake lights and make sure you find a turn out when they do (to clear oncoming traffic).

OBSERVE AND OBEY THE SIGNS

Signs communicate information about the road, traffic you can expect, active worksites or hazardous conditions; take time to read and understand signs at the start of the road and along the way.

STOP IN THE RIGHT SPOT

If you must stop along the road find a pull out or straight section that provides good visibility from both directions and is wide enough for traffic to pass. Pull over onto the shoulder; avoid stopping in a curve or on the crest of a hill.

BE PREPARED

Plan your trip before you go! Beware of road conditions and traffic; share trip information with a reliable contact, bring a map and GPS. Carry extra clothing, footwear, food, water and fuel. Have an emergency first aid kit. Make sure your vehicle is ready for the trip — good tires, a spare, chains in winter, tools including a shovel and a fire extinguisher.

BC Forest
Safety Council
1-877-741-1060
VINBC.CA

KEEP AN EYE OUT FOR THE **VIN** PROGRAM

◯ **BC Forest Safety**
Unsafe is Unacceptable

REPORT A CONCERN OR
COMPLIMENT ABOUT A VEHICLE
AT 1 877 741 1060
OR VINBC.CA

GET ANSWERS TO YOUR TRAVEL QUESTIONS!

- ❖ What to see
- ❖ What to do
- ❖ How to get there
- ❖ Transportation
- ❖ Accommodations
- ❖ Tours
- ❖ Attractions
- ❖ Special Events
- ❖ ...and more

BRITISH COLUMBIA

Lillooet

Located in Coastal Mountains with hot dry summers and mild winters. Boundless natural beauty for the outdoor enthusiasts. Don't forget to visit the Museum.

(Seasonal April to October)

Lillooet Visitor Centre
790 Main St
Lillooet, BC V0K 1V0
250-256-4308 Phone

www.lillooetbc.ca

See Map 60

McBride

Robson Valley is an outdoor recreation paradise for backcountry hiking, ATV, snowmobiling, skiing, trail rides, boating on the Fraser, and wildlife viewing.

(Year Round)

McBride Visitor Centre
1000- 1st Ave
McBride, BC V0J 2E0
250-569-3366 Phone
866-569-3366 Toll-free

www.visitmcbride.ca

See Map 59

Quesnel

Visit the Museum, see the amazing "hoodoos" at Pinnacles Provincial Park. Enjoy the Riverfront Trail. World Class fly fishing and canoeing as well as many other recreational activities to explore. Come and enjoy some true North Cariboo hospitality.

(Year Round)

Quesnel Visitor Centre
703 Carson Ave
Quesnel, BC V2J 2B6
250-992-8716 Phone
800-992-4922 Toll-free

www.quesnelchamber.com

See Map 42

South Cariboo

100's of clean clear lakes, miles of multi-use trails, wildlife, birding, gold rush history, log home industry, tours, guest ranches, resorts and RV parks.

(Year Round)

100 Mile House Visitor Centre
155 Airport Rd
100 Mile House, BC V0K 2E0
250-395-5353 Phone
877-511-5353 Toll-free

www.southcaribootourism.ca

See Map 18

Wells

Wells, an arts and outdoor adventure community is the Gateway to the Historic town of Barkerville and the amazing Bowron Lakes canoe circuit.

(Seasonal May to September)

Wells Visitor Centre
11900 Barkerville Hwy
Wells, BC V0K 2R0
250-994-2323 Phone
877-451-9355 Toll-free

www.wellsbc.com

See Map 57

Williams Lake

Western Heritage and the Williams Lake Stampede, Thousands of fishing spots and tons of outdoor recreation, Thriving Arts & Culture, Gateway to the Chilcotin Coast

(Year Round)

Williams Lake Visitor Centre
1660 Broadway Ave South
Williams Lake, BC V2G 2V8
250-392-5025 Phone
877-967-5253 Toll-free

www.williamslakechamber.com

See Map 29

Legend

Line and Area Classifications:

Freeways	Trans Canada Trail
Highways	Long Distance Trail
Secondary Highways	Snowmobile Trails
Arterial Paved Roads	Motorized Trails ATV/OHV/Snowmobile
Rural Paved Roads	Developed Trail
Local Paved Roads	Routes (Undeveloped Trails)
Forest Service / Main Industry Roads	Portage Route
Active Industry Roads (2wd)	Ferry Routes
Other Industry Roads (2wd / 4wd)	Lake / River Paddling Routes
Unclassified / 4wd Roads	Powerlines
Deactivated Roads	Pipelines
Railways	WMU - Wildlife Management Zones
Cut / Seismic Lines	

Scale Bar

Scale 1:250 000   1 Centimetre = 2.5 Kilometres

2.5km   0km   4km   8km   12km

Map Information

Elevation Bar:

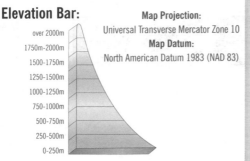

over 2000m
1750m-2000m
1500-1750m
1250-1500m
1000-1250m
750-1000m
500-750m
250-500m
0-250m

Map Projection:
Universal Transverse Mercator Zone 10

Map Datum:
North American Datum 1983 (NAD 83)

Recreational Activities:

ATV / Motorbiking	Golf Course
Boat Launch	Fish Hatchery
Beach	Fish Spawning / Ladder
BRMB Geocache	Hiking
Campsite / Limited Facilities	Horseback Riding
BC Recreation Site (Camping)	Interpretive Trail
RV Campsite / Trailer Park	Paddling (canoe-kayak)
BC Recreation Site (Camping-RV)	Picnic Site
Campsite (back country / water access only)	Portage
Canoe Access Put-in / Take-out	Portage Distance (P2100m)
Caving / Spelunking	Rock Climbing
Cross Country Skiing / Back Country Ski Touring	Snowmobiling
Cycling	Snowshoeing
Diving	Trailhead
Downhill Skiing	Wildlife Viewing

Area Indicators:

National / Provincial / Regional Parks	City
Recreation Sites	First Nations
Conservation / Protected Area / Ecological Reserve	Glaciers
Motorized Closures / Restricted Area	Water
	Swamps

Miscellaneous:

Airport / Airstrip	Marsh
Anchorage	Microwave Tower
Arrow / Location Pointer	Mine Site (abandoned)
Beacon	Parking
Cabin / Chalet / Hut / Shelter	Pictograph
City, Town, Village Indicator	Point of Interest
Dam	Ranger Station
Ferry	Resort
Float Plane Landing	Resort (BCFROA)
Gate	Viewpoint / Forestry Lookout (abandoned)
Highway: Trans Canada	Visitor Centre
Highway: Primary	Waterfall
Hotspring	Wilderness Area / Wildlife Area / Wildlife Reserve
	Workcamp

Contour Lines:

	100m Intervals
	500m Intervals
	Contour Intervals approximately 100m

Visit backroadmapbooks.com to see tutorials on how to use different elements of our Legend.

VI

Navigating
Your Backroad Mapbook Outdoor Recreation Guide

Introduction

This section has many valuable planning tools such as information on Travel/Tourism & Visitor Centres. One of the main tools will be your Legend.

Topographic Maps

This section starts with the Map Key for the region. Use our Topographic Maps and Insets to guide you to your Adventure destination.

Service Directory

Find details on some of the best Accommodations, Sales/Services and Tours/Guides in the area to help select the one that is the right fit with your travel style and needs.

Adventures

For each activity and experience this section will help you plan your trip and ensure you get the best experience of working with our maps and all of the great features.

Index

A full index of the guides' contents is included with page numbers and map coordinates for easy reference. Other tools included are Important Numbers, a Distance Chart and an Advertiser List.

YOUR *BRMB* EXPERIENCE

Each of our Backroad Mapbooks is filled with amazing experiences that show you how to enjoy the outdoors and create unforgettable memories. Visit **backroadmapbooks.com** *for our other great products, tips & tutorials, features and updates to further enhance your outdoor experiences.*

WELLS BARKERVILLE
MOUNTAIN TRAILS
BRITISH COLUMBIA

Cornish Mtn 1519m

Sugar Creek Loop

Cornish Mtn Rd

2200 Rd

Sliding Mtn

Bowron Lake Rd

Mt Murray 1993m

Jubilee Trail

Downey Pass

One Mile Lake Rd

The Hump Bypass

Yellowhawk Trail

Island Mtn 1786m

Willow River

Wendle Lake Provincial Park

Coronado Rd
B Loop Connector
Coronado Connector
A Loop

Mt Greenberry 1895m

Meadows Ski Trail
Mouse Island Loop

WELLS

Meadows Trail

Lowhee Dyke Trail

26

Valley Mtn Trail

Valley Mtn 1526m

Wells-Barkerville Winter Connector

Forest Rose Campground

Bowron Lake Rd

Waverly Mtn 1752m

70km to Quesnel

26

Jack of Clubs Lake

Lowhee Creek

Reduction Rd

3100 Rd

Lowhee Campground
Lowhee Campground Trail
Cemetery Ditch Trail

Russian Creek

1600 Rd

Barkerville Mtn 1627m

Government Hill Campground

Jack of Clubs Lake Rd

Cow Mtn Ditch

Ned's Connector

Goldfields Ditch

Bruce Trail

P

Mt Patchett Trail

Stout's Gulch

BARKERVILLE

Mt Conklin

French Creek

Pleasant Valley Creek

Antler Creek

Tucker Lake

Cow Mtn 1784m

Richfield Cemetery Trail

RICHFIELD

Conklin Gulch

Williams Creek

Mt Amador

Jack of Clubs Creek Rd

Richfield Mtn Route

Grouse Creek Route

Mt Howley

1600 Rd

Richfield Mtn 1827m

Proserpine Mining Rd

Grouse Creek

Stoney Creek

Jack of Clubs Creek

Mt Pinkerton

Ella Lake

Summit Rock

Williams Creek Trail

1861 Pack Trail

Old Cariboo Hudson Rd

Mt Guyet

Mt Agnes Hiking & Skiing Route

McCallum Gulch

Cariboo Waggon Rd

Mt Agnes Multi-Use Route

Proserpine Multi-Use Connector

Brough Lake

Cooper's Cabin

Powderhouse Trail

Beggs Gulch

Van Winkle Trail

Elk Mtn 1891m

Mt Proserpine 1861m

Proserpine Hiking & Skiing Connector

Williams Creek

White Grouse Creek

Stevens Gulch

Whiskey Flats

3100 Rd

Lightning Creek

Lower Van Winkle Trail

Groundhog Lake

Bald Mtn 1900m

Bald Mtn Connector

Roadhouse site

Grouse Creek

Loskey Creek

Mt Agnes 1937m

Racetrack Creek

Racetrack Flats

Wolf Creek

Antler Creek

Begbie Campsite

Maloney Campsite

Antler Mtn 1829m

1861 Pack Trail

Rhubarb Cabin

3100 Rd

Sawmill Flats

0   1km   2km
SCALE 1:110,000

OVERVIEW MAP

Two Sisters Trail

2300 Rd

Bowron Lake Park

Sugar Creek Loop

Little Swift River

Bowron Lake Rd

Jubilee Trail

WELLS

26

Yellowhawk Trail

BARKERVILLE

3100 Rd

1600 Rd

RICHFIELD

STANLEY

Mt Patchett Trail

Cariboo Waggon Rd

Old Cariboo Hudson Rd

3100 Rd

1861 Pack Trail

Yanks Peak Route | Roundtop Mtn Route

LEGEND

⌂	Shelter
★	Historic Landmark
△	Campsite
⚒	Mining
⊞	Picnic Area
26	Paved Highway
——	Gravel Road
- - -	Industry Road
▪▪▪▪	Snowmobile Corridor
▦	Protected Caribou Area (pink tint)

TRAIL ETIQUETTE

Please respect other trail users at all times – we are all out there to have an enjoyable experience. Leave no trace; do not litter or damage the natural environment. Be prepared for the fact that most trails do not have toilet facilities. Many of the trails cross mining claims or private property. Stay on the trails and do not disturb any equipment or workings.

Please report any damage or problematic trail conditions to the District of Wells.

Original base map: Angelique Justason
Maps & Design: Bill Horne
Amazing Space Studio www.claireart.ca
Photos: Thomas Drasdauskis, Bill Horne, Whitegold Adventures, Justin Scott.

WELLS INSET

Sugar Creek Loop

A Loop

One Mile Rd

Coronado Rd

B Loop Connector

Coronado-Cornish Connector

B Loop

One Mile Lake

Cornish Mtn Rd

Willow River

Hardscrabble Road

Meadows Ski Trail

Williams Creek

Sugar Creek Loop

Meadows Trail

Moose Island Loop

WELLS

Dawson St

26

Wells-Barkerville Winter Connector

Willow River

Pooley St

Sanders Ave

Visitor Centre

Lowhee

Lowhee Dyke Trail

Goldfields Rd

Lowhee Dr

Cow Mtn Ditch

0   500m
SCALE 1:45,000

VALHALLA PURE
OUTFITTERS

SKI • BACKPACK • TRAVEL

CLIMB • RACE • PADDLE

Photos: Arc'teryx images

The *best* gear is here.

🍁 Since 1990 🍁

VANCOUVER

VERNON

SMITHERS

Victoria/Langford, BC
109 - 2401D Millstream Rd
250 412-2356
millstream@vpo.ca

Nanaimo, BC
5773 Turner Rd
250 751-8686
nanaimo@vpo.ca

Courtenay, BC
Unit F, 2885 Cliffe Avenue
250-871-3963
courtenay@vpo.ca

Vancouver, BC
88 W. Broadway
604 872-8872
vancouver@vpo.ca

Abbotsford, BC
2, 1707 Salton Rd.
604 850-5523
abbotsford@vpo.ca

Squamish, BC
Squamish Station
1-877-892-9092
squamish@vpo.ca

Vernon, BC
2814 - 48th Ave
250-542-3537
vernon@vpo.ca

Smithers, BC
1122 Main St
250 847-0200
smithers@vpo.ca

Revelstoke, BC
213 MacKenzie Ave
250 837-5517
revelstoke@vpo.ca

Nelson, BC
624 Baker St
250 354-1006
nelson@vpo.ca

New Denver, BC
101 Eldorado St
250 358-7755
newdenver@vpo.ca

Canmore, AB
726 Main St
403 678-5610
canmore@vpo.ca

Red Deer, AB
A3, 2319 Taylor Dr
403 343-3658
reddeer@vpo.ca

Medicine Hat, AB
1667 Dunmore Rd. SE
403 487-5474
mh@vpo.ca

Now Shop Online!
vpo.ca
Product differs slightly from store to store

With 14 locations across British Columbia and Alberta to serve you.

Map Key
Cariboo Chilcotin Coast BC

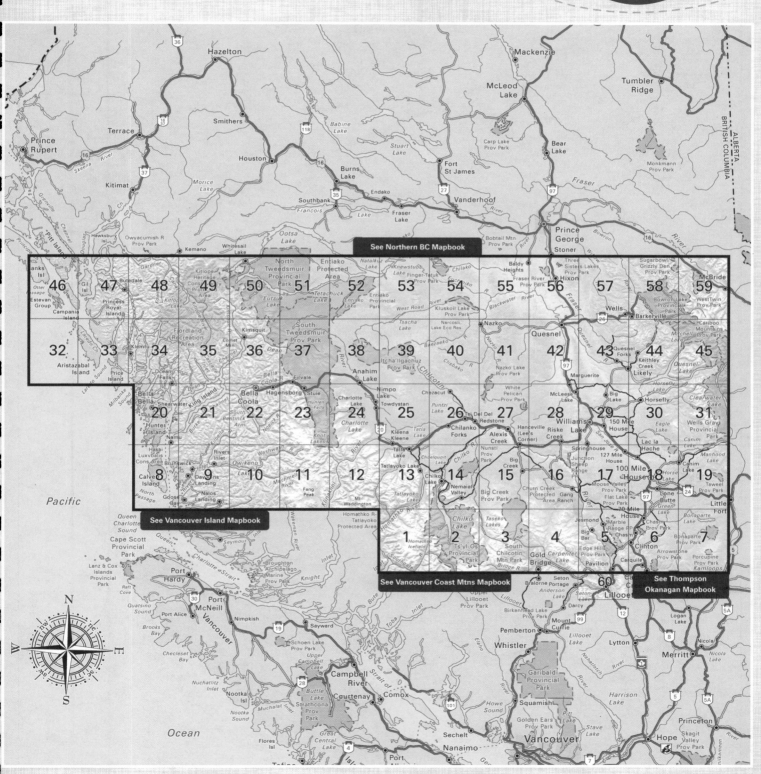

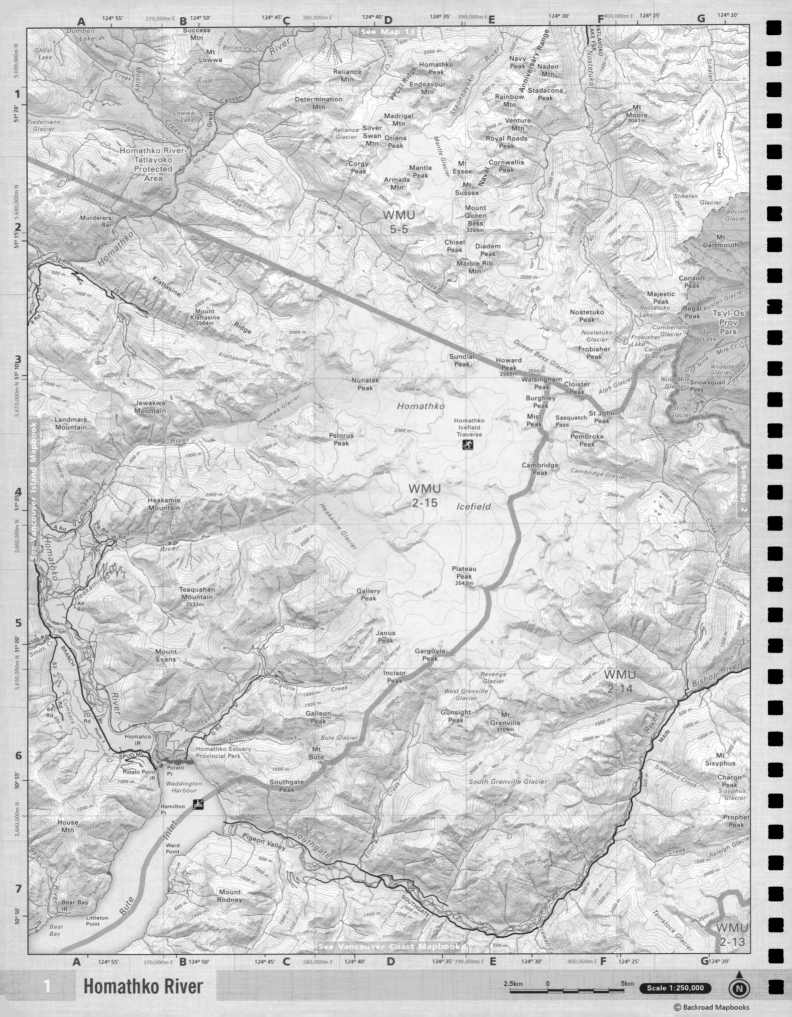

Scale 1:250,000

© Backroad Mapbooks

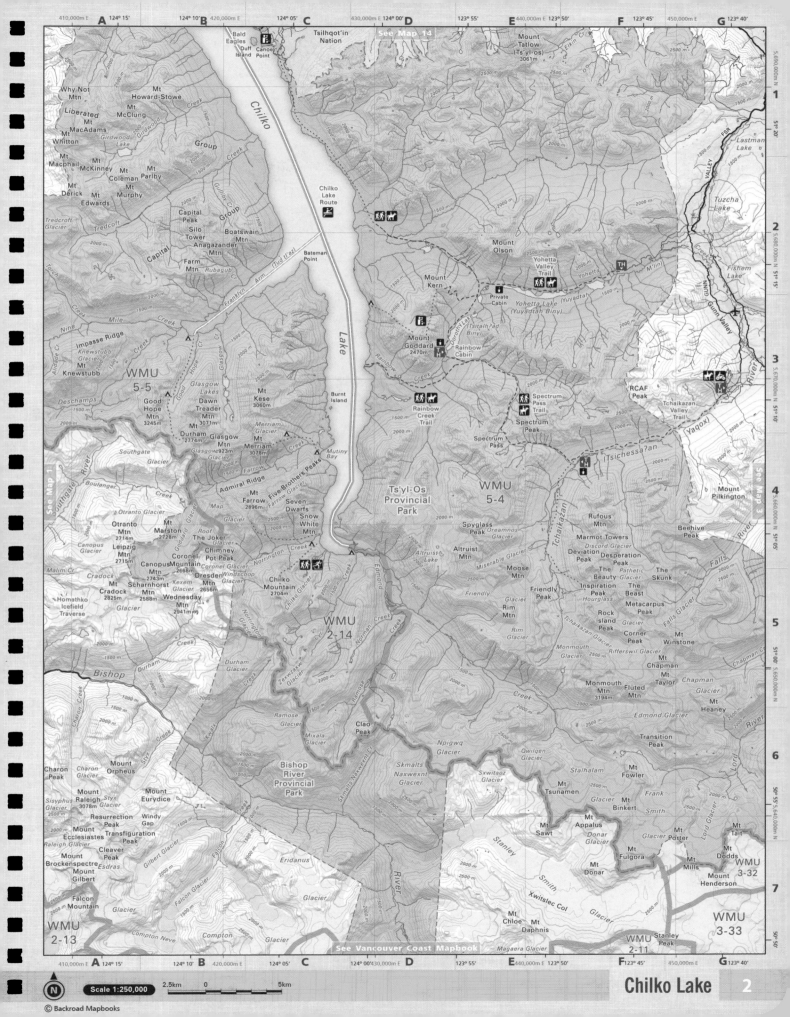

Chilko Lake

Scale 1:250,000

© Backroad Mapbooks

2

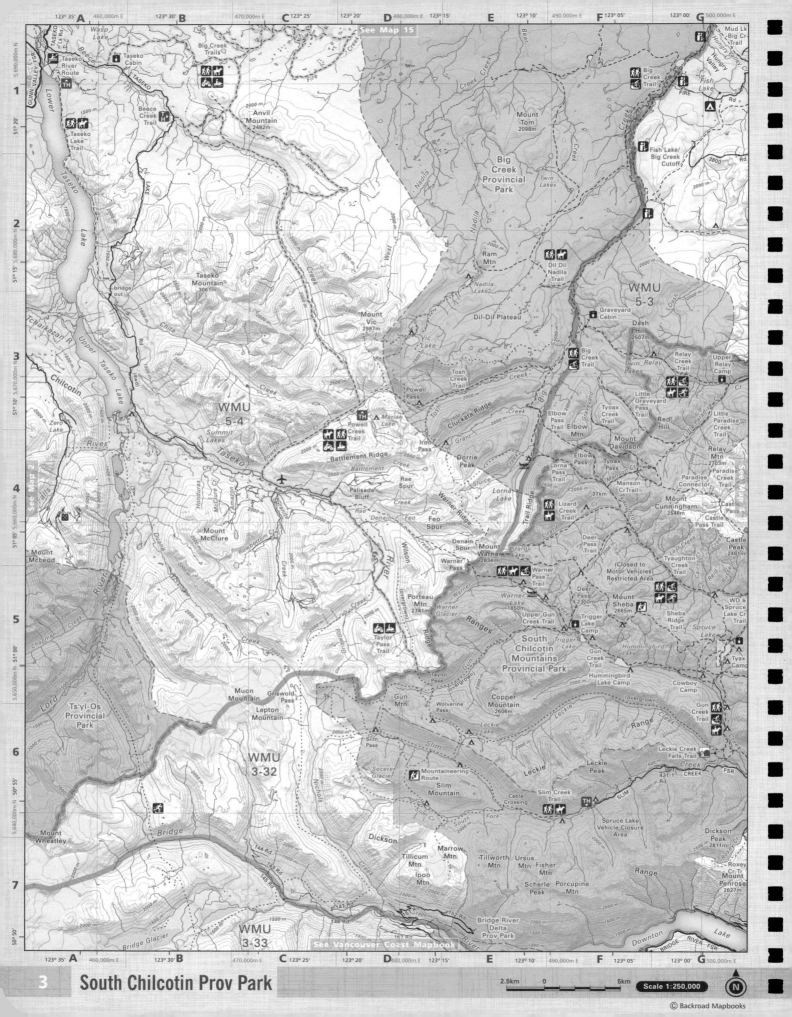

3 **South Chilcotin Prov Park**

Scale 1:250,000

2.5km   0   5km

© Backroad Mapbooks

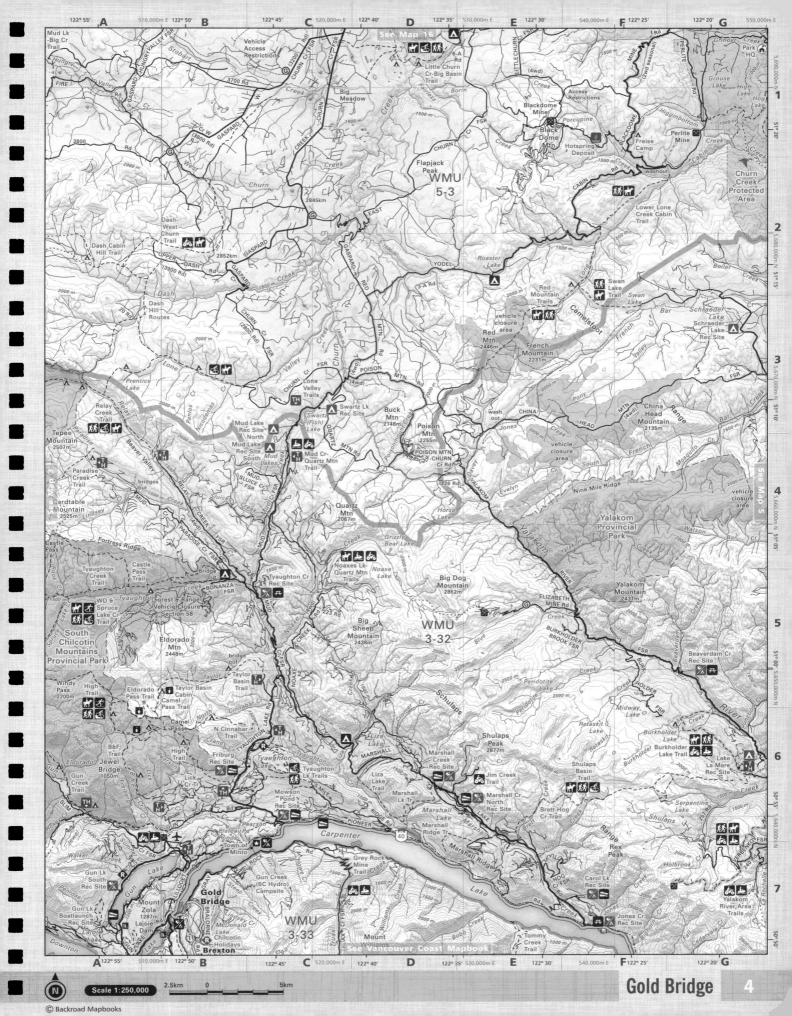

Gold Bridge

4

Scale 1:250,000

© Backroad Mapbooks

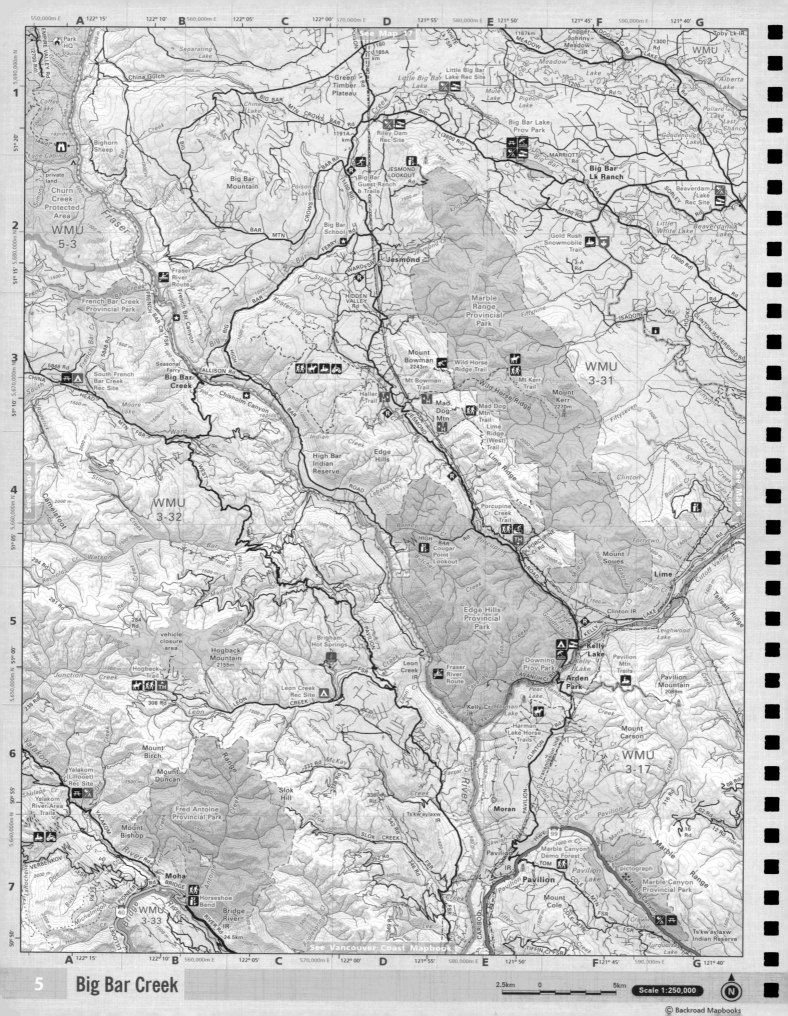

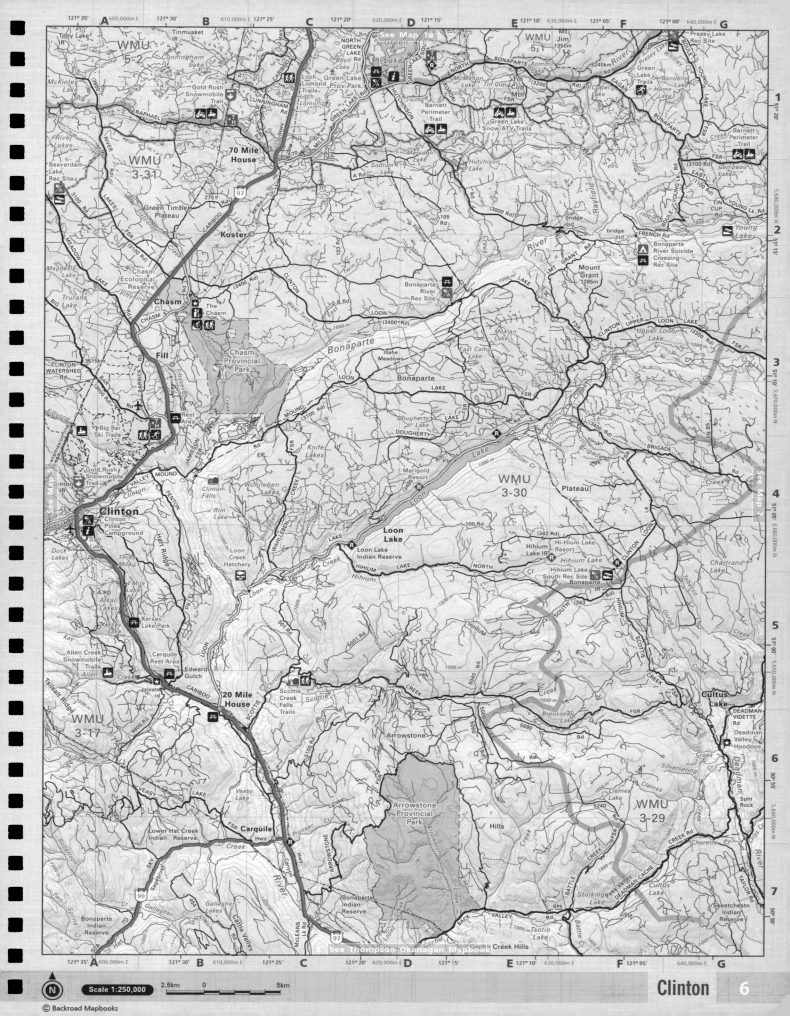

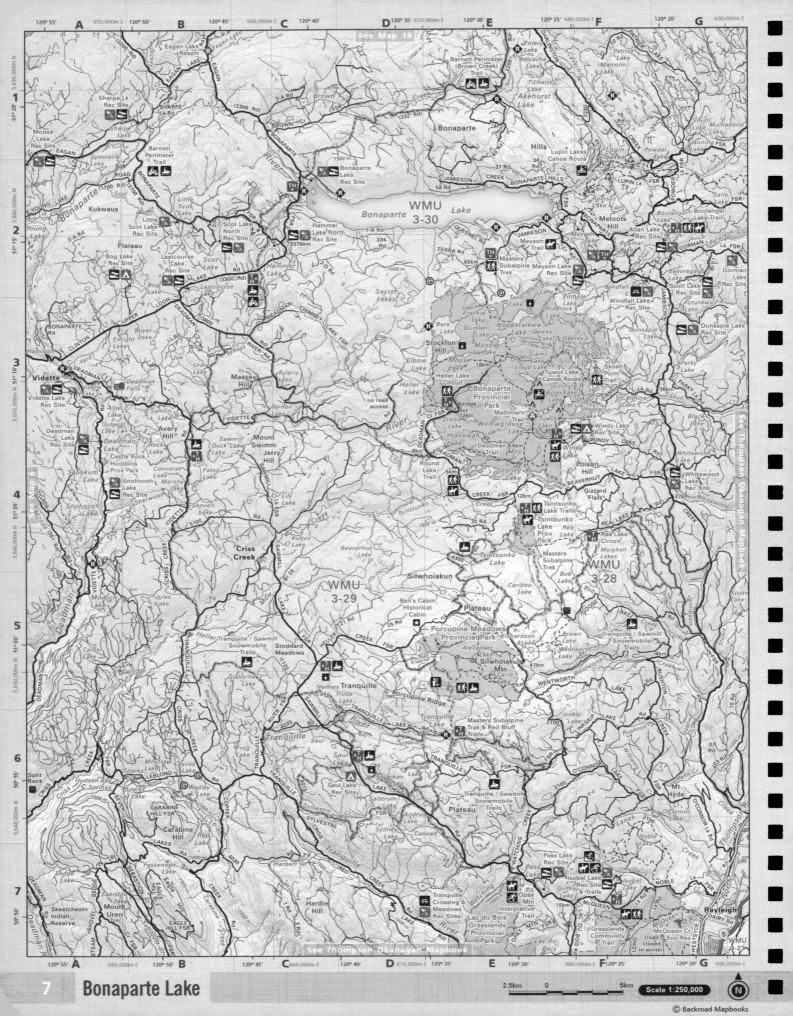

2.5km 0 5km

Scale 1:250,000

© Backroad Mapbooks

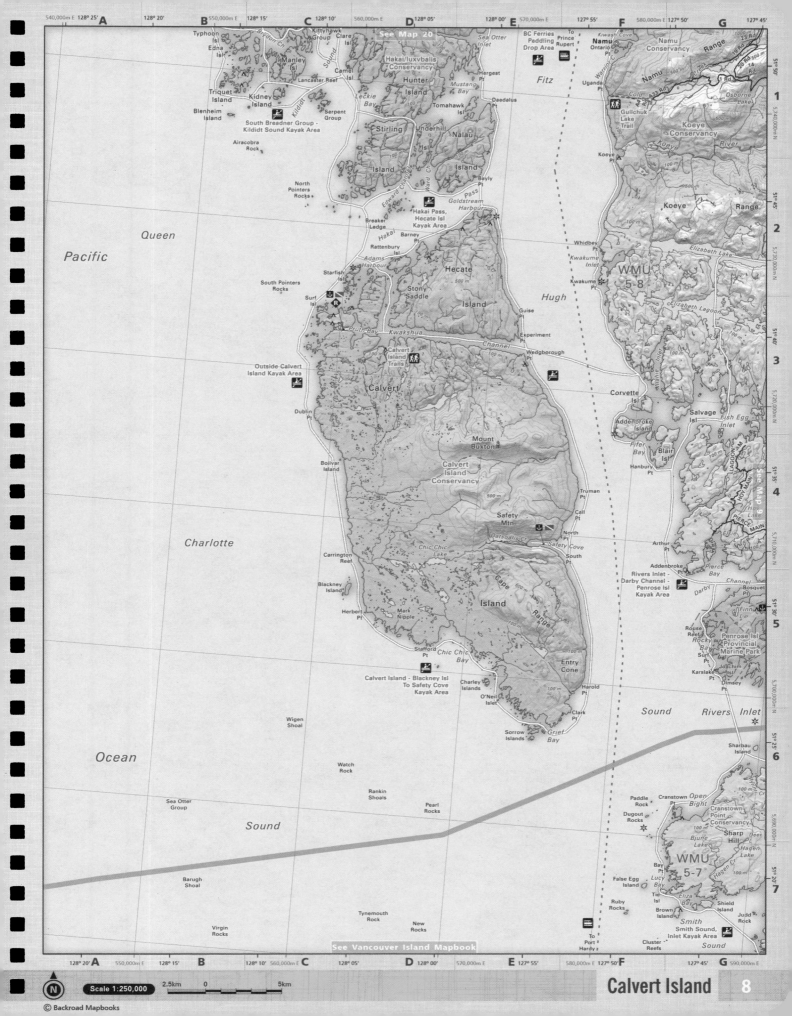

See Vancouver Island Mapbook

See Map 9

Scale 1:250,000

2.5km 0 5km

© Backroad Mapbooks

Calvert Island 8

Scale 1:250,000

© Backroad Mapbooks

Scale 1:250,000

© Backroad Mapbooks

Scale 1:250,000

© Backroad Mapbooks

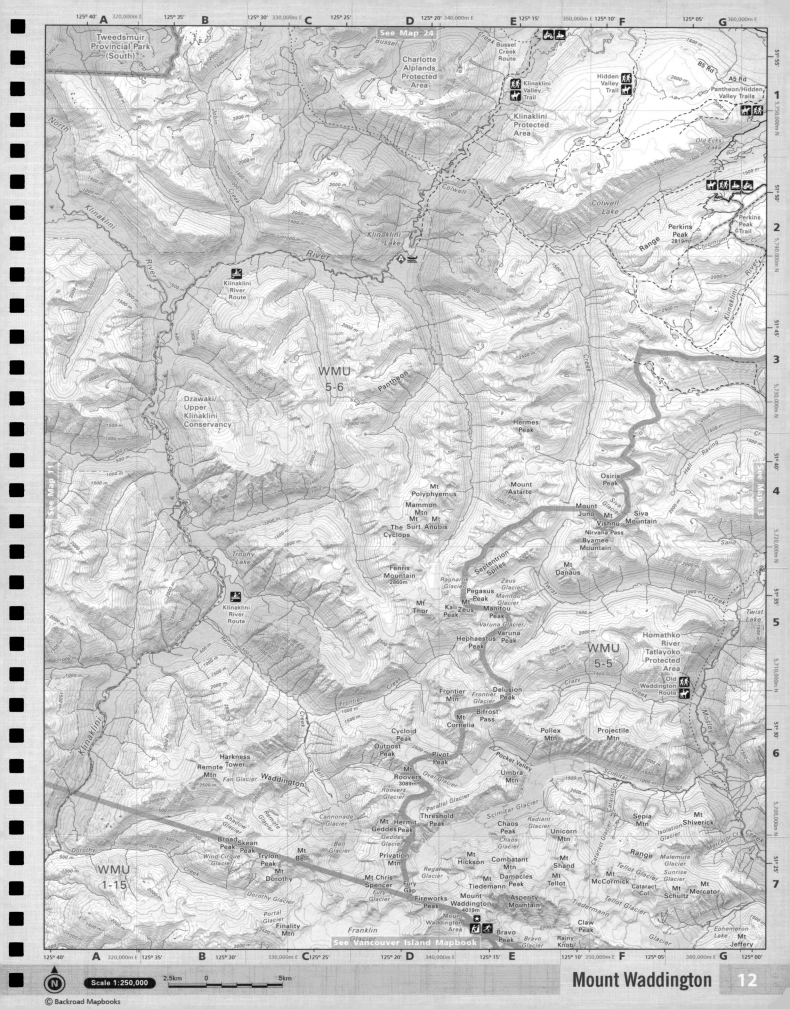

Tweedsmuir
Provincial Park
(South)

Charlotte
Alplands
Protected
Area

Bussel Creek
Route

Klinaklini
Valley
Trail

Hidden
Valley
Trail

Pantheon/Hidden
Valley Trails

B5 Rd

A5 Rd

Klinaklini
Protected
Area

Colwell
Lake

Old Ecks
Lake

Perkins
Peak
2819m

Perkins
Peak
Trail

Range

Chromium

Klinaklini Lake

Klinaklini
River
Route

Klinaklini River

WMU
5-6

Pantheon

Dzawaki/
Upper
Klinaklini
Conservancy

Hermes
Peak

Osiris
Peak

Mt
Polyphyemus

Mount
Astarte

Mammon
Mtn

Mount
Juno

Mt
Vishnu

Siva
Mountain

The Surt
Cyclops

Mt
Anubis

Nirvana Pass

Byamee
Mountain

Trophy
Lake

Fenris
Mountain
2860m

Septentrion
Spires

Mt
Danaus

Klinaklini
River
Route

Ragnarok
Glacier

Pegasus
Peak

Zeus
Glacier

Manitou
Glacier

Mt
Thor

Kali
Peak

Mt
Zeus

Manitou
Peak

Varuna Glacier

Homathko
River
Tatlayoko
Protected
Area

Twist
Lake

Hephaestus
Peak

Varuna
Peak

WMU
5-5

Old
Waddington
Route

Frontier
Mtn

Delusion
Peak

Frontier
Glacier

Bifrost
Pass

Pollex
Mtn

Projectile
Mtn

Cycloid
Peak

Mt
Cornelia

Outpost
Peak

Pivot
Peak

Pocket Valley

Umbra
Mtn

Harkness
Tower

Mt
Roovers
3089m

Oval Glacier

Waddington

Remote
Mtn

Fan Glacier

Roovers
Glacier

Parallel Glacier

Scimitar Glacier

Radiant
Glacier

Sepia
Mtn

Mt
Shiverick

Shadow
Glacier

Cannonade
Glacier

Mt Hermit
Geddes Peak

Threshold
Peak

Chaos
Peak

Chaos
Glacier

Unicorn
Mtn

Range

Malemute
Glacier

Sunrise
Glacier

Broad
Peak

Skean
Peak

Bell
Glacier

Geddes
Glacier

Privation
Mtn

Mt
Hickson

Combatant
Mtn

Mt
Shand

Mt
Tellot

Mt
McCormick

Cataract
Col

Mt
Schultz

Mt
Mercator

Wind Cirque
Glacier

Trylon
Peak

Mt
Bell

Mt
Dorothy

Regal
Glacier

Mt
Tiedemann

Damocles
Peak

Tellot Glacier

Dorothy

WMU
1-15

Mt Chris
Spencer

Fury
Gap

Mount
Waddington
4019m

Asperity
Mountain

Claw
Peak

Ephemeron
Lake

Mt
Jeffery

Dorothy Glacier

Fury
Glacier

Fireworks
Peak

Mount
Waddington
Area

Bravo
Peak

Rainy
Knob

Portal
Glacier

Finality
Mtn

Franklin

See Vancouver Island Mapbook

Bravo
Glacier

Tiedemann Glacier

© Backroad Mapbooks

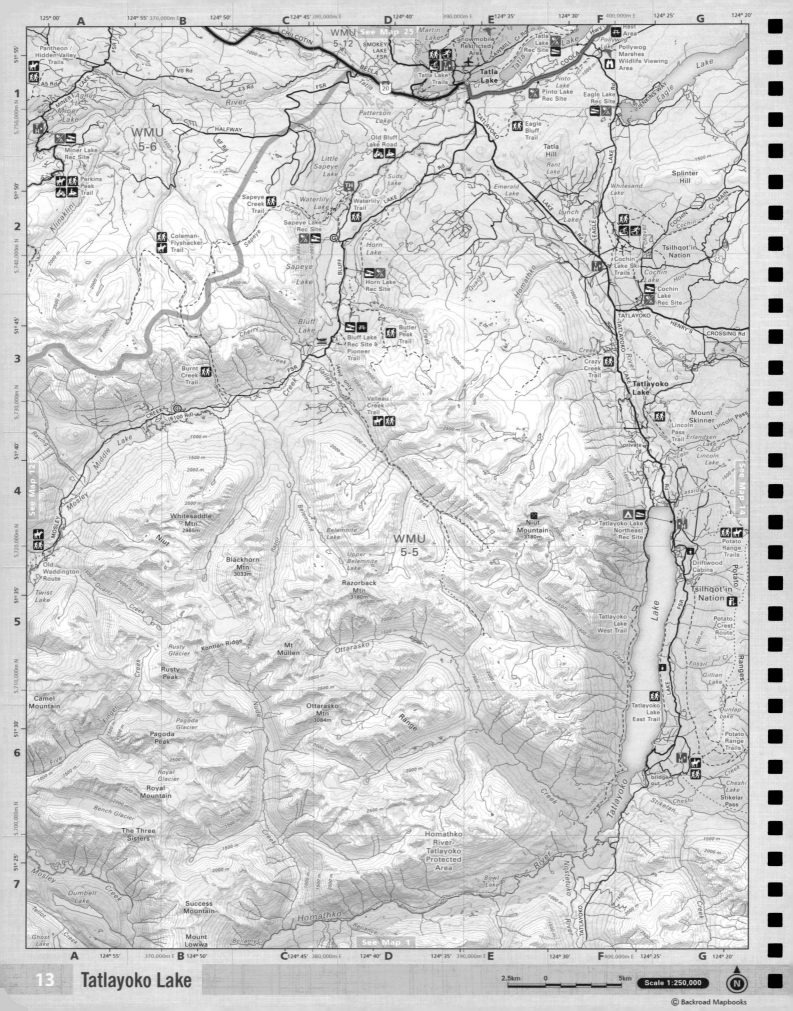

Scale 1:250,000

© Backroad Mapbooks

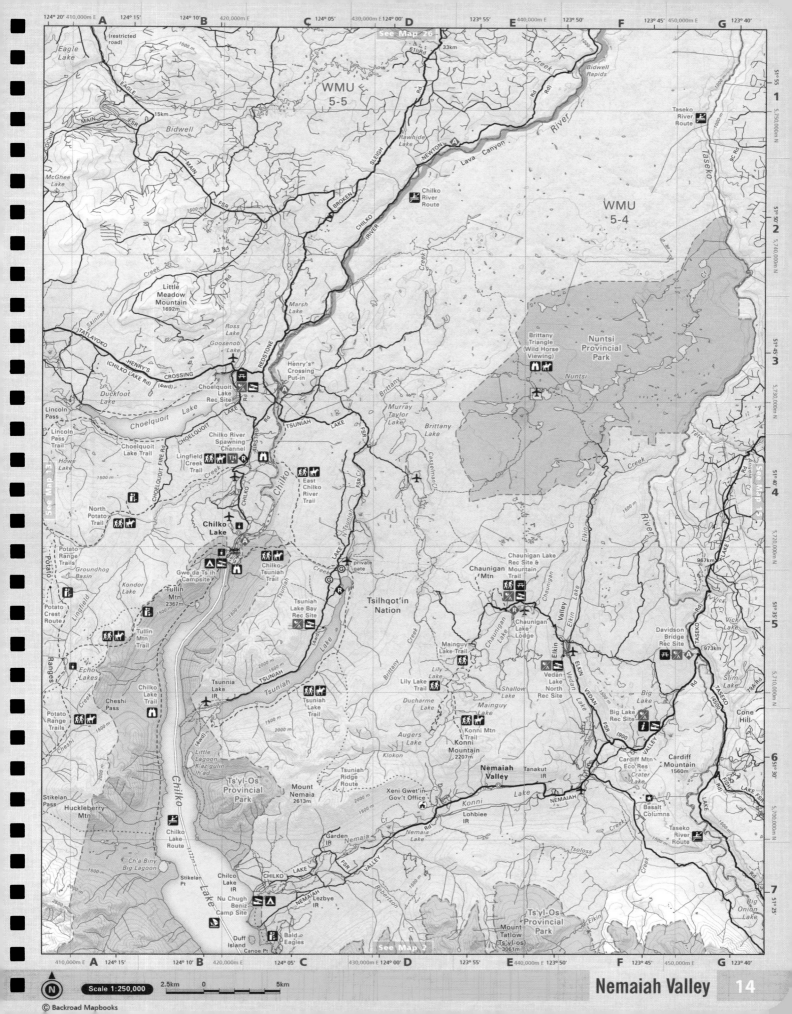

Scale 1:250,000

2.5km   0   5km

© Backroad Mapbooks

Nemaiah Valley 14

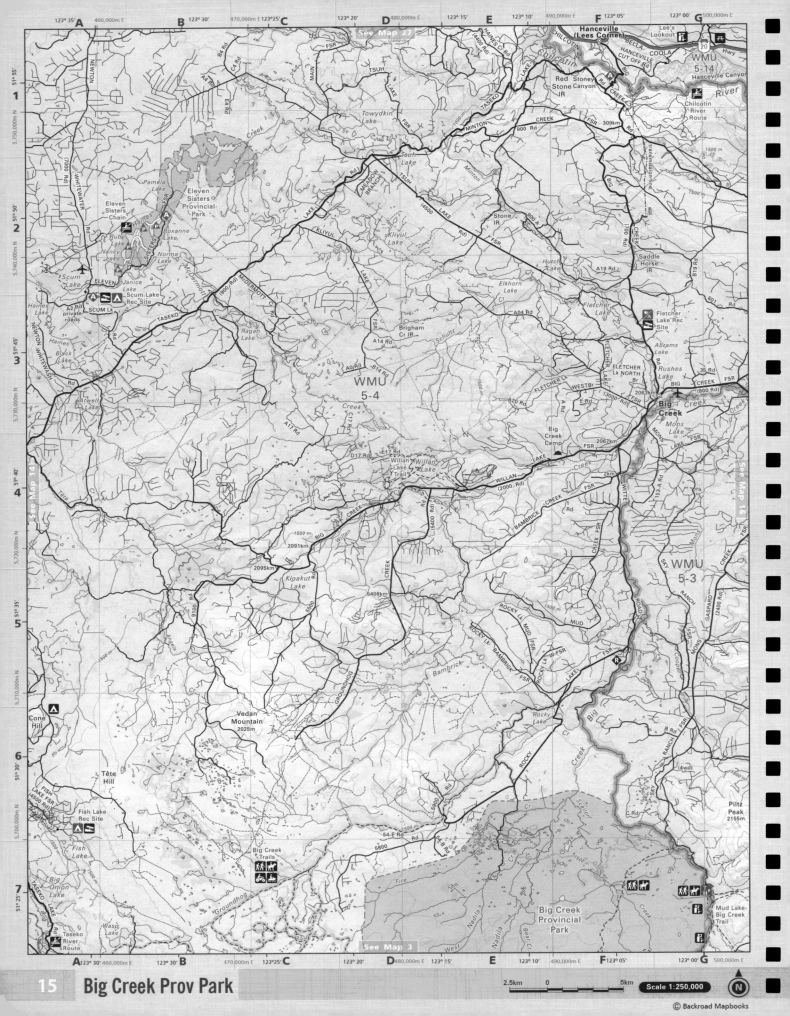

Big Creek Prov Park

2.5km 0 5km

Scale 1:250,000

© Backroad Mapbooks

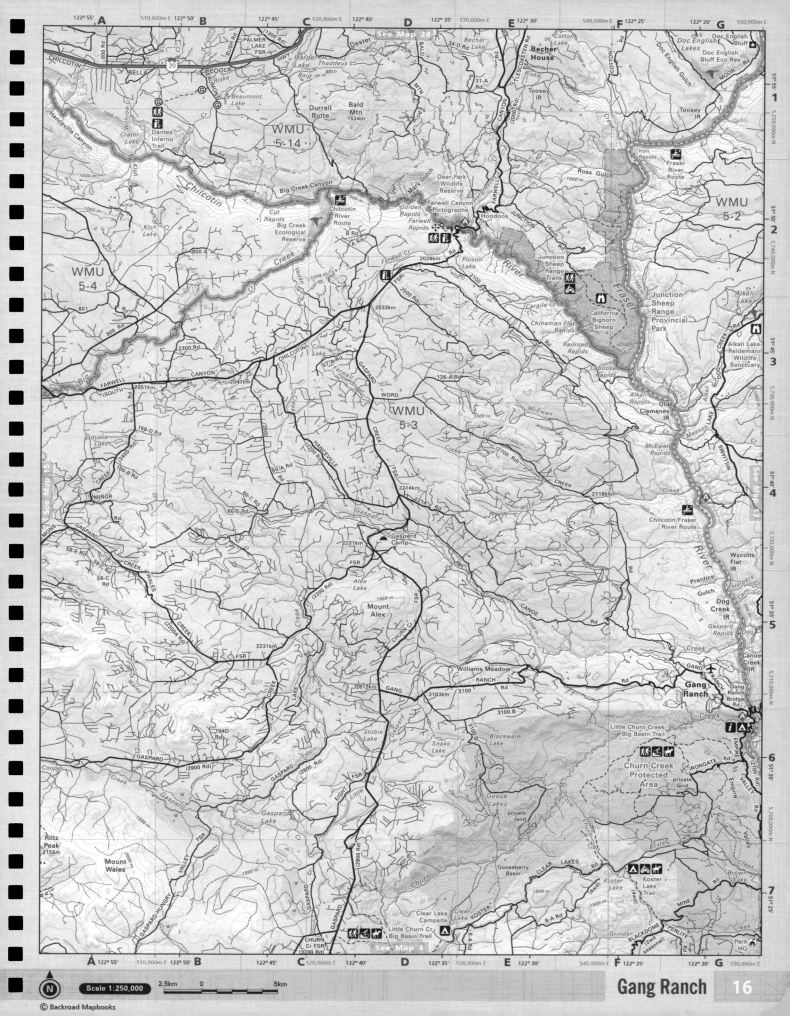

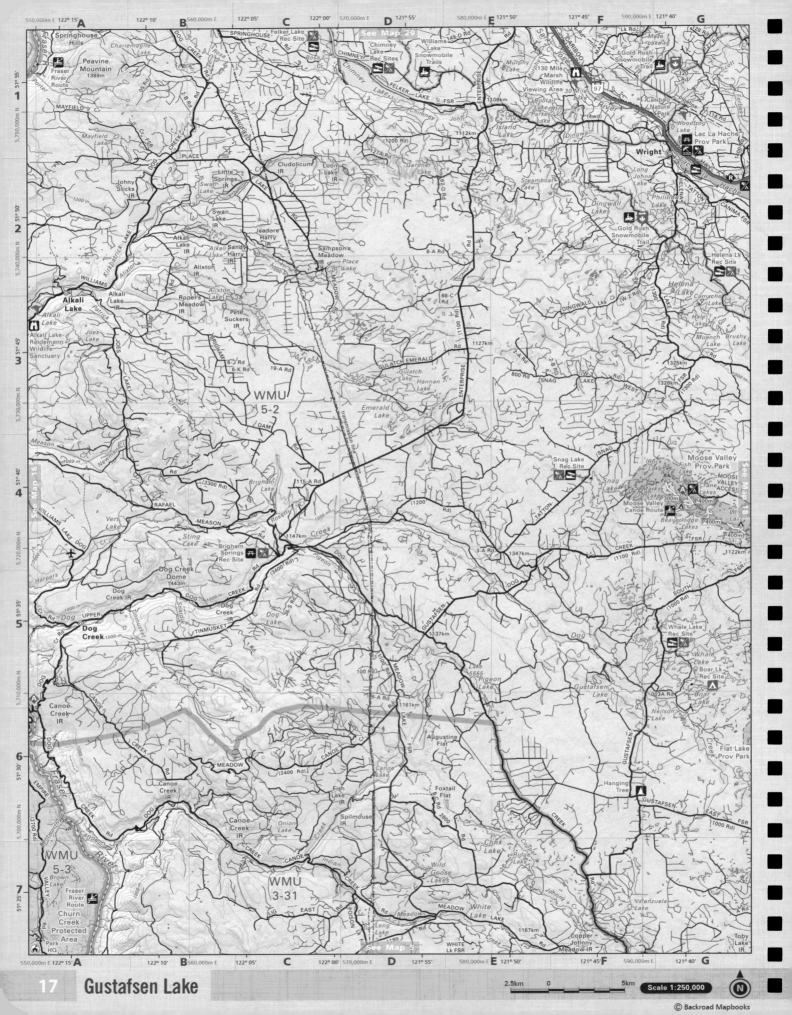

Scale 1:250,000

© Backroad Mapbooks

100 Mile House

18

Scale 1:250,000

© Backroad Mapbooks

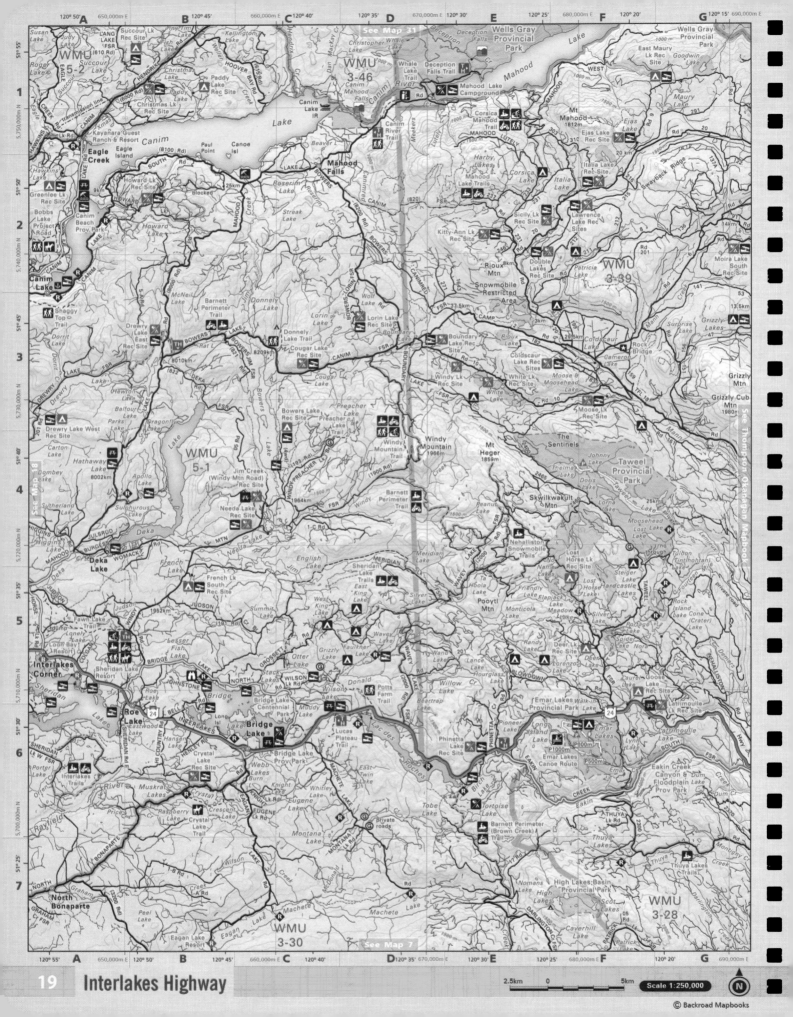

Scale 1:250,000

© Backroad Mapbooks

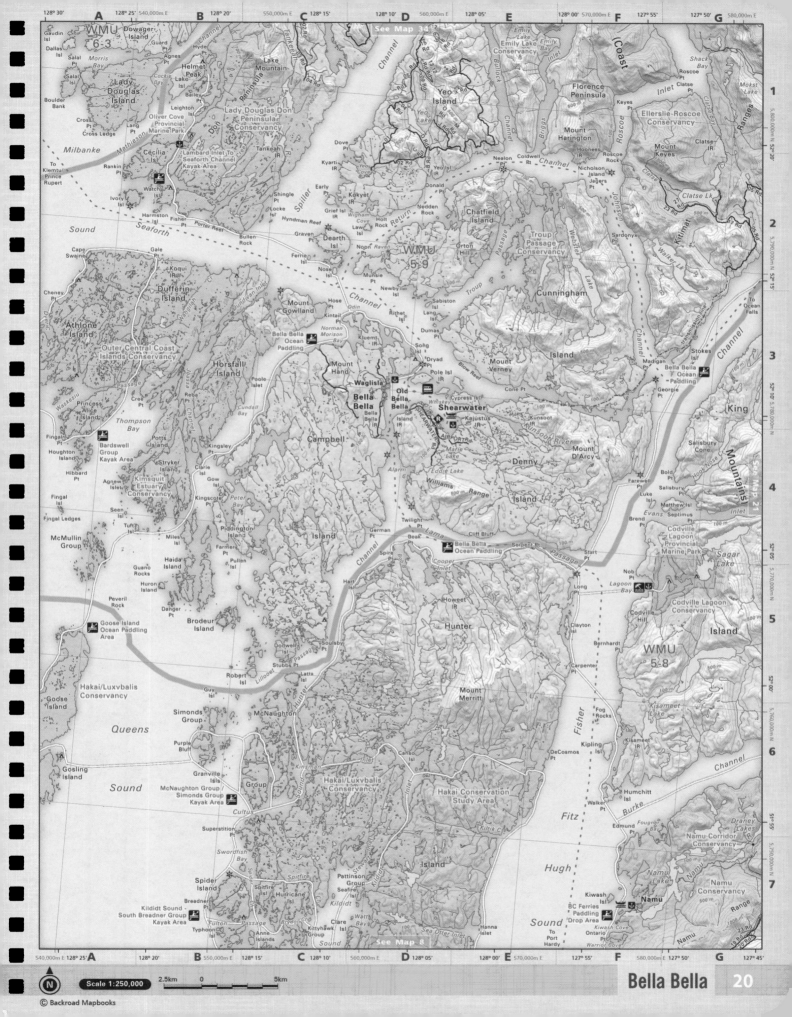

Scale 1:250,000

© Backroad Mapbooks

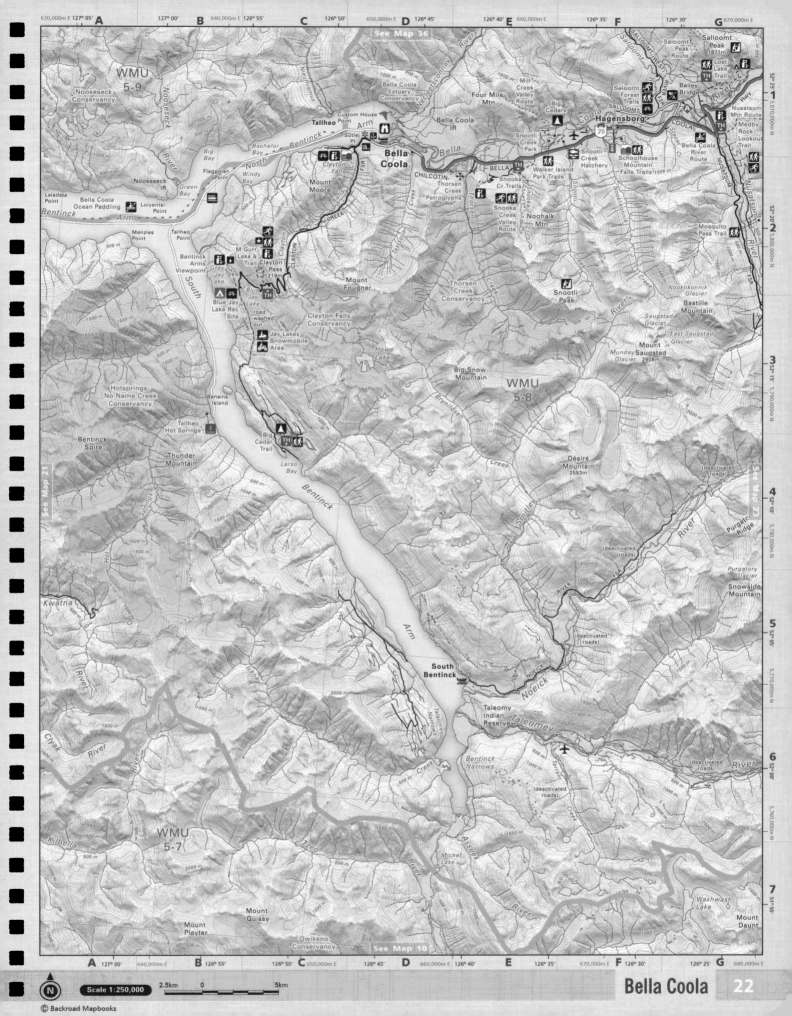

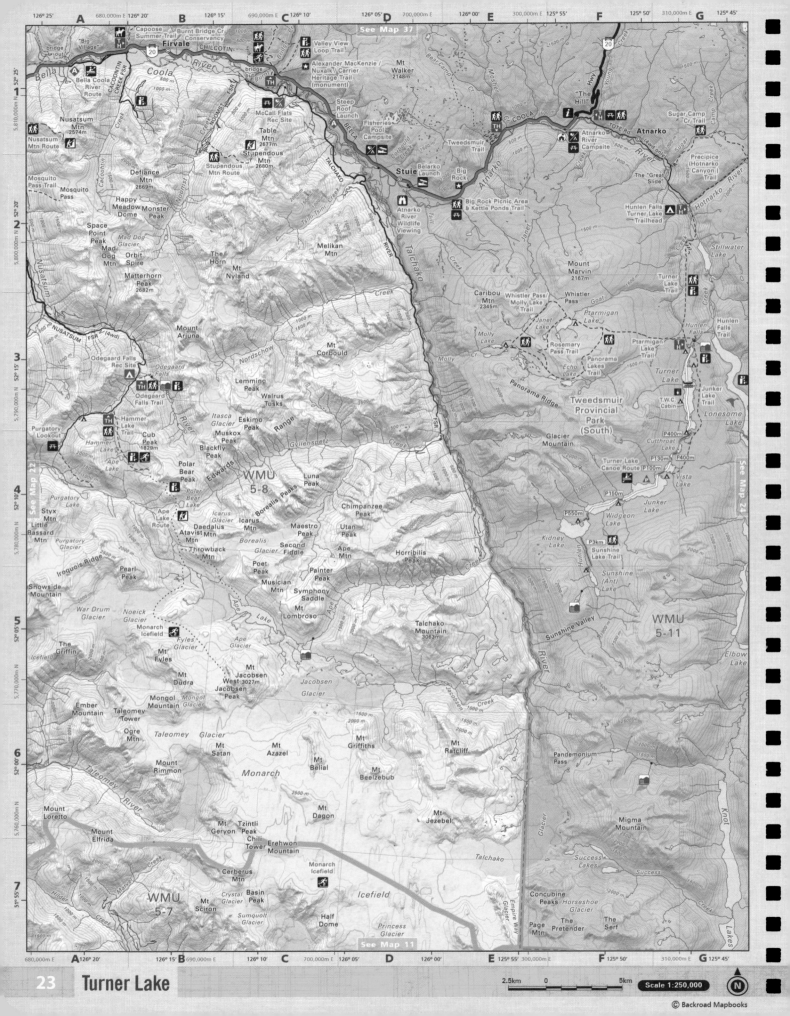

Scale 1:250,000

© Backroad Mapbooks

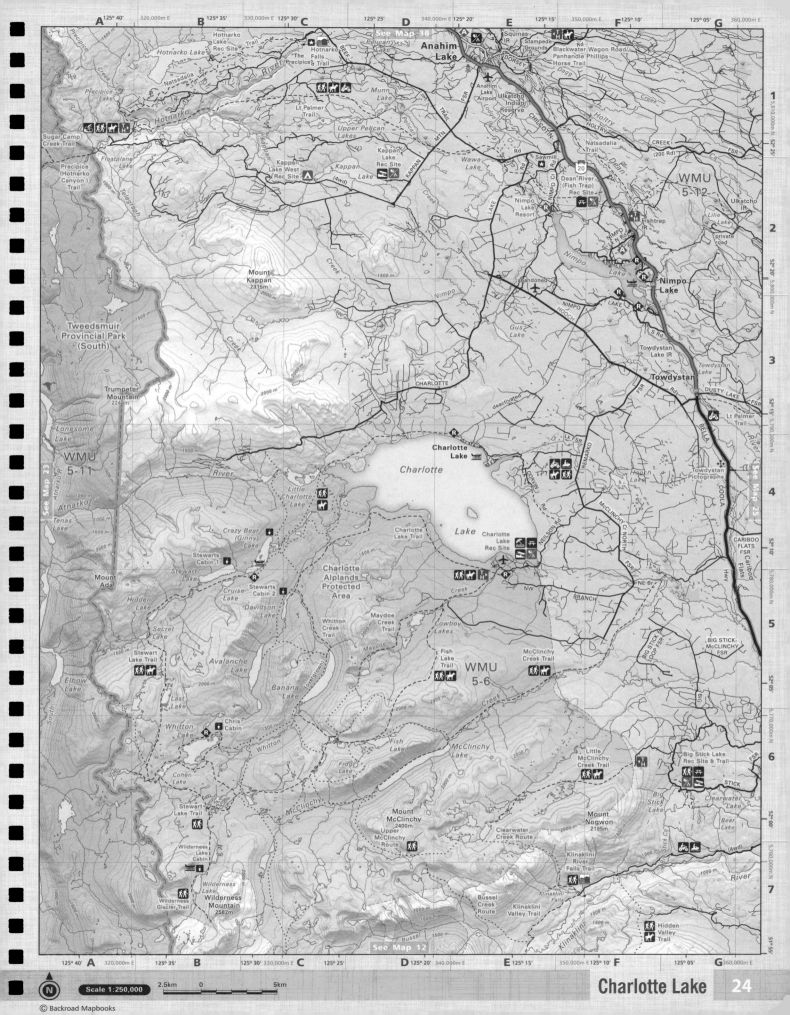

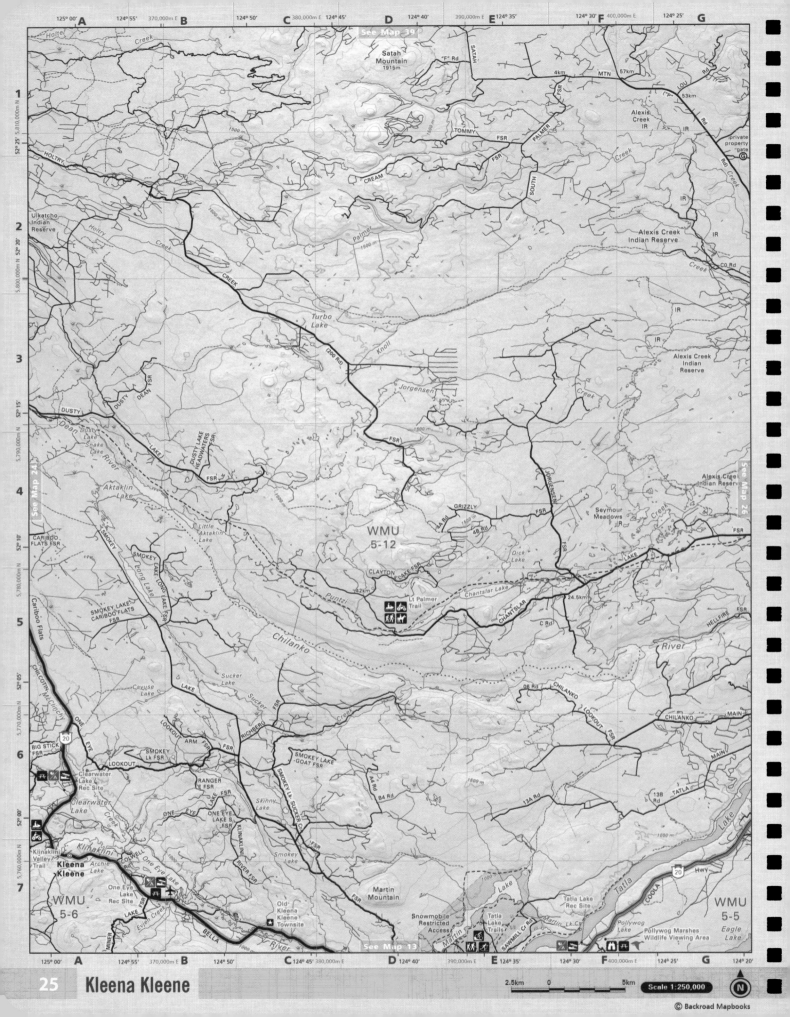

Scale 1:250,000

© Backroad Mapbooks

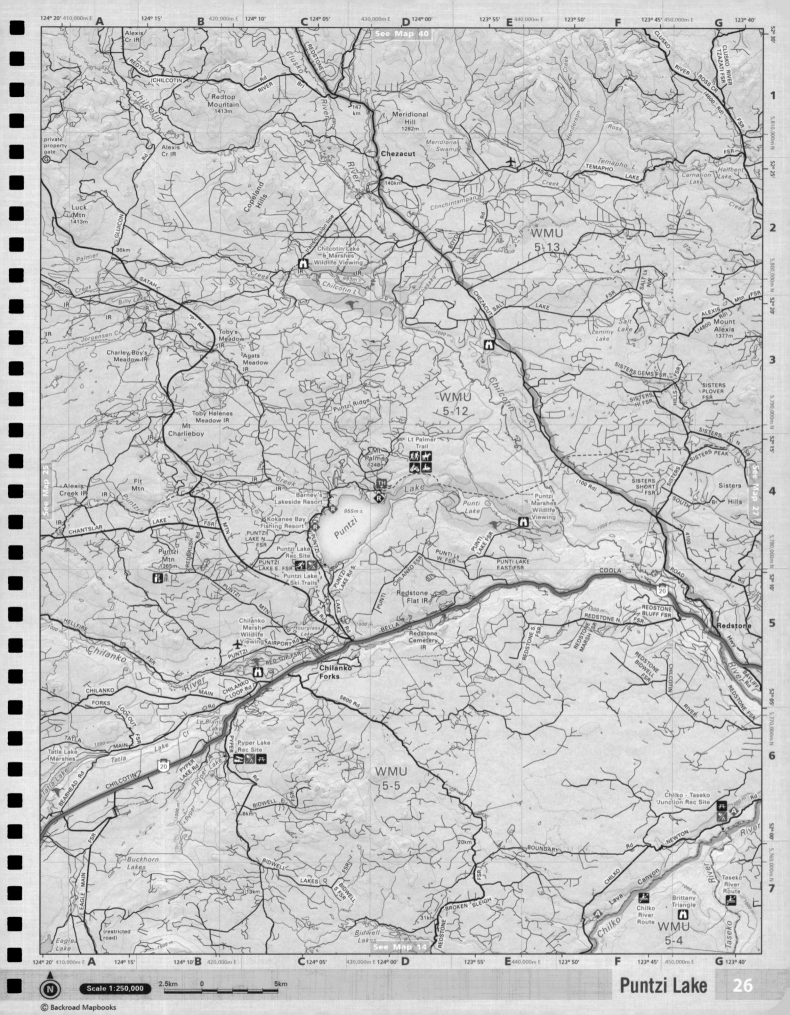

Scale 1:250,000

© Backroad Mapbooks

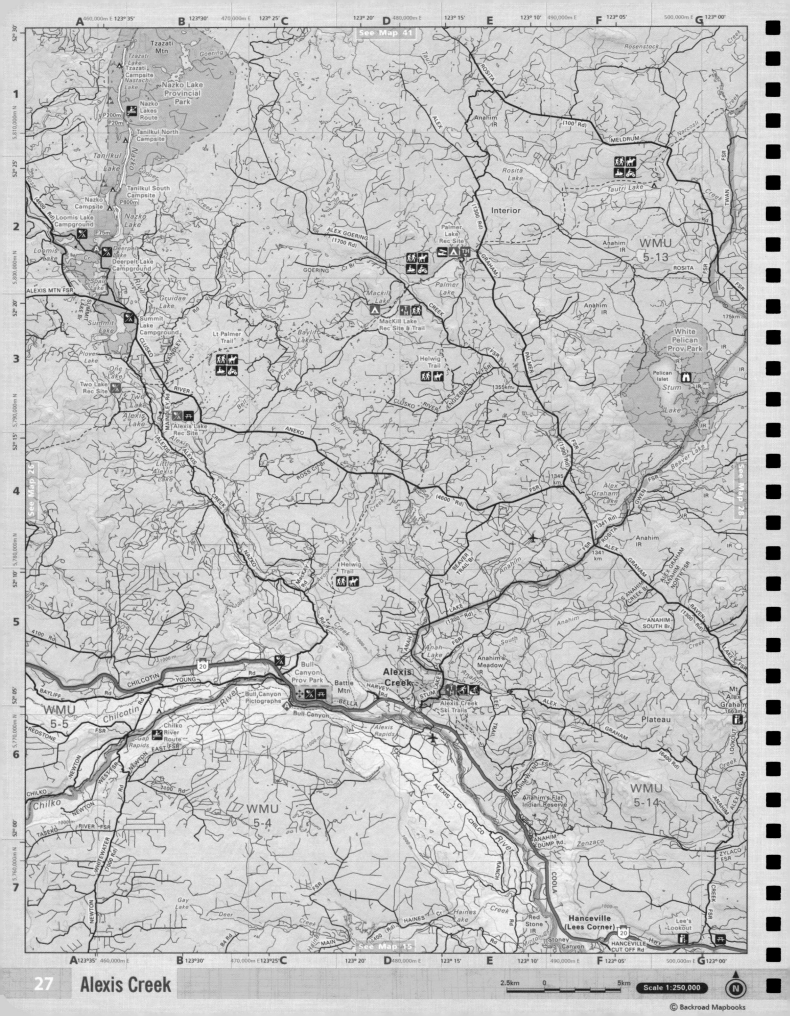

Scale 1:250,000

© Backroad Mapbooks

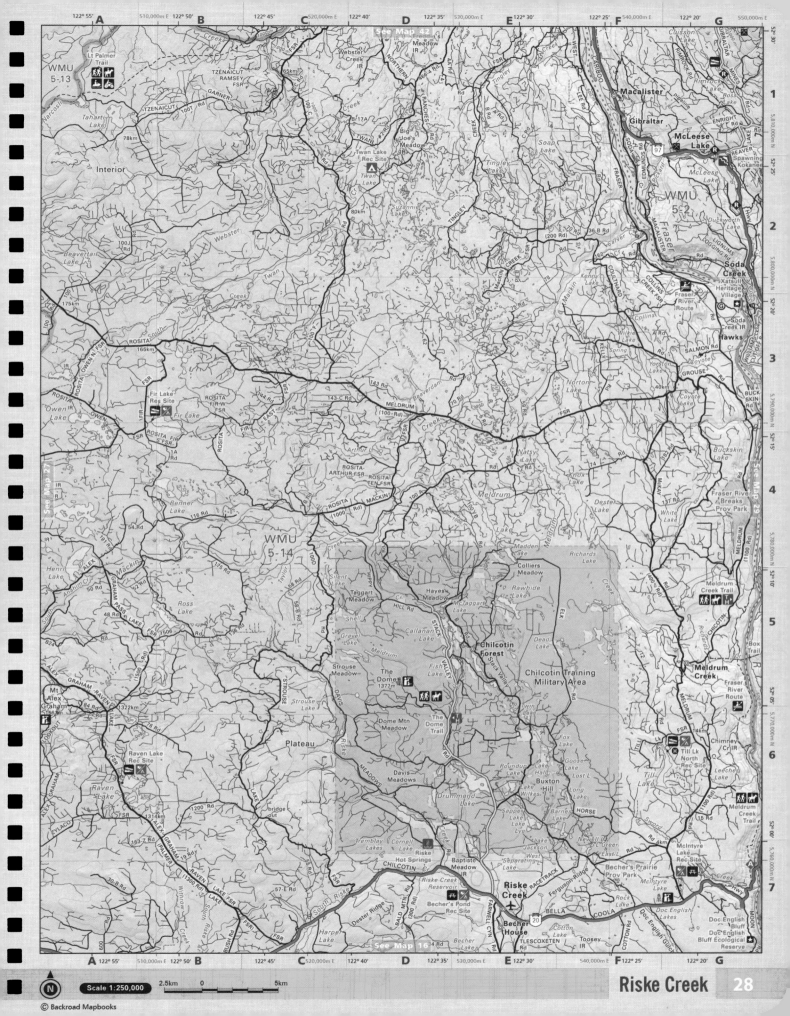

Scale 1:250,000

© Backroad Mapbooks

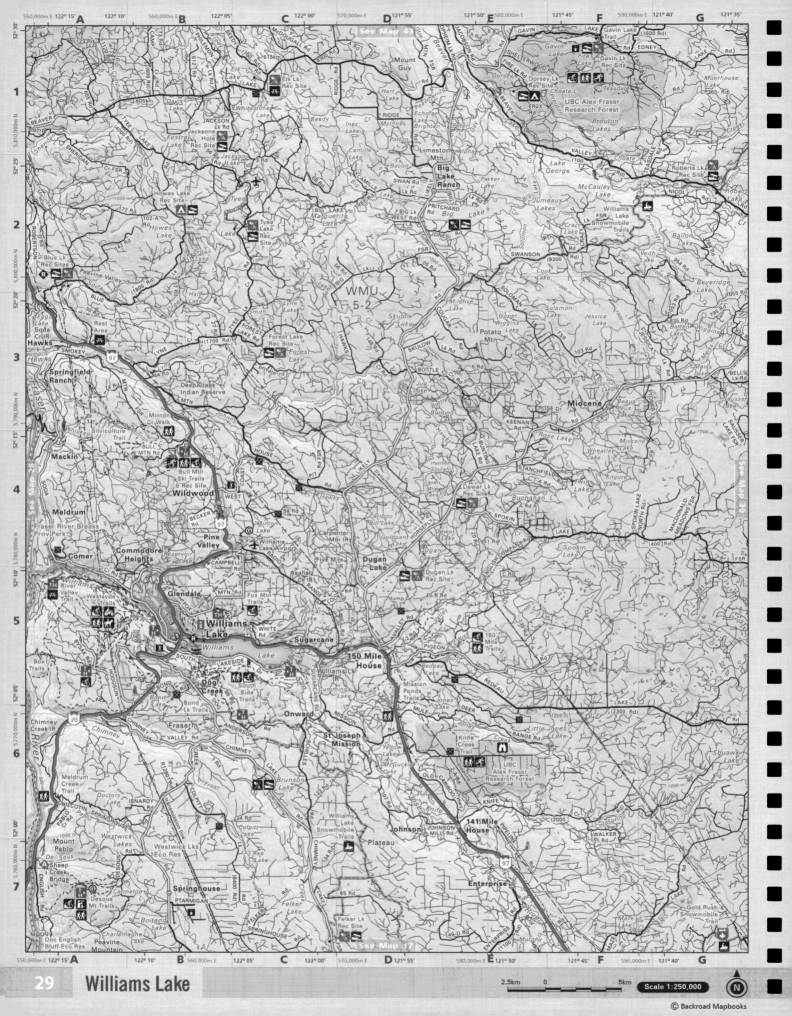

Scale 1:250,000

© Backroad Mapbooks

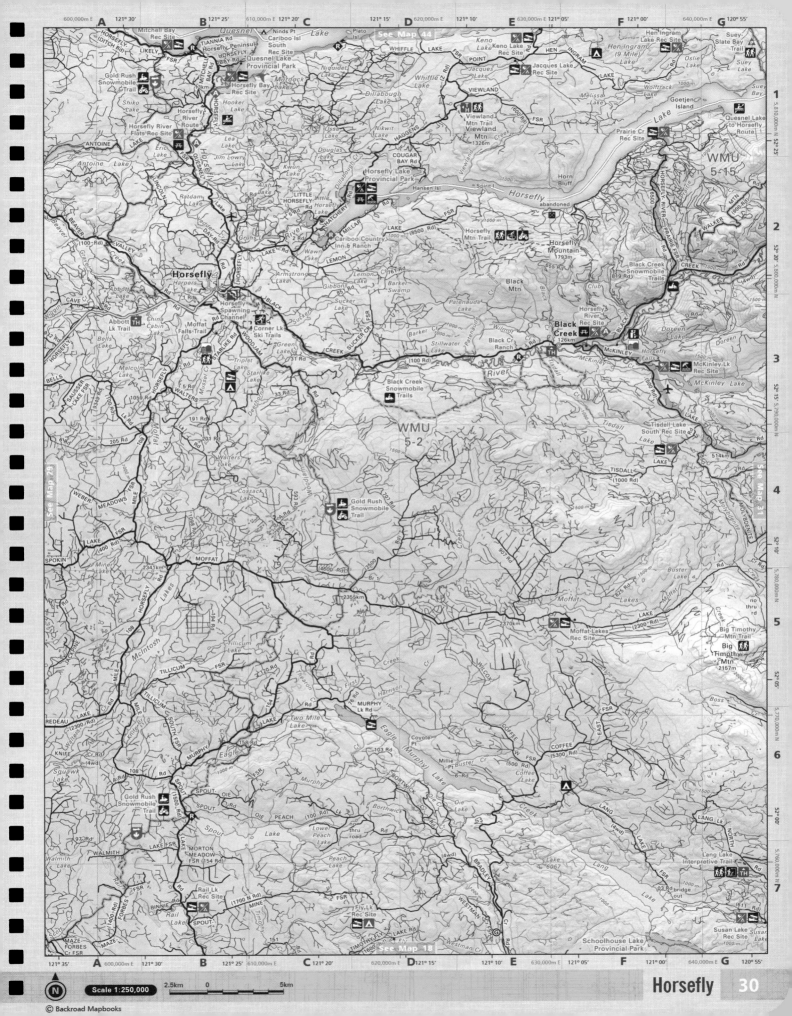

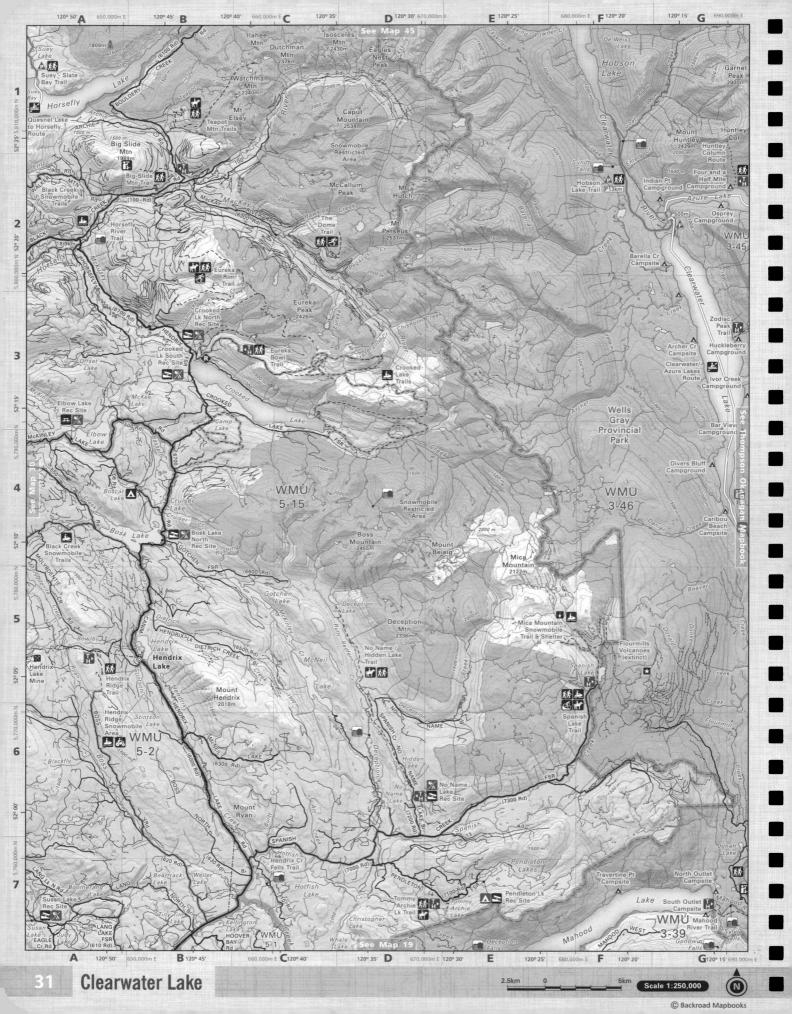

Scale 1:250,000

2.5km   0   5km

© Backroad Mapbooks

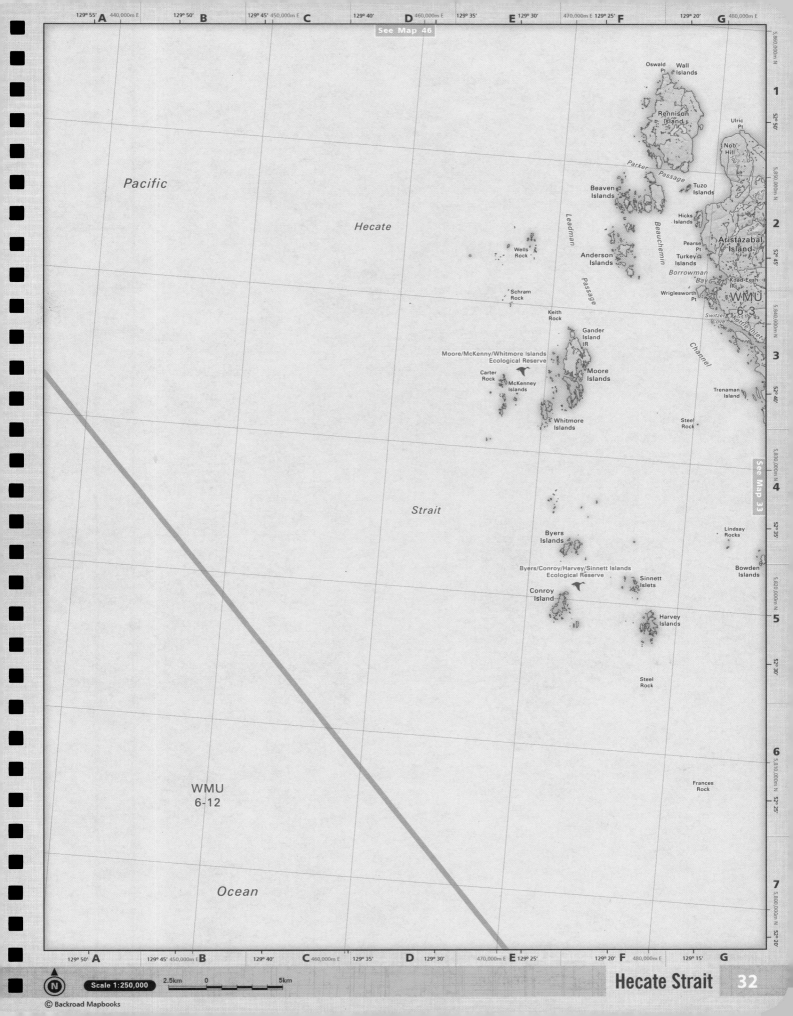

Pacific

Hecate

Strait

Ocean

WMU
6-12

Oswald
Pt
Wall
Islands

Rennison
Island

Ulric
Pt

Nob
Hill

Parker Passage

Beaven
Islands

Tuzo
Islands

Hicks
Islands

Aristazabal
Island

Leadman

Beauchemin

Pearse
Pt
Turkey
Islands

Borrowman
Bay

Kdaa-Eesh
IR

WMU
6-3

Wells
Rock

Anderson
Islands

passage

Wriglesworth
Pt

Switzer
Cove

Kettle Inlet

Schram
Rock

Keith
Rock

Channel

Trenaman
Island

Gander
Island
IR

Moore/McKenny/Whitmore Islands
Ecological Reserve

Carter
Rock

McKenney
Islands

Moore
Islands

Whitmore
Islands

Steel
Rock

See Map 33

Byers
Islands

Lindsay
Rocks

Byers/Conroy/Harvey/Sinnett Islands
Ecological Reserve

Sinnett
Islets

Bowden
Islands

Conroy
Island

Harvey
Islands

Steel
Rock

Frances
Rock

N

Scale 1:250,000

2.5km   0   5km

© Backroad Mapbooks

Hecate Strait **32**

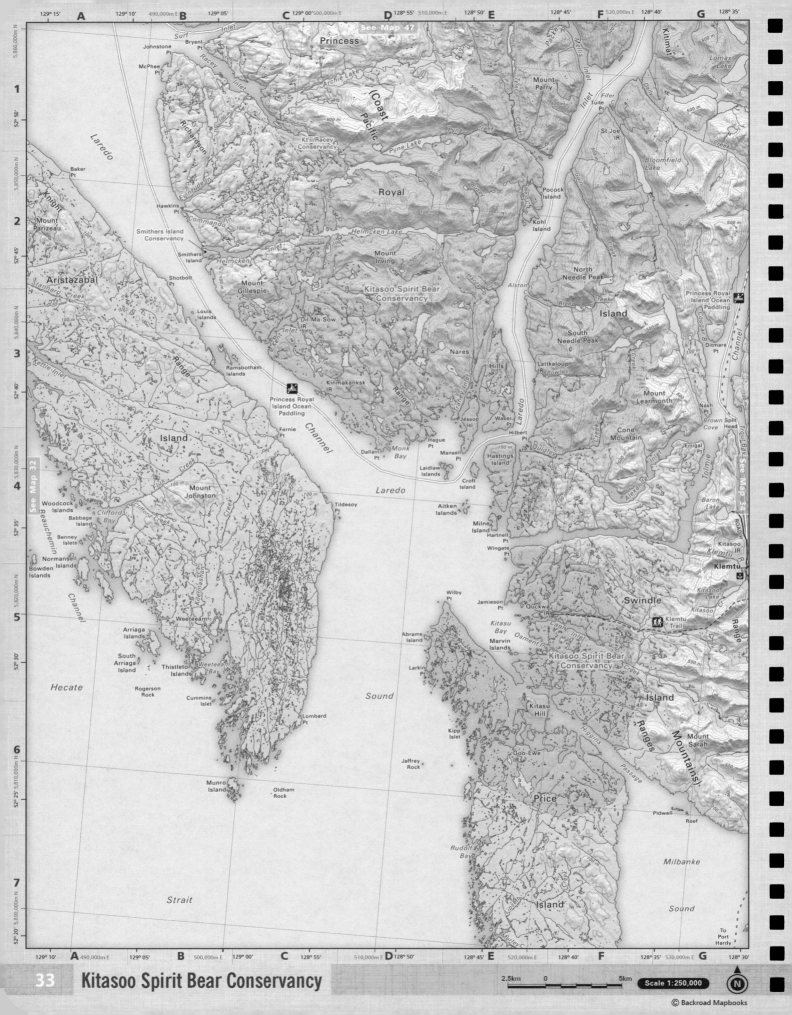

Kitasoo Spirit Bear Conservancy

2.5km 0 5km Scale 1:250,000

© Backroad Mapbooks

Scale 1:250,000

2.5km 0 5km

© Backroad Mapbooks

Roderick Island

34

Huchsduwachsdu
Nuyem Jees / Kitlope
Heritage Conservancy

WMU
6-3

Fiordland
Conservancy

Cascade-Sutslem
Conservancy

Mountains)

Ranges

WMU
5-9

Ikesumkah Lake

Ellerslie
Roscoe
Conservancy

Thumb
Pt

Noota
IR

Latch
Pt

Martin
Lake

Cornice
Peak

Pollard
Peak

Comet
Mountain

Skowquiltz
River IR

Skowquiltz
Pt

Skowquiltz
Bay

Channel

White Cliff
Pt

Nascall Bay
Hot Springs

Nascall
Island

Nascall
Rocks

Nascal
Bay

Eucott Bay
Hot Springs

Ram Bluff
Hot Springs

Eucott
Bay

Edward
Pt

Labouchere

Ovsen
Pt

Dean

Channel

2.5km   0   5km   Scale 1:250,000

© Backroad Mapbooks

See Map 36
See Map 38

37 **South Tweedsmuir Prov Park**

2.5km 0 5km

Scale 1:250,000

© Backroad Mapbooks

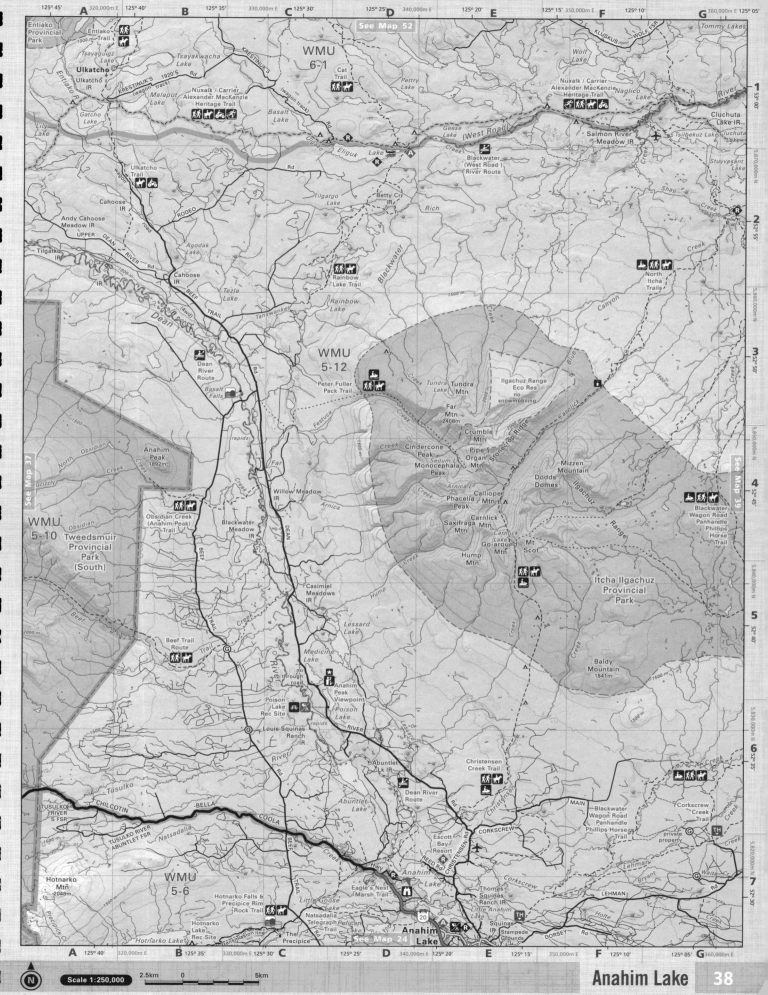

Scale 1:250,000

2.5km · 0 · 5km

© Backroad Mapbooks

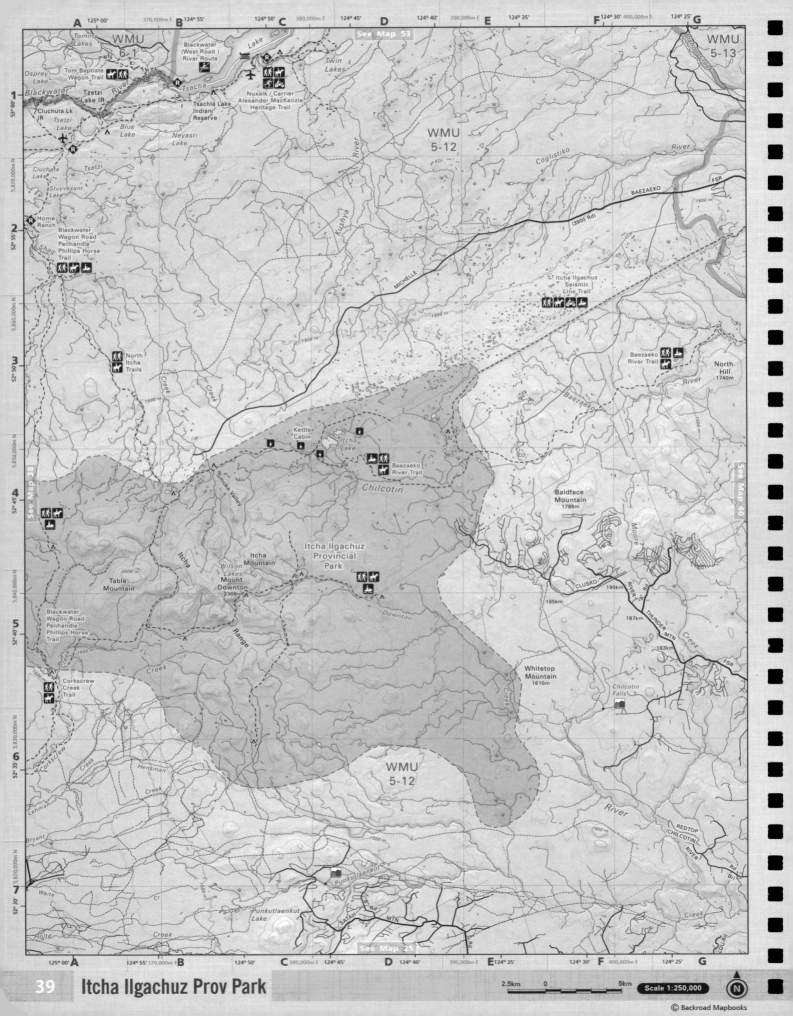

Scale 1:250,000

© Backroad Mapbooks

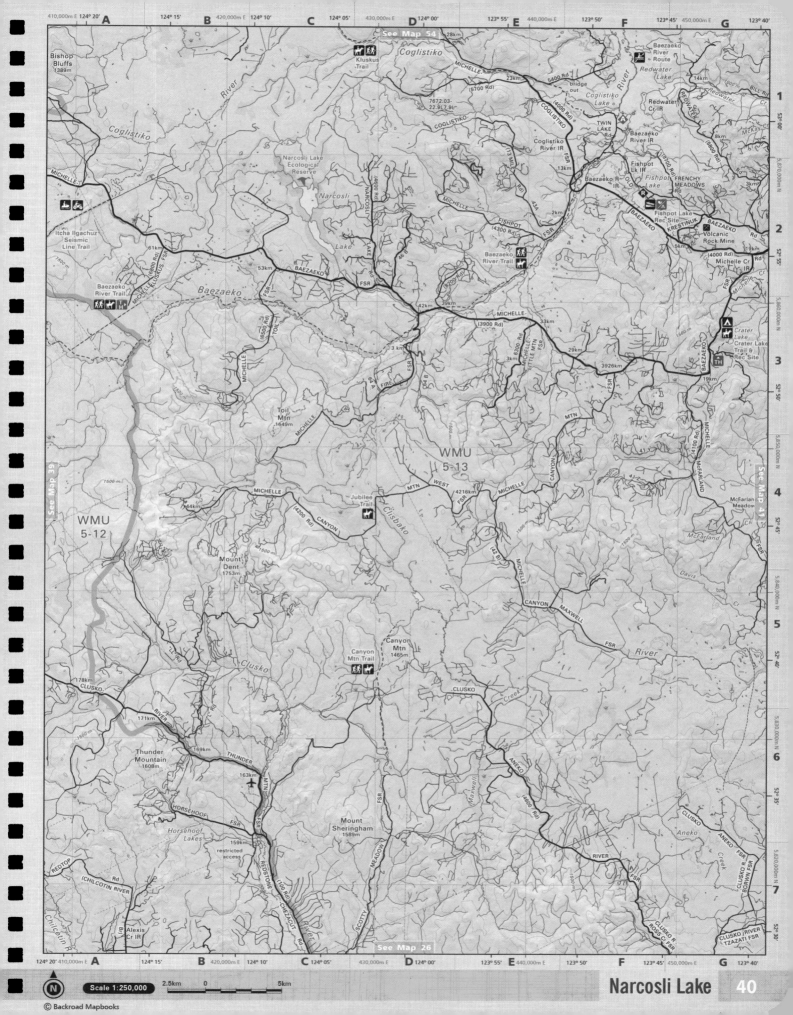

See Map 39
See Map 41

Narcosli Lake

40

Scale 1:250,000

2.5km   0   5km

© Backroad Mapbooks

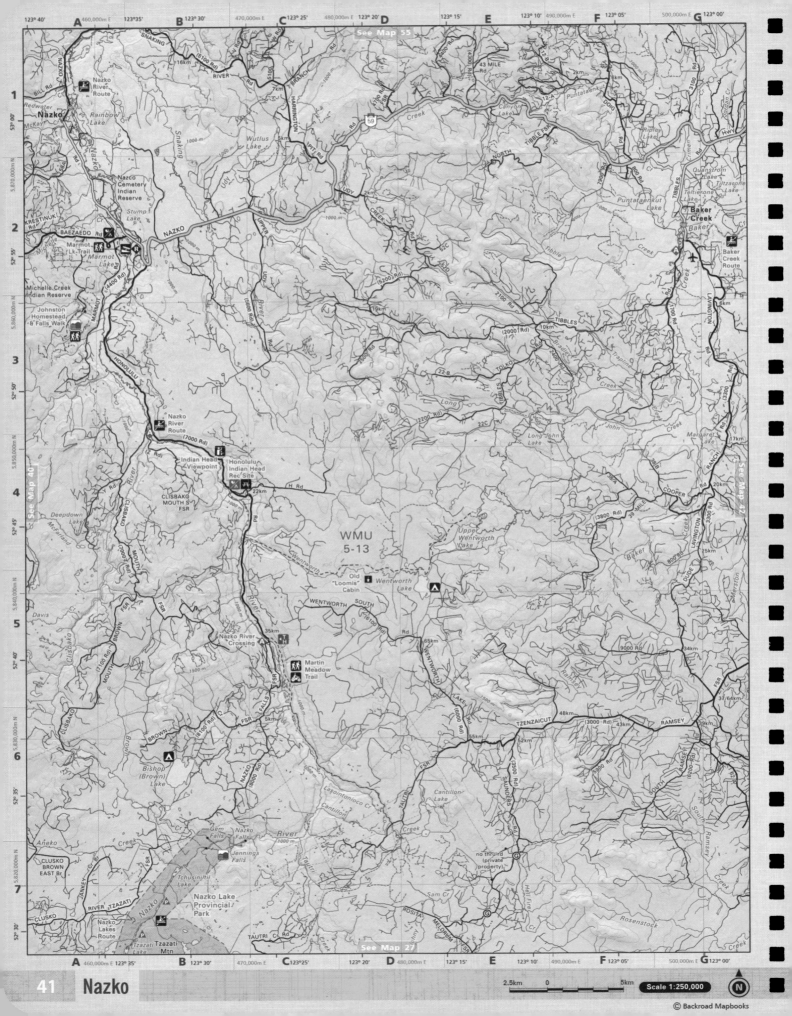

Scale 1:250,000

© Backroad Mapbooks

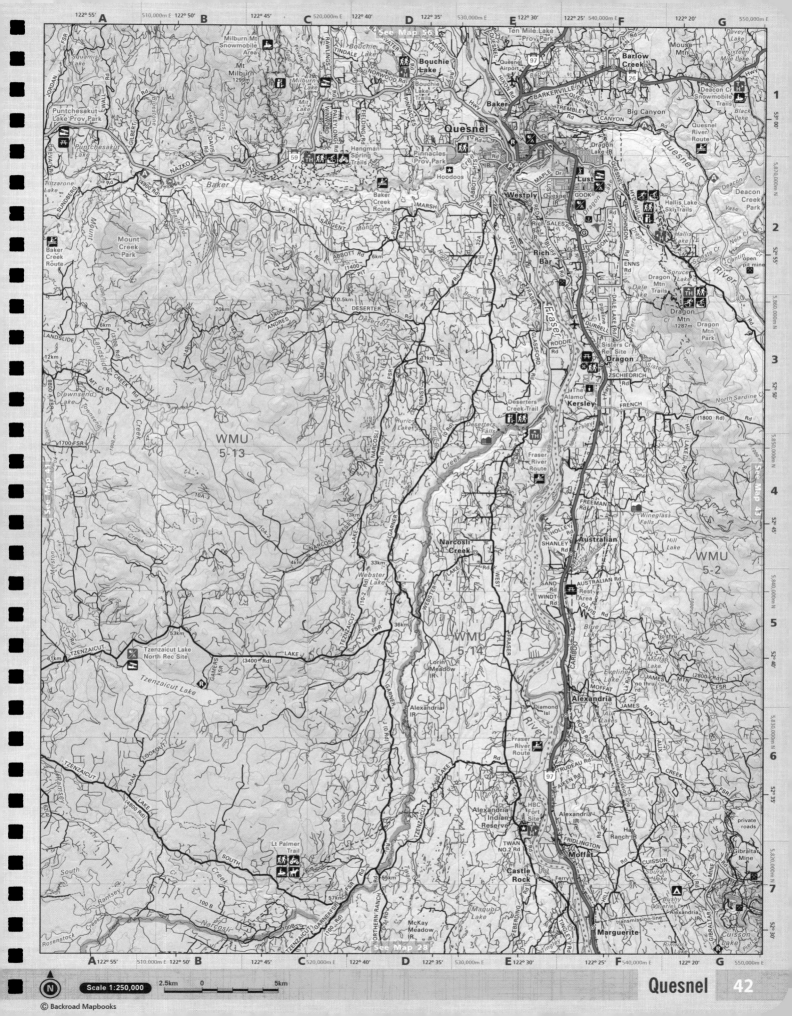

Scale 1:250,000

© Backroad Mapbooks

Scale 1:250,000

© Backroad Mapbooks

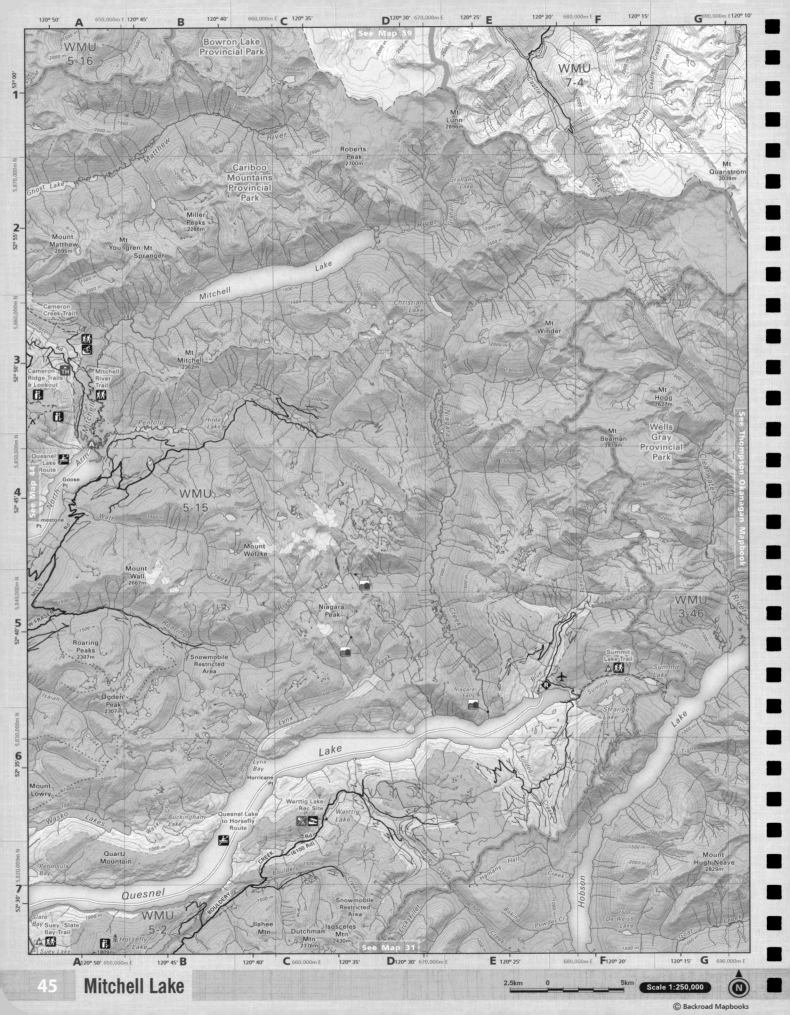

Mitchell Lake

Scale 1:250,000

© Backroad Mapbooks

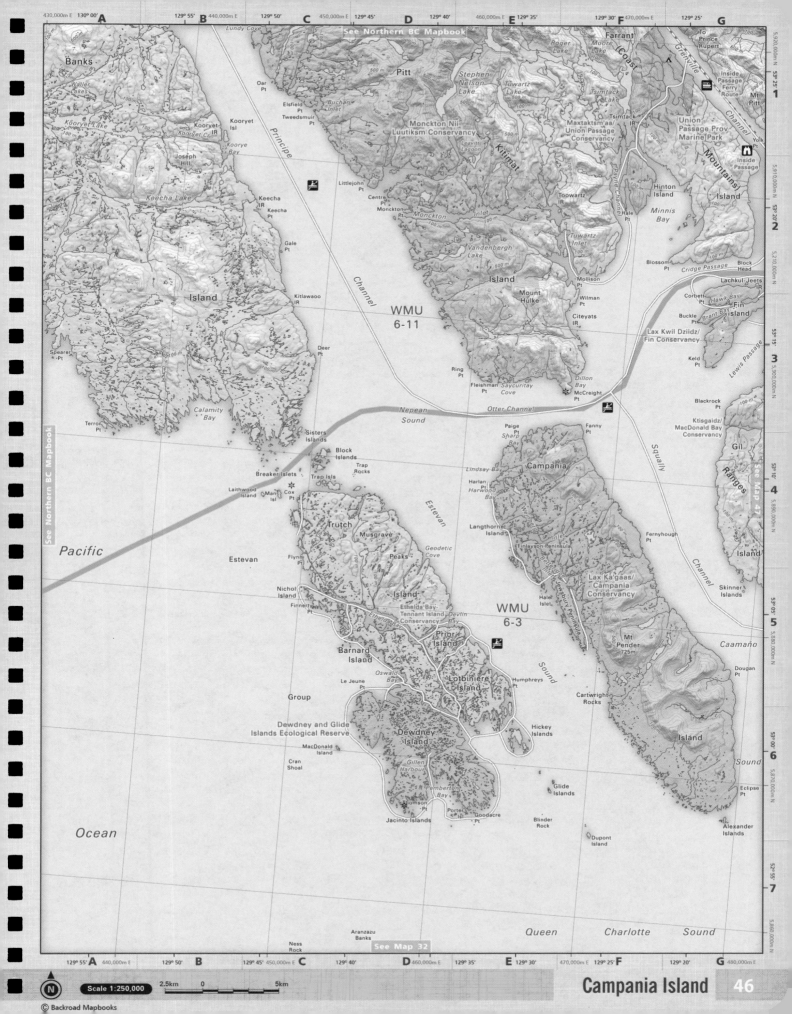

WMU
6-11

WMU
6-3

Pacific

Ocean

Queen   Charlotte   Sound

See Map 32

© Backroad Mapbooks

Scale 1:250,000
2.5km   0   5km

Campania Island   46

Scale 1:250,000

2.5km   0   5km

© Backroad Mapbooks

Scale 1:250,000

2.5km 0 5km

© Backroad Mapbooks

See Map 47

See Map 49

See Map 34

Scale 1:250,000

© Backroad Mapbooks

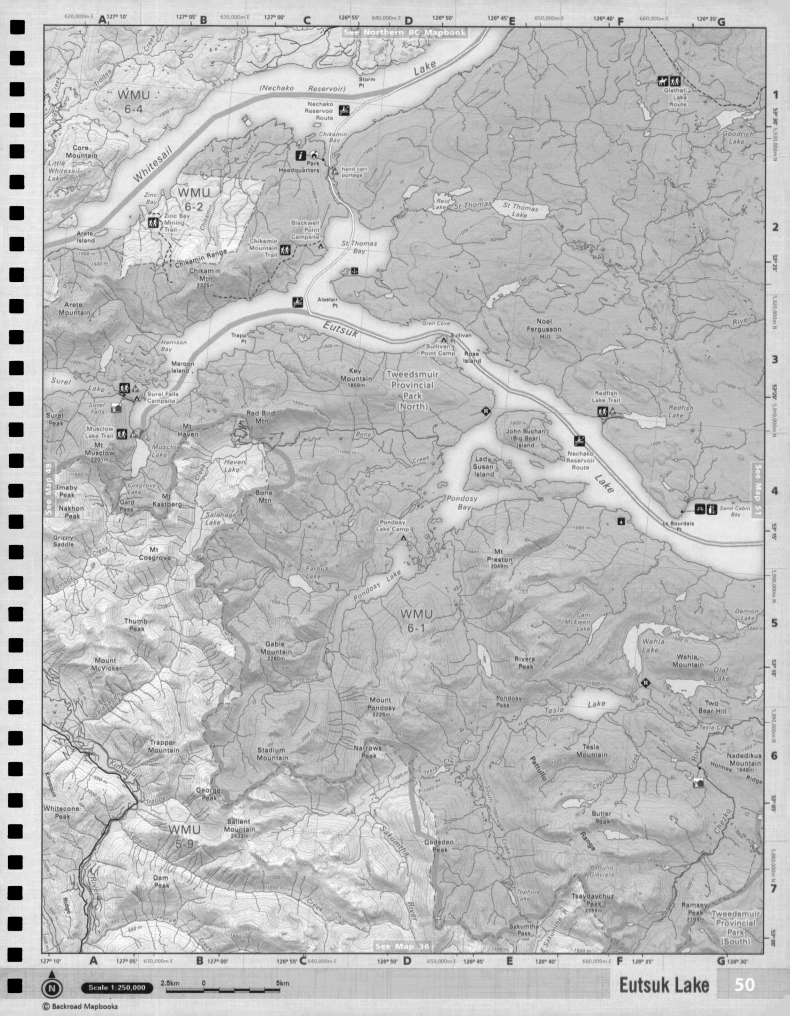

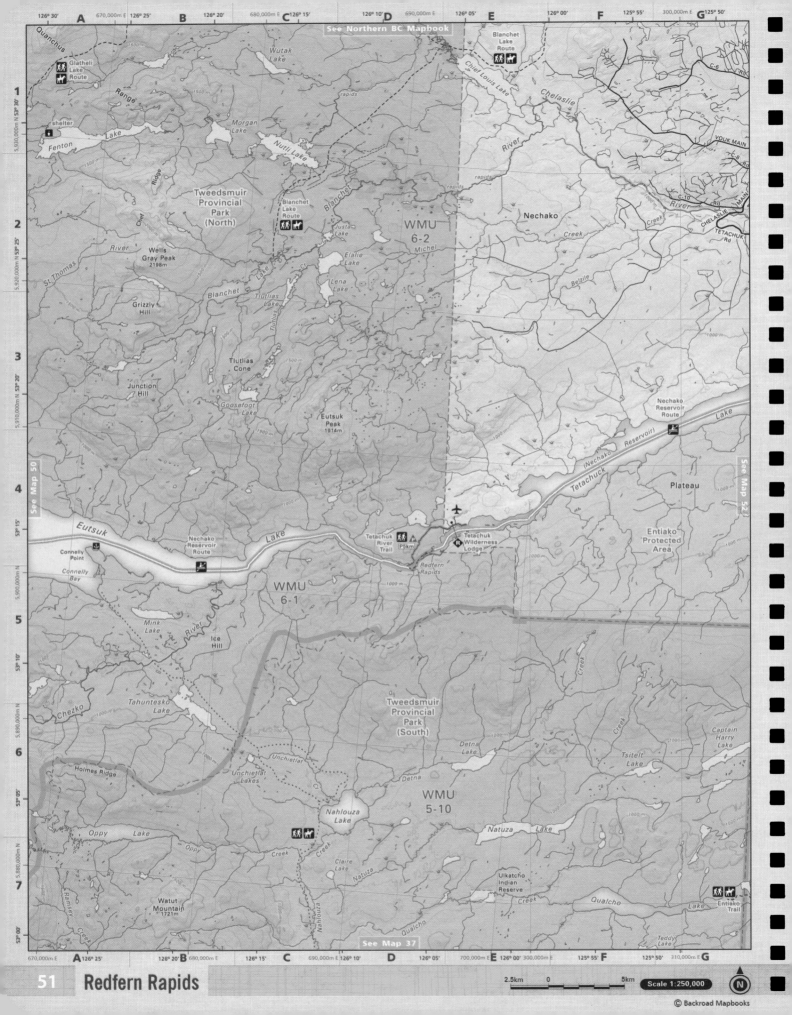

Scale 1:250,000

© Backroad Mapbooks

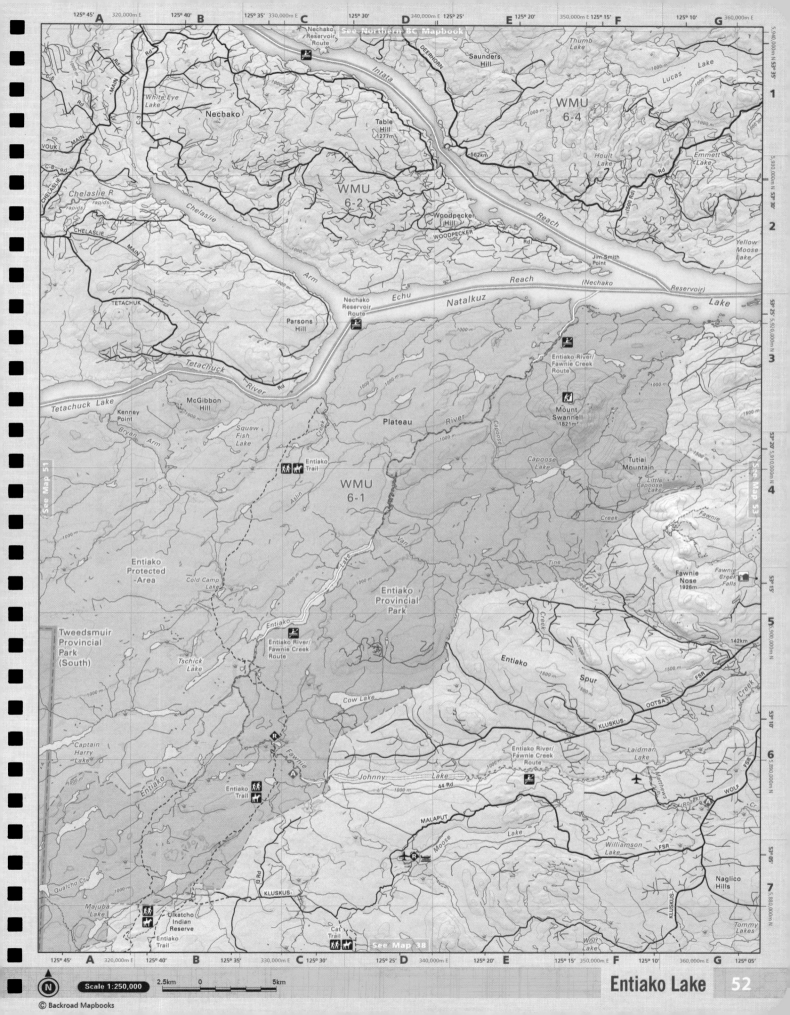

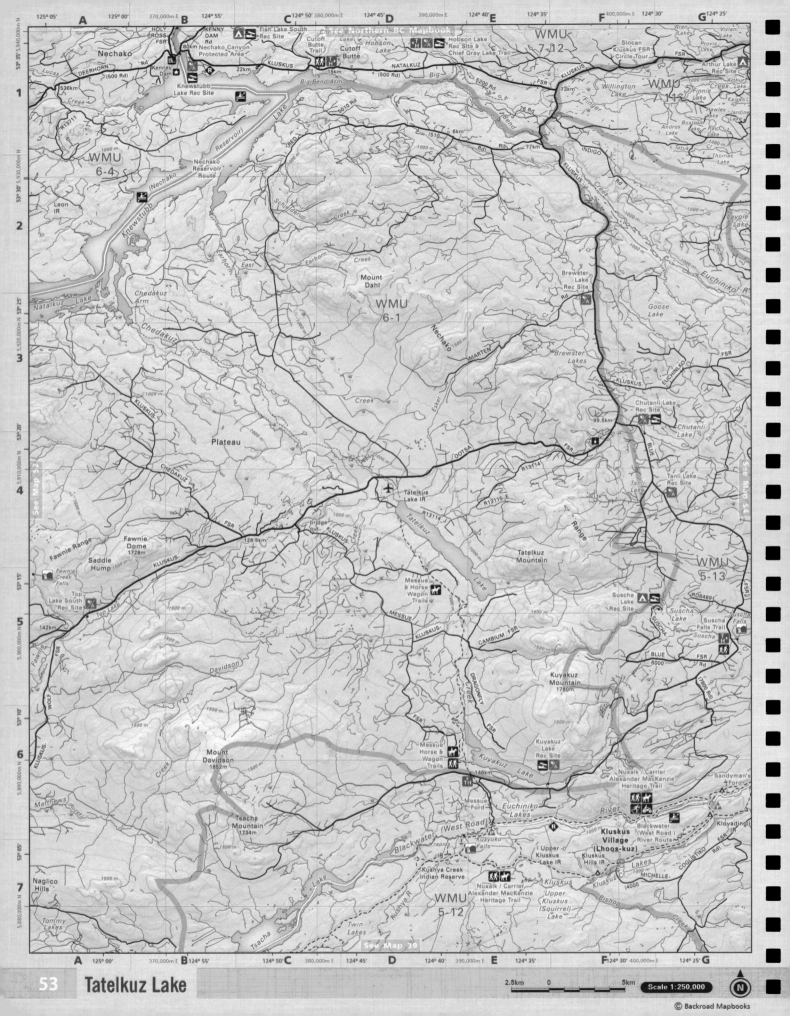

Tatelkuz Lake

2.5km 0 5km

Scale 1:250,000

© Backroad Mapbooks

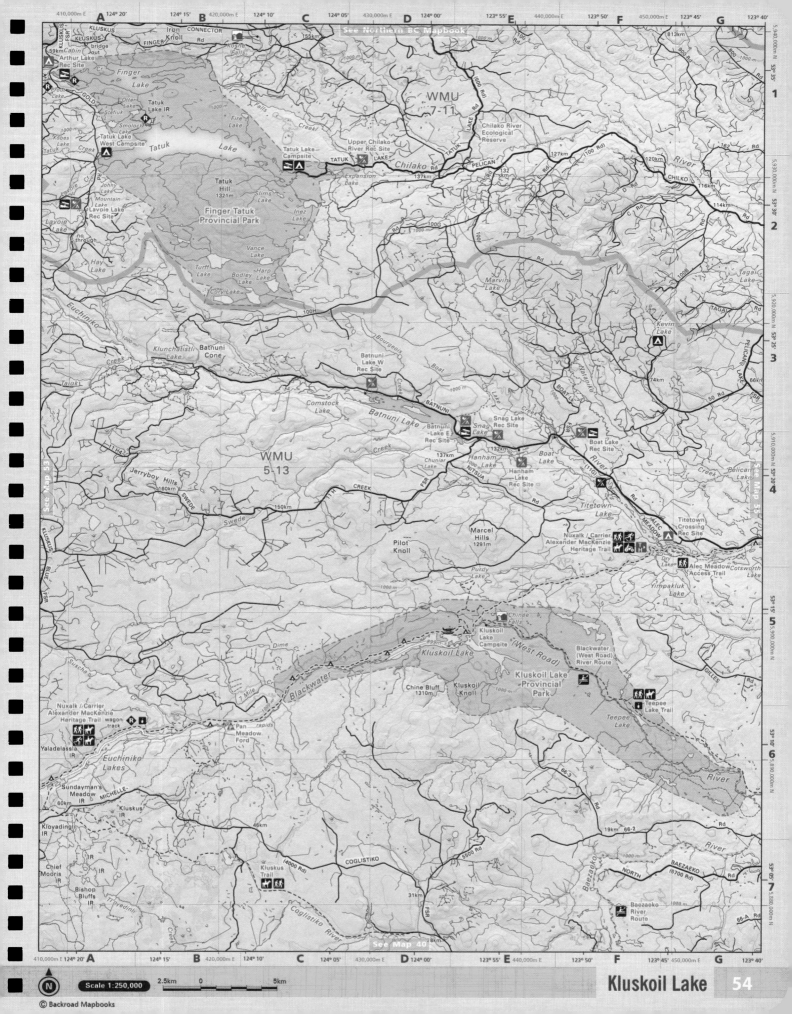

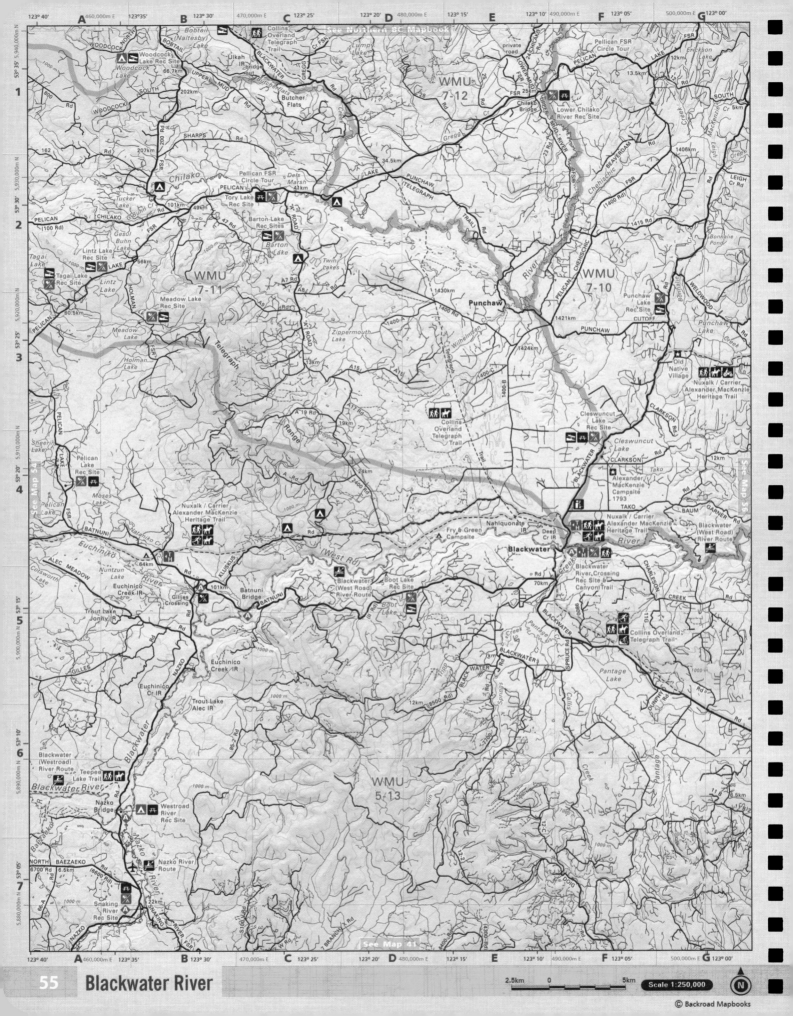

Blackwater River

2.5km 0 5km Scale 1:250,000

© Backroad Mapbooks

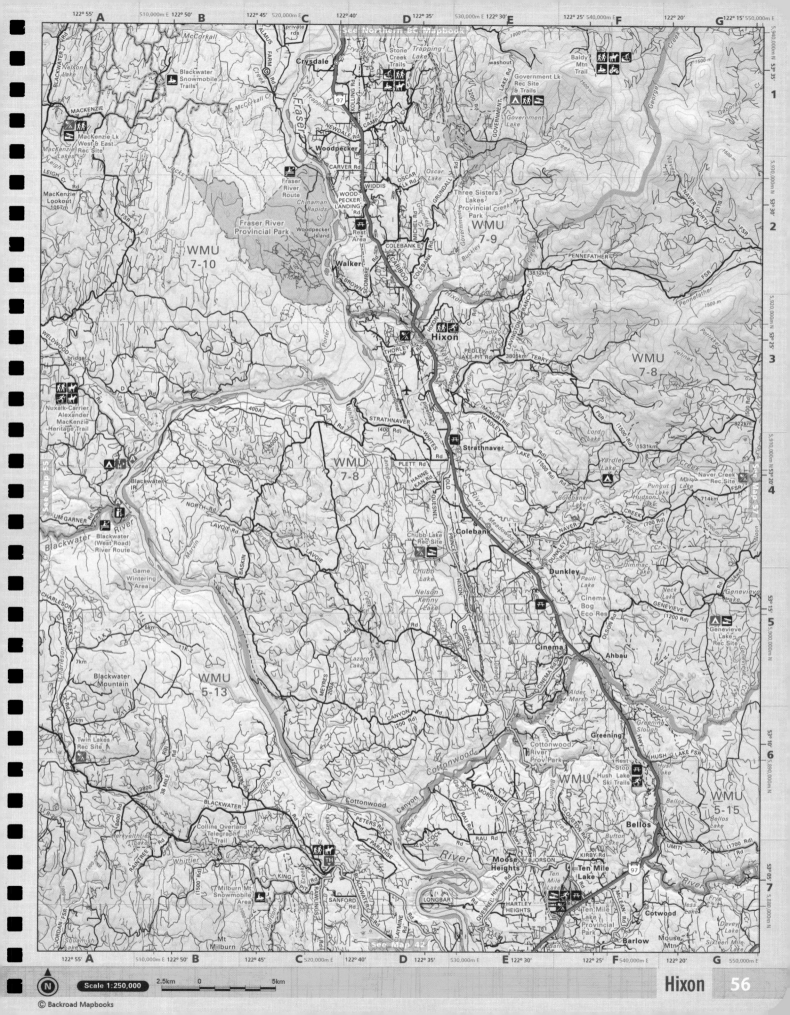

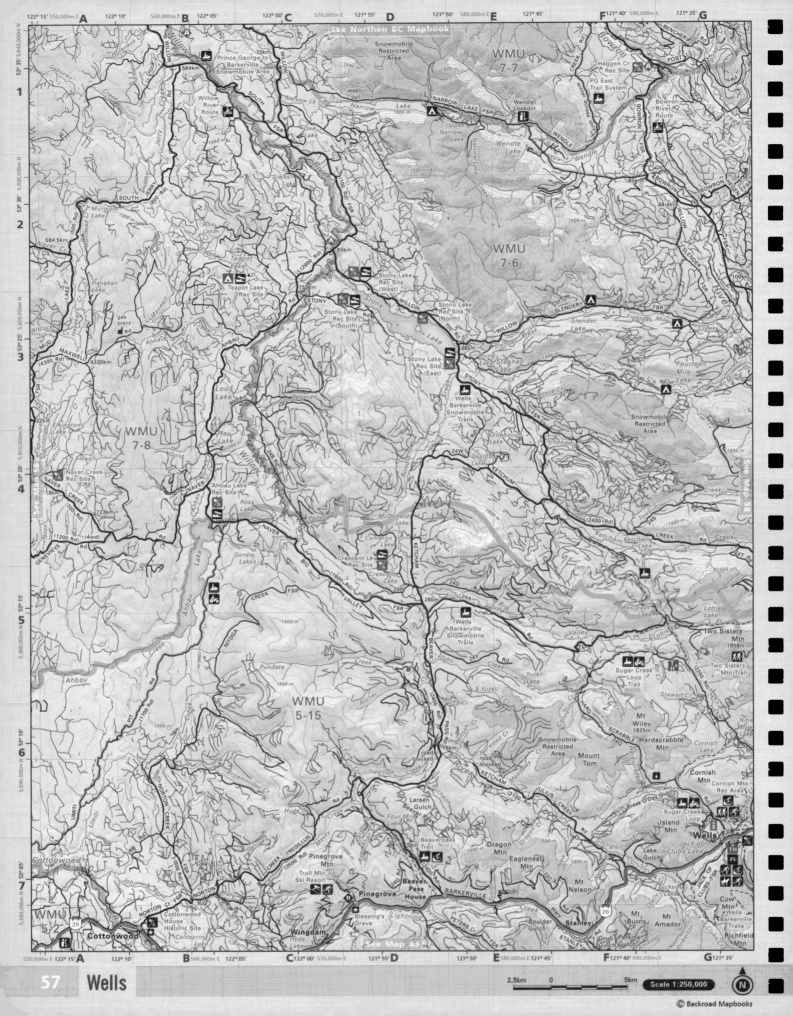

Scale 1:250,000

© Backroad Mapbooks

© Backroad Mapbooks

Scale 1:250,000

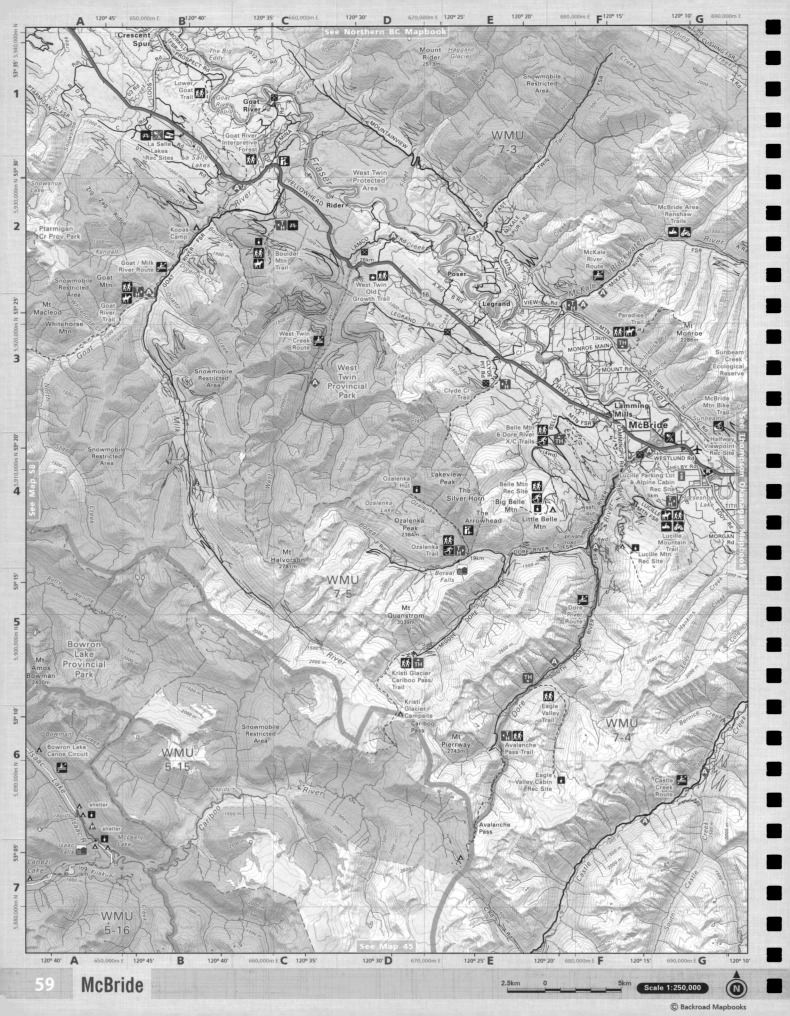

Scale 1:250,000

© Backroad Mapbooks

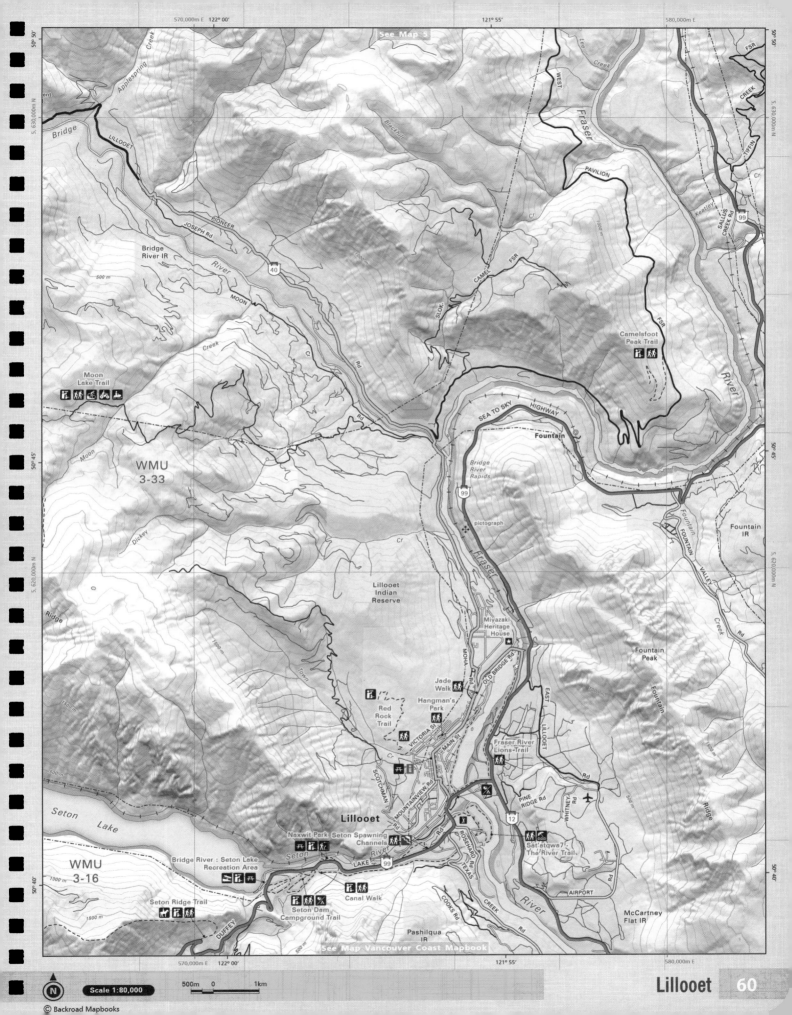

570,000m E 122° 00'

121° 55'

580,000m E

50° 50'

5,630,000m N

Bridge

Appplespring Creek

LILLOOET

River

Bridge
River IR

JOSEPH Rd

PIONEER

40

MOON

Creek

Moon
Lake Trail

WMU
3-33

Moon

Dickey

500 m

Ridge

5,620,000m N

Seton Lake

WMU
3-16

1000 m

Seton Ridge Trail

1500 m

DUFFEY

Bridge River : Seton Lake
Recreation Area

Naxwit Park

Lilllooet

Seton Spawning
Channels

Seton

Canal Walk

Seton Dam
Campground Trail

LAKE RIVER

99

Pashilqua
IR

Cr

Blackhill

Cr

Rd

Cr

FSR

CAMEL

SLOK.

Lilllooet Indian
Reserve

Town

Red
Rock
Trail

Cr

Cr

SCOTCHMAN

MOUNTAINVIEW Rd

VICTORIA St

MAIN St

Jade
Walk

Hangman's
Park

ROSEHARD Rd

TEXAS

COOKS Rd

CREEK

Fraser

WEST

Lee Creek

PAVILION

1000 m

Camelsfoot
Peak Trail

SEA TO SKY HIGHWAY

Fountain

Bridge
River
Rapids

99

pictograph

Fraser

MOHA Rd

OLD BRIDGE Rd

Miyazaki
Heritage
House

EAST LILLOOET

Fraser River
Lions Trail

PINE RIDGE Rd

WHITNEY Rd

12

Sat'atqwa7
The River Trail

AIRPORT

McCartney
Flat IR

River

KEATLEY Rd

SALUS CREEK Rd

99

TIFFIN CREEK

FSR

Cr

River

50° 45'

Fountain
FOUNTAIN

Fountain
IR

FOUNTAIN VALLEY

5,620,000m N

Fountain
Peak

Creek

Rd

Fountain

Ridge

Rd

50° 40'

570,000m E 122° 00'

121° 55'

580,000m E

N

Scale 1:80,000

500m 0 1km

© Backroad Mapbooks

Lilllooet   **60**

CAMPING & RV IN BC

Go where your spirit takes you!

British Columbia's backyard provides campers and RVers with numerous choices of camping sweet spots. Search Camping and RV BC's mapping tool to locate over 1,500 campgrounds, offering four unique camping experiences:

- **Privately operated campgrounds and RV parks** (including municipal campgrounds)
- **Provincial campgrounds** (BC Parks)
- **National campgrounds** (Parks Canada)
- **Recreation Sites and Trails BC** (operated by the provincial government)

Plan to gear up and get on the road!

RVCAMPINGBC.COM
Your one stop for campgrounds and RV parks in British Columbia

CONNECT WITH US f y p •• You Tube

SCAN ME!

Reservations:

_____

_____

_____

_____

_____

_____

_____

_____

_____

_____

_____

_____

_____

_____

_____

_____

_____

Service Directory

Find what you are looking for, from our trusted
Service Directory Members.

▶**Accommodations** ▶ **Tours & Guides** ▶ **Sales & Services**

LITTLEFORT
FLY AND TACKLE
QUALITY FLYFISHING PRODUCTS

25 YEARS EXPERIENCE

VISIT OUR ONLINE STORE
flyanglers
warehouse.com

YOUR FISHING HEADQUATERS ON THE FISHING HIGHWAY 24
FOR INFO AND GUIDING ON LOCAL LAKES AND RIVERS
VISIT OUR WEBSITE:

www.littlefort.com

136 HWY. 24 (BOX 75), LITTLE FORT, B.C., V0E 2C0 | PHONE (250) 677-4366

CHAUNIGAN LAKE LODGE
British Columbia's Legendary Southern Chilcotin

**Deluxe & Rustic Log Cabins
Large Native Rainbow Trout
Horseback Riding**

Toll Free:
1-888-879-8885
Local: 250-394-7077
www.chaunigan.com

Chilcotin Holidays
Authentic Wilderness Adventures

Mountain Adventures   Ranch Based Adventures

Native Tours   Custom Adventures

Excited to start your adventure?
250-238-2274 www.chilcotinholidays.com

Gun Creek Road, Gold Bridge, B.C., V0K 1P0   Find us on **facebook**

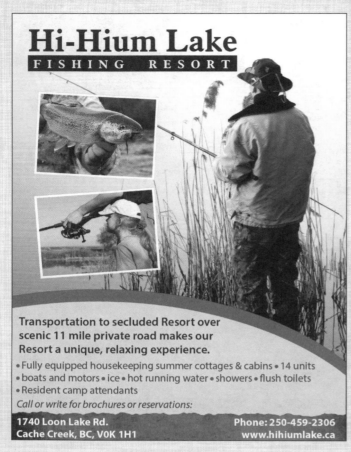

Hi-Hium Lake
FISHING RESORT

Transportation to secluded Resort over scenic 11 mile private road makes our Resort a unique, relaxing experience.

• Fully equipped housekeeping summer cottages & cabins • 14 units
• boats and motors • ice • hot running water • showers • flush toilets
• Resident camp attendants
Call or write for brochures or reservations:

1740 Loon Lake Rd.
Cache Creek, BC, V0K 1H1

Phone: 250-459-2306
www.hihiumlake.ca

Kokanee Bay
FISHING RESORT
on beautiful Puntzi Lake

Lake Front CABINS
with full kitchen and bath
Lake Front CAMPING
with boat rentals

Fishing | Hiking
Bird Watching
ATVing | Biking
Hunting

3904 Puntzi Lake Rd, Chilanko Forks, B.C.
Ph: 250-481-1130 | kokaneebayfishingresort.ca

Measured in Pounds... not Inches.

SHERIDAN LAKE RESORT

• Trolling • Fly-Fishing • Cabins • Camping • Grassy RV Sites • Tackle Shop
• Boat Launch • Hunting • Water Sports • Boat & Motor Rental
• Wildlife Viewing • Internet Access

Please Call for Directions/Reservations
P: 250-593-4611

www.sheridanlakeresort.com

CABINS | CAMPING | FISHING | RECREATION

Biking
Canoeing
Boat Rentals
Swimming
Camping
Jogging
and more!

Fishing
Rainbow Trout
Hiking
ATVing
Sandy beach
Water Ski

COME AS STRANGERS
LEAVE AS FRIENDS

THE PERFECT WAY
TO RELAX!

SHERIDAN
PARK RESORT

7118 Boulanger Road
Lone Butte, B.C., V0K 1X1

250-593-4643
sheridanlake.com

BARNEY'S
LAKESIDE RESORT
www.barneyslakesideresort.com
Puntzi Lake, British Columbia

Activities Barney's Lakeside Resort:
Fishing • Canoeing • Bird watching • Swimming
Kayaking • Hunting • Hiking • ATV Riding
Mountain Biking • And much much more ......

Book Now: 250-481-1100 | markchipman61@hotmail.com

CARIBOO COUNTRY
INN & RANCH
Experience the Seasons...

* **OPEN 365 DAYS A YEAR!**
Full service campground
Cozy cabin rentals

CALL US TODAY
for more information
250-620-3434

Birch Bay Rd, Horsefly, BC
caribooncountryinn.com

Fish - Hike - Canoe - Kayak - Swimming - and more

Eagan Lake Resort
Your hosts Kris & Cheryl Verheul
• Limited large RV campsites
• Private lakefront log cabins & docks
• Kokanee & Rainbow fishing
• Mountain Biking   • Hunting
• X-country Skiing   • Snowmobiling
• Hiking   • Water Sports
• and much more!

P.O. Box 139, Bridge Lake, BC, V0K 1E0
P: 250-593-4343
www.eaganlake.com

Rejuvenate and recharge in BC's finest wilderness
ELYSIA RESORT
QUESNEL LAKE, B.C.

250-243-2433
Email: rainbow@elysiaresort.com
www.elysiaresort.com | **www.fishrainbowwaters.com**

Escott Bay
Resort
escottbay.com

📍 P.O. Box 3375, Anahim Lake, BC, V0L 1C0
📠 Phone: (250) 742-3233 Fax: (250) 742-3233
Toll Free: 1-888-380-8802 ✉ escottb@xplornet.com

Relax & watch the world go by...

Fawn Lake Resort

Fly Fishing / Lakefront Log Cabins / RV Campground / Boat Rentals
Fawn Lake Resort / Lone Butte / British Columbia
250 - 593 - 4654 / www.fawnlakeresort.com

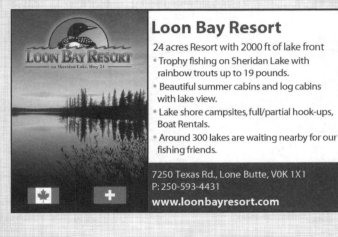

LOON BAY RESORT
on Sheridan Lake, Hwy 24

Loon Bay Resort
24 acres Resort with 2000 ft of lake front
• Trophy fishing on Sheridan Lake with rainbow trouts up to 19 pounds.
• Beautiful summer cabins and log cabins with lake view.
• Lake shore campsites, full/partial hook-ups, Boat Rentals.
• Around 300 lakes are waiting nearby for our fishing friends.

7250 Texas Rd., Lone Butte, V0K 1X1
P: 250-593-4431
www.loonbayresort.com

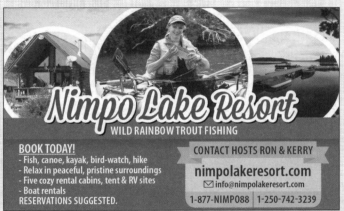

Nimpo Lake Resort
WILD RAINBOW TROUT FISHING

BOOK TODAY!
- Fish, canoe, kayak, bird-watch, hike
- Relax in peaceful, pristine surroundings
- Five cozy rental cabins, tent & RV sites
- Boat rentals
RESERVATIONS SUGGESTED.

CONTACT HOSTS RON & KERRY
nimpolakeresort.com
✉ info@nimpolakeresort.com
1-877-NIMPO88 | 1-250-742-3239

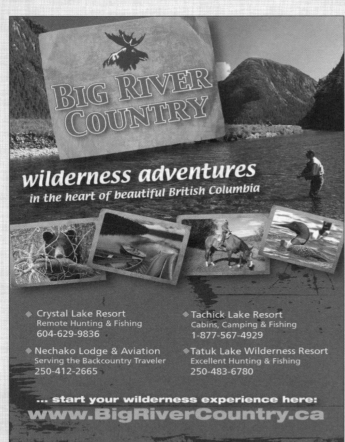

BIG RIVER COUNTRY

wilderness adventures
in the heart of beautiful British Columbia

◆ Crystal Lake Resort
Remote Hunting & Fishing
604-629-9836

◆ Tachick Lake Resort
Cabins, Camping & Fishing
1-877-567-4929

◆ Nechako Lodge & Aviation
Serving the Backcountry Traveler
250-412-2665

◆ Tatuk Lake Wilderness Resort
Excellent Hunting & Fishing
250-483-6780

... start your wilderness experience here:
www.BigRiverCountry.ca

Two Stop Shopping on Highway 24

Coffee Shop   Groceries   Produce

From...
Groceries to Gas, Propane, Liquor Store, Fishing Supplies, Deli/Bakery, Laundromat, Coffee Shop, ATM, Fireworks, Ultra-pure Water refill station, Fresh Local Produce, Lottery, Canada Post Office & More!

Interlakes Market & Esso
Corner of Horse Lake Rd & HWY 24
250-593-2242

Sheridan Lake Market
Sheridan Frontage Rd.
250-593-4616

B.C.'s Fishing Highway
Lakes Markets

FRANK'S SUPERMARKET

PROVIDING BOTH LOCALS & TRAVELLERS WITH A HUGE SELECTION OF **FISHING** AND **HUNTING** GEAR ALONG WITH **GROCERIES** AND THEIR FAMOUS HARD **ICE CREAM** SELECTION.

2310 QUESNEL-HYDRAULIC RD
QUESNEL, BRITISH COLUMBIA V2J4C4
PHONE: (250) 747-2092

Surplus Herby's
"The craziest store in town"

○ Fishing Gear
○ Camping Equipment
○ Outdoor Equipment
○ International Military Surplus
○ Closeout Merchandise

Pick from 500,000 items

Kamloops
248 Tranquille Road
1-800-665-4533

Vernon
3325- 31st Ave
1-800-663-2887

Williams Lake
527 Mackenzie Ave S.
1-800-661-5188

Prince George
1175 2nd Ave
250-562-8000

www.surplusherbys.com

Chilcotin Guns

One stop source for all your outdoor needs.

○ Fishing   ○ Paintball Equipment
○ Hunting   ○ Outdoor Equipment

P: 250-392-6800   1542 S. Broadway, Williams Lake, BC

"Your most diversified sporting goods store in the cariboo"

eXeter SPORTING GOODS LTD.

100 MILE HOUSE, BC CANADA

320 Birch Ave. South

We carry a large selection of

- Fishing Tackle
- Fly Fishing
- Firearms & Acc.
- Ammunition
- Camping Supplies
- Skates & Hockey Equip.
- Pawn Shop
- X-country & Accessories
- Reloading
- Misc. Sporting Goods

Jude Dion P: 250.395.4626 or 1.888.729.5507 exeter@bcinternet.net

HORSEFLY hardware

FISHING TACKLE & HANDMADE FLIES   CAMPING SUPPLIES   AMMUNITION & HUNTING SUPPLIES   GIFTS & SOUVENIRS   PLUMBING & ELECTRIC   GENERAL PAINT

📞 (250) 620-3338   📍 3-3044 BOSWELL ST, HORSEFLY, BC, V0L 1L0

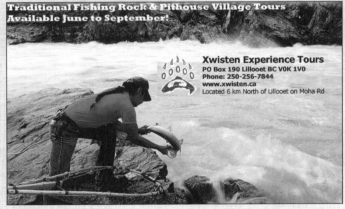

GAS STATION • GENERAL STORE
PUB
POST OFFICE • ICE • RESTAURANT
JACK O'CLUBS

GAS STATION | POST OFFICE | GENERAL STORE

We sell pretty much anything ya need getting new things in all the time, stop on in and ask, if we dont have it than it goes on the list!

JACK O'CLUBS GENERAL

12383 Barkerville HWY
Barkerville, B.C.
V0K 2R0

FIND US ON 📘

📞 (250)994-3242

Your Local Store is:

Home hardware

288 Reid Street,
Quesnel, BC

Willis-Harper Hardware

Serving hunters, anglers & outdoor enthusiasts for over 50 years.

Phone: (250) 992 - 2135   • FISHING • HUNTING • CAMPING

Traditional Fishing Rock & Pithouse Village Tours Available June to September!

Xwisten Experience Tours
PO Box 190 Lillooet BC V0K 1V0
Phone: 250-256-7844
www.xwisten.ca
Located 6 km North of Lillooet on Moha Rd

DELUXE WALL TENTS

FREE SHIPPING IN CANADA
★ custom wall tents ★
★ wood stoves ★
★ aluminum frames ★ tarps ★
★ game bags ★ bedrolls ★
★ diesel heaters ★ cots ★
www.deluxewalltents.com
250-704-2534
perry@deluxewalltents.com

100 Mile House

Century Hardware Ltd.

For Home & Outdoor
Recreation Supplies
Houseware & Plumbing
Heating & More

P: 250-395-2216

488 Birch Ave, Box 608
100 Mile House, BC, V0K 2E0

www.homehardware.ca

Quesnel

Nazko Cafe

Restaurant, Convenience Store, Laundry mat, Showers, Cabin Rentals, Gas & Diesel, Crew Meals Available.

Right across from Marmot Lake.

Fishing Year Round.

P: 250-249-5226
F: 250-249-5226

9480 Nazko Rd.
Quesnel, BC V2J 3H9

Come Visit Us Today!

Williams Lake

The Open Book

Books * Magazines * Newspapers
Local History * Maps & Travel Books

THE LARGEST SELECTION OF BOOKS & MAGAZINES IN THE CARIBOO!

P: 250-392-2665
openbook.wl@gmail.com

247 Oliver Street
Williams Lake, BC, V2G 1M2

www.theopenbook.ca

We've Got Your Back in the Back Country!

HORSE COUNCIL
BRITISH COLUMBIA

HCBC supports recreational and trail riders in BC by providing excellent third party liability and accidental death and dismemberment coverage from Capri Insurance with our yearly membership.

Preservation, access to trails, and safety is of great importance to all those who enjoy the pleasure of a ride through the countryside. Horse Council BC provides safety manuals, educational resources, funding, and guidance and support to members interested in building, maintaining, and using the trail systems in BC.

For more information please visit the Horse Council BC website at: www.hcbc.ca or contact us directly at recreation@hcbc.ca

Follow Us Online!

Trip Planning Notes:

_____

_____

_____

_____

_____

_____

_____

_____

_____

_____

_____

_____

_____

_____

Adventures
Cariboo Chilcotin Coast BC

The following is a how-to for navigating the Adventure section of this guide. For each activity we showcase alternatives to help you plan your trip. We then link these adventures to the maps and surrounding areas to help you discover more of the region and all that there is to experience.

▶ Adventure Summary

For each Adventure section we have provided a quick overview summary of that activity as it pertains to the region. This write-up will give you a feel for what the region has to offer as well as a better understanding of what the given area offers relative to that particular activity.

▶ Listing & Descriptions

Each Adventure section is made up of countless listings and descriptions of different activities. From a great fishing spot, recreation site or park to visit, to a great trail, natural attraction or area to explore. Each guidebook offers endless possibilities when it comes to planning your next adventure.

Sarah Point (Map 46/A5)
Sarah Point marks the northern tip of Malaspina Peninsula. It is a good spot for fishing because fish entering Desolation Sound must pass by the point. There are some wintering Chinook but the main fishery is from May and June for Chinook and late August to early September for Coho. Trolling around the point seems to work the best.

Thacker Regional Park (Map 15/F6)
Found in Hope, this 9 hectare park is home to a new spawning channel, built in 2001 for Coho, pink and chum salmon. The trail along the channel is part of the Trans Canada Trail and is very popular in fall when the salmon spawn. In summer, there is a popular swimming hole at the confluence of Sucker Creek and the Coquihalla River.

▶ Activities

Another great feature many of our listings have is the symbols that showcase the numerous activities that can be done on the trail or in the area. Most of the symbols are easy to decipher, but the Legend on Page VII provides a description for each symbol.

▶ Map references/navigating

Probably the most popular feature of each listing is the map reference that tells you where to find and explore these great adventures on our maps.

Cheam Peak (Map 5/A3)
Cheam is one of the most prominent peaks in the Fraser Valley. How far you have to ski depends on how high you can get a vehicle up the Chipmunk Creek Forest Service Road to the south. At the base of Cheam Peak is a lovely open meadow and the ascent, while stiff, isn't too difficult. Nearby Knight Peak is another popular ski destination.

** Note: we have provided you with a trip planning page where you can write down important notes about your adventures, updates, errors or omissions.

Backroad
Adventures

When exploring the backroads of the Cariboo Chilcotin region, you will be mesmerized by a vast, ever-changing landscape. From the waters of the Pacific Coast to the sprawling Cariboo Mountains, discover forests, hidden lakes and a vast plateau in between. The Cariboo Chilcotin is an area of striking contrasts and beauty.

You will encounter rolling grasslands and dense forests, snow-capped mountain peaks, lush valleys, glacier-fed lakes and secluded saltwater inlets. With few paved roads, access will be granted to only the most adventurous and savvy map readers.

The Cariboo Chilcotin region is sparsely populated, with most residents living in and around the three largest towns of Williams Lake, Quesnel and 100 Mile House. All of these towns are situated on Highway 97, the main route north from Cache Creek to Prince George. The Canadian census states that there are 62,392 people residing in the Cariboo, on a land area of 80,629 km^2.

Highway 97 links with Highway 20 at Williams Lake, paved in sections and gravel in others. The notorious stretch east of Bella Coola, known locally as the Hill, comprises 43 kilometres of steep, narrow road with sharp hairpin turns and two major switchbacks as the highway descends from the Chilcotin Plateau. Definitely not for drivers with a fear of heights, the Hill has a 9 km stretch of up to 18 percent grade. Westbound drivers towing heavy loads may wish to leave their trailers in the parking lot at the top of the Hill. Safety measures include using low gear on steep sections and stopping several times to allow your vehicle's brakes to cool.

Secondary highways in the region include Highway 24 to Bridge Lake and Highway 26 to Wells. Highway 24, also known as the Interlakes Highway, begins in the west at 93 Mile House, passing through the small community of Lone Butte at km 9. After passing several turn-offs to resort lakes, including Sheridan Lake, the highway passes through the community of Bridge Lake, 38 km later. It then proceeds another 50 km east through the forest and over a large hill, before reaching its final stop at Little Fort. Highway 26 leads to the community of Wells and the famous gold rush town of Barkerville at the foot of the Cariboo Mountains. As this highway is lightly travelled, it has not seen major improvements since its opening. Its route is roughly the same as that of the famous Cariboo Wagon Road that helped to open up this area back in 1861.

GOLD COUNTRY
GEOTOURISM ADVENTURES
— MODERN DAY TREASURE HUNT —

**Field Guide providers
can be found at www.goldtrail.com**
Available in English and French

Gold
Country
GEOTOURISM
PROGRAM
www.goldtrail.com

Backroad Adventures

108 Mile Ranch Heritage Site (Map 18/C3)
The heritage site is located at the 108 Mile House Rest Area on Highway 97. Starting in 1867, the ranch played a big part in the development of the region as a service centre for the miners and trappers travelling the legendary Cariboo Wagon Road during gold rush days. Today, visitors will find several heritage buildings, including the 105 Mile Roadhouse, a one-room schoolhouse, a trapper's cabin, a blacksmith shop and much more. The heritage site is open from the May long weekend until Labour Day in September, from 10 am to 5 pm daily. Visit their website at www.historical.bc.ca for more information.

Anahim Peak Viewpoint (Map 38/C5)
This sacred peak is located 39 km northwest of Anahim Lake. The volcanic cone stands alone as it rises from the Chilcotin Plateau to 1,897 metres (6,224 ft) in elevation. There is a pullout in between Medicine Lake and Poison Lake that offers a view of the peak, which resembles a First Nation Chief's head and torso lying on his treasure as he looks up at the sky.

Barkerville (Map 58/A7)
Barkerville is BC's largest historical site and one of the largest on the continent. It was the heart of the Cariboo Gold Rush, and much of the town has been restored to its former glory. Highlights include a re-enactment of the courtroom once ruled by Judge Begbie, a well-preserved Chinatown, a blacksmith shop, saloons and hotels. Opening hours and attractions vary throughout the year. As there are many different programs and events, many visitors spend two days here. For full details and to plan a visit, check out their website at www.barkerville.ca.

Boreal Falls (Map 59/E5)
A short 500 metre trail leads to a beautiful 20 metre (66 ft) waterfall. The trailhead can be found near the 21 km mark along the Dore River Forest Service Road.

Bridge Creek Falls (Map 18/D4)
The Bridge Creek Falls are located in downtown 100 Mile House at Centennial Park. Found off Highway 97, these falls are accessible along a nice park trail.

Bull Canyon Pictographs (Map 27/C6)
Preserved as a provincial park, the Bull Canyon has been a significant area with First Nations people for thousands of years. A set of pictographs can be seen from the highway at the base of the cliffs atop a rock slope. The site is at the second cave from the westernmost slope. The Chilcotin River Interpretive Trail also provides access to a series of shallow caves to explore.

Bullion Pit (Map 43/G6)
Located on Likely Road, about 5 km west of Likely, is the Bullion Pit. This large, man-made chasm was a gold mine operated from the 1870s until 1942. The mine covers a big area that is roughly 125 metres (410 ft) deep by 300 metres (985 ft) and over 3 km (1.9 mi) wide.

Canim and Mahood Falls (Map 19/D1)
The trail to Canim and Mahood Falls can be found via Mahood Lake Road near the border of Wells Gray Park. It is a short hike from the trailhead to the 15 metre (49 ft) high Mahood Falls. A few hundred metres further along the trail, you will find Canim, a dual cascade that descends 20 metres (66 ft) to the river below. There is also a short trail that leads down the gorge to the river below the falls, which is a pretty amazing sight. While the main 1 km trail to the falls is wheelchair accessible, the trail down to the base of Canim Falls is steep and covered with loose gravel and exposed tree roots.

Chilko Lake (Map 14/B5)
One of the great things about owning a high clearance four-wheel drive vehicle in this part of British Columbia is some of the places you can explore. Chilko Lake is the largest, natural, high-elevation freshwater lake in North America. And you can drive there along an often-rough, 80 km (50 mi) long gravel road. There are a number of recreation sites in the area, along with a park campsite where you can set up a base camp and explore the numerous trails. And there's a good chance you will have the area pretty much to yourself.

Clayton Falls (Map 22/C1)
This waterfall, located just west of Bella Coola, is one of the most popular sights in the valley. BC Hydro has built an oceanfront recreation area here providing a nice picnic site and a viewing platform of the falls. Depending on the season or the current weather, the falls can be a full apron or narrow streamlets flowing through ancient grooves.

Cottonwood House Historic Site (Map 57/B7)
Located off the south side of Highway 26, this historic site is found about 26 km east of Quesnel. The preserved road house was part of the Gold Rush Trail to Barkerville and includes a number of historic buildings including a general store, interpretive building and horse barn. Camping and picnicking, pitch & putt golf, trails and a host of other activities are possible at the site, which is open from early May to September for a fee. Further east, Blessing's Grave is a lonely road stop, marking the site of an infamous murder. More details about this wheelchair accessible historic site can be found at www.cottonwoodhouse.ca.

Deserters Creek Falls (Map 42/E4)
A moderate 2.6 km trail is located off West Fraser Road, south of Quesnel. The route traverses along Narcosli and Deserters Creeks to the scenic 61 metre (200 ft) waterfall. Caution is advised, as the trail can be steep and rough in sections.

Doc English Bluff (Map 28/G7)
An interesting half dome of rock, rising above the Fraser River, is now protected by an ecological reserve. Home to rare plants and cliff-nesting birds, the riverside of the bluff is a sheer limestone cliff. Access is off Highway 20 on the west bank of the Fraser River, 24 km south of Williams Lake. The short 600 metre trail climbs steeply to the top of the bluff, passing close to the cliff edge on the top.

Eucott Bay Hot Springs (Map 35/F7)
Some of the largest springs on the coast, the Eucott Bay Hot Springs are also among the most popular, due to the good anchorage for boaters. The large, odourless hot springs are encased by natural boulders and concrete slabs placed by locals working at the former mill at Ocean Falls. While soaking in the pools, some guests have spotted whales in the Dean Channel or heard the howl of a Central Coast grey wolf later in the day.

Farwell Canyon Pictographs (Map 16/E2)
Found near the junction of the Chilcotin and Fraser Rivers off the Chilcotin South Forest Service Road, the canyon view will amaze you. If you have the time and energy, try hiking down to the Chilcotin River to check out native pictographs and sandstone hoodoos among the largest moving sand dunes in Canada.

Historic Driving Tours
There are a number of paved, unpaved or combination road tours to visit historic sites in the Cariboo Chilcotin area. Listed below are a few of them:

Dog Creek Road to 70 Mile House (Map 29/B5–17/G6–6/C1)
This day trip starts out paved as it leads south from Highway 20, just outside of Williams Lake. It heads past Springhouse, where the Dog Creek Road turns to gravel. Continuing south, you will visit Alkali Lake Ranch, Dog Creek Airport, the Churn Creek Protected Area and Gang Ranch. Here the Meadow Lake and Dog Creek Roads provide a couple of options to continue southeast past Meadow Lake to Highway 97 and 70 Mile House.

Highway 24 (Map 18/D5)
This trip takes the traveller to Lone Butte, which is named for the 49 metre (160 ft) high butte rock. One of the interesting historic attractions here is an original Diefenbunker bomb shelter. Most continue east to Sheridan and Bridge Lake along what is rightfully known today as the Fishing Highway.

Horsefly Road (Map 29/D5–30/B2)
This trip takes you from Highway 97 to where gold was originally found in 1859. Be sure to visit the Horsefly Museum and take a side trip to Black Creek or Horsefly Lake. Following the Beaver Valley Road northwest will form a circle route as it joins the Likely Road north of Big Lake.

Keithley Creek Road to Wells and Barkerville (Map 44/A6–58/A7)
This trip follows the roads between Likely and Barkerville. It's a great day trip for those fascinated with Gold Rush history as it visits Keithley Creek, Antler Creek, Cunningham Creek and Whiskey Flats. Be sure to check in either Likely or Barkerville for current road conditions.

Huckleberry Butte (Map 18/F5)
East of Lone Butte, look for Holmes Road off the south side of Highway 24. You can park off the side of the road and cross the highway and follow it east for about 500 metres to the trail up Huckleberry Butte. The trail scrambles up through the timber to the top of the scenic butte, which sits 1,263 metres (4,143 ft) above sea level.

Hunlen Falls (Map 23/G3)

Hunlen Falls, in Tweedsmuir Provincial Park, boasts the highest continuous unbroken drop in Canada at 401 metres (1,316 ft). The best way to see the falls is by air and then canoeing and portaging. There is also a difficult 16.4 km trail that takes you from Highway 20 to the falls at the base of the sheer granite cliff below Turner Lake. This trail features 78 switchbacks and an elevation gain of 800 metres (2,625 ft), and takes about six to nine hours one-way. Most base camp at Turner Lake and enjoy the 30-minute walk to the falls. Be wary as a large number of grizzly and black bears reside at the start of the trail. To avoid them, travel between late morning and early afternoon.

Klekane Hot Springs (Map 47/G3)

These hot springs are located in the K'Lgaan/Klekane Conservancy which is located on the east side of the Princess Royal Channel. There is an 8'x12' bath house and an 8'x8' concrete block pool. The odorless, but non-drinkable water comes out of a crevice about 150 metres away from the pool. The water at the source is 53.2°C (128°F) while it drops to 41.3°C (106°F) at the bath house. The Conservancy protects grizzly bears and as there are no roads into the area, be aware of bears while following the shoreline.

M. Gurr Lookout (Map 22/C2)

If you have a high clearance four-wheel drive vehicle, the M. Gurr Lake area is well worth the trip. The scenic area offers great views of the Coastal Mountains with the fjord-like Bentinck Arm shimmering in the distance. To find the trailhead to the viewpoint, head south out of Bella Coola on the Clayton Falls Forest Service Road for approximately 17 km. The moderate trail runs 1 km to M. Gurr Lake and 1.7 km to the viewpoint climbing about 215 metres (705 ft) in elevation. Just beyond the trailhead, Summit Pass also offers a panoramic view of the area.

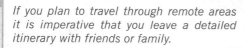

If you plan to travel through remote areas it is imperative that you leave a detailed itinerary with friends or family.

Moffat Falls (Map 30/B3)

Found 7 km east of the town of Horsefly via a short three-minute walk off the east side of 108 Mile Road is Moffat Falls. You can climb down to the bottom of the falls and relax on a sandy beach on a hot summer day. As the water flows over layers of loose basalt, the falls continue to get higher year after year. While in the area, also look for remnants of turn-of-the century mining activity.

Mount Begbie Lookout (Map 18/C6)

Off the east side of Highway 97, about 20 km south of 100 Mile House, visitors will find a parking area and picnic tables. From here, a short, but steep trail ascends a steep grade to the summit of Mount Begbie and the site of a 1923 Forest Fire Lookout Station. The station sits at 1,276 metres (4,186 ft) and provides a 360 degree view of the area. It is said that on a clear day you can see over 100 miles in any direction. Watch your footing as the trail climbs a number of switchbacks and over loose rocks, exposed tree roots and large boulders along a ridge.

Mount Waddington (Map 12/E7)

Mount Waddington is the highest peak to lie solely within BC. Also known as Mystery Mountain, it was not discovered until the 1920s. The first summit of the 4,019 metre (13,186 ft) peak occurred almost a decade later. Despite the remote and dramatic terrain, it remains a popular mountaineering destination. Those that do venture in come in through the Homathko River and up the glacier from there. Most, however, simply view the mountain from afar, or from a plane.

Nascall Bay Hot Springs (Map 35/F7)

Located 48 km northwest of Bella Coola, Nascall Bay is only accessible by boat and plane. The springs are remote, but have been developed by a private resort, making a perfect complement to the good fishing or sea kayaking in the area.

Odegaard Falls (Map 23/B3)

Estimated to be about 280 metres (918 ft) high, Odegaard Falls remain a fine backroad attraction in the heart of the Coastal Mountains. The trails to the viewpoint pass through old mossy forests of western hemlock, Sitka spruce and amabilis fir. Located near Bella Coola south of Highway 20, access to the area is best left to high clearance vehicles.

Off-Road Exploring

A quick browse through this mapbook can give you lots of great ideas for off-road exploration. Many of these roads were originally built for mining and forestry. In addition, many old rail beds that are now disused routes have been opened up to all forms of travel. Although a number of the roads are accessible by car, deactivated roads will usually require a four-wheel drive vehicle to explore. Yellow gates are meant to keep vehicles out; please respect these gates and the areas behind them as there are plenty of other trails anyway. Some popular routes include the Lillooet to Gold Bridge to Pemberton roads that reveal high cliffs overlooking a number of lakes. Other popular road networks include the roads leading from 100 Mile House towards Canim Lake and the roads west of Williams Lake and near Anahim Lake. If you are unsure and still want to explore, there are numerous off-road adventure companies that offer tours on ATVs, dirt bikes, open air jeeps or four-wheel drive trucks.

Pinnacles Provincial Park Hoodoos (Map 42/D2)

West of Quesnel, there is an easy trail taking less than an hour which offers great views of the hoodoos. Stick to the side of the fence for the best views. The access road has a few switchbacks to get to the parking area.

Quesnel Forks (Map 43/F5)

Located where the Cariboo and Quesnel Rivers meet, 13 km west of Likely, is a fascinating ghost town. One of the earliest mining camps in the Cariboo, it became one of the main communities in the Cariboo until the Cariboo Wagon Road was built and prospectors no longer had to travel by water. By 1875, the town dwindled to 200 residents, and in 1958, it was abandoned. Many of the buildings have been restored.

Sheemahant Hot Springs (Map 10/F2)

One of the hardest-to-reach hot springs along the coast, about the only access here is via air to the logging camp near the mouth of the Sheemahant River on Owikeno Lake. From here, follow the road north for about 2 km to the Sheemahant River Road, which you follow for another 10 km.

Sir Alexander Mackenzie Provincial Park (Map 21/D1)

In 1793, Alexander Mackenzie became the first European to travel overland across North America, north of Mexico. The last section of his historic route is preserved as the Alexander Mackenzie Heritage (Grease) Trail that stretches west from near Prince George through South Tweedsmuir Provincial Park, to near Bella Coola. To reach the end of his journey, however, you need to take a boat to this small park, out in the Dean Channel. Here you will find the rock where he inscribed his famous words: "Alex Mackenzie from Canada by land 22nd July 1793".

Tallheo Hot Springs (Map 22/B3)

This beautiful set of hot springs is located in the south Bentinck Arm, far away from the nearest road access. For those with access to a boat (there are charters out of Bella Coola) or float plane, these are some of the nicest springs in the province, carved into the rock overlooking the fjord and covered with a canopy of thick rainforest. The fjords from Bella Coola offer little in the way of landing spots, so kayaking to the springs is not recommended. The main soaking pool is about 69°C (156°F), but the entire area is full of hot seeps.

Thorsen Creek Petroglyphs (Map 22/E2)

On a high bank surrounded by forest, you can see these petroglyphs, which are weathered etchings of faces, animals and geometric patterns. They were created hundreds of years ago, and pieces have fallen from the cliff-face and lie scattered amongst the tree roots deep in the forest west of Bella Coola. A Nuxalk First Nations guide is recommended as the petroglyphs are on private land.

Towdystan Pictographs (Map 24/G4)

These pictographs are well known and in very good condition. Look for them 5.5 kilometres south of the settlement of Towdystan right beside Highway 20. They can be seen on a boulder about 30 metres from the road.

Xatsull Heritage Village (Map 29/C4)

Located on Mountain House Road, north of Williams Lake, the Xatsull Heritage Village offers visitors an opportunity to experience the spiritual, cultural and traditional way of life of the Xatsull community. There are educational activities along with daily scheduled tours that include a visit with village elders. Here you get a sample of their storytelling which has passed down from generation to generation. Visit their website at www.xatsullheritagevillage.com for additional details.

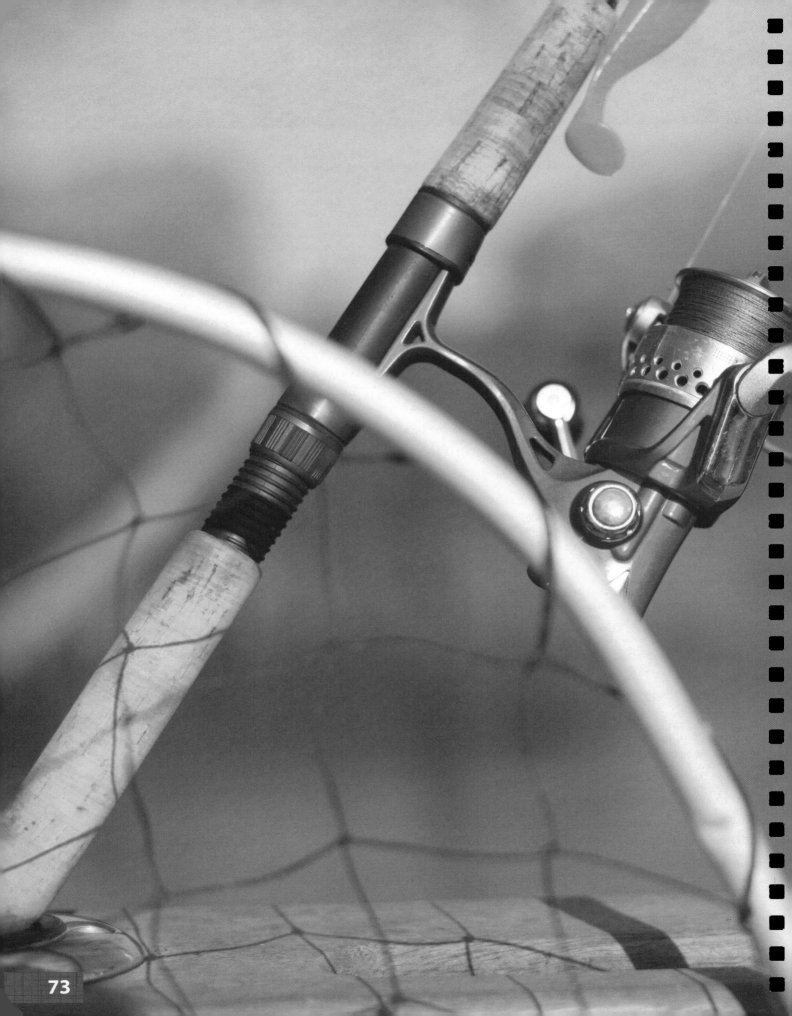

Fishing
Adventures

The Cariboo Chilcotin Coast is famous for big mountains, sprawling plateaus and large fish residing in secluded lakes and streams. Perhaps the most popular destination in the Cariboo is the lakes around the Interlakes Highway (Hwy 24) between 100 Mile House and Little Fort. The Chilcotin Plateau to the west is equally impressive and even more remote.

Nimpo Lake is the floatplane capital of BC, and many of the nearby lakes and streams are only accessible by plane (or a long, long walk). This makes the region a great place to fish for those famous wild rainbow trout.

Lake fishing is at its best in the spring and fall, when the lakes are cooler and the fish are more active. Fishing can start as early as April, and by mid-May, most lakes are open. Summers can be long and hot, and fishing in smaller lakes will slow down as the water warms up. During this time it is best to hit the higher elevation or bigger lakes. Come November, the lakes start to freeze. When the ice is thick enough, those lakes with brook trout and whitefish make fine ice fishing destinations.

The clear water lakes in the area contain a lot of leeches and freshwater shrimp that help the trout grow rapidly. Chironomids, mayflies, stoneflies, caddisflies and dragonflies are other common insects in the area for fly anglers to test. Anglers interested in trolling will find that the gang troll continues to be the gear of choice. Outside of a few popular fishing holes, the remote nature of the area allows anglers to use almost anything they choose.

There are two distinct styles of stream fishing in this large area. The world-famous Dean River is a classic example: while the Lower Dean River is a salmon stream, well-known for its impressive steelhead runs, rivers in the high country of the Chilcotin Plateau and Cariboo region, such as the Upper Dean, are best known as trout streams. Separated from its lower reaches by rapids and falls, the Upper Dean is bursting with feisty rainbow trout.

Our stream section only mentions the major river and creek systems in the area. Many of the tributaries to these systems share their characteristics; therefore, the fishing will be similar. If you are out there touring around and see an inviting hole, why not try casting a line? It is important to note, however, that the rivers and creeks have a limited season and are usually more regulated to help protect spawning trout and salmon.

Lakes that have been stocked within the last five years are noted with the ⬛ symbol. Be sure to check the Freshwater Fishing Regulations before heading out.

Screamin' REEL FLY & TACKLE

RODS - REELS - LURES

- Flies - Fly Tying Supplies - Waders
- Float Tubes - Fins - Line - Nets
- Tackle Boxes - Knives - Boat Seats - Electric Motors
- Downriggers - Rod Holders - Depth Sounders - Saltwater Tackle
- Inflatable Fishing Vests - Ice Fishing Supplies - Binoculars
- Spotting Scopes - Garmin GPS - Smokers - Sunglasses
- Fishing & Hunting Licenses - Live Bait
- Navigation - Spot and Globalstar

ALSO
- Hunting & Camping Supplies - Digital Cameras–Nikon
- Magazines & Map Books - Souvenirs - Toys & Games
- Small Appliances - Cards & Stationery - Luggage
- Pet & Veterinarian - Cosmetics
- Health & Beauty
- Giftware

Plus all your Pharmacy needs

Doney Pharmacy & Department Store

I·D·A· CANADA POST / POSTES CANADA   EVERY DAY LOW PRICES

Downtown 100 Mile House, 145 Birch Ave   250-395-4004

Lake Fishing

108 Mile Lake (Map 18/C3) 🐟
108 Mile Lake is a resort destination 12 km north of 100 Mile House. The lake is known more for its golf course and Nordic ski centre than its fishing. Stocked every year, the rainbow trout can grow to 1.5 kg (3 lbs), although they tend to be much smaller. This is partly due to the large number of coarse fish that compete for the food resources. Boats are restricted to electric motor only, and there is a public access day-use picnic site and cartop boat launch at the lake.

Abbott Lake (Map 30/A2) 🐟
Abbott Lake is a small lake found 6 km west of the town of Horsefly. The lake is inhabited by rainbow trout and lake trout. It is stocked annually with trout that grow up to 3 kg (6.5 lbs), but the average is closer to 1 kg (2 lbs). There is a single barbless hook restriction as well as a ban on ice fishing and bait fishing. There is also an electric motor only restriction at the lake.

Abuntlet Lake (Map 38/D6)
Abuntlet Lake is a pretty, 230 ha (568 ac) waterbody on the Dean River system, 17 km northwest of the town Anahim Lake. Fishing is best near where the river flows out of the lake. The lake contains cuttbows (a cross between rainbow and cutthroats), most of which will weigh less than 1.5 kg (3 lbs). It is an artificial fly only lake and there is a single barbless hook restriction in place.

Agnus Lake (Map 13/A1)
Agnus Lake rests north of Miner Lake and is rumoured to be good for rainbow. It has a bait ban and single barbless hook restrictions.

Ahbau Lake (Map 57/B5)
This is a popular recreation lake located northeast of Quesnel. To access, turn east off Highway 97 at the Naver Creek Road. Fishing in the lake is fair for rainbow trout. Both trolling and fly-fishing will produce results. A boat launch and recreation site are located at the north end of the lake.

Akehurst Lake (Map 7/E1)
A large 220 ha (543 ac) lake located north of Bonaparte Lake, access is off Darlington Creek Forest Service Road. This high elevation lake has rainbow that reach 2 kg (4.5 lbs). The best time to fish is in the spring or fall by fly-fishing or trolling. There is a resort on the lake.

Aktaklin Lake (Map 25/B4)
Found at 1,200 m (3,940 ft), this 207 ha (511 ac) lake offers fishing for rainbow. 26 km southeast of Nimpo Lake, head east at Towdystan. You can connect to the Lt. Palmer Trail on the north shore of this scenic lake.

Alexis Lake (Map 27/B3) 🐟
Stocked with rainbow trout, this 103 ha (254 ac) lake is a constant producer. The lake is accessible off Alexis Lakes Road, a good two-wheel drive road, which is in turn accessed off Highway 20, west of Alexis Creek. Fishing remains good from May to October. Alexis Lake has a recreation site and an electric motor only restriction.

Allan Lake (Map 7/G2) 🐟
West of Barriere, off Jamieson Creek Forest Service Road, this 149 ha (368 ac) lake sees heavy fishing pressure throughout the ice-free season for rainbow trout. At the east end of the lake there is a recreation site with a cartop boat launch and camping facilities.

Anahim Lake (Map 38/E7)
Anahim Lake is located on Highway 20, about 320 km west of Williams Lake. The lake's many small bays filled with reeds make it ideal for fly-fishing using waders or float tubes. It is also suited to spin-casting or trolling for rainbow trout ranging from 1–1.5 kg (2–3 lbs) or larger. Cuttbow, found exclusively in Anahim Lake, are a cross between cutthroat and bull trout.

Annette Lake (Map 44/C7)
About 32 km south of Likely, off Spanish Lake Road, Annette Lake is a small, seldom-fished lake. Rainbow can reach 2.5 kg (5.5 lbs) in size here. There is an old trail to Annette Lake from Freshette Lake and rough logging road access.

Antoine Lake (Map 30/A1) 🐟
Antoine Lake is found within the Horsefly River Valley, 15 km north of Horsefly. The lake offers fair fishing for small rainbow and kokanee. Over half of the lake contains shoals, ideal locations to find cruising trout and kokanee. Unfortunately there are many coarse fish. Public access is limited.

Avalanche Lake (Map 24/B5)
Accessed by a remote trail, this shallow lake makes for very good fishing. The cutthroat trout that inhabit this very cold and sterile lake tend to be quite small in size. There is a bait ban and single barbless hook restriction.

Ballon Lake (Map 29/G2) 🐟
Ballon Lake is a popular catch-and-release lake for fly anglers willing to pack in small watercrafts. The tough access allows the stocked rainbow to grow to 60–70 cm (23–28 in). There is a bait ban and single barbless hook restriction.

Banana Lake (Map 24/C5)
It is a long walk along the rugged May Doe Creek Trail, but those willing to lug in a float tube will find very good fishing for wild rainbow trout throughout the summer. There is a bait ban and single barbless hook restriction.

Bare Lake (Map 7/E3) 🐟
Bare Lake is a large, remote lake reached by a 6 km hike along the Heller Lake Trail or by floatplane. This 230 ha (568 ac) lake offers good fishing throughout the ice-free season for rainbow reaching 1.5 kg (3 lbs).

Barton Lake (Map 55/C2) 🐟
Barton Lake is 78 km southwest of Prince George via the Blackwater and Pelican Lake road systems. A popular 67 ha (165 ac) fly-fishing lake, it is stocked with rainbow and brook trout and is home to a pair of small recreation sites.

Basalt Lake (Map 38/C1)
Basalt Lake is accessed via the Alexander MacKenzie Heritage Trail. The remote location and catch-and-release (single barbless hooks) fishery helps the fish grow to good sizes. The lake contains bull and rainbow trout, Dolly Varden and a handful of other non-sportfish species. There is a bait ban and no ice fishing allowed here.

Batnuni Lake (Map 54/D3)
Batnuni Lake is a 9 km (5.5 mi) long lake, found about 135 km west of Quesnel. It is third in a chain of lakes including Boat and Hanham lakes. These lakes are linked by the Euchiniko River and all provide similar fisheries for small rainbow and kokanee as well as dollies. Rainbow are best caught near the shore with fly gear, while the kokanee and dollies are best caught on the troll. There are two recreation sites on this lake.

Beaver Lake (Map 27/G4)
Beaver Lake is a very shallow waterbody, 30 km northeast of Alexis Creek. During the hot summer months fishing usually drops off, however, early and late season fishing for the lake's large rainbow can be excellent. Access is off a rough four-wheel drive access road.

Beaver Valley Lakes (Map 29/G2–43/D6)
The Beaver Valley Lakes are a collection of nine lakes along Jacobson and Beaver Valley Roads west of Horsefly. They start with the small, shallow lakes found just north of Joan Lake and end with Roberts Lake to the southeast. The lakes hold good numbers of kokanee and rainbow trout that have been known to top the 1.5 kg (3 lb) range. Roberts Lake has a day-use recreation site with a boat launch, while the other lakes have rustic launches and places to pitch a tent.

Beaverdam Lake (Map 5/G2)
Meadow Lake Road is a good gravel road that leads right by the eastern shore of Beaverdam Lake, 11 km north of Highway 97. Fishing in the 146 ha (360 ac) lake is best in the early summer or fall for brook trout that can grow to 2 kg (4.5 lbs) in size. Ice fishing can be a lot of fun on this lake, while the recreation site provides camping and a boat launch.

Becher Pond (Map 28/D7)
Also known as the Riske Creek Reservoir, this small lake is 45 km west of Williams Lake, alongside Highway 20. Even with all the pressure, the small rainbows that inhabit the lake still take well to flies. There is a recreation site on the lake.

Bellos Lake (Map 56/G6) 🐟
This small lake lies just north of Quesnel and is only 4 km east of Highway 97. The lake is stocked annually with rainbow trout that can be in the 50 cm (20 in) range. It is best to work the shoals around the deeper hole near the west end. It is possible to launch small boats from the north end of the lake.

Benny Lake (Map 44/C7)
Benny Lake is a small walk-in lake found southeast of Spanish Lake. The lake has some big rainbow trout which can grow to 2 kg (4.5 lbs) in size. The best way to fish the lake is to pack a float tube during the spring or fall.

Fishing Adventures

Benson Lake (Map 43/B2)
Found about 24 km south off Highway 26, Benson Lake offers good rainbow trout fishing from late May to early June and again in the fall. Fishing can slow down during summer heat. The lake has extensive shoal areas and trolling is best near the east end. It is possible to launch a small boat at the lake and to camp at roadside.

Bidwell Lakes (Map 26/D7)
This chain of small lakes is located along Bidwell Creek, which is south of Highway 20. The lake contains a few different species of fish, including rainbow trout. The lakes are rarely fished due to their remote location.

Big Bar Lake (Map 5/E1)
Big Bar Lake is a destination style lake that is easily accessed off Big Bar Road west of Clinton. The lake is stocked yearly and at times rainbow trout reach 3 kg (6.5 lbs) in size. Fly anglers do well casting the shoals in the quieter bays, while trollers often work the drop-off area. The park provides camping and a paved boat launch.

Big Lake (Map 14/F6)
Big Lake is a fairly popular fishing lake found on the rough Nemaiah Valley Road. The rainbow are stocked periodically and grow to 1.5 kg (3 lbs) and there are also native kokanee and lake trout. A scenic recreation site is available for visitors to enjoy.

Big Lake (Map 18/B4)
Despite the name, this lake is only 100 ha (247 ac) in size. Found 14 km west of 100 Mile House, off the Big Lake Forest Service Road, the lake sees few anglers partly due to the elusive nature of the trout in the lake. Rainbow, brook and lake trout do grow to 3 kg (6.5 lbs) here. There is a bait ban and single barbless hook restriction at this lake.

Big Lake (Map 29/E2)
This Big Lake is 571 ha (1,410 ac) and a popular recreation lake, just off the Likely Road near Big Lake Ranch. The lake holds rainbow trout, steelhead, kokanee, brook trout, burbot and lake trout. There are big fish here, with rainbow reaching 4.5 kg (10 lbs) and lake trout 14 kg (30 lbs). The lake is best suited for trolling in the late spring and early fall. Fly anglers will find the expansive shallows around the northeast end appealing. There is a campground and boat launch on the lake.

Big Onion Lake (Map 15/A7)
Sandwiched between the road and the Taseko River, this 59 ha (145 ac) lake contains wild dollies and stocked rainbow trout. Like most of the lakes in the Southern Chilcotin, the surrounding scenery is very impressive.

Big Stick Lake (Map 24/G6)
This 141 ha (348 ac) lake holds a few rainbow, but is not a popular fishing destination. It does make a nice camping destination 10 km west off Highway 20, on Big Stick Lake Forest Service Road. A boat launch is also available at the recreation site on the lake.

Birch Lake (Map 19/E6)
Found 22 km east of Bridge Lake off Highway 20, there is a cartop boat launch and a resort. The lake is best fished by fly-fishing or trolling throughout the ice-free season for burbot and rainbow. The rainbow can reach 2 kg (4.5 lbs) in size.

Bishop Lake [Brown Lake] (Map 41/B6)
Located just north of Nazko Lake Park, off Nazko Falls Forest Service Road, this lake is a consistent producer of good sized trout around 3 kg (6.5 lbs). Special regulations include a two trout limit, as well as single, barbless, baitless hook restrictions. Fly anglers will find that chironomids and leeches work well in this lake, on account of its nice shoals.

Blanchet Lake (Map 51/B3)
Blanchet Lake is found at the end of a 30 km trail, which is accessed on the far side of Ootsa Lake that requires crossing a 5 km stretch of open water. Needless to say, the lake doesn't see much fishing pressure for its resident rainbow.

Blue Jay & Gray Lakes (Map 22/B3)
These two small lakes, combined for only 10 ha (24 ac) in size, are stocked with cutthroat. Despite the road that seems to wind to the top of the world, the low elevation makes these lakes a better spring or fall fishing destination. There is a recreation site on Blue Jay Lake.

Blue Lake (Map 29/A2)
Found 35 km northwest of Williams Lake, Blue Lake is a 34 ha (84 ac) waterbody that produces the odd rainbow to 2.5 kg (5.5 lbs). Kokanee are also found in good numbers as well as a number of non-sportfish. Spinners and flies do well, however the bigger rainbow are notoriously hard to catch in the clear waters. There is a popular resort and two recreation sites on the lake. Only electric motors are allowed.

Blue Lake (Map 42/F5)
This lake covers 14 ha (34 ac) and is located off Highway 97 north of Alexandria. The lake is stocked with rainbow.

Bluff Lake (Map 13/C3)
Located just south of Sapeye Lake and Horn Lake, 23 km south of Tatla Lake, Bluff Lake is a beautiful waterbody with views of the Niut Range looking south from the recreation site. Fishing is good for bull trout to 4.5 kg (10 lbs), rainbow trout to 1.5 kg (3 lbs) and Dolly Varden. There is a day-use recreation site, but no powered boats allowed on the deep lake.

Boar Lake (Map 17/G5)
Accessed by four-wheel drive off the Gustafsen South Forest Service Road (1000 Rd), Boar Lake offers stocked rainbow that grow to decent sizes. The 30 ha (74 ac) lake is home to a small recreation site, but fishing slows considerably during the summer. There is a bait ban and single barbless hook restriction at this lake.

Boat Lake (Map 54/E4)
Boat Lake is located northwest of Titetown Lake on the Batnuni Lake Forest Service Road and offers a campsite and boat launch. Wild rainbow and Dolly Varden commonly reach 1 kg (2 lbs) in this small lake.

Bobbs Lake (Map 18/G2)
Accessed by an old road cum trail off the Canim Lake Road, Bobbs Lake is home to rainbow and kokanee. An aggressive stocking program ensures a quality fishery at this 107 ha (264 ac) lake.

Bobtail Lake [Naltesby Lake] (Map 55/B1)
Found off the Blackwater/Telegraph Trail Road, there is an improved recreation site and a boat launch on the eastern shore. Kokanee and rainbow inhabit the lake and can reach 0.5 and 2 kg (1 and 4.5 lbs) respectively. The lake is stocked annually to offset the heavy fishing pressure this lake sees.

Bogmar Lake (Map 7/F2)
Bogmar Lake is located to the east of Bonaparte Lake, 40 km southwest of Little Fort. A short hike is required to reach the 15 ha (37 ac) lake. The lake contains a variety of fish including bull and rainbow trout, sucker and carp.

Bonaparte Lake (Map 7/C2–E2)
Bonaparte Lake is the largest lake on the Bonaparte Plateau, north of Kamloops at 33,674 ha (83,210 ac). The lake is high enough at 1,169 m (3,834 ft) and deep enough to stay cool through summer. It is a good ice fishing lake and can produce rainbows in the 5.5 kg (12 lb) range (2 kg/4.5 lbs is the norm), and smaller kokanee. There are a number of resorts on the lake, as well as a recreation site with a cartop boat launch and camping. Trolling is the mainstay of the lake.

Boot Lake (Map 55/D5)
Off the south side of the Batnuni Lake Forest Service Road, anglers will find a variety of fish including stocked rainbow and moderate populations of walleye. There is a small recreation site with cartop boat launch on the lake.

Bootjack Lake (Map 43/G7)
Accessed of Moorehead-Bootjack Forest Service Road, Bootjack Lake does not receive a lot of fishing pressure and has a generous catch limit of eight fish per day. The rainbow grow to 30 cm (12 in) and are often caught on the troll. There is a nice recreation site and boat launch at the north end of the lake.

Bosk Lake [Boss Lake] (Map 31/B4)
Bosk Lake is connected to Cruiser Lake by a short channel. The lake has rainbow trout, lake trout, mountain whitefish, burbot and kokanee as well as a number of coarse fish. Covering 126 ha (311 ac), the shoals are best worked in late May to early July. There is a sandy beach at the recreation site along with a cartop boat launch.

Bouchie Lake [Six Mile Lake] (Map 42/D1)
Also known as Six Mile Lake, Bouchie Lake is a 127 ha (313 ac) lake found west of Quesnel. There are a number of full time residences on the lake. Bouchie contains stocked rainbow trout to 2 kg (4.5 lbs) if not winterkilled, as well as steelhead. Given the shallow depth of the lake, try fly-fishing or spincasting the drop-off area, as the fish tend to congregate in the fringe area.

Boulanger Lake (Map 7/G2)
There is a mess of lakes southeast of Bonaparte Lake; this tiny lake is one of them. It is accessed by trail only and holds rainbows.

Bowers Lake (Map 19/C4)
Bowers Lake is a 602 ha (1,478 ac) lake found in a narrow valley that is prone to sudden winds. Fishing for rainbow trout to 1 kg (2 lbs) begins in late May and remains steady into the fall. There is a recreation site on the eastern shore that requires a four-wheel drive vehicle to access.

Bowron Lake (Map 58/B5)
This popular lake has a campground and boat launch. The big lake offers bull trout, kokanee, rainbow trout and lake trout with June and September proven to be the best fishing months. Spincasters and fly anglers can work the north end of the lake at the inflow of the Bowron River. During summer, it is best to troll deep. There is a bait ban and single barbless hook restriction.

Bowron Lakes (Map 58/B5–59/A7)
Within Bowron Lake Park, there are eleven portage-connected lakes. The fishing is better in the first few lakes (Kibbee, Indianpoint and Isaac Lake) during the late spring or early fall. After Isaac the silty waters of the Cariboo River make fishing slow until the canoe route veers north past Unna Lake. The big bull, lake and rainbow trout are best caught by trolling closer to the creek mouths. There is also a population of hard-to-catch kokanee. Swan and Spectacle Lakes are connected lakes offering fishing opportunities for bull trout, kokanee, burbot, whitefish and rainbow trout along with coarse fish. There is a bait ban and single barbless hook restriction.

Brewster Lakes (Map 53/F3)
The Kluskus Forest Service Road is a good two-wheel drive road that leads past the access road into the small recreation site on the first of three Brewster Lakes, 100 km southwest of Vanderhoof. Expect average-sized rainbow here. Despite the difficult access, the second lake is the better lake as it is smaller and not very deep at a maximum of 4.3 m (14 ft).

Bridge Lake (Map 19/C6)
Bridge Lake is a very popular fishing retreat found on Highway 24. The 1,370 ha (3,385 ac) lake holds arctic char that are best caught shortly after ice-off in early to mid-May when they congregate in the shallows. In addition, the lake is stocked with rainbow, lake trout as well as kokanee and also holds burbot and a number of coarse fish. Kokanee are best fished in June before the fish retreat to the depths of the lake in late summer. Rainbow trout can grow to 3 kg (6.5 lbs), with the best fishing in the early spring or just before ice-over in the fall. The lake trout grow up to 9 kg (110 lbs) and are best caught on a deep troll using a large spoon such as an Apex. It is catch-and-release only for lake trout. There are also numerous resorts and access areas scattered around the lake.

Brittany Lake (Map 14/D4)
Found above Murray Taylor Lake, Brittany Lake sits quite high in elevation. The 149 ha (368 ac) lake also has coarse fish competing with the rainbow for available food.

Brunson Lake (Map 29/C6)
Brunson Lake is the slowest of the lakes in the Chimney Creek Chain. The rainbow here tend to be smaller and more difficult to catch than nearby Felker or Chimney. A rough cartop boat launch is available at the north end.

Buchanan Lake (Map 29/E4)
About 35 km northeast of Williams Lake, Buchanan Lake offers good fishing for stocked rainbow. The trout are usually small, but can be found up to 1 kg (2 lbs) on occasion.

Buckskin Lake (Map 28/G4)
Buckskin Lake is accessed via a rough road, south from Grouse Road. The lake offers fair to good fishing for rainbow that can reach 3 kg (6.5 lbs). Trolling, fly-fishing and spincasting all produce results.

Buffalo Lake (Map 18/F3)
Northeast of 100 Mile House, about 18 km down the Canim Lake Road is Buffalo Lake. Small trout begin taking flies, bait and small lures by mid-May. Try casting around the near shore area off Buffalo Creek for good results. The fish often hold in the deeper east end, near the Buffalo Lake Ranch, in summer.

Burkholder Lake (Map 4/G6)
Located to the west of Yalakom River, this small lake receives light fishing pressure. As a result, it offers some good fishing for small rainbow, bullhead and walleye.

Bushy Lake [Valerie Lake] (Map 42/G7)
Found just 8 km east of Highway 97 and the Fraser River, this lake offers an early season for rainbow, but slows during the summer. The best access comes from the south of Gibraltar Mine Road. There is a recreation site with a cartop boat launch on the lake.

Camp Lake (Map 31/B3)
Found about 5 km south of the bigger Crooked Lake, Camp Lake is a tiny roadside lake that is home to a few rainbow trout.

Canim Lake (Map 19/A2–C1)
This large 5,611 ha (13,865 ac) lake makes a fine fishing destination, with several campsites, resorts and access points. Trolling or spinning gear is popular for rainbow trout up to 1.5 kg (3 lbs), lake trout up to 10 kg (22 lbs) and smaller stocked kokanee. Fly-fishing near creek mouths and around the islands in the spring can be effective for trout. This lake is prone to sudden winds. Be sure to note the no fishing zone on the northwest corner of the lake; look for the signs on either side of the shore.

Cariboo Lake (Map 44/C4)
This large 1,109 ha (2,740 ac) lake holds kokanee, lake trout, mountain whitefish, bull trout, burbot and rainbow trout. The lake trout can grow to 5.5 kg (12 lbs), while bull trout grow to 2.5 kg (5.5 lbs). Chinook and Coho salmon also enter the lake in the fall. Most anglers troll along the drop-off in the early summer or early fall. Ladies Creek Recreation Site is located along the eastern shore of the lake.

Carpenter Lake (Map 4/B7–F7)
Stretching approximately 50 km from Gold Bridge and at a maximum depth of 654 m (2,145 ft), this massive lake is fished quite frequently as there are numerous spots to drop a boat or fly-fish from shore. Most target the rainbow trout, but Dolly Varden and kokanee are also available. Trout vary in size from 1 kg (2 lbs) all the way up to 10 kg (22 lbs) plus. Trolling is the mainstay of the lake but boaters should be wary of deadheads and drawdown on the lake.

Caverhill Lake (Map 7/F1)
Caverhill Lake is 542 ha (1,339 ac) and has many bays and islands that are ideal for casting a line. Rainbow to 1 kg (2 lbs) are found throughout the ice-free season. There is a resort, accessible by boat or air from Kamloops, providing an ideal getaway with hiking trails and rentals.

Charlotte Lake (Map 24/E4)
Charlotte Lake is a beautiful lake that is best known for its large rainbow. The trout average an impressive 2 kg (4.5 lbs) and are often found bigger. The big 6,596 ha (16,299 ac) lake is found southwest of Nimpo Lake and offers a small recreation site with a wonderful sandy beach.

Chaunigan Lake (Map 14/E5)
A beautiful 461 ha (1,139 ac) lake that has yielded some equally beautiful fish, Chaunigan Lake is found 100 km southwest of Hanceville, where the Coast Mountains rise above the plateau. Wild rainbow up to 3.5 kg (7.5 lb) are caught fairly regularly from late spring to early fall. There is a recreation site with cartop boat launch on the lake, which also has a single barbless hook restriction.

Cheshi Lake (Map 13/G6)
This small lake lies between Tatlayoko and Chilko Lakes and offers small rainbow trout. There are multiple trails in the surrounding area to enjoy as well as a lodge offering cabins.

Chief Gray Lake [Bitch Lake] (Map 53/D1)
This 33 ha (81 ac) lake is an excellent walk-in lake found off a 4 km trail leading from Hobson Lake. Stocked annually, it is deep enough to maintain good sized rainbow (averaging 50 cm/20 in but getting up to 65 cm/26 in) throughout the summer. The best time to go is during the damsel hatch in late July. The lake is catch-and-release, with a single barbless, baitless hook. Chief Gray is also closed to angling November 1 to April 30.

Chilcotin Lake (Map 26/C3)
Drained by the Chilcotin River, this lake is found in a marshy area that is popular with bird watchers. Anglers will find rainbow trout to 2 kg (4.5 lbs) if they bring in a small boat or canoe to get beyond the weeds. There is a bait ban and single hook restriction.

Chilko Lake (Maps 2, 14)
At 20,032 ha (49,500 ac), Chilko Lake is the largest high-elevation lake in North America, stretching 84 km (52 mi) into the heart of the Coast Mountains. The lake contains plenty of large fish, with bull trout to 4.5 kg (10 lbs) and rainbow up to 3 kg (6.5 lbs). The lake is also home to one of the largest runs of sockeye in BC. A good place to start is around creek mouths. Trolling or fly-fishing near the drop-off and the feed lines can produce some large fish. There is a bait ban and single barbless hook restriction at this lake, plus no powered boats allowed on Big Lagoon (on the west side of the lake). All services and facilities are available at Chilko Lake.

Chimney Lake (Map 17/D1)
Chimney Lake is a popular recreational lake for Williams Lake residents found about 50 km southeast of town. The lake is best fished in the early spring and late fall while the summer months are better for water sports. Stocked annually, the most productive method of fishing is trolling a lake troll along the shoreline, opposite the recreation sites and boat launch. The rainbow are usually found in the 25–46 cm (10–18 in) category. There are also a number of coarse fish.

Choelquoit Lake (Map 14/B4)
Choelquoit Lake is rumoured to have some very large wild rainbow that are very hard to catch. Access is off Tatlayoko Henry's Crossing Road, 38 km southeast of Tatla Lake. There is a recreation site on the northeast side of the lake. The lake is subject to sudden violent storms.

Chubb Lake (Map 56/D5)
Found about 7 km from Highway 97, this 67 ha (165 ac) lake offers fair fishing for rainbow trout to 2 kg (4.5 lbs) and brook trout to 1 kg (2 lbs). There are also suckers and redside shiners. Fly-fishing is the most productive method at the lake, although trolling a small spinner or spoon can produce some results. There is a recreation site and launch located along the north shore of the lake.

Chutanli Lake (Map 53/G4)
Found 120 km west of Blackwater, Chutanli Lake offers a huge shoal area full of insect life. The shallow lake is better for casting than trolling. Rainbow are the main sportfish, but kokanee and whitefish are also available. A recreation site and a boat launch are also present.

Check www.env.gov.bc.ca/fw/fish/regulations for changes to freshwater fishing or www.pac.dfo-mpo.gc.ca for changes to salmon and steelhead regulations. To receive notifications on regulation changes, subscribe to the In-Season Regulation Changes feed at www.env.gov.bc.ca/fw/news.

Clearwater Lake (Map 25/A6)
Located just off Highway 20, this 214 ha (528 ac) lake contains wild rainbow, which average 1 kg (2 lbs). Fly-fishing is popular here because of the large shoal area. There is a small lakeside recreation campsite with a cartop launch.

Clearwater Lake (Map 31/G2–G4)
Clearwater Lake is a big lake within Wells Gray Provincial Park. Although the trout in this lake are hard to come by, rainbow and bull trout can be found to 3 kg (6.5 lbs), while lake trout can top 6 kg (13 lbs) in size. The most successful areas are at either end of both lakes, as well as creek mouths such as Barella Creek and Angus Horne Creek.

Cleswuncut Lake (Map 55/F4)
Found off the Blackwater Road between Prince George and Quesnel, this small lake offers anglers fair fishing for small rainbow. The lake is subject to winterkill, which accounts for the slow fishing. There is a recreation site with a boat launch on the shores of the lake.

Club & Next Lakes (Map 19/F6)
Club Lake lies south of Highway 24 and can only be accessed via portage from Long Island (Janice) Lake. The small lake offers very good fly-fishing or spincasting for rainbow trout from 1.5 kg (3 lbs) up to 4.5 kg (10 lbs). Next Lake is actually connected to Club Lake by a small shallow channel and offers a similar fishery.

Cochin Lake (Map 13/F2)
Cochin Lake has wild rainbow that average in the 2 kg (4.5 lb) range that are best caught with trolling gear, but are equally attracted to flies. Bigger trout to 4.5 kg (10 lbs) are not that uncommon. Hot weather can slow the fishing down. There is a cartop boat launch at the lakeside recreation site.

Cogistiko Lake (Map 40/F1)
A rough two-wheel drive branch road leads to the southern shores of this small, shallow lake. Winterkill is a problem. Anglers will find brook trout, rainbow trout and salmon all migrate up the river on occasion. If fishing is slow, it is possible to venture down the river from here.

Coldscaur & Cameron Lakes (Map 19/F3)
Coldscaur Lake is a narrow lake that can be found via the Camp 2 Road, 27 km west of Clearwater. The lake offers productive fishing for rainbow trout to 1.5 kg (3 lbs). A recreation site complete with a boat launch is also found at the lake. Off the southeast shore is the small, but productive Cameron Lake, which holds generally small rainbow and brook trout.

Colwell Lake (Map 12/F2)
Located in the shadows of the Pantheon Mountain Range with Perkins Peak at 2,819 m (9,248 ft) towering above, Colwell Lake is a serene, secluded rainbow trout lake with average weights of 1 kg (2 lbs). Access is at the end of Miner Lake Forest Service Road, then a short hike along the Moose Valley Trail.

Comstock Lake (Map 54/C3)
There is only a short patch of river separating Comstock Lake from its bigger neighbour, Batnuni. As a result, the two share similar fishing patterns. The rainbow here grow to 2 kg (4.5 lbs).

Cone Lake [Crater Lake] (Map 19/G5)
This small lake can be found via a rough four-wheel drive road northwest of Little Fort. The lake is a perfect lake for float tubes. With the steep hike in deterring most anglers, the lake can produce large rainbow to 1.5 kg (3 lbs).

Cook Lake [Camp Lake] (Map 29/E2)
This tiny lake sits southeast of Big Lake off Swanson Road (8200 Rd). Stocked every fall with the Pennask strain of rainbow, Cook or Camp Lake is often overlooked and boasts high populations of rainbows in the 1 kg (2 lb) range, although reports suggest larger fish have been caught here.

Corsica Lake (Map 19/E2)
Off the Branch 233 forestry road, Corsica Lake offers good fishing for rainbow trout that can reach up to 2 kg (4.5 lbs). Trolling, fly-fishing and spincasting all produce results. A high clearance vehicle is required to access the lake.

Cowboy Lakes (Map 24/D5)
Accessed by the Maydoe Creek Trail, these high elevation lakes are very shallow. Winterkill can be a problem, especially in the northern lake. They are still rumoured to provide a very good fishery for rainbow trout for those able to work beyond the marshy shoreline.

Crater Lake (Map 40/G3)
Tucked to the east of the Michelle-Baezakeko Road (4100 Rd), this tiny, 10 ha (24 ac) lake is accessed by a short trail. It is stocked with rainbow every other year to help maintain the fishery. It is possible to camp at lakeside.

Crazy Bear and Area Lakes (Map 24/C4)
Crazy Bear Lake is a fly-in waterbody southwest of Charlotte Lake. The wild rainbow are 35–50 cm (14–20 in) long, making this a good summer fishing destination. There is a lodge offering cabins, which operates from June until September. Walking trails lead to five other trout lakes in the region.

Crescent Lake (Map 57/D5)
Crescent Lake is located 82 km northeast of Quesnel. Home to bull and rainbow trout as well as several coarse species, this lake is best trolled in the deeper water towards the northwest end. There is a rustic recreation site found at the north end of the lake with a cartop boat launch.

Fishing Adventures

Crooked Lake (Map 31/C3)
Crooked Lake is a deep lake covering 1,092 ha (2,698 ac), found 62 km east of Horsefly. The lake contains a good population of rainbow trout and few coarse fish. The trout average 25–30 cm (10–12 in) in size, but some fish can grow to 45 cm (18 in). Trout are readily caught from late May through September. Working the inflow at the east end of the lake or at the outflow at the west end provides good results. There are two resorts as well as two recreation sites on the popular lake.

Crown & Turquoise Lakes (Map 5/G7)
This pair of lakes is found in Marble Canyon Park southeast of Pavilion, directly off Highway 99. Crown Lake is slightly bigger and provides a cartop boat launch and camping. Both lakes hold rainbow to 1 kg (2 lbs).

Crystal Lake (Map 19/B6) 🐟
Aptly named Crystal Lake is located off the North Bonaparte Road, south of Bridge Lake. The lake is stocked annually with rainbow trout, which provide for good fishing at times. Most trout are 2 kg (4.5 lbs), although a 6.3 kg (14 lb) rainbow is on record. The lake is best in the spring and fall. The lake also produces well during the ice fishing period. There is a recreation site on the north shore of the lake, complete with a car boat launch.

Cuisson Lake (Map 28/G1) 🐟
Cuisson Lake is found 11 km north of the town of McLeese Lake off the Gibraltar Mine Road. The lake offers a good spring and fall fishery for rainbow trout, which are stocked annually. A recreation site and boat launch is found at the south end of the lake.

Cultus Lake (Map 6/F7)
This 48 ha (118 ac) lake is easily accessed of the Deadman-Cache Creek Road and offers fair fishing for small rainbow. The shallow lake suffers from the summer doldrums.

Dagger Lake (Map 7/F3) 🐟
This remote 49 ha (121 ac) lake is only accessed by trail or by the horse drawn car service of Skitchine Lodge. As a result, the lake sees few anglers and can be very good fishing for rainbow trout.

Dante's Inferno (Map 16/B1) 🐟
This tiny trail access lake is found in a canyon famous for the heat in the summer months (thus the name). Dante's Inferno is a good place to catch stocked rainbow to 1 kg (2 lbs), as long as you try in the spring and fall when the temperature is cooler.

Davidson Lake (Map 24/C5)
Accessed by the Whitton Creek Trail in the Charlotte Alplands Protected Area, Davidson Lake is a shallow lake that can suffer from winterkill during severe winters. This mid-elevation lake opens earlier than others in the area and is known to produce good fishing for rainbow. There is a bait ban and single barbless hook restriction.

Davis Lake (Map 18/C6)
Found in Flat Lake Park, just 3 km west of Highway 97, Davis Lake is surrounded by private property and anglers will need to portage in from the start of the popular canoe route. When winterkill is not a problem, fishing can be great in the spring and fall. Work the fringe area south of the island located in the middle of the lake.

Deadman Lake (Map 7/A4)
Deadman Lake, located at the 47 km mark on the Deadman Vidette Road, sports a recreation site with cartop boat launch on the western shore. The 49 ha (121 ac) lake has reasonably good fishing for rainbow and kokanee that can reach 1 kg (2 lbs) in size. Fly-fishing or trolling are your best bets.

Deer Lake [Lakeview Lake] (Map 19/F5)
You can access Deer Lake from the rustic campsite and boat launch off the Taweel Road. The lake provides fishing opportunities for rainbow trout that can reach up to 1 kg (2 lbs). Fly anglers should try a leech imitation like a Woolly Bugger for added success.

Deka Lake (Map 19/B4) 🐟
This 1,153 ha (2,849 ac) lake offers boat launches and a bed and breakfast at the southwest end of the lake. Rainbow and kokanee are stocked and you will find lake trout as well. Lakers can grow up to 4.5 kg (10 lbs) and are caught on a deep troll using a spoon or larger lure such as an Apex. Increased stocking of kokanee should improve this fishery.

Dempsey Lake (Map 18/D2)
Dempsey Lake is best accessed through the shallow channel from Timothy Lake to the north. Rainbow to 1 kg (2 lbs) are possible, but so is landing suckers and squawfish. Try working the inflow area at the north end of the lake.

Dewar Lake (Map 29/E4) 🐟
Dewar Lake is a 41 ha (101 ac) lake found 28 km northeast of Williams Lake, off the paved Horsefly Road. The deeper part of the lake is at the south end away from the recreation site and boat launch. Working the fringe area of the deeper water with a fly or lure produces well for stocked rainbow trout. Ice fishing is not recommended as the lake is aerated.

Dixon Lake (Map 18/B2)
This lake holds numerous small rainbow, which are easily caught by trolling or fly-fishing. The shallow shore area of the lake makes shore fishing a challenge. You can find the lake just south of Lac La Hache off the Tatton-Canima Forest Service Road.

Dog Lake (Map 17/C5) 🐟
Rough logging roads branch from the Tinmusket Road (3400 Rd) to the east of Dog Creek and provide access to this tiny lake. The lake is stocked annually with rainbow. There is a bait ban and single barbless hook restriction along with no ice fishing allowed at this lake.

Donnely Lake (Map 19/C3) 🐟
Donnely Lake is a hike-in lake situated to the north of Bowers Lake. The hike and shallow depth of the lake discourages trollers, although a float tube will help you work the best spots. There is a good population of stocked rainbow trout, but note the bait ban and a single barbless hook restriction. There is no ice fishing or powered boats allowed on this lake.

Dor Lake (Map 18/F1) 🐟
Located in Lang Lake Schoolhouse Park, this lake can be accessed via a rough road off the Bradley Creek Road. The lakes are not fished often due to their location, but there are stocked rainbow for those that make the effort to get there.

Doreen Lake (Map 30/G3)
This seldom-visited lake requires a good four-wheel drive vehicle and some patience to find. The lake offers an early season beginning in early May and plenty of small rainbow. It is possible to launch a small boat and to camp at roadside.

Doris Lake (Map 19/F4)
Doris Lake lies within Taweel Park and can be reached by a short trail from Taweel Lake. The lake suffers from winterkill so any fish in the lake will be small.

Dorsey Lake (Map 29/E1) 🐟
Found within the UBC Alex Fraser Research Forest, this small lake has been stocked heavily with rainbow trout over the past several years, making for some excellent trout fishing. Reports have rainbows in the 1–2 kg (2–4.5 lb) range. Four-wheel drive access limits visitors.

Double Lakes (Map 19/E2)
Double Lakes is really one lake that gives the illusion of two lakes if viewed from above. The lake is accessible off Road 20 west of Clearwater. Fishing is fair for rainbow trout to 1 kg (2 lbs). There is a recreation site available at the lake, equipped with a boat launch.

Dragon Lake (Map 42/F2) 🐟
Dragon Lake is a popular lake found south of Quesnel where big brook and rainbow trout to 5.5 kg (12 lbs) are not uncommon. It is one of the first lakes in the region to ice off in early spring. The nutrient-rich lake has plenty of weed beds that are ideal for insect rearing, and the trout tend to move a lot. Fly anglers who work the south weed beds during spring with a wet fly may lure a trophy trout. Fishing is slow in the summer, but picks up again in the fall. In addition to the boat launch off Gook Road, there is a private campsite and lodging on the lake, which is lined by private residents. Check the regulations for closures.

Drewry Lake (Map 19/A3)
Drewry Lake is a beautiful 565 ha (1,396 ac) lake surrounded by a thick Douglas-fir forest. Fishing begins in late May and remains active until early July. The lake does not offer much in the way of a summer fishery. There are a good number of wild rainbow trout growing to 2 kg (4.5 lbs), but averaging only about 20–30 cm (8–12 in). Trolling is popular, while casting from shore is limited. There are two recreation sites with cartop boat launches.

Fishing Adventures

Dugan Lake (Map 29/D5) 🐟
Dugan Lake is a popular fishing spot during ice fishing season. Just 107 ha (264 ac) and stocked with brook and rainbow it is a highly productive lake. Brook trout are the main focus, with fish reaching 1–2 kg (2–4.5 lbs) in size. Brown trout also inhabit the lake and trolling for kokanee is very popular. The biggest fish are rainbow, which reach 3 kg (6.5 lbs) on occasion. There is a large recreation site located in a meadow next to the lake.

Dum Lake (Map 19/G6)
You can find Dum Lake off a rough four-wheel drive road, 20 km west of Little Fort. The lake offers good fishing for small rainbow trout that can reach 1 kg (2 lbs) on occasion. Fly-fishing can be very good in the spring or fall with a caddisfly or dragonfly pattern.

Dunsapie Lake (Map 7/G3)
This 10 ha (24 ac) lake is located along the Jamieson Creek Road 30 km west of Barriere and has a nice recreation site with camping and a cartop boat launch. The high elevation lake is home to a fair number of rainbow and trolling seems to be the preferred method, especially in the summer.

Eagan Lake (Map 19/C7)
Found 14 km south of Bridge Lake, this 410 ha (1,013 ac) lake offers fairly good fishing for rainbow that can reach 1 kg (2 lbs) in size. There are also some small kokanee that inhabit the lake. The lake is 1,050 m (3,413 ft) above sea level and has a resort on the north end.

Eagle Lake (Map 13/G1)
South of Highway 20, this clear, 1,187 ha (4,662 ac) lake is a popular destination with anglers. All services can be found nearby in Tatla Lake. The rainbow average 1 kg (2 lbs), but the odd trout can reach 3.5 kg (8 lbs) in size. Smaller kokanee are also present and fishing is good during the summer, providing it isn't too hot. The lake has a recreation site on the west end.

Eagle Lake [Murphy Lake] (Map 30/D6) 🐟
Eagle Lake offers decent fishing for rainbow trout to 2.5 kg (5.5 lbs) beginning in late May to early June. Trolling around the holes at the northwest and southeast ends of the lake is effective, while spincasters or fly anglers can have luck around the creek mouths or the sunken island in the middle of the lake. There are a number of private cabins along both shorelines, along with a boat launch towards the northwest end of the lake.

Earle Lake (Map 18/F4) 🐟
Earle Lake is stocked annually and offers a good fishery for rainbow trout averaging 20–30 cm (8–12 in), however reports show some fish in the 51 cm (20 in) range. The lake is well suited for a belly boat or canoe and is also a great place for fly anglers. The road is overgrown and you might need to walk in. There is a bait ban and single barbless hook restriction along with no ice fishing allowed at this lake.

East & West King Lakes (Map 19/D5)
Found about 10 km down the rough Grossett Road, off the Bridge Lake North Road, East and West King Lakes remain popular destinations. This is due to the good fishing for rainbow trout. There is an artificial fly only and engine size restriction of 7.5 kW (10 hp) on the lakes. Check the regulations for other restrictions.

Edmund Lake (Map 18/B5) 🐟
West of 100 Mile House, the better road access is from the north, off the Gustafsen Lake Forest Service Road (1100 Rd). There are lots of islands and structures for the fish to hide in, but most of the action is found in the deeper west end. Rainbow grow big here with occasional 2 kg (4.5 lb) fish. Winterkill can be an issue on cold years so the lake is stocked.

Ejas Lake (Map 19/F1)
Ejas Lake offers good fishing for rainbow trout to 2 kg (4.5 lbs). Trolling or fly-fishing are your best bets for success, especially during the spring or fall periods. A recreation site with a boat launch is found at the lake.

Elbow Lake (Map 31/A4)
Elbow Lake is located 27 km east of Black Creek off the McKinley Lake Road (500 Rd). The lake is 126 m (413 ft) at its deepest point and can be fished throughout the ice-free season with reasonable success. The fish are spread out and are hard to catch so trolling is the preferred angling method. There is a recreation site with a beach area and boat launch.

Elbow Lake (Map 7/D3) 🐟
Home to a resort on the west end, visitors can also access the lake along the Heller Lake Trail. High enough to stay cool through summer, the lake offers great fishing for stocked rainbow trout to 1 kg (2 lbs). Fly anglers can try chironomids, mayflies, damselflies or leeches around the shoals.

Eleven Sisters Chain (Map 15/B2)
Access is via the 7000 Road to the Scum Lake Recreation Site. This series of lakes (Norma, Nancy, Roxanne, Ruby, etc.) offers fishing for wild rainbow. There is limited access to the lakes, but it is possible to bushwhack along Haines Creek to get to the more remote lakes in the chain. Haines Lake, to the west of Scum Lake is also part of the group.

Eliguk Lake (Map 38/D2)
Eliguk Lake is a great fly-fishing lake that produces well throughout the year. The dry fly season peaks in late summer for the abundant rainbow that reach a chunky 1.5 kg (3 lbs). Access is by floatplane or via an eight day hike along the Alexander Mackenzie Trail. There is a private resort, as well as wilderness tenting spots next to the lake. Check the regulations for special limits and regulations.

Elk Lake (Map 29/C1) 🐟
Elk Lake is a scenic, little, 58 ha (143 ac) lake with huge shoals and extensive weed beds. While the lake does not contain large numbers of trout, it is stocked with trout that grow to 2.5 kg (6 lbs). If you are planning a trip to the lake, late spring to early summer or later into fall are the most productive times. The lake is well suited for float tubes and is designated a fly only lake. The recreation site offers a small dock and hand launch for electric motor boats only.

Elkhorn Lake (Map 15/E2)
You will find this secluded but productive lake off the Tsuh Lake Forest Service Road, south of Highway 20. Rainbow trout are in abundance here and can be found in the 1–3 kg (2–6.5 lb) range. Fly-fishing can be quite productive here.

Elkin Lake (Map 14/F5)
Elkin Lake is situated north of Vedan Lake and offers a similar fishery, with wild Chilcotin rainbow to 1 kg (2lbs) and Dolly Varden to 7 kg (15 lbs). Trolling is the most common method of catching these fish.

Emar Lake (Map 19/F6)
Accessed off Highway 24, Emar Lake is inhabited by rainbow trout that can reach up to 2 kg (4.5 lbs). There are some superb shoals found around the lake that produce well for fly anglers. There is a bait ban in effect on the lake.

Emerald Lake (Map 17/D3) 🐟
You can reach this remote lake via Gulatch Emerald Road, a very rough logging road. The lake has been stocked annually with moderate amounts of rainbow trout since 2005.

English Lake (Map 19/C5)
English Lake is off Meridian Lake Forest Service Road, just north of Bridge Lake. The high elevation lake does not become fishable until mid to late May and the fishing will remain somewhat active for rainbow throughout the ice-free season.

Euchiniko Lakes (Map 53/E7–54/B6)
The lakes along the Blackwater River are wonderful trout lakes with the aggressive Blackwater strain of rainbow that grow to 2 kg (4.5 lbs). The problem is the access. The lakes are accessed by plane, canoe or trail along the Alexander Mackenzie Trail. There are wilderness resorts in the area.

Eutsuk Lake (Map 50/B3–51/D4)
Eutsuk Lake is the largest natural lake in BC, at 84 km (52 mi) long. There are good populations of rainbow trout, kokanee, burbot and mountain whitefish. Rainbow in this lake have been known to top 7 kg (15 lbs), with the largest being a whopping 15.5 kg (34 lbs). Access is by boat from Ootsa or Whitesail Lake or by floatplane.

Exeter Lake (Map 18/C4)
Found just 4 km west of 100 Mile House off Exeter Road, Exeter Lake is a good family lake. The fish are small, but feisty. It holds rainbow trout and lake whitefish and some coarse fish. Exeter Lake is only 4.3 m (14 ft) deep, so it is subject to winterkill. Fishing is best in spring and fall; the lake becomes rather swampy during summer.

Faulkner Lake (Map 19/D5)
Found 18 km northeast of Bridge Lake, Faulkner Lake is stocked with trout reaching 2.5 kg (5.5 lbs). These big trout can be a challenge to catch, especially in the dog days of summer. There is a small camping area on the northern shore where a small boat can be launched. A four-wheel drive vehicle is recommended to access the lake.

Fawn Lake (Map 18/G5)
Fawn Lake is situated north off Highway 24, about 27 km west of Bridge Lake. The popular fishing hole is home to a resort and regularly yields rainbow trout in the 2–3 kg (4.5–6.5 lbs) size range on the fly. There are also rumours of some fish exceeding 5 kg (11 lbs). The lake is stocked and there is public access with a boat launch for electric motors only.

Felker Lake (Map 29/C7)
This lake is found 28 km south of Williams Lake off the Chimney Lake Road. It is inhabited by burbot and stocked rainbow along with some coarse fish. At only 227 ha (560 ac) this lake is free of ice earlier than most of the Cariboo lakes and most of the action can be found in the deeper north end. The improved recreation site offers a boat launch on the north end of the lake.

Finger Lake (Map 54/A1)
Access to this lake is limited through a private resort, although the whole area is part of Tatuk Finger Provincial Park. The 877 ha (2,167 ac) lake is 9 km (5.5 mi) long with several islands and bays. The lake offers consistent fishing for rainbow reaching 2.5 kg (5 lbs), kokanee and dollies to 1 kg (2 lbs). The two islands and outflow of Finger Creek are a few areas to work.

Fire Lake (Map 29/F1)
South of Gavin Lake in the UBC Alex Fraser Research Forest, there is a road/trail leading to the east side of this 15 ha (37 ac) lake. Stocked every fall with the Pennask strain of rainbow, this lake offers better fishing around dusk working near the bottom. There is a bait ban and single barbless hook restriction along with no ice fishing allowed at this lake.

Fir Lake (Map 28/B4)
This clear, shallow, 877 ha (2,167 ac) lake offers wary rainbow trout in the 2 kg (4.5 lb) range. Fly anglers do well by anchoring and casting towards shore, although trolling small leeches can work too. Mayflies, damselflies and sedges are other common fly patterns. There is a recreation site with boat launch found 8 km south off the Rosita-Meldrum Forest Service Road.

Fiset Lake (Map 18/F4)
This small lake is located east of 100 Mile House off the Kaluza Road. Small rainbow are reported here.

Fish Lake (Map 15/A7)
Rumours of a mine wiping this lake out in 2009 surfaced. Thankfully this has not materialized, and the lake, which is situated about 16 km southeast of the Taseko River (Davidson) Bridge, is a good place to chase wild rainbow. The lake offers a small recreation site with a cartop boat launch and a great view of Anvil Mountain. Check the regulations for restrictions.

Fishem Lake (Map 2/G2)
Fishem Lake is one of a series of lakes in the valley between Ts'ylos and the Taseko Mountain. It only has an average depth of 4.8 m (16 ft) and is 141 ha (348 ac), but produces wild rainbow and bull trout. Access is off Gunn Valley Forest Service Road.

Fishpot Lake (Map 40/F2)
Accessed off the Michelle-Coglistiko Road (4000 Rd) 120 km west of Quesnel, this 87 ha (214 ac) lake has been known to produce rainbow up to 3 kg (6.5 lbs). The small lake fishes well from a float tube throughout the year. There is a resort on the lake, and the recreation site provides camping and a gravel boat launch.

Flapjack Lake (Map 19/F5)
This small lake can be found 34 km northeast of Bridge Lake via a short trail from a rough access road. The lake offers good fishing for small rainbow trout around 1–2 kg (2–4.5 lbs), which are best caught on the fly. There is camping and a resort nearby.

Fletcher Lake (Map 15/F3)
Found 26 km south of Hanceville, there are accommodations, boat rentals and some services available at Fletcher Lake. There is also a grassy recreation site near the north end of the lake. Wild rainbow up to 4.5 kg (10 lbs) are caught regularly, although the average is only 1 kg (2 lbs). The lake is best fished from May through October and trolling seems to be the preferred method.

Fly Lake (Map 18/C1)
Fly Lake is a small lake located just west of the Mount Timothy Ski Area. Fishing can be decent for small rainbow trout, especially on a fly. There is a rustic recreation site available at the lake for overnight camping and small boat access. No power boats.

Forest Lake (Map 29/C3)
Only 37 km from Williams Lake, Forest Lake is a popular fishing lake that produces some trophy fish. Ice is gone by April and fishing is good through May and early June. Lurking in the deeper holes are fish rumoured to be over 8 kg (17.5 lbs) in size, although most are 2 kg (4.5 lbs). It is an artificial fly lake only and there is a good caddisfly hatch towards the middle of June. Dragonfly and damselfly nymphs, chironomids and shrimp are other popular patterns. There is a recreation site complete with a boat launch on the northern shore of the 98 ha (242 ac) lake. Restrictions include a bait ban and artificial flies as well as no ice fishing or powered boats allowed.

Fourteen Mile Lake (Map 57/G3)
Access can be a challenge but is best from the northeast, off the Bowron Forest Service Road. The lake provides fishing opportunities for rainbow trout, although the shallow nature of this lake makes it subject to winterkill during harsh winters. A pleasant, secluded campsite overlooks the lake.

French Lake (Map 19/B5)
French Lake is located 22 km north of Bridge Lake on a steep four-wheel drive road off the Windy Mountain Forest Service Road (1900 Rd). Fishing for the high populations of stocked rainbow trout is best from late May into June. Most of the popular Cariboo region flies work well at this lake. Barbless hooks, no ice fishing, bait ban and powerboat restrictions are in effect. Camping and a boat launch are available at the lakeside recreation site.

Freshette Lake (Map 44/C7)
It is a short hike from a spur road off the Spanish Lake Road to reach the lake, but is worth it to lure a large rainbow. Due to limited fishing pressure, the trout grow to 3.6 kg (8 lbs) on occasion.

Friendly Lake (Map 19/F5)
Friendly Lake is inhabited by good numbers of rainbow trout, some of which reach 2 kg (4.5 lbs) in size. The lake is quite deep; therefore, it is not subject to winterkill. The lake can be reached off Wavey Lake Forest Service Road, north of Highway 24.

Gardner Lake (Map 17/E2)
Another in a series of small stocked lakes around Williams Lake, this small lake rests to the west of the Enterprise Road (1100 Rd), south of Chimney Lake. The lake is stocked annually with rainbow.

Gavin Lake (Map 29/F1)
Gavin Lake is the main lake in the UBC Alex Fraser Research Forest and is easily reached by car. The small, 95 ha (234 ac) lake is deep and allows for decent fishing throughout the summer months. Rainbow reach 1 kg (2 lbs) or 35 cm (14 in) here. The recreation site offers a good boat launch.

Genevieve Lake (Map 56/G5)
Genevieve Lake can be accessed by the Olson Road, which links to the Genevieve Road (700 Rd) to the east of Highway 97 north of Quesnel. The lake provides good fishing in the spring and fall for rainbow trout that can reach 1.5 kg (3 lbs). There is a small, rustic recreation site that can be challenging to reach during the wet season.

Ghost Lake (Map 44/G2–45/A2)
Forming the main access point into the Cariboo Mountains Park, Ghost Lake also offers decent fishing for rainbow trout. There are also bull trout and kokanee. In the fall Chinook, Coho and sockeye salmon spawn here creating eggs and smelt in the spring for the trout to feast on. From the campsite, it is a short walk down to the lake. For those willing to hand launch, trolling can be effective.

Goodwin Lake (Map 19/G1)
This small lake is found off the rough Road 9, south of Mahood Lake. Goodwin offers fishing opportunities for rainbow trout to 1 kg (2 lbs) that are best taken on the fly. The lake is home to a small recreation site complete with a cartop boat access.

Goose Lake (Map 18/B3)
Goose Lake can be found by trail from the McKinley-Ogden Road. The lake is inhabited by a good population of rainbow that can grow to 1 kg (2 lbs). Fly-fishing can be quite good at times, especially in the spring during chironomid hatches.

Gotchen Lake (Map 31/C5)

Nestled under the shadows of Deception and Boss Mountains, Gotchen Lake produces moderate amounts of rainbow trout and the odd lake trout. Unfortunately, lake trout populations have declined in recent years. There is a bait ban and single barbless hook restriction at this lake.

Government Lake (Map 56/E1)

Found in the hills above Highway 97, 28 km north of Hixon, Government Lake is a small lake with a fine recreation site and trail system. Fishing can be good for rainbow trout to 1.5 kg (3.5 lbs), especially on the fly. Spincasters will find a few areas suitable for casting.

Green Lake (Map 18/D7–E7)

Green Lake is renowned for its beautiful green waters. The popular lake is 15 km long and contains rainbow trout and kokanee, both of which are stocked. Rainbow can reach up to 3 kg (6.5 lbs) in size and are best found by trolling. The 2,760 ha (6,820 ac) lake is home to a number of camps and resorts, as well as the several locales of Green Lake Park that provide good boat access around the lake.

Greenlee Lake (Map 19/A2)

Greenlee Lake is located near the large Canim Lake. The smaller 29 ha (71 ac) lake is a productive fly-fishing lake with rainbow trout that can grow to 2 kg (4.5 lbs). Greenlee Lake is stocked annually with rainbow, but receives very little fishing pressure except from locals. There is a recreation site with a rough cartop boat launch on the eastern shores of the lake. Only electric motors are allowed on the lake.

Greeny Lake [Greene Lake] (Map 18/C2)

Access to Greeny Lake is off Timothy Lake Road (1500 Rd), 12 km northeast of Lac La Hache. The lake is 75 ha (185 ac) and 14 m (46 ft) deep. It contains rainbow and burbot along with redside shiners and squawfish. A recreation site is situated on the northern shore of the lake. There is a 7.5 kW (10 hp) engine power restriction.

Grizzly Bear Lake (Map 4/D4)

Grizzly Lake is a small lake, accessed by four-wheel drive or ATV off the Noaxe Creek Forest Service Road. Anglers can find small rainbow later in the year at this mountain lake.

Grizzly Lake (Map 19/C5)

Located just north of Bridge Lake, Grizzly Lake offers fishing opportunities for stocked rainbow, averaging 30 cm (12 in). It is a deep lake that sees few visitors due to the rough road access. There is a rustic camping area and boat launch available. There is a bait ban and single barbless hook restriction at this lake as well as no ice fishing.

Grizzly Lakes (Map 19/G3)

Grizzly Lakes offers fishing opportunities for big rainbow (stocked annually) to 3 kg (6.5 lbs). The deeper lake is over 30 m (98 ft) deep, allowing the lake to avoid winterkill. A good area to focus fishing efforts is near the inflow or outflow creeks found on the lake. There is a place to camp and launch a boat on the lake.

Groundhog Lake (Map 44/A1)

This scenic lake lies south of Barkerville in the popular recreational area around Mount Agnes. Accessed by trail, the mountain lake offers small rainbow trout.

Grouse Lake (Map 19/F6)

Grouse Lake can be reached via portage or by a trail from Emar Lake. This smaller lake provides good fly-fishing for rainbow trout to 2 kg (4.5 lbs), especially during spring chironomid hatches.

Gun Lake (Map 4/A7)

Gun Lake is a popular recreational lake to the west of Goldbridge. The lake is lined with cabins and has a resort, a boat launch and a recreation site on the west side. The lake offers fair fishing for rainbow to 1 kg (2 lbs), small kokanee and dollies to 4 kg (9 lbs). Trolling is the mainstay of the lake.

Gustafsen Lake (Map 17/F6)

Gustafsen Lake is a 142 ha (350 ac) lake, situated about 40 km southwest of 100 Mile House. Access to the lake is through private property; the current owners allow public access, but that is subject to change without notice. Gustafsen Lake has good fishing for rainbow trout beginning in the late spring. Rainbow trout can grow to 1.5 kg (3 lbs), but average about 40–51 cm (16–20 in). The clear lake can be a challenge to fish; anglers should work the drop-off area near the middle of the lake. There is a cartop boat launch at the popular lake.

Haines Lake (Map 27/E7)

Haines Lake is noted for the biggest trout of the Eleven Sisters Lakes. Only 16 km south of Alexis Creek, access to the lake is off Haines Creek Road (4400 Rd), which can be difficult in wet weather. Fishing is best in spring and fall.

Hammer Lake (Map 7/C2)

Hammer Lake has a good sedge fly hatch, which means that fly-fishing is best in late June and into July. Be forewarned that the 68 ha (168 ac) lake can be quite moody, especially in the summer when the water is warm. The lake contains rainbow in the 1–2 kg (2–4.5 lb) range, although there is the odd fish that reaches 3 kg (6.5 lbs). A recreation site is found along the Egan-Bonaparte Forest Service Road (3700 Rd). Boaters should note the electric motor only restriction.

Hanham Lake (Map 54/E4)

Hanham Lake is 3 km west of Boat Lake. There is a little-used recreation site that sits above the east end of the lake; the steep incline makes it inconvenient for anything but light boats and canoes.

> *Rainbow trout will take readily to small spinners, spoons, roe, worms and flies. Fly anglers should match the hatch carrying with them larval, pupal and adult forms of chironomids, caddisflies, stoneflies, and mayflies.*

Hardcastle Lakes (Map 19/F5)

These two secluded lakes can be accessed off the Taweel Lake Forest Service Road. The lakes offer fishing opportunities for rainbow that reach 2 kg (4.5 lbs) in size on occasion. The Lower Hardcastle Lake is quite shallow and experiences winterkill from time to time.

Hathaway Lake (Map 19/A4)

Hathaway Lake offers a good fishery for stocked rainbow trout and wild lake trout that begins in late May. The rainbow trout average 2.5 kg (5.5 lbs), whereas the lake trout average 3.5 kg (8 lbs). At 152 ha (375 ac), Hathaway Lake is a good trolling lake. Access is off Mahood Lake Forest Service Road; there is a resort on the south end of the lake and a picnic site and boat launch on the western shore.

Hawkins Lake (Map 18/G1–19/A2)

Hawkins Lake is located on Hawkins Lake Road and is inhabited by a fair population of rainbow trout that average about 25–35 cm (10–14 in); however, the odd rainbow in the 1 kg (2 lb) range is caught periodically. Trolling is an effective angling method, although spincasting and fly-fishing can provide some success. There is a cartop boat launch at the lake. There is an engine power restriction of 7.5 Kw (10 HP) here.

Hay & Lodi Lakes (Map 57/B3)

Hay and Lodi Lakes are connected lakes that contain rainbow trout as well as an abundance of coarse fish, which impact the trout's ability to grow and survive. As a result, angling success suffers. Hay Lake is too shallow to troll, but fly anglers will like the appealing shoals. Lodi Lake is a little deeper and trollers will find success working the northern end of the lake. Hay Lake offers a recreation site. Access is off the Naver-Ahbau Forest Service Road (700 Rd).

Helena Lake (Map 17/G2)

Helena Lake is situated to the southwest of Lac la Hache in the heart of the Cariboo. Helena Lake is a notoriously moody lake with rainbow trout that average 1 kg (2 lbs), but can grow to 4.5 kg (10 lbs). The spotty fishing is a surprise given that the lake is stocked with 30,000 rainbow trout annually and is only 238 ha (588 ac) in size. Fish grow rapidly in this lake given the abundance of shrimp and aquatic insects. After ice-over in November, the lake becomes a good ice fishing destination. The lake has a recreation site with a boat launch situated at the northeast end.

Fishing Adventures

Heller Lake (Map 7/D3)

Heller Lake is another hike-in lake just south of Elbow Lake and accessed along the Heller Lake Trail, which starts at the south end of the Bonaparte Provincial Park. The lake is high enough, at 1,220 m (3,965 ft), to provide very good fishing for rainbow trout to 1.5 kg (3 lbs) throughout the ice-free season.

Hen Ingram Lake [9 Mile Lake] (Map 30/F1) 🐟

Hen Ingram Lake is also known as 9 Mile Lake and is nestled in the mountains between Horsefly and Quesnel Lakes. The lake has good fishing for rainbow despite redside shiners, which compete for food. The trout are stocked annually and grow rapidly, averaging 35–45 cm (14–18 in) in size and can grow up to 3–4 kg (6.5–9 lbs). Since the lake is fairly deep, it allows for a decent fishery throughout the season. Trolling is the preferred angling method. The improved but busy recreation site has a good boat launch.

Henri Lake (Map 28/A5)

One of several medium-sized lakes in the area, Henri Lake is your basic hit-or-miss lake. Rainbows here fall into the 1 kg (2 lb) category, with lake trout topping the 4.5 kg (10 lb) mark. Access is off the Alex Graham Pass Lake Forest Service Road. It is best to work the drop-off points within this lake.

Hiahkwah Lake (Map 7/E4)

This lake can be reached by a four-wheel drive road or the Deadman Trail from Bonaparte Provincial Park. There is a good population of rainbow that can grow to 1 kg (2 lbs). Fly-fishing around the shoals with sedge flies at dusk in June and July is quite effective. Chironomids, mayflies and leeches also work.

Hidden and Secret Lakes (Map 24/B5)

Found in the Crazy Bear Valley, southwest of Charlotte Lake, few anglers ever make it into these high elevation lakes, and fishing can be very good for wild rainbow. Some trout are over 36 cm (14 in) long. There is a bait ban and single barbless hook restriction as well as no ice fishing at this lake.

Higgins Lake (Map 19/A4) 🐟

Covering 22 ha (54 ac), Higgins Lake is a consistent producer of stocked rainbow trout in the 25 cm (10 in) range. The lake has had a history with winterkill, but an aerator was installed to reduce the problem. However, that means that ice fishing can be dangerous and the ice can be thin. There is a cartop boat launch for electric motors only at the public access to the lake.

Hihium Lake (Map 6/F5) 🐟

This 350 ha (864 ac) waterbody is located near Loon Lake and is known as an excellent fly-fishing lake, given its abundant weed beds and rocky shoals. The rainbow trout can reach 2 kg (4.5 lbs) due in part to the good hatches that include chironomids and mayflies in spring as well as the smaller damselflies and sedges (in June and July). The high elevation lake has two recreation sites and a boat access fish camp on its shores. Restrictions include motor size (max 7.5 kW/10 hp), single hooks and bans on ice fishing and bait use.

Hobson Lake (Map 53/D1)

Located east of the Kinney Dam, Hobson Lake is a small trophy lake and one of the best fly-fishing spots in the Nechako Reservoir area. The lake is accessed off the Klukus-Kenny Dam Road (500 Rd). A rough two-wheel drive road leads to a recreation campsite with a cartop launch on the shores of the lake. The lake can produce large trout up to and over 5 kg (11 lbs). The extensive shoals can create exciting sight fishing if the wind isn't blowing.

Hoopatatkwa Lake (Map 7/E3)

Located within Bonaparte Provincial Park, this lake is accessible only by trail or float plane. This lake covers 104 ha (256 ac) and has good fishing for rainbow trout to 2 kg (4.5 lbs). Fly-fishing (chironomids, damselflies and sedges), bait fishing or spincasting are all effective. There is a resort at the lake.

Horn Lake (Map 13/D2) 🐟

One of the nicest recreation sites in the Chilcotin accentuates this lovely lake, which has big views of the Niut Range to the south. The lake contains rainbow to 1.5 kg (3 lbs) as well as bull trout. Access is off Bluff Lake Road, 17 km south of Tatla Lake.

Horse Lake (Map 18/E5–F5) 🐟

Horse Lake is a 1,162 ha (2,871 ac), 18 km (11 mi) long lake found southeast of 100 Mile House. It receives heavy fishing pressure due to its easy access. Deep trolling is preferred for the lake trout, while spinning lures are the most effective for rainbow and kokanee. The rainbow can grow over 2 kg (4.5 lbs). There are full facilities at the lake including cottages, resorts, camping and a boat launch.

Horsefly Lake (Map 30/C2–31/B1)

Horsefly Lake is a large, 5,868 ha (14,500 ac) lake northeast of Horsefly. The lake is best fished by trolling in the late spring. Some big fish are caught annually with rainbow trout to 5.5 kg (12 lbs), lake trout to 10 kg (22 lbs), bull trout to 6 kg (13 lbs) and kokanee to 2 kg (4.5 lbs), offering a good selection to choose from. Horsefly Lake Park is located on the western shore of the lake and offers a paved boat launch. Wind can be a problem for anglers and boaters on this big lake.

Hotfish Lake (Map 31/C7)

North of Canim Lake, you can find this secluded lake via trail from the Spanish Creek Forest Service Road. The trail is steep but worth it as the fishing is normally very good for rainbow trout to 1 kg (2 lbs). Both fly-fishing and spincasting can produce good results. It is recommended to pack a float tube in.

Hotnarko Lake (Map 24/B1)

The trophy trout have all but disappeared, but rainbow that average about 30–40 cm (12–16 in) in size still thrive. The clear, 524 ha (1,294 ac) lake has many islands and shoals for the fly angler. Similar to most lakes in the area, leeches, shrimp or dragonflies are the most effective fly patterns. Access is limited to plane, foot or bike as the road that runs past the lake has been blocked off to preserve the wilderness setting. Anglers are well advised to haul in a canoe or small boat as shore fishing is difficult and the lake is too windy for float tubes. There is a bait ban and a single hook restriction on the lake.

Hourglass Lake (Map 19/E6)

Hourglass Lake can be accessed off a four-wheel drive branch from the Blowdown Road. The rainbow trout can reach 2 kg (4.5 lbs), although they average about 25–30 cm (10–12 in) in size. Fly-fishing and spincasting are both productive. There is a good caddis hatch on this lake during the late spring and summer periods.

Howard Lake (Map 19/B2) 🐟

Howard Lake is a scenic, 167 ha (412 ac) lake set in the forest-covered hills south of Canim Lake. Despite the heavy fishing pressure, Howard Lake still produces well for stocked rainbow trout up to 2 kg (5 lbs). With some very nice shoals, drop-offs and weed beds to focus around, fly anglers will find may places to work their magic. There are two recreation sites on the lake, one with a boat launch in an open meadow that was once a sawmill. A maximum 7.5 kW (10 hp) restriction exists for powerboats.

Howes Lake (Map 29/B2) 🐟

This is a shallow, 65 ha (160 ac) lake southeast of McLeese Lake. Winterkill is a problem here. The lake is best in its deeper southwest end. There is a recreation site with a boat launch on the east side of the lake off Blue Lake Road (1800 Rd).

Hunter Lake (Map 44/E1)

Hunter Lake is located within Bowron Lake Park and can be accessed by trail from Sandy Lake to the north or by trail from the Matthew River Road to the south. The lake is rarely visited and fishing can be quite good for rainbow trout that average 25–35 cm (10–14 in). Fly-fishing is particularly good on this lake since the rainbow are rarely picky.

Hush Lake (Map 56/F6) 🐟

Hush Lake is a small, 5.3 ha (13 ac) lake found north of Quesnel next to Highway 97. The lake is stocked with brook trout and rainbow trout that average about 0.5 kg (1 lb). Fishing is surprisingly good on the fly. Try casting a dragonfly or damselfly pattern towards the lily pads. Although no powerboats are allowed, a small boat would be helpful to get past the lily pads; you can cast from shore near the boat launch.

Hutchison Lake (Map 6/E2)

East of 70 Mile House, Hutchison Lake is accessed via Hutchison Forest Service Road (3000 Rd), south of Green Lake. This small lake provides reasonably good fishing for small rainbow, with the larger reaching approximately 1.5 kg (3 lbs) in size.

Indian Lake (Map 58/B4)

This medium-sized lake sits north of Bowron Lake and offers bull trout, kokanee, lake trout and rainbow trout. Access is from a rough off-shoot road from Kruger Lake Road leading to the southern shores. June and September have proven to be the best months for fishing this peaceful lake.

Irish Lake (Map 18/E5) 🐟

Irish Lake is a popular 28 ha (69 ac) lake found 2 km east of Lone Butte directly off Highway 24. The lake has rainbow trout in the 35–46 cm (14–18 in) class and the odd brook trout. The lake receives heavy fishing pressure, but the an-

nual stocking program helps maintain the fishery. The lake is best suited for fly anglers and spincasters as the lake is too shallow to troll. The recreation site offers a boat launch for electric motor only boats and an aerator has been installed at the lake to reduce winterkill. Ice fishing is not recommended.

Isobel Lake (Map 7/F7)
Isobel Lake is a small, 14 ha (34 ac) lake, found 20 km northwest of Kamloops. The population of stocked brook trout are best caught in the fall or through the ice. There is a recreation site providing camping and a rough cartop boat launch at the lake.

Italia Lake (Map 19/F2)
Italia Lake offers good spring or fall fishing for small rainbow trout. By summer the water warms and the fishing slows down. A fishing camp and recreation site is found at the lake, which is accessible via a well-maintained Road 20.

Jack of Clubs Lake (Map 57/G7)
Located off the south side of Highway 24, within walking distance from Wells, this is a very scenic lake. Fishing in the lake is good for rainbow trout, bull trout and lake trout. Due to mining activity the lake has a high level of mercury and it is recommended not to eat lake trout over 45 cm (18 in).

Jackson Lake [Jacks' Hole Lake] (Map 29/C1)
The difficult access, combined with an intensive stocking program and fly-fishing only restriction results in good fishing. There are large numbers of trout in the 1 kg (2 lb) range. The lake has crystal clear water allowing you to see the shoals and drop-offs over which you can cast your fly. Try using a dragonfly nymph or chironomid imitation in the spring. Attractor type patterns like the Woolly Bugger and the leech also work well. There is a recreation site with a rough boat launch for electric motors only. There is a bait ban, artificial fly only and electric motor only restriction at this lake.

Jacobie Lake (Map 43/F7)
Just off Likely Road on Jacobie Lake Forest Service Road lies this 91 ha (224 ac) lake. It is clear of ice by mid-May and fishing is best during the early summer and fall periods. The rainbow trout grow rapidly in the nutrient-rich waters with the average fish being in the 25–35 cm (10–14 in) range. A popular recreation site is situated on the west end of the lake and offers a cartop boat launch. Check the regulations for special catch limits.

Jacques Lake (Map 30/E1)
Jacques Lake is found off the Hen Ingram Lake Road (Z Road), 29 km northeast of Horsefly. This 3 km (1.8 mi) long lake contains stocked rainbow that often reach 2.5 kg (5 lbs). Fishing is good in the early part of the season and there are some nice shoal areas to focus around. Although trolling is the preferred fishing method, fly anglers and spincasters can find success working the sunken island near the middle of the lake. A nice recreation site provides lakeside camping as well as a boat launch.

Jim Lake (Map 18/F7)
Stocked heavily with rainbow trout, Jim Lake is a popular lake to the south of the bigger Green Lake. If you can hand launch a small boat, trolling is recommended. Otherwise try working the shoals at either end of the lake with a fly or small lure.

Johnny Lake (Map 19/F4)
This small, secluded lake can only be accessed by trail from the much larger Taweel Lake. This has helped keep the fishing pressure low, and as a result fishing can be quite good for rainbow trout that average about 20–30 cm (8–12 in) in size. However, the lake can be subject to winterkill since it only averages about 6 m (20 ft) in depth.

Johnny Lake (Map 52/C6)
Located on the east side of Entiako Provincial Park, this high elevation lake is reached by the Kluskus-Malaput Road or by canoe on the Fawnie Creek Paddling Route. It has fair fishing for rainbow trout to 1 kg (2 lbs) throughout the spring and fall.

Kappan Lake (Map 24/C2)
Located 15 km south of Anahim Lake, off Kappan Lake Forest Service Road, Kappan Lake is 345 ha (852 ac) and contains wild rainbow. The lake sees fairly heavy angling pressure and has two recreation sites and boat launch. There is a bait ban/single barbless hook restriction on the lake.

Kelly Lake (Map 5/F5)
Kelly Lake lies within Downing Park, only 16 km southwest of Clinton, and is easily reached by car. The lake offers rainbow trout that can reach up to 1 kg (2 lbs) in size. Strong afternoon winds can play havoc with boaters. The scenic lake has a long sandy beach and camping and day-use facilities.

Keno Lake (Map 30/E1; Map 44/E7)
Keno Lake is located north of Jacques Lake and contains rainbow trout. The trout average under 0.5 kg (1 lb), but can grow to 2 kg (4.5 lbs) or more. Anglers will find good fishing early in the spring or later in the fall. It is best to troll around the three deep holes in the lake, especially in the summer. The recreation site on the eastern shores of the lake receives heavy use during the summer months and is equipped with a boat launch.

Kersey Lake [5 Mile Lake] (Map 6/A5)
Kersey Lake is located 8 km or 5 miles south of Clinton, off the east side of Highway 97. There is a pullout on the roadside. The lake has been stocked in the past with brook trout, which can provide good fishing at times. Brookies are best fished in the spring or fall as well as through the ice in winter.

Kestrel Lake (Map 29/B1)
South of the Beaver Valley Road north of Williams Lake, Kestrel Lake is stocked annually with rainbow trout. Try fishing for these trout near the bottom at dusk. There is a bait ban and single barbless hook restriction along with no ice fishing allowed at this lake.

Kevin Lake (Map 54/F3)
Stocked in the past with rainbow trout, Kevin Lake is a remote lake. There is an informal camping area on the south shore and decent access off the Pelican Lake Forest Service Road.

Kitty Ann Lake (Map 19/E2)
This small lake has fair fishing for rainbow to 1 kg (2 lbs), which are caught primarily in the spring or fall. Fly-fishing is one of the best methods to have success on this lake, although trolling can produce results. The lake can be reached via the Branch 231 forestry road and is home to a recreation site equipped with a cartop boat launch. The access road requires a high clearance vehicle.

Klinne Lake (Map 44/E7)
Klinne Lake is stocked annually with rainbow trout, which provide for good fishing for rainbow to 1 kg (2 lbs), but average 20–30 cm (8–12 in). The 20 ha (49 ac) lake can be found off the Haggens Point Road and is designated a fly-fishing only lake. Fishing in Klinne Lake is best in the late spring and fall. The lake also has a recreation site and a boat launch.

Kloakut Lake (Map 15/C5)
Kloakut is an excellent fishing lake off Big Creek Forest Service Road. The most popular fishing methods are spincasting and trolling, but fly-fishing works for the wild rainbow up to (and over) 4 kg (9 lbs). June and September are the best months, since fishing slows down in the heat of summer. The lake is subject to winterkill. Check the regulations for special catch limits.

Kluskoil Lake (Map 54/E5)
Kluskoil Lake is another lake along the Blackwater River that the Alexander Mackenzie Trail passes by. It is about 18 km from the deep crossing of the Euchinko River that will deter most people. Kluskoil Lake features great fishing for rainbow, plus a good population of bull trout. Kokanee and whitefish are also found in the 471 ha (1,163 ac) lake.

Klunchatistli Lake (Map 54/B3)
Found near the end of the Batnuni Lake Forest Service Road, this long, narrow lake boasts moderate populations of rainbow trout averaging 1–2 kg (2–4.5 lbs). Be aware that the road does get quite rough just past Comstock Lake.

Kluskus Lakes (Map 53/F7)
This remote Blackwater River lake offers excellent rainbow fishing. The problem, as always, is the access. The lakes are accessed by plane, canoe, on foot or by four-wheel drive. The Alexander Mackenzie Trail is a very rough four-wheel drive route and should be attempted only by multiple self-sufficient vehicles.

Knewstubb Lake (Map 53/B2)
Part of the Nechako Reservoir, Knewstubb Lake is a flooded forest. While this makes for a good fish habitat (as the rainbow that are pulled out of here look more like good-sized Coho), it can play havoc with your gear. There is a resort and recreation site providing good access to the north shore of the lake.

Knox Lake (Map 28/F4)
Sandwiched between Natsy Lake to the north and Dester Lake to the south, Knox Lake is a typical rainbow trout lake with the odd laker as well. Fishing is better in the spring and fall for both species.

Konni Lake (Map 14/E6)
Directly off Nemaiah Valley Road, this 565 ha (1,396 ac) lake contains wild rainbow that can grow up to 2.5 kg (5 lbs) in size. The lake also contains a small contingent of small dollies averaging 1 kg (2 lbs). Fishing starts in May and stays strong into October. Trolling is the preferred method, but boaters should be aware that strong winds are common.

Lac Des Roches (Map 19/D6) 🐟
Lac Des Roches is 16 km east of Bridge Lake on the south side of Highway 24. The 657 ha (1,623 ac) lake is separated into two distinct bays by a narrow channel. There are a few burbot and the stocked rainbow trout average 1–1.5 kg (2–3 lbs) with some growing to the 3.5 kg (8 lb) category. For fly anglers, the lake offers a good spring chironomid hatch as well as one of the best mayfly hatches in the Cariboo that begins in late May and extends into the early part of June. By summer, the fishing at Lac Des Roche slows off significantly before picking up again in fall. Try focusing around the deeper water and along the steep drop-offs. There are boat launches and a few resorts scattered around the lake.

Lajoie Lake [Little Gun Lake] (Map 4/A7)
Located just south of Gun Lake, this 40 ha (98 ac) lake provides good fishing for rainbow trout and dollies to 1 kg (2 lbs), which can be caught with a fly or with a small lure. There is a cartop boat launch here, but an electric motor only restriction. It is 900 m (2,925 ft) above sea level and is best fished in the spring and fall.

Lake 5565 (Map 17/E5) 🐟
Another lake with an odd name, Lake 5565 is stocked with the Blackwater strain of rainbow trout every year and is a favourite for catching small to medium sized trout. This lake rests along the Dog Creek Road, just north of Pigeon Lake.

Lake 6067 (Map 30/E7) 🐟
Sandwiched between Spout Lake in the west and Lang Lake to the east, Lake 6067 can be accessed by bushwhacking off the Coffee East Forest Service Road. At a maximum depth of 26 m (85 ft), the fishery should hold into early summer. The lake is stocked moderately with rainbow trout and reports have them in the 1 kg (2 lb) range, but larger ones have been caught as well.

La Salle Lakes (Map 59/B1) 🐟
Situated 46 km north of McBride off the west side of Highway 16, there is a short but rough road that leads from the highway to the west lake. From the west lake there is a short trail to Little La Salle Lake. Both small lakes are inhabited by plenty of stocked rainbow trout that can be easily coaxed into hitting a fly. Rustic camping is available at the lakes, which have an electric motor only restriction.

Lastman Lake (Map 2/G1)
Lastman is a remote lake that yields moderate amounts of wild rainbow and bull trout. Part of a series of lakes along the Gunn Valley Forest Service Road between Ts'ylos and the Taseko Mountain, trout here range from 1–2 kg (2–4.5 lbs).

Latremouille Lake (Map 19/G6)
This 96 ha (237 ac) lake is located just off Highway 24. There is consistent fishing for rainbow trout to 1.5 kg (3 lbs) that are reported to come readily to chironomid and leech fly patterns. There is a recreation site providing camping and a cartop boat launch along the east end of the lake.

Laurel Lake (Map 19/F6) 🐟
Laurel Lake can be reached by a short trail from Taweel Road 18 km west of Little Fort. It is a productive fly-fishing lake inhabited by numerous small rainbow trout, although the odd rainbow can reach up to 2 kg (4.5 lbs). Try working chironomids off the shoal areas in the spring. There are a few hike-in lakes beyond Laurel Lake that see few people and as a result offer excellent fishing.

Lac La Hache (Map 17/G2–18/B2) 🐟
This popular recreational lake offers all the amenities needed for a relaxing holiday, including campgrounds, resorts and a helpful tackle shop. Although rainbow trout and kokanee are the main sportfish in the lake, there are burbot, lake trout and mountain whitefish. The lake contains extensive shoals, which are ideal for insect rearing and fly-fishing. Trolling remains the preferred method of fishing this large water body.

Lavoie Lake (Map 54/A2)
Lavoie Lake is a 231 ha (570 ac) lake just south of Tatuk Lake and contains rainbow to 2 kg (4.5 lbs). The average depth is only 3.8 m (12 ft) so winterkill can be a problem. There is undeveloped camping and a cartop boat launch on the lake, and rustic footpaths leading to smaller lakes nearby.

Lawrence Lake (Map 19/F2)
Lawrence Lake is found next to the popular Italia Lake via Road 20, northwest of Clearwater. The lake offers very good fishing for small rainbow trout. Trolling and spincasting can work quite well at this lake, although fly-fishing can out-produce any other method when matching the hatch. There is a recreation site and boat launch on the lake.

Le Bourdais Lake (Map 43/E4)
Found in the shadows of Kangaroo Mountain, the best time to try Le Bourdais Lake is during the spring or fall, as summer fishing is extremely slow. The lake holds good numbers of rainbow trout that can reach up to 2 kg (4.5 lbs) in size. Due to the larger size of this lake, trolling is the preferred method of angling.

Lessard Lake (Map 38/D5)
Lessard Lake contains hybrid cuttbow, which are a cross between rainbow and cutthroat. These fish are rare elsewhere in BC, but thrive here. The average catch is about 35 cm (16 in). The scenic lake also contains wild rainbow, averaging 1.5 kg (3 lbs). With large shoal areas, this 179 ha (442 ac) lake is ideal for fly-fishing. Found 32 km north of Anahim Lake, there is a cleared area for launching a boat at the north end of the lake.

Lesser Fish Lake (Map 19/B5)
Lesser Lake lies just west of Bridge Lake, off Bridge Lake North Road. Lesser Lake produces well for rainbow trout that average 35–40 cm (14–16 in) and can reach up to 2 kg (4.5 lbs). The depth of the lake enables fishing to remain somewhat steady throughout the ice-free season.

Link Lake (Map 21/B2–35/B6)
Link Lake is a 19 km (12 mi) long reservoir behind a large dam within the town of Ocean Falls. Unknown to most, the lake has great freshwater fishing for cutthroat trout up to 2 kg (5 lbs), and there are also Dolly Varden, kokanee and rainbow trout. Access from Ocean Falls is by car or foot, but Ocean Falls itself is only accessible by air or water. The fiord-like lake features vertical cliffs that fall straight into the water. There is a small dock maintained by Ocean Falls Fishing Lodge.

Lintz Lake (Map 55/A2) 🐟
Located along the Pelican Lake Forest Service Road, this popular lake has rainbow to 1 kg (2 lbs). The 212 ha (523 ac) lake is best fished for rainbow by trolling or fly casting. The recreation site provides a good boat launch onto the lake.

Little Big Bar Lake (Map 5/D1) 🐟
This 65 ha (160 ac) lake is stocked regularly and provides good fishing at times for average-sized rainbow up to 1 kg (2 lbs). The lake is subject to winterkill and is also home to a popular recreation site with a cartop boat launch.

Little Charlotte Lake (Map 24/C4)
Little Charlotte Lake is accessible by boat across Charlotte Lake and then a short hike in, or you can drive fairly close then hike in as well. The 159 ha (392 ac) lake is known for producing small but feisty wild rainbow, which take well to fly-fishing and spincasting. The rapids connecting the lakes are really good for fly-fishing. The lake is over 9 m (30 ft) deep on average and stays cool during summer, so fishing is good throughout the ice-free season. There is a bait ban and single barbless hook restriction as well as a two trout daily quota at this lake.

Little Green Lake (Map 18/F7) 🐟
Found to the northeast of the much larger Green Lake, Little Green is a shallow, 125 ha (308 ac) water body that is basically one big shoal. The shoal area is ideal for insect rearing and fly-fishing. The lake is stocked with rainbow each year, and although the trout are small, they are found in good numbers. Try fly-fishing or spincasting the eastern end of the lake for best results. It is possible to launch a boat.

Little Jones Lake (Map 29/F6) 🐟
Accessing this little stocked lake to the east of 150 Mile House may be the hardest part. Follow the Redeau Lake Road east from the Pigeon Road for about 12.7 km to the powerline and head south. The next road branching west leads past the north end of this hidden lake. There is a bait ban and single barbless hook restriction along with no ice fishing allowed at this lake.

Little White Lake (Map 5/G2)
Little White Lake is one of the many small waterbodies found in the Big Bar Lake area. Fishing in the lake is generally fair for small rainbow that can reach 1.5 kg (3 lbs) on occasion. Spring and fall are the best times to fish here as the shallow lake heats up considerably during the summer, reducing angling success.

Liza Lake (Map 4/D6)
Liza Lake is located off the Marshall Lake Forest Service Road, 52 km northeast of Goldbridge. The lake offers good fishing for small rainbow that are best caught by fly-fishing. Dry flies can be a lot of fun here.

Long Island Lake [Janice Lake] (Map 19/F6)
Providing the main access to the Emar Lake, this 146 ha (360 ac) lake is accessed off Highway 24, west of Little Fort. The lake has plenty of shoals and shallows, ideal for fly-fishing. Fly-fishers should look forward to a good spring mayfly hatch. The rainbow in the lake can grow to 1.5 kg (3 lbs) in size. There is a fishing camp as well as a rustic camping area with rough boat launch on the lake. To maintain the fishery, there is an ice fishing ban, bait ban and single hook regulations in effect.

Long Lake (Map 28/F6)
Located inside the Chilcotin Military Training Area, near Riske Creek, Long Lake contains rainbow to 1 kg (2 lbs). Please respect all signage and closures in the area.

Loon Lake (Map 6/D4)
This long, narrow lake is another popular recreational lake found southeast of Clinton. The lake provides reasonably good fishing for generally small rainbow, although the odd trout reaches 1.5 kg (3 lbs) in size. There are a few resorts on the 970 ha (2,396 ac) lake.

Lorenzo Lake (Map 19/F6)
Accessible via a rough spur road from Blowdown Road, Lorenzo Lake offers fair fishing for rainbow trout that can reach up to 3 kg (6.5 lbs). Fly-fishing or spincasting along the deep holes found in the northern portion of the lake is your best bet for results. Rustic camping and a cartop boat launch are available at the lake.

During summer it is best to hit the higher elevation or bigger lakes.

Lorin Lake (Map 19/C3)
Lorin Lake is 276 ha (682 ac) and offers a good rainbow trout fishery. The lake is stocked with rainbow trout that can reach 2 kg (4.5 lbs). Fly-fishing and trolling are the preferred fishing methods with the shoals near the recreation site creating tremendous mayfly hatches.

Lorna Lake (Map 19/F4)
Access to this remote lake is limited as it is hike-in only within Taweel Provincial Park. As a result, rainbow can reach 2 kg (4.5 lbs). Fly-fishing is the preferred angling method used at this lake.

Lost Horse Lake (Map 19/F5)
You can find this lake via a branch road off the Taweel Lake Road north of Highway 24. The lake is good for rainbow trout that can reach up to 1 kg (2 lbs). There are ample shoal areas around the lake ideal for insect activity and perfect for fly anglers and spincasters to work their magic. The Lost Horse Lake Recreation Site is on the north end of the lake.

Lost Lake (Map 19/F4)
Lost Lake can be found via a rough trail off Taweel Road, west of Clearwater. The lake provides some good fishing for stocked rainbow trout in the 1–3 kg (2–6.5 lb) range.

Lower Lake (Map 18/E3)
Off Canim Lake Road, a rough road provides access to a small recreation site and boat launch on the eastern shore of the lake. There are also a series of trails in the area allowing good shore access for the rainbow and brook trout that reside in this 15 ha (37 ac) lake. The lake is stocked annually with rainbow.

Lunch Lake (Map 13/F2)
Southeast of the community of Tatla Lake, rainbow are the main catch here, although smaller kokanee are also present. Trout average about 1 kg (2 lbs), but the trout can reach 3.5 kg (8 lbs) in size. Fishing is best during the summer, providing it isn't too hot.

Lupin Lakes (Map 7/F2)
Better known for canoeing than fishing, this series of mountain lakes, strung along Caverhill Creek, offers rainbow to 1 kg (2 lbs) by spincasting or fly-fishing. At 1,350 m (4,430 ft), the lake remains fairly active for fishing throughout the ice-free season. A paddling route connects the lakes.

Lynn Lake (Map 19/F6)
Lynn Lake can be found by an access road that branches south off Highway 24. It is a clear, shallow lake stocked annually with a good number of rainbow and brook trout to 1 kg (2 lbs). Try fly-fishing near the small creek mouths or trolling the lake. There is a resort nearby and a fishing camp, but is closed to ice fishing.

Machete Lake (Map 19/D7)
Machete Lake is a 440 ha (1,087 ac) lake, 18 km south of Highway 24 on Machete Lake Road. It is a popular recreation lake, complete with camping, resorts, picnicking and boat launching facilities. It has fair fishing for rainbow trout and kokanee to 1 kg (2 lbs). The preferred methods of fishing are by trolling (lures or leech patterns) and ice fishing.

MacKenzie Lakes (Map 56/A1)
Found south of Prince George off the Blackwater-Mud Road, these three small lakes hold rainbow, which grow to about 1 kg (2 lbs). Fly-fishing can be surprisingly good on occasion. There are recreation sites complete with areas to launch small boats on the first two lakes. The third lake would require bushwhacking to get to.

MacKill Lake (Map 27/D3)
MacKill Lake is accessed by a short, easy hike-in from the road. The stocked lake is designated as a children's fishery and there are a lot of small fish. It is also possible to camp at the lake.

Mahood Lake (Map 19/E1)
This big, 3,311 ha (8,181 ac) lake forms the southwest boundary of Wells Gray Park. The lake offers fishing for rainbow trout to 4.5 kg (10 lbs) and lake trout to 9 kg (110 lbs) along with the odd kokanee. Fishing can be steady right from May to October. Ice fishing is also possible. Trolling is the most productive angling method used; for fly anglers and spincasters, try near one of the creek or river mouths. There is a campground with a boat launch as well as a number of boat access lakeshore campsites on the lake.

Marguerite Lake (Map 29/C2)
Marguerite Lake is just west of Big Lake off the rough two-wheel drive Marguerite Lake Road, not far off the rough Big Lake-Tyee Road. The fishing can be good at times for rainbow trout to 1 kg (2 lbs); fly-fishing, spincasting and trolling are the best methods, but try this lake well before the heat of summer. There are some rustic camping areas at the lake.

Marmot Lake (Map 41/A2)
Found 2 km west of the Nazko Store, the 55 ha (135 ac) Marmot Lake is stocked annually with rainbow. Recent reports indicate there are a lot of rainbow in the 1–1.5 kg (2–3 lb) class. The private campsite maintains the boat launch and a trail circles the lake.

Marshall Lake (Map 4/D6)
Marshall Lake has good fishing for rainbow to 1 kg (2 lbs), primarily by trolling a gang troll with a wedding band and worm. Casting a Krocodile or a Dick Nite also meets with success. There are two recreation sites on the south end of the lake, which is 65 ha (160 ac) in size and 1,150 m (3,738 ft) above sea level.

Martin Lake (Map 25/E7)
Martin Lake is located just 10 minutes north of the community of Tatla Lake. Martin is stocked with rainbow and is a popular swimming, horseback riding and winter recreation area.

Maud Lake (Map 43/D5)
Located adjacent to the Maud Lake Recreation Site (boat launch and camping facilities), this lake is known for its above-average rainbow trout fishing. Due to its remote location, it often gets overlooked, meaning there are some big fish here. There is a bait ban and single barbless hook restriction at this lake.

Maury Lake (Map 19/G1)

Maury Lake is off Road 9, 5 km from Road 20. The lake offers good fishing for rainbow trout that can reach 1 kg (2 lbs) and there is a recreation site and a gravel boat launch available.

McClinchy Lake (Map 24/D6)

Another good fishing lake found in the Charlotte Alplands Protected Area, Mc-Clinchy Lake rests in a valley below a prominent ridge. The trail access and elevation of the lake limit the fishing season to the summer months. Anglers will find bull and rainbow trout that can reach fair sizes. Check the regulations for special limits. There is a bait ban and single barbless hook restriction.

McDonald Lake (Map 4/B7)

Home to rainbow trout, this decent trolling lake can be found east of Gold Bridge. However, the difficult access may deter some from bringing in a boat.

McIntosh Lakes (Map 30/B5)

These two good-sized lakes can be reached via the Moffat Lake Forest Service Road (2300 Rd). The lakes provide inconsistent success for rainbow trout to 1.5 kg (3 lbs), partly due to the coarse fish that are a big problem in these lakes. The best time to try your luck is in the spring. It is possible to hand launch a boat onto the lakes.

McIntyre Lake (Map 28/G7) 🛥

Lying 500 metres from Highway 20 and having a recreation site does not bode well for this lake's fishery. Luckily, this 18 ha (44 ac) lake is stocked with both rainbow and brook trout. The lake warms quickly in the summer, making early spring and fall the best times to fish. Ice fishing is also popular.

McKinley Lake (Map 30/G3)

Home to a nice recreation site with boat launch, this scenic lake is 512 ha (1,265 ac) in size. The main fishery is for lake trout to 4 kg (9 lbs) and rainbow trout to 1.5 kg (3 lbs). The spawning salmon in fall create eggs in fall and smelt in spring that attract the trout. There are also kokanee, burbot and coarse fish in the lake.

McLeese Lake (Map 28/G2) 🛥

McLeese Lake is a 340 ha (840 ac) lake that is easily accessed off the west side of Highway 97. The lake is monitored and stocked with rainbow and kokanee. White-fish also inhabit the lake, which is easily accessed from the north end or from the resort at the south end. Opening up early in the year, trolling is the favoured method.

McNeil Lake (Map 19/B3) 🛥

McNeil Lake is a smaller lake found next to the Mahood Lake Road, 46 km north of Bridge Lake. There is a good population of rainbow trout. One downfall of this lake is that there are large populations of suckers and squawfish. Check the regulations for special limits. There is a bait ban and single barbless hook restriction.

McTaggart Lake (Map 28/D5)

Accessed via a rough two-wheel drive road (high clearance may be necessary), McTaggart Lake offers fair fishing for rainbow that can reach 1 kg (2 lbs). Fly-fishing during the hatches can produce well. There is a rough cartop boat launch at the lake, but access may be restricted as it lies in the Chilcotin Military Training Area.

Meadow Lake (Map 19/F5)

Meadow Lake is one of the many pothole lakes found northwest of Little Fort, off Taweel Road. Fishing in the lake is generally fair for small rainbow that can reach 1.5 kg (3 lbs) on occasion. The shallow lake heats up considerably during the summer, reducing angling success at that time. There is a private fishing camp located on the lake.

Medicine Lake (Map 38/C6) 🛥

The northern of the Poison Lakes that are found 30 km north of Anahim Lake off the Upper Dean River Road, this lake requires you to carry a canoe about 100 metres to get onto it. Stocked with rainbow, this scenic lake produces the odd trout that grows to 2.5 kg (5 lbs).

Meldrum Lake (Map 28/E4)

Stocked in the 1940s, this lake still holds a few rainbow trout. Like most lakes in the area, the 167 ha (412 ac) lake is best fished in the spring and fall due to its elevation.

Melissa Lake (Map 30/F1) 🛥

Found south of Hen Ingram Lake and road, Melissa Lake is a 58 ha (143 ac) lake that is home to stocked rainbow trout. The Pennask strain of rainbow are often more active at dusk and feed near the bottom. Reports have trout in the 1.5 kg (3 lb) range.

Middle Lake (Map 13/A4)

At last reports, the road is gated just before Middle Lake, creating even more difficult access to this deep, 5 km long by 1 km wide lake. Those that make it in should find good fishing for bull trout, Dolly Varden and rainbow. There is a limit of two trout per day allowed here.

Milburn Lake (Map 42/C1) 🛥

Milburn Lake is a small 33 ha (81 ac) lake located to the west of Quesnel. The lake is heavily stocked with brook trout and rainbow that grow to 1 kg (2 lbs). There are plenty of shoal areas along this lake, which provide for excellent insect populations. The lake is also a popular ice fishing destination in winter.

Miner Lake (Map 13/A1)

This lake holds a variety of sportfish including bull trout and dollies, kokanee and rainbow. There is a recreation site with a boat launch on Miner Lake, which is best fished on the fly or by casting from a small boat.

Mitchell Lake (Map 45/C3)

This remote, fly-in lake lies within the heart of the Cariboo Mountains. The lake has excellent rainbow and bull trout fishing; the rainbow are in the 1–2.5 kg (2–5 lb) range and the bull trout up to 7 kg (15 lbs). Be sure to check the regulations before heading out.

Moira Lake (Map 19/G2)

Easily accessed off a main haul logging road, Moira Lake offers quite good fishing throughout the ice-free season for rainbow trout to 1 kg (2 lbs). Fly anglers can do exceptionally well at the lake, although if you troll a small spoon or spinner you should also find some success. For overnight campers, there is a recreation site with boat launch.

Mons Lake (Map 15/G4)

Accessed by a rough two-wheel drive road system, Mons Lake offers fair fishing for rainbow trout. The 135 ha (333 ac) lake is best fished in the spring and fall.

Monticola Lake (Map 19/E5)

Accessible via trail from a rough road off the Blowdown Road, this 74 ha (182 ac) lake offers some good fishing for rainbow trout that can reach 1.5 kg (3 lbs) in size. Trolling is a popular angling method on the lake. One of the more popular flies for this lake is a Woolly Bugger or similar leech patterns. Since this lake is deep, winterkill is not a problem. Rustic camping is available at the lake.

Morehead Lake (Map 43/F6)

Morehead Lake lies next to the road to Likely and has a resort and boat launch to accommodate visitors. The lake holds good numbers of rainbow trout that can reach up to 2 kg (4.5 lbs) in size. The best time to try Moorehead Lake is during the spring or again later in the fall, as the summer heat slows fishing considerably. Due to the larger size of this lake, trolling is the preferred method of angling.

Moose Lake (Map 7/E3)

This high elevation hike-in lake is reached by the Heller Lake Trail. It has fair fishing for rainbow trout to 1 kg (2 lbs) in size throughout the spring and fall.

Moose Lake (Map 52/E7) 🛥

Moose Lake is a fly-in lake about 100 km north of Nimpo Lake, which is the best place to find a floatplane. The lake contains stocked rainbow to 1.5 kg (3 lbs), which take well to spinning lures or fly-fishing. Fishing remains strong from late May to September.

Moose & Moosehead Lakes (Map 19/F3)

Moose Lake is a small, shallow lake which has a few rainbow trout. Moosehead Lake offers good fishing for smaller rainbow trout. Try working the drop-off areas around the lake for best results. Fly-fishing can create a frenzy of action at times during good hatch periods. You can find the lakes on either side of the Taweel Lake Forest Service Road and the south end of Taweel Provincial Park.

Mowich Lake (Map 7/A5)

The 29 ha (71 ac) Mowich Lake has fair fishing for small rainbow and kokanee, best caught by fly-fishing or spincasting throughout the spring and fall. There is a resort on the north end of the lake.

Mowson Pond (Map 4/C7) 🛥

Severely affected by the forest fire in 2009, Mowson Pond now has a heavy stocking program to restore the fishery that once produced nice-sized rainbow trout to 36 cm (14 in). Dry fly-fishing can be a lot of fun on this lake, which warms significantly in the summer. There is a recreation site along with a boat launch on the lake.

Mud Lakes (Map 4/C4)

Access is difficult into these small lakes found south of Swartz Lake. The lakes are known to hold rainbow trout and a float tube is recommended to get away from the mosquitoes and the swampy shoreline. Four-wheel drive enthusiasts can access the recreation sites on the lake via the Mud Creek Forest Service Road.

Murphy Lake (Map 17/E1)

Access to this small lake is found off the Enterprise Road (1100 Rd) south of Highway 97. The main access travels through private land; be sure to obtain permission before approaching the lake. The lake is lightly fished and offers some good fishing for rainbow trout that can reach up to 2.5 kg (5.5 lbs) in size.

Murray Taylor Lake (Map 14/D4)

This shallow 7.6 m (25 ft) lake is all but overrun with coarse fish. There are a few rainbow trout in the 95 ha (234 ac) lake.

Musclow Lake (Map 50/B4)

Another fly-in or boat-in lake found in Tweedsmuir Park, Musclow Lake is a great fly-fishing lake. Rainbow up to 3 kg (6.5 lbs) make the long journey well worth the effort.

Narrow Lake (Map 57/D1)

This 353 ha (872 ac) lake can be unpredictable, but has a wide range of species. The rainbow grow to 1 kg (2 lbs), kokanee to 0.5 kg (1 lb) and the odd lake trout to 3 kg (6.5 lbs). The lake can be accessed by the rough Narrow Lake Forest Service Road.

Nazko Lake (Map 27/A2)

The second lake (or first, depending if you can get your vehicle down the rough four-wheel drive track to the boat launch at the south end of the lake) in the Nazko Lake chain, this 117 ha (289 ac) lake was regularly stocked with 20,000 rainbow, up until 2000. Currently, the fish grow to pan size. Fishing is best in spring, as the fish become muddy as the weather warms up. Powerboats are allowed.

Needa Lake (Map 19/C4)

Windy Mountain Forest Service Road (1900 Rd) provides good access to the 188 ha (464 ac) Needa Lake. The lake offers good fishing for rainbow to 0.5 kg (1 lb), mainly by trolling. A popular recreation site with a steep cartop boat launch provides a good base from which to explore the lake.

Nelson Kenny Lake (Map 56/E5)

Located off the Quesnel Hixon Road, visitors can expect fair fishing for rainbow trout that can be found to 2 kg (4.5 lbs) on occasion. Fly-fishing can be more effective on this lake, although spincasting can provide some success as well.

Nimpo Lake (Map 24/F2)

Nimpo Lake is often used as the launching point for fly-in fishing trips in the area. After all, it is the floatplane capital of BC. The lake itself is an excellent rainbow lake, with the average catch in the 1.5 kg (3 lb) range. Fly-fishing is the most popular way of catching these fish, but spincasting and trolling are certainly possible. The lake was the site of the 1993 Commonwealth Fly-Fishing Championships.

No Name Lakes (Map 19/F5)

These lakes take some effort to find; as a result, there is good fishing for small rainbow trout. If you can pack a float tube or canoe in, try working the shoal areas with a fly. Camping is located at nearby Lost Horse Lake Recreation Site.

Noaxe Lake (Map 4/D5)

This mountain lake is only accessed by trail. It offers good fishing for small trout. Due to the elevation, fishing is better in the summer (later June) and holds through the fall.

Noble Lake (Map 7/F7)

Noble Lake is located on a four-wheel drive access road off Dairy Creek Road, north of Isobel Lake. It is a small lake with good fishing for stocked rainbow that can reach 1 kg (2 lbs) in size. It is possible to launch a small boat onto the clear water lake.

Nolan Lake (Map 18/E7)

A rough side road leads south from the Green Lake South Road to the western edge of Nolan Lake. The lake is stocked annually with rainbow trout.

Nora & Spider Lakes (Map 19/F5)

Nora Lake is accessible east of the Taweel Road and provides fishing opportunities for rainbow. The trout average 20–30 cm (8–12 in) in size, although there is a chance to find bigger fish in this lake. The north end of the lake seems to be the hot spot on the lake, although working off any shoal area should produce. Spider Lake to the north is accessible by trail from Nora Lake and also offers small trout.

Olaf Lake (Map 50/G6)

Olaf Lake is a hike-in lake, from a fly-in lake. Lake District Air maintains a cabin on Tesla Lake and it's a 40 minute hike from there to this lake. Expect fast fly-fishing for pan-sized rainbow up to 1 kg (2 lbs).

One Eye Lake (Map 25/B7)

Located right next to Highway 20, One Eye Lake has wild rainbow that get up to 1.5 kg (3 lbs) and Dolly Varden to 4.5 kg (10 lbs). The easy access means the lake sees its fair share of anglers. Fishing is fair from June to October. There is a recreation site on the lake with a cartop boat launch.

One Lake (Map 27/A3)

One Lake is the first of a pair of small lakes at the north end of Alexis Lake and is accessed off the Alexis Lake Road. It is possible to line a canoe or small boat between the lakes, which offer similar fishing for rainbow to 2.5 kg (5 lbs) and brook trout to 1 kg (2 lbs). Fly-fishing and spincasting yield the best results. There is a recreation site on Two Lake and an electric motor only restriction.

Life jackets and personal flotation devices are known to save lives; they only work when they are worn and fitted correctly.

Oslie Lake (Map 30/G1)

Sandwiched between Horsefly and Quesnel Lakes to the east of Hen Ingram Lake, little Oslie Lake is often overlooked. Those that make it in will find stocked rainbow trout.

Owen Lake (Map 28/A4)

Owen Lake is a 297 ha (733 ac) lake with clear shallow waters. It supports a fishery for both rainbow and lake trout. The rainbow can reach 1 kg (2 lbs), while the lakers can grow beyond 9 kg (110 lbs). However, this lake can be hit-or-miss at best. There are good mayfly, damselfly and sedge hatches on this lake, but the shrimp that once thrived are on the decline due to minnows. It is best to work the drop-offs near the small group of islands across from the access point.

Owikeno Lake (Map 10/A3–E2)

A massive lake that spreads over approximately 40 km (25 mi), Owikeno Lake is located 23 km from Rivers Inlet on the west coast of British Columbia. There are a variety of fish species found here; the main draw are the Chinook, Coho and sockeye salmon that run through the lake in fall.

Paddy Lake (Map 19/B1)

They don't get much smaller than this. Just 2.9 ha (7 ac), the lake is surprisingly deep as it rests on the tip of Squirrel Lake. There is rough road access to the recreation site on the lake. It is a short walk to the lake where anglers will find plenty of stocked rainbow.

Palmer Lake (Map 27/E2)

Located along the Alex Graham Road and off the Lt. Palmer Trail, Palmer Lake is a popular 210 ha (518 ac) lake. The lake produces stocked rainbow that grow to 3 kg (6.5 lbs) on occasion. This is partly due to the difficult access – the last 6.5 km into the recreation site are very steep and rough – and partly due to the special regulations on the lake.

Pantage Lake (Map 55/F5)

Known for its small rainbow that take readily to flies, this lake is extremely popular throughout the season. It is easily accessed from the community of Blackwater by travelling south along the Blackwater Road. Trolling and fly-fishing are the popular angling methods on the lake.

Pass Lake (Map 7/E7)

Pass Lake is located on the Lac Du Bois Road (two-wheel drive) and drains into Watching Creek. Managed as a quality fishery, there are many restrictions that help grow the rainbow to 4 kg (9 lbs). Of course, the bigger fish are notoriously hard to catch. The 28 ha (69 ac) lake is a fly-fishing only lake and is best fished in the early season, given its elevation, or again in late September to October. Try matching the early spring chironomid or mayfly hatches and casting near the northeastern shoals. Later in the spring or into the fall, leech, dragonfly, sedge or caddisfly patterns work. A recreation site offers a nice place to camp and launch a small boat.

Fishing Adventures

Patrick Lake (Map 7/F1)
At 1,375 m (4,469 ft) above sea level, Patrick Lake provides good fishing throughout the summer months for rainbow to 1 kg (2 lbs) by spincasting or fly-fishing. The lake covers an area of 15 ha (37 ac) and is accessed by an undeveloped trail off Patrick Lake Forest Service Road.

Pavilion Lake (Map 5/F7)
Pavilion Lake—the largest lake in the Marble Canyon Area—has fair fishing for rainbow to 1.5 kg (3 lbs), primarily caught by trolling a gang troll with a Wedding Ring and worm or a Flatfish. The lake also offers good ice fishing. A cartop boat launch is available, as is camping and a resort. The lake is 260 ha (642 ac), 825 m (2,681 ft) above sea level and heavily stocked on an annual basis.

Peanut Lake (Map 19/E4)
This small, secluded lake can only be accessed by trail from Horse Lake, which is accessed off the Wavey Lake Forest Service Road (2000 Rd). Peanut Lake holds rainbow to 1.5 kg (3 lbs) although the trout generally average about 30–40 cm (12–16 in). Fly-fishing is the preferred angling method with spincasting or bait fishing providing some success.

Pearson Pond (Map 4/B7)
Pearson Pond is a small, 8 ha (19 ac) lake, which is a little more difficult to access and fish than nearby Mowson Pond. In addition to rainbow, there are stocked brook trout that reached 1.5 kg (3 lbs) in size before the devastating forest fire in 2009. A boat is a definite asset here, and there is a cartop boat launch and camping at the former recreation site.

Pelican Lake (Map 38/D7)
Found west of Anahim Lake, Pelican Lake is a shallow, swampy lake that on first glance does not look like a great fishing hole. Rumour has it that it does provide good fishing for rainbow. There are also coarse fish that compete for food, so the trout that are found here are often bigger.

Pelican Lake (Map 55/A4)
Found 46 km west of Blackwater, this lake has good road access, and the recreation site can be busy. Despite its heavy summer time use, Pelican continues to provide good fishing for wild rainbow.

Pendleton Lake (Map 31/E7)
Pendleton Lake can be reached via the rough Pendleton Lake Forest Service Road (7100 Rd); a four-wheel drive vehicle is recommended. The lake is inhabited by small rainbow trout that can reach up to 1.5 kg (3 lbs) on occasion. A good place to try is off one of the small islands found on the lake. There is a recreation site and a steep boat launch.

Phinetta Lake (Map 19/E6)
Accessed via Eakin Creek Road off Highway 24, Phinetta Lake has many shoals ideal for insect growth. It is a productive fly-fishing lake for rainbow trout (stocked annually) that is home to a small forest recreation site with a boat launch.

Pigeon Lake (Map 17/E5)
Found on the east side of the Dog Creek Road, about 18 km south of the Enterprise Road junction, this is one of a series of stocked lakes in the area. The lakes are stocked annually with the Blackwater strain of rainbow trout that prefer shallow water.

Pioneer Lake (Map 19/E6)
Located not far from Highway 24 off a rough access road, Pioneer Lake offers fair fishing for rainbow trout that can reach up to 2 kg (4.5 lbs) in size. Try a leech pattern, such as a Woolly Bugger.

Poison Lake (Map 38/C6)
A pair of pretty lakes known as the Poison Lakes are found 28 km north of Anahim Lake off the Upper Dean River Road. There is a recreation site on Poison Lake, but you will have to carry a canoe about 100 metres to get onto the lake. The lakes are stocked with rainbow that can get up to 2.5 kg (5 lbs) to help maintain a good fishery.

Polley Lake (Map 43/G7)
Due to a breach of the Mount Polley Mine tailings pond in August of 2014, this lake and the recreation site remain closed until more information becomes available. The road access has been washed out and the lakes' water has been adversely affected, which will ultimately affect the former rainbow trout fishery. A public information line has been established at 250-398-5581.

Portage Lake (Map 19/F5)
Portage Lake can be reached by rough trail from Taweel Road and offers fishing for average-sized rainbow trout. Try fly-fishing or spincasting the inflow or outflow of the lake for added success.

Preacher Lake (Map 19/D4)
Since the road is gated, Preacher Lake is a walk-in lake that can produce some big trout in the spring and fall. The shallow lake has a grassy shoreline ideal for fly-fishing or casting from shore. Check the regulations for special limits.

Pressy Lake (Map 18/F7)
Located along North Bonaparte Road, Pressy Lake is a long, thin, 57 ha (140 ac) lake with a recreation site and a boat launch as well as cabins and a private campsite. The lake offers a good fishery for rainbow trout to 1 kg (2 lbs) in size throughout the spring and fall.

Punchaw Lake (Map 55/G3)
Known for its small rainbow to 1 kg (2 lbs) that take readily to flies, this lake is extremely popular throughout the season. It is easily accessed from both Prince George and Quesnel along Blackwater Road. The busy recreation site is RV accessible and sports a boat launch. Trolling and fly-fishing are the popular angling methods on the lake.

Punkutlaenkut Lake (Map 39/C7)
Also known as Punky Lake (much to the relief of outsiders trying to ask for directions), Punkutlaenkut Lake contains small rainbow that are well known for their ability to evade anglers. The lake was stocked during the 40s and 50s, yet the fish remain small, mostly under 0.5 kg (1 lb).

Puntchesakut Lake (Map 42/A1)
Puntchesakut is a popular recreation lake 44 km west of Quesnel. The lake is free of ice in early May, but the fishing can be slow for rainbow; this is due to the redside shiners. The deepest part of the lake is near the north end where trolling a gang troll or a lure such as a flatfish can produce. There is a park with a boat launch and a nice beach.

Punti Lake (Map 26/E4)
This 384 ha (948 ac) lake is nowhere near as popular as its larger neighbour, Puntzi Lake. This smaller lake does offer a sports fishery for whitefish.

Puntzi Lake (Map 26/C4–D4)
Puntzi Lake is a popular, 1,706 ha (4,215 ac) lake that is home to a couple of fishing resorts and a recreation site. Located 11 km north of Highway 20, this lake is very deep for the Chilcotin area, averaging 33 m (108 ft). Spinning and trolling are the most popular ways to fish the lake, but fly-fishing works well early and late in the season. There is good fishing for kokanee and rainbow both averaging 0.75 kg (1.5 lbs).

Pyper Lake (Map 26/B6)
Pyper Lake is found less than a kilometre off Highway 20. Needless to say, the recreation site is often quite busy. The lake is occasionally stocked with rainbow (the last time was in 2007). The recreation site has a cartop boat launch.

Quesnel Lake (Maps 30, 44, 45)
One of the deepest freshwater lakes in the world, Quesnel Lake is a very scenic fjord lake. The lake is a popular destination for outdoor enthusiasts with a lot of development, including a number of resorts, boat launches and recreation sites, found on the western end of the lake. It holds trophy class fish with rainbow trout over 8 kg (18 lbs), lake trout to 20 kg (44 lbs), bull trout to 8 kg (18 lbs) and kokanee to 2 kg (4.5 lbs). Trolling can be quite effective year-round, while fly anglers and spincasters will find some success near the creek mouths during the spring and fall periods. There is a bait ban and single barbless hook restriction at this lake as well as many no fishing zones here. Be sure to check regulations before heading out.

Rail Lake (Map 30/B7)
Deep in the heart of the Cariboo, Rail Lake is a 230 ha (568 ac) lake found off Spout Lake Road (1500 Rd). The lake has some good numbers of rainbow trout as well as burbot; there are also coarse fish like squawfish and chub. The rainbow are stocked and average about 1.5 kg (3 lbs). There are extensive shoals at the southern end of the lake along with a small recreation site, which offers a boat launch for small trailers.

Rainbow Lake (Map 38/C3)
Rainbow Lake is north of Anahim Lake off Upper Dean River Road then east on a deactivated road system. The lake contains wild rainbow that average about 1.5 kg (3 lbs). Despite the name, the lake also contains kokanee and lake trout.

Randy Lake (Map 19/E5)
Randy Lake is a small, secluded lake that can only be found by trail from Lorenzo Lake. This smaller lake holds good numbers of rainbow that are best caught from a float tube or other water device.

Raven Lake (Map 28/A6)
Raven Lake is a smaller lake northeast of Hanceville and next to a main haul logging road. The lake is found off Palmer Lake Road and contains Eastern Brook Trout averaging 1 kg (2 lbs) and rainbow up to 2.5 kg (5 lbs). There is a large recreation site complete with a boat launch on the lake. There is a 7.5 kW (10 hp) engine power restriction on the lake.

Red Lake (Map 7/B6)
Red Lake is 56 km northwest of Kamloops off Copper Creek Road. It has a good population of brook trout in the 1 kg (2 lb) range, which are best fished during the fall or ice fishing seasons. Fly-fishing with chironomids, shrimp patterns and leeches, slow trolling and spincasting around the shoals can all produce. The 109 ha (269 ac) lake has an undeveloped boat launch with a rustic camping area. The water warms significantly in the summer and the fish are subject to winterkill.

Redfish Lake (Map 50/F4)
After a long boat ride, a short 1.6 km trail leads from the northern shores of Eutsuk Lake to this popular fly-fishing lake. Bringing in a canoe or tube (or waders) will help you work the lake a lot better.

Redwater Lake (Map 40/F1)
One of the bigger lakes in the region, Redwater Lake can be found close to the end of Redwater Road travelling north. Anglers here will find moderate populations of rainbow and brook trout.

Reservoir Lake (Map 29/B5)
Just outside of the town of Williams Lake, this reservoir is stocked with brook trout. It is also home to a few rainbow.

Rimrock Lake (Map 28/G1)
North of McLeese Lake, the Rimrock Road branches from the Gibraltar Mines Road providing good access to this lake. It is the smaller, shallower cousin of Cuisson Lake and provides decent fishing for stocked rainbow.

Roaster Lake (Map 4/E2)
Hidden in the popular off-roading area north of Carpenter Lake and south of Churn Creek Park, Roaster Lake is reported to have rainbow trout. Access is found off the south side of Yodel Cabin Road.

Robertson Lake (Map 43/B2)
Robertson Lake is located southeast of Quesnel and can be accessed south from Highway 26 via the Nyland Lake Forest Service Road system. The lake has good numbers of rainbow trout together with some burbot. The large shoal areas make the lake an ideal destination for fly-fishing. Although a floatation device is better, shore casting into the deeper water is possible.

Rock Island Lake (Map 19/G5)
Rock Island Lake is a good fly-fishing lake that holds rainbow trout in the 1 kg (2 lb) range, although the largest on record is 3.6 kg (8 lbs). Try fishing the shoals and along the deep pockets that are found around the lake. There is a rustic campsite at the southern end of the lake and a resort along the north shore. No ice fishing is permitted here.

Rock Lake (Map 7/B4)
This tiny 4 ha (9 ac) lake located southeast of Deadman Falls is worth noting because it provides a surprisingly good fishery for small rainbow easily taken by fly-fishing or spincasting. The lake requires a hike along an undeveloped trail. Since the lake warms during the summer, it is best to try your luck in the spring.

Rollie Lake (Map 44/A4)
A four-wheel drive vehicle is recommended to access this lake north of Likely. Rollie Lake has average-sized rainbow that are naturally reproducing. Trollers should work in a circle out from the middle of the lake, while spincasters and fly anglers should work the fringe area or try casting at the outflow and inflow areas. It is possible to launch a boat at roadside.

Rose Lake (Map 29/E3)
Found about 21 km down the Horsefly Road, Rose Lake is home to a few private residences. There are also rainbow and kokanee that take well to trolling a lake troll with Wedding Ring or Flatfish.

Roserim Lake (Map 19/C2)
This 41 ha (101 ac) lake is relatively shallow as it is only 10 m (33 ft) deep. Last stocked in 2003, there are decent-sized rainbow in this lake. It is found south of the Mahood Lake Road only a couple of kilometres east of the community Mahood Falls.

Rosita Lake (Map 27/E2)
Rosita Lake is a secluded rainbow trout lake with reports up to 2 kg (4.5 lbs). Adjacent to Tautri Lake to the east, access is south from the Rosita Meldrum Forest Service Road.

Rushes Lake (Map 15/G3)
Similar to Abrams to the north, at 4 m (13 ft) in depth, Rushes Lake is almost too shallow to hold fish. Rainbow do migrate up the creek system and can be found by fly anglers working the expansive shoals.

Ruth Lake (Map 18/F2)
Ruth Lake is situated 33 km northeast of 100 Mile House and contains a good number of rainbow trout. The rainbow are stocked and compete with the non-sportfish (squawfish, redside shiner, suckers and peamouth chub) for food. The lake is deep enough to troll if you stick around the three distinct holes found in the middle, at the north end and in the western bay. Several islands provide some nice, productive drop-off areas where you can cast a fly or lure tipped with a worm. There is a day-use area at the east end of the lake together with a cartop boat launch.

Sabiston Lake (Map 7/A7)
Sabiston Lake is located along Sabiston Creek Road and provides a good fishery for brook trout to 1 kg (2 lbs) during the fall or during ice fishing season. Sabiston Lake is subject to winterkill, but the stocking program has helped to maintain the fish population.

Sandell Lake (Map 9/C4)
Located a short bushwhack from Rivers Inlet, Sandell Lake has good numbers of cutthroat and rainbow trout and some Dolly Varden. The remote lake is not frequently fished. If you can get there, you may find a trophy trout to 5 kg (11 lbs).

Sapeye Lake (Map 13/C2)
Sapeye Lake is across the road from Horn Lake, but is 50 m (164 ft) lower, down a steep, narrow access road. The road leads to a recreation site at the north end of the lake. The lake is an excellent fly only lake, with wild rainbow averaging 1.5 kg (3 lbs). The lake also contains big bull trout, with lots of fish caught in the 2.5 kg (5.5 lb) size range.

Safe ice usually forms by December and often runs well into March, sometimes even early April. When the ice is thick enough, those lakes with brook trout and whitefish make fine ice fishing destinations.

Sardine Lake (Map 43/A4)
This small lake is located near the confluence of the North and South Sardine Creeks. The lake has rainbow trout (stocked in 2014), which provide for good fishing much of the time.

Saul Lake (Map 7/D6)
This 25 ha (61 ac) lake is located on Sawmill Lake Forest Service Road and has a recreation site with a campground. The popular lake offers good fishing throughout the ice-free season for small rainbow that are easily taken on a fly (shrimp or attractor patterns) or by a gang troll.

Schoolhouse Lake (Map 18/G1) 🐟

Found within the Schoolhouse Lake Provincial Park, the lake can be reached by trail from Hawkins Lake Road. The lake has been stocked over the past few years with rainbow that have been reported to reach 3 kg (6.5 lbs) in size. The access limits the fishing pressure here.

Scot Lakes (Map 7/C2)

Accessed off Egan-Bonaparte Forest Service Road, Scot Lake offers a recreation site with camping and a boat launch. There are nice shoals around the inflow and outflow streams for fly anglers to try their luck for the rainbow trout. This 29 ha (71 ac) lake can be fished throughout the ice-free season. Nearby Little Scot Lake also offers a recreation site with camping. The smaller lake is best fished in the spring and fall for average-sized rainbow.

Scum Lake (Map 15/A3)

Despite the name, Scum Lake isn't that bad a spot and the fishing for wild rainbow to 0.75 kg (1.5 lbs) is pretty good. The 68 ha (168 ac) lake offers a recreation site with a cartop boat launch. A four-wheel drive vehicle may be necessary to reach the lake.

Sedge Lake (Map 7/A7)

Sedge Lake is a 10 ha (24 ac) lake located high in the hills north of Kamloops Lake. It offers good fishing for rainbow trout in the 1 kg (2 lb) range throughout the spring and fall by fly-fishing and spincasting. The lake is accessed by a four-wheel drive spur road.

Sharpe Lake (Map 7/B1)

Known for having a fair number of good-sized rainbow to 2.5 kg (5 lbs), this small 69 ha (170 ac) lake is found south of Bridge Lake on the Egan-Bonaparte Forest Service Road. The trout are best caught on the fly. There is a recreation site providing camping and a cartop boat launch along the west side of the lake.

Shelley Lake (Map 7/E4)

Shelley Lake is a small hike-in lake along Deadman Trail. The 40 ha (98 ac) lake offers good fishing for rainbow trout by fly-fishing or spincasting, and because it is a high elevation lake, the fishing remains constant throughout the summer and fall.

Sheridan Lake (Map 18/G5–19/A6) 🐟

Sheridan Lake is one of the premier trout lakes in the province and it receives heavy fishing pressure year-round. The 1,659 ha (4,099 ac) lake is highly productive due to an abundance of freshwater shrimp (scuds). Each year it is stocked with thousands of rainbow to help maintain the fishery. The rainbow average 1–3 kg (2–6.5 lbs), with some reaching 8 kg (17.6 lbs) in size. Trolling is the best method of fishing the lake, and fly anglers can test their luck in the southwest bay. The spring chironomid hatch, the evening mayfly hatch in mid-June to late June, and the evening sedge hatch beginning in late June and July are famous for producing good results. There are numerous resorts, boat launches, private residences and a nearby store with a café and a gas station.

Sicily Lake (Map 19/E2)

Located on Road 20 east of Clearwater, Sicily Lake is a good fly-fishing lake for rainbow trout to 1.5 kg (3 lbs). The more popular fly patterns used on the lake include caddisflies, mayflies and leeches. Be sure to bring a floatation device, as the marshy shallow shoreline makes it all but impossible to have success from shore. There is a recreation site with a cartop boat launch available.

Simon Lake (Map 18/D3) 🐟

Just 12 km east of 108 Mile Ranch, you can find Simon Lake off the Simon Lake Road. The lake has been stocked recently with rainbow trout and there are reports of some success in the lake for generally small trout. There is a bait ban and single barbless hook restriction at this lake as well as no ice fishing allowed due to aeration.

Skookum Lake (Map 7/A4)

Because of the relatively low elevation, this 19 ha (46 ac) lake is best fished in the spring or fall for rainbow and kokanee that can reach 1 kg (2 lbs) in size. The shallow lake has some nice shoals for fly anglers to work, while trollers will want to stick to light gear.

Skulow Lake (Map 29/D3) 🐟

Skulow Lake has a good population of brook and rainbow trout, with rainbows to 1 kg (2 lbs). Both species are stocked and grow rapidly in the nutrient-rich waters. The shallow lake is best suited for spincasting and fly-fishing. Try casting a fly or lure tipped with a worm towards the weeds that line the lake. An aeration system is in place at the lake to reduce the winterkill problem, but makes ice fishing dangerous. An electric motor only restriction applies at the lake.

Slender Lake (Map 57/F3)

Slender Lake is a 144 ha (355 ac) lake that can be found via Slender Forest Service Road. Rainbow, bull trout, Dolly Varden and whitefish are abundant in the lake. Trolling is perhaps the best method for success in this lake, especially for bull trout. The lake is home to a recreation site complete with a cartop boat launch.

Slim and Vick Lakes (Map 14/G5) 🐟

West of Taseko Lake Road, Slim Lake is a hidden trout lake that was stocked in 2008 with rainbow trout. The access is best off the 4500 Road, which passed Vick Lake en route. Vick also offers rainbow. There is a bait ban and single barbless hook restriction at this lake.

Snag Lake (Map 17/F4) 🐟

Snag Lake is a 91 ha (224 ac) lake west of the Moose Valley Park and 100 Mile House. Fishing is very good after spring turnover, or in the fall when using a lure tipped with a worm or an attractor type fly. By summer, the shallow lake warms up considerably and fishing slows. The fall is the best time to fish for stocked brookies as the males are very aggressive just before spawning and strike at most anything. There is a recreation site with a boat launch on the western shoreline. There is a bait ban and single barbless hook restriction at this lake.

Snag Lake (Map 54/E4)

Snag Lake is found east of the much larger Batnuni Lake. It is a small lake with steep banks making shore fishing rather difficult. It is a fly-fishing only lake with special catch limits, a bait ban and no power boats allowed.

Snohoosh Lake (Map 7/A4)

This long, thin 91 ha (224 ac) lake has a recreation site at its north end with a boat launch and camping, as well as a private campground at its south end. The lake contains rainbow trout and kokanee up to 1 kg (2 lbs). The elevation is relatively low, meaning the spring and fall are best times to fish here.

Spanish Lake (Map 44/B6)

Spanish Lake is a 454 ha (1,121 ac) lake just east of Likely via Spanish Lake Road (1300 Rd). The lake is one of the larger ones in the area and is best trolled for its rainbow trout to 2 kg (4.5 lbs) and bull trout to 3 kg (6.5 lbs). Spincasting and fly-fishing near creek mouths can provide results from time to time. You will find a recreation site with a boat launch along the southeast shore of the lake.

Spectacle Lake (Map 7/A1)

Off the 3700 Road (two-wheel drive), Spectacle Lake is a small 12 ha (29 ac) lake. It offers fair fishing for rainbow trout to 1 kg (2 lbs). Fly anglers should try a shrimp or dragonfly pattern.

Spout Lake (Map 30/B7)

Accessed off Spout Lake Road (1500 Rd) north of Lac La Hache, there is a lodge on the lake that provides the best access. Rainbow to 1 kg (2 lbs) are caught here.

Spruce Lake (Map 3/G5)

This remote backcountry lake is accessed on foot, by bike, by horse or float plane. The lake is known for its excellent fly-fishing for rainbow that can grow to 1.5 kg (3 lbs). Working from a float tube is your best bet since the 40 ha (98 ac) lake is quite shallow and shore fishing can be difficult. There are private cabins found on the lake, which also holds Dolly Varden and whitefish. The high elevation lake offers a good fishery throughout the season.

Squawk Lake (Map 29/G6–30/A6)

Squawk Lake offers a good fishery for rainbow trout in the spring and fall. Access is off the four-wheel drive Knife Creek Road (2000 Rd) from Highway 97. Trout in the 2 kg (4.5 lb) range have been reported. Fishing Squawk Lake is best from a small boat or float tube in order to cast your line towards the shallows.

Starlike Lake (Map 30/B3) 🐟

Stocked in the past with rainbow, the 57 ha (140 ac) lake is found about 8.5 km from the Horsefly Road. The trout can grow to 2 kg (4.5 lbs) since they feed on the redside shiners that have infested the lake. There is an old forestry site offering a rustic place to camp and launch on the lake.

Steiger Lake (Map 19/F5)

Accessible by a short trail from the rough Taweel Road, the lake provides some good fishing for small rainbow trout as long as it affected by winterkill on cold years.

Stillwater Lake (Map 23/G2)

Most people walk past Stillwater Lake on their way to Turner Lake. This is partly due to the shallow nature of the lake as it is only 5 m (16 ft) deep. But the At-narko River feeds the 106 ha (261 ac) lake and all sorts of sportfish make their way into it. Rainbow, Dolly Varden, cutthroat, whitefish and even salmon can be found. The low elevation lake is best fished in the early spring or fall.

Stinking Lake (Map 6/F7)

This shallow lake offers good fishing for brook trout in the spring and fall. Try spincasting with bait and fishing near the bottom. Good access is provided along the Deadman-Cache Creek Road.

Stony Lake (Map 57/D3)

This large, 851 ha (2,102 ac) lake can be found off the Willow-Stony Forest Service Road and it provides fishing opportunities for rainbow trout, bull trout, lake trout and kokanee. Trolling is the most effective method of angling used on this big lake. There are four separate recreation sites found along the shores of Stony Lake.

Succour Lake (Map 19/A1)

Succour Lake is found 10 km northeast of Canim Lake. The lake offers a good fishery for rainbow trout beginning in late May until late October. Since the lake is deep, trollers will find success during the summer months. Spincasters and fly anglers should try near the shore area off the northwest shoreline where there are expansive shallows. A recreation site is located on the southeast shoreline and has a cartop boat launch available.

Suey Lake (Map 31/A1)

There is a portage/trail that travels from Slate Bay on Quesnel Lake to Suey Bay on Horsefly Lake that passes by the small Suey Lake. The lake is seldom visited and provides good fishing for rainbow trout that grow to 3 kg (6.5 lbs). Fly-fishing can be quite effective on this lake.

Sulphurous Lake (Map 19/A4)

Sulphurous Lake is squeezed between Hathaway and Deka Lakes. The lake offers stocked rainbow and kokanee. The trout often reach 1.5–3 kg (3–6.5 lbs) in size as they feed on the coarse fish in the lake. Covering 380 ha (939 ac), the lake is a trolling lake as it is very deep. Spincasters and fly anglers can still work the near shore area including around the island at the middle of the lake or off the large shoal near the west end of the lake. There is a lake trout daily quota of one; lake trout must be released from Oct 1st to Nov 30th.

Summit Lake (Map 19/C5)

North of Bridge Lake, this 19.5 ha (48 ac) lake is home to rainbow trout and was last stocked in 2004. The rough road access limits visitors to the lake.

Surprise Lake (Map 19/G3)

Surprise Lake lies to the west of the Grizzly Lakes and is accessible via the 156 spur road. It is recommended to travel the road with a high clearance vehicle. Fishing for rainbow trout is generally fair throughout the open water season.

Susan and Judy Lakes (Map 19/A1–31/A7)

A four-wheel drive vehicle and a bit of patience is needed to find these small rainbow trout lakes north of Canim Lake. Access is best off the Lang Lake Road (610 Rd) to the north. Susan Lake is home to a small recreation site and rustic boat launch.

Swartz Lake [Fish Lake] (Map 4/C3)

A popular destination with four-wheel drive and ATV enthusiasts, this 14 ha (34 ac) lake holds rainbow trout. It is a higher elevation lake that offers fair fishing throughout the ice-free season.

Ta Hoola Lake (Map 19/E5)

With road access off Wavey Lake Forest Service Road (2000 Rd), the fishing in Ta Hoola Lake is not as good as it once was. Regardless, there are still plenty of rainbow that grow to 1 kg (2 lbs) in size.

Tagai Lake (Map 54/G2–55/A2)

Covering 252 ha (622 ac), Tagai Lake is not high enough or deep enough at an average of 6.5 m (21 ft) to stay cool in the summer. Anglers will find the fishing much better in the spring or fall. The lake had about 40,000 rainbow trout dumped in it back in the early 80s and is now a self-sustaining population. The trout come readily to fly gear or by trolling and grow to about 1 kg (2 lbs). The recreation site offers camping and a cartop boat launch.

Taseko Lakes (Map 3/A1–A3)

These two high mountain lakes stretch south, deep into the heart of the Coast Mountains. While they are not popular fishing lakes (too remote, too windy, too big, too much glacial till and too few fish are some of the common reasons not to go) they have wild rainbow and dollies. The best-known place to catch these fish is near the outflow of the Taseko River at the north end of Lower Taseko Lake. Spincasters and fly anglers also have luck near any inflowing creek.

Tatla Lake (Map 13/E1–26/A6)

A long, narrow 1,816 ha (4,487 ac) lake that parallels Highway 20, Tatla Lake is not noted for its fishing. It offers a few decent-sized rainbow and ko-kanee. In fact, the average catch is rumoured to be a chunky 37 cm (15 in). In addition to a recreation site with a steep boat launch, there is a resort with much better access to the lake.

Tatlayoko Lake (Map 13/F7–G4)

Records show that in 1927, 146 Dolly Varden were deposited into Tatlayoko Lake. Although there still are some dollies and native bull trout, the lake is better known for its rainbow trout fishing. Rainbow average from 1–2.5 kg (2–5 lbs) and can be caught by trolling, spincasting or fly-fishing. Boaters should be wary of the heavy winds common on the lake. There is a recreation site on the lake, but permits are required for hunting and fishing since the lake falling in the Tsilhqot'in First Nation area. Visit www.tsilhqotin.ca for more information.

Tatuk Lake (Map 54/B2)

South of the town of Vanderhoof, via Tatuk Road or the Kluskus Forest Service Road, you can find Tatuk Lake. This is a beautiful, 1,894 ha (4,680 ac) lake, which gets its name from the Carrier word for "three hills." There are recreation sites with boat launches available at both ends of the lake with the eastern site better for larger boats. The popular fishing destination offers rainbow to 2 kg (4.5 lbs) and abundant kokanee that also grow to about 2 kg (4.5 lbs). Most people fish by trolling.

Taweel Lake (Map 19/F4)

This 440 ha (1,087 ac) lake lies within the Taweel Park, but there are resorts that restrict road access. There is no public boat launch, but if you are interested in a resort-based fishing trip, the fishing can be good for rainbow trout to 2 kg (4.5 lbs).

Taylor Lake (Map 18/D6)

Taylor Lake was stocked periodically until the 1970s. The lake now holds good numbers of rainbow trout that can grow to 1 kg (2 lbs) in size. Most of the 103 ha (254 ac) lake is comprised of a large shoal area and is only suited for spincasting or fly-fishing. The fishing heats up in the later part of May and continues until the summer doldrums kick in, in early July. The shallow nature of this lake makes it subject to winterkill.

Teapot Lake (Map 57/C2)

A rough 5.5 km road leads west from the Naver-Ahbau Forest Service Road (700 Rd) to Teapot Lake. The small lake contains average-sized rainbow trout. Trolling is the preferred method, although fly-fishing along shoal areas during spring can be effective. A recreation site complete with a cartop boat launch is available at the lake.

Teepee Lake (Map 54/F6)

An old road leads into this lake, which is one of those local hideaways. In fact, an old ranger cabin has been kept clean and stocked by a few individuals. Since few people venture in, the fishing is quite good for rainbow. Please help keep the cabin clean and stocked for the next person to enjoy. The lake is a fly-fishing only lake, with special catch limits. There is a bait ban, single barbless hook and artificial fly only restriction at the lake.

Ten Mile Lake (Map 56/F7)

The 243 ha (600 ac) Ten Mile Lake is a popular retreat. It has a number of private residences lining its shores, as well as a quaint park. The lake has good numbers of rainbow trout and kokanee as well as some mountain whitefish, lake chub and redside shiners. The trout are stocked each year and can grow up to 3 kg (6.5 lbs) in size. The kokanee help make this a good year-round fishery. For fly anglers, the shallows contain lilies and other weeds to work, while trollers should work the hole at the northwest end of the lake. The park offers campsites, a boat launch and picnic area.

Tesla Lake (Map 50/E6–F6)

This is a big Tweedsmuir Park Lake that offers trophy rainbow trout up to 7 kg (15 lbs). The fishing is amazing and the setting gorgeous. Too bad the access is limited to floatplane. Then again, maybe not! There is a fishing lodge on the shores of the lake.

Fishing Adventures

Tezla Lake (Map 38/B3)

Another shallow Chilcotin Lake that suffers from winterkill, the rainbow and coarse fish that are found here travel in from the nearby Dean River. The lake, which is accessed from the rough four-wheel drive access Dean River Road, is rumoured to provide a good fishery in the spring and fall.

Thelma Lake (Map 19/F4)

Thelma Lake lies within the Taweel Park and is best accessed by rough trail from Taweel Lake. The road access is gated. If you do find the lake, the fishing can be quite good for rainbow trout that can reach 1 kg (2 lbs). The trout are usually aggressive and can be caught using flies, bait or lures.

Thuya Lakes (Map 19/F7)

Most anglers use the lodge as a base to explore this chain of lakes, which are found off the 2300 Road south of Eakin Creek Road. There are a series of ATV accessible trails that connect the lakes, which hold rainbow trout. There is an electric motor only restriction.

Till Lake (Map 28/G6) 🐟

The 78 ha (192 ac) lake is stocked with rainbow, which can grow up to 1.5 kg (3.5 lbs), although the lake is subject to winterkill. Home to a recreation site at the north end, Till Lake is found off the Meldrum Creek Road (1100 Rd), which leads north from Highway 20.

Tiltzarone Lake (Map 41/G2)

A small, 59 ha (145 ac) lake just south of the Nazko Road, Tiltzarone Lake is known for producing some fairly big wild rainbow, up to 2.5 kg (5 lbs). The lake is accessed via a short trail. The use of a canoe or a float tube can dramatically increase your success on this lake.

Timothy Lake (Map 18/D2) 🐟

Timothy Lake is a 444 ha (1,097 ac) resort destination lake that is easily reached 18 km east of Lac La Hache. Getting a 1.5 kg (3 lb) rainbow trout in Timothy Lake is not uncommon, but so is catching some coarse fish (redside shiners, squawfish, suckers and chub). The good fishing is partly due to the annual stocking program. The lake is deep enough to troll and there are a few resorts on the lake that offer camping, launching facilities and boat rentals.

Tisdall Lake (Map 30/F4)

Found south of Black Creek, Tisdall is a popular fishing destination with a recreation site and boat launch. The 491 ha (1,213 ac) lake is best trolled for the rainbow in the 30–40 cm (12–16 in) range. The lake is big and deep enough to maintain a summer fishery.

Titetown Lake (Map 54/F4)

Titetown Lake is located about 24 km west of the Nazko-Euchiniko Road junction along the Batnuni Lake Forest Service Road and offers anglers an opportunity to fish for wild stock rainbow and Dolly Varden. There is a recreation site on the east end of this long lake.

Tobe Lake (Map 19/D6)

An overgrown road/trail leads from the Machete Lake Road to the western shore of Tobe Lake. Due to the difficult access few visitors make it into the remote lake. Fly-fishing is for rainbow trout that reach above average sizes.

Tommy Archie Lake (Map 31/D7)

This small, secluded lake can be reached by a trail from the Pendleton Lake Forest Service Road (7100 Rd). The first section is quite steep. The lake is not heavily fished and fishing can be quite good at times for rainbow trout to 1 kg (2 lbs).

Tortoise Lake (Map 19/E6)

Accessible by trail from Birch Lake, this lake offers the chance to catch a rainbow in the 2 kg (4.5 lb) range. Unfortunately, squawfish compete for available food and the trout are not as plentiful as they could be. Casting off the rock bluff along the western shore is a good spot to try your luck. There are plenty of weed beds and shoals that line the lake.

Tory Lake (Map 55/C2) 🐟

Tory Lake is located alongside the Pelican Lake Forest Service Road and sports a small recreation site. There is a boat launch at the campsite, but the access is steep. This small 19 ha (46 ac) lake is occasionally stocked with rainbow, which don't grow too big. Fly-fishing towards the marshy shoreline is the most effective method.

Towydkin Lake (Map 15/D1)

Towydkin Lake is located just 16.7 km from Hanceville off Highway 20 and the Minton Creek Forest Service Road. Anglers will find rainbow and lake trout in the 1–2 kg (2–4.5 lb) range. This lake is best fished from May through October and trolling seems to be the preferred method.

Tranquille Lake (Map 7/E6) 🐟

This 58 ha (143 ac) lake is located on a rough two-wheel drive road north of Kamloops. It is a high elevation lake is considered a good option throughout the ice-free season for the abundant small rainbow in the 1 kg (2 lb) range and ko-kanee. Fly-fishing (Doc Spratley, leeches or small attractors), trolling (Willow Leaf and maggots) and spincasting (small lures) all work. There is a resort on the lake.

Trio Lake (Map 43/F7)

This small lake is located west of the larger Bootjack Lake off the Moorehead-Bootjack Forest Service Road (100 Rd). Trio Lake is inhabited by rainbow trout to 1 kg (2 lbs), which are best caught by fly-fishing in the late spring or early fall. There is a cartop boat launch available at the lake.

Tubbs Lake (Map 18/D3)

Southeast of Lac La Hache, you will find this fairly productive lake about 6 km down Hickling Road. Rainbow flourish here, with trout in the 1–2 kg (2–4.5 lb) range.

Tsacha Lake (Map 39/B1–53/C7)

Fishing Tsacha can be good for rainbow, but you've got to get there first. Tsacha is a 15 km long remote lake. You can fly-in, paddle along the Blackwater River or access it along the Alexander Mackenzie Trail. There is a lodge on the lake.

Tsintsunko Lake (Map 7/E4)

The 100 ha (247 ac) lake offers reasonable fishing for small rainbow trout on a fly or by trolling throughout the summer months and into the fall. The lake is found along the Tsintsunko Lake Trail, which leads off the 4300 Road.

Tsuniah Lake (Map 14/C5)

Tsuniah Lake doesn't produce big fish, but they usually come at your hook fast and furious. Rainbow average up to 1 kg (2 lbs) and are fairly indiscriminate. Fishing stays strong June through October, but is subject to strong winds that filter down the high mountain valley. You will need a four-wheel drive vehicle to access the recreation site on the west side of the 1,079 ha (2,666 ac) lake. There is a bait ban and single barbless hook restriction. Since the lake falls in the Tsilhqot'in First Nation area, permits are required for hunting and fishing. Visit www.tsilhqotin.ca for more information.

Tuloon Lake [Tintlhohtan Lake] (Map 19/G5)

This is another fine lake with a resort from which to base your efforts. The lake is inhabited by good numbers of rainbow trout that can reach 1 kg (2 lbs). Dragonfly and leech fly patterns are two of the popular fly patterns used at this lake.

Turbo Lake (Map 25/C3)

A medium-sized lake in a secluded region, Turbo Lake can be accessed by the Holtry Creek Forest Service Road (200 Rd), southeast of Anahim Lake and Highway 20. If you are willing to make the long, rough trek this lake is productive with rainbows in the 2 kg (4.5 lb) range.

Turner Lake (Map 23/G3)

The Tote Road, a rough four-wheel drive road, heads south from Highway 20 to the trailhead for the hike up to Turner Lake. It's 16 km from the end of the road to the lake, much of that slogging uphill. Many people prefer to fly-in with their canoes. The seven lakes in the chain (including Turner, Junker, Widgeon and Kidney Lakes) form the headwaters of the Atnarko River and contain cutthroat trout, which grow up to 35 cm (14 in). There is a bait ban and single barbless hook restriction as well as a two trout daily limit at these lakes.

Tuzcha Lake (Map 2/F2)

Sandwiched between Fishem Lake to the south and Lastman Lake to the north, Tuzcha Lake is one of a series of lakes in the valley between Ts'ylos and the Taseko Mountain. Producing moderate to high populations of both wild rainbow and bull trout, this excellent fishing region can be accessed off Gunn Valley Forest Service Road.

Twin Lake (Map 7/E3)

Found near the northern border of the Bonaparte Provincial Park, Twin Lake is a hike-in angling destination. Due to the remote access, fishing can be good for rainbow to 2 kg (4.5 lbs). The lake can be fished throughout the ice-free season.

Twin Lakes (Map 29/F4)
Getting a boat down onto the Twin Lakes is a difficult proposition, as the banks are very steep and there is no launch. Most of the fishing for the generally small trout is done from shore or on a float tube.

Twin Lakes [Ikt and Mokst Lakes] (Map 21/A1)
Located near Ocean Falls (water or air access only), getting to the Twin Lakes or Ikt and Mokst is not the easiest accomplishment. The lake sees little fishing pressure for the good numbers of cutthroat trout, Dolly Varden and kokanee that reside here.

Twist Lake (Map 12/G5)
This lake sits south of the Old Waddington Route and north of Homathko River Protected Area along Mosley Creek. Best known for its rainbow trout that average in the 1–2.5 kg (2–5 lb) range, bull trout and Dolly Varden can also be caught by trolling, spincasting or fly-fishing.

Two Lake (Map 27/B3)
Two Lake is located just past Alexis Lake. As the name implies, Two Lake is the second of a pair of small lakes, joined together by a short channel. The lake is well stocked with rainbow that grow to 2.5 kg (5 lbs) and native brook trout to 1 kg (2 lbs). There is a small recreation site on the shore and a cartop boat launch for electric motors only.

> *Kokanee are a soft-mouthed fish found in many BC lakes. They are best caught by trolling slowly in an "S" pattern using a lake troll with a Wedding Ring or Dick Nite and maggot, Flatfish or small pink Spin-N-Glo lure.*

Two Mile Lake (Map 30/C6)
Two Mile Lake can be found off the Murphy Lake Road and offers fishing opportunities for rainbow trout to 1 kg (2 lbs) in size. There is a large private lot on this lake, therefore, please be sure not to trespass.

Tyaughton Lake (Map 4/C6)
"Tyaughton" is native for flying fish. On any given evening, you will know why. Trolling a Willow Leaf and Wedding Band has caught good numbers of dollies and rainbow here. The lake is quite deep and clear making fly-fishing difficult, but casting towards shore with a fly or small lure can be effective. There is a resort and recreation site on the lake.

Tyee Lake (Map 29/B2)
Found 30 km east of McLeese Lake, Tyee Lake is stocked with rainbow trout and kokanee. The kokanee fishery is quite active in summer and winter, and the lake is now stocked with the Gerrard strain of rainbow – so expect bigger fish. The lake is ideal to troll since the water depth drops off rapidly from shore. Alternatively, the inflow and outflow creeks are good areas to try casting a fly or lure. A recreation site offers camping and a boat launch. Check the regulations for special limits.

Tzenzaicut Lake [Fish Lake] (Map 42/B6)
Locals unwilling to wrap their mouths around the name call this Fish Lake, a tribute to both the number and the quality of the fish here. Early summer is the best time to catch wild rainbow in the 20–38 cm (10–15 in) range. Found 58 km southwest of Quesnel, the road to the lake is in good condition and there is a popular recreation site with a boat launch on the lake.

Valentine Lake (Map 18/B5)
Valentine Lake is stocked with thousands of rainbow each year ensuring a healthy trout population despite the heavy pressure. The lake is 56 ha (138 ac), but quite deep so trolling (electric motors only) is certainly possible without too many hang ups. The lake produces rainbow up to 3.6 kg (8 lbs) on rare occasion. The fly-fishing only lake also has an electric motor only and no ice fishing restriction. Visitors will find a recreation site with cartop boat launch on the lake.

Vedan Lake (Map 14/F5)
Vedan Lake contains wild rainbow averaging 1 kg (2 lbs), but the real draw here is the bull trout, which can get up to 7 kg (15 lbs). Angling remains strong throughout the late spring and early fall, mostly by trolling. Although flies work well for the rainbow, you will have to get deeper to lure the bull trout. There is a recreation site at the lake that provides a good boat launch onto the often windy, 307 ha (758 ac) lake. Since the lake falls in the Tsilhqot'in First Nation area, permits are required for hunting and fishing. Visit www.tsilhqotin.ca for more information.

Vidette Lake (Map 7/A3)
This 35 ha (86 ac) lake is found at a relatively low elevation. Although this is a deep lake, fishing is still best during spring and fall. The lake is also a popular ice fishing location in winter. Both the small kokanee and average-sized rainbow are best caught by trolling (try deeper for the trout). There is a resort as well as a recreation site on this popular lake.

Wahla Lake (Map 50/F5)
Wahla Lake is a hike-in lake in Tweedsmuir Provincial Park, with rainbow to 7 kg (15 lbs). Although the walk from nearby Tesla Lake is short, getting to the bigger Tesla Lake requires a floatplane.

Walk in Lake (Map 19/F6)
This small lake can be easily reached by a short trail off the west side of Taweel Road, not far from Highway 24. The rainbow average about 25–30 cm (10–12 in) in size. Fly-fishing can be particularly effective on this lake.

Warttig Lake (Map 45/C6)
This secluded, 51 ha (126 ac) lake can be reached via the Bouldrey Creek Road (6100 Rd) east of Horsefly Lake. The lake has a good population of naturally spawning rainbow trout that often cruise the shallow southern and middle parts of the lake in search of insects. The drop-off areas around the deeper water are good spots to troll or cast a line. On the southern shore of the lake, a recreation site offers camping and a cartop boat launch.

Watch Lake (Map 18/F6)
Watch Lake is a popular destination with multiple resorts. The 261 ha (644 ac) lake has a good number of rainbow trout that grow to 5 kg (11 lbs) on occasion. The best time to the fish the lake is from the early part of May until mid-July and then mid-August to October.

Waterlily Lake (Map 13/D2)
Sandwiched between Sapeye and Little Sapeye lakes, Waterlily Lake has a decent trail system for those without a boat. High populations of wild rainbow averaging in the 1.5 kg (3 lb) range flourish here, with moderate numbers of big bull trout caught in the 2.5 kg (5.5 lb) size range as well.

Wavey Lake (Map 19/D5)
The fishing at Wavey Lake begins later than other lakes in the Cariboo. The lake is 91 ha (224 ac) and contains large shoal areas ideal for fly-fishing. Towards the summer months, focus out from shore in the deeper water or troll the drop-off area around the inflow and outflow creeks. The lake contains good numbers of rainbow trout, but also has some coarse fish (suckers, squawfish and redside shiners). There is a fish camp on the lake.

Wawa Lake (Map 24/E2)
Northwest of Nimpo Lake, Wawa Lake is home to rainbow trout in the 1 kg (2 lb) range. Access is south of the city of Anahim Lake along Highway 20.

Wendle Lake (Map 58/A7)
This small, roadside lake is the highlight of the day-use Wendle Park found north of Barkerville. The lake is stocked with rainbow trout, which provide for decent fishing opportunities for generally small trout.

Whale Lake (Map 17/G5)
West of 100 Mile House, this small lake provides fair to good fishing for small kokanee. Try small flies from a float tube for added success on this lake. There is camping and a boat launch available at the recreation site. There is a bait ban and single barbless hook restriction at this lake.

Whale Lake (Map 19/D1)
Whale Lake can be reached by trail from the Mahood Lake Road. The remote lake is stocked with rainbow trout, which provide good fishing throughout the year. There is a bait ban and single barbless hook restriction at this lake.

Whitewood Lake (Map 7/G4)

Located along the Jamieson Creek Forest Service Road (two-wheel drive access), this 15 ha (37 ac) lake has a recreation site complete with camping and boat launching facilities. The lake is fairly good for trolling and fly-fishing for rainbow that can reach 1 kg (2 lbs). Fishing is best during the spring and fall given the elevation of the lake.

Whitton Lake & Area (Map 24/B6)

At 1,494 m (4,900 ft), this 235 ha (580 ac) lake offers good fishing for rainbow trout from June through fall. Nearby Cohen Lake is much smaller at 45 ha (111 ac) and is easier to fish than its bigger neighbour.

Williams Lake (Map 29/B5)

Williams Lake is a large, 723 ha (1,786 ac) lake next to Highway 97 and the city of the same name. The lake is one of the first ice-free lakes in the Cariboo and contains a few burbot, kokanee, rainbow trout and whitefish. The fish are most active in the spring and are best caught on the troll. Be sure to visit one of the local tackle shops to find out what is working in the area.

Willow & Wand Lakes (Map 19/E5)

Willow Lake offers a good fishery for rainbow trout. The lake is best fished beginning in late May to early June and is well suited to trolling. Wand Lake is the smaller lake to the north that is inhabited by numerous small rainbow.

Willowgrouse Lake (Map 7/E3)

Willowgrouse provides good fishing for rainbow to 1 kg (2 lbs) by fly-fishing or spincasting. The 105 ha (259 ac) lake is best fished in the spring and fall. The lake can be accessed along the Tuwut Lake Canoe Route or by the Masters Sub-Alpine Trek.

Wilson Lake (Map 19/C6)

Despite the good access, a lodge and cabins on the lake, few anglers stop to sample this lake. With improvements to the spawning channels, look for the angling success to pick up. The lake is best trolled, although shore casting for rainbow is possible. There is a boat launch on the west side.

Windy Lake (Map 7/F4)

Windy Lake is located just outside of Bonaparte Provincial Park, on the Windy Lake Road. The recreation site on the lake is popular with both hikers and anglers. The lake is not quite high enough to sustain summer fishing, but has fair fishing for rainbow to 1 kg (2 lbs) during the spring and fall. The preferred methods are trolling and fly-fishing.

Wolverine Lake (Map 44/A5)

Wolverine Lake is situated north of Likely off Keithley Creek Road. The lake contains rainbow trout as well as some lake char. Fishing pressure is low despite the fact that the lake regularly produces rainbow trout in the 2 kg (4.5 lb) category. The small, 24 ha (59 ac) lake has large shoal areas well suited for a vibrant insect population. A recreation site is situated on the southern shores of the lake and offers a cartop boat launch.

Yardley Lake (Map 56/F4)

Only 11 km northeast from Highway 97, the Yardley Lake Road skirts this nice lake. In addition to good fishing for small rainbow trout, there is a former recreation site at the lake that some people still use to camp at.

Yimpakluk Lake (Map 54/G5)

Very few people fish this lake; mostly due to the rough four-wheel drive access (fording of the Euchinko River along the Alexander MacKenzie Trail is necessary). The lake has been stocked with rainbow trout and contains lots of fish in the 1 kg (2 lb) range. Fly anglers will find ample shoals and there is a rustic campsite available.

Young Lake (Map 6/G2)

Located southeast of Green Lake, this 252 ha (622 ac) lake holds good numbers of rainbow trout to 2 kg (4.5 lbs) and some kokanee. There is a boat launch at the lake.

Zippermouth Lake (Map 55/D3)

West of the communities of Blackwater and Punchaw in the shadows of the Telegraph Mountain Range, Zippermouth Lake is your typical rainbow trout lake, with average weights in the 1–2 kg (2–4.5 lb) range. Although roads come close, be prepared to bushwhack your way into this one.

River & Stream Fishing

Below we have described most of the fishable streams in the area. Access into many of the other streams hinders both the fish and anglers from enjoying these wild waters. There are also many smaller streams that we have not mentioned. Some of these dry out in the summer, while others are simply tributaries of the bigger creeks and rivers that have similar characteristics and fish species as the bigger streams. To receive notifications on freshwater regulation changes, subscribe to the In-Season Regulation Changes feed at www.env.gov.bc.ca/fw/news; changes to the salmon and steelhead regulations can be found at www.pac.dfo-mpo.gc.ca.

Ahbau Creek (Map 56/F5–57/B5)

This stream flows south from Lodi Lake and west of Ahbau Lake into the Cottonwood River north of Quesnel. The stream crosses under Highway 97, which is a popular spot for parking and beginning to fish the creek. Chinook, kokanee and rainbow trout are found in Ahbau Creek up to Lodi Lake.

Atnarko River (Map 23/D2–24/C4)

One of the most popular angling destinations in the area, the Atnarko River is a lovely place to be. There is a strong Chinook run mid-May to mid-July, Coho in September and October and chum and pink in late July to August. The Upper River is accessed by boat from its headwaters on Charlotte Lake or along the Turner Lakes Canoe Chain in Tweedsmuir Provincial Park. Access to much of this section of the river is difficult, if not impossible. Hunlen Falls separates the upper section from the lower section. This is a pretty insurmountable barrier to the spawning salmon and steelhead. However, the upper river is well known as a fly-fishing river for rainbow trout. Consult your regulations before heading out, as there are many restrictions on this big river.

Baezaeko River (Map 39/E3–55/A6)

The Baezaeko is a major tributary of the Blackwater, flowing through a vast wilderness near Itcha Ilgachuz Provincial Park. There are few road crossings to be found west of Nazko; however, there is a trail that follows the Baezaeko to its headwaters in the Itcha Mountains for over 100 km (60 mi). The easiest place to access the river is near Nazko, where it flows into the much larger Coglistiko River. The banks of the river here are muddy and steep, and the river is slow-moving with a lot of weeds and shallows that make shore casting difficult, though not impossible. A small boat or tube would be very helpful. The river has excellent fly-fishing for wild rainbow in the 2 kg (4.5 lb) range and bull trout to 4.5 kg (10 lbs).

If you cannot find your favourite river or stream in the write-ups, look for a stream in the area. Most nearby creeks have similar characteristics to one another.

Bella Coola River (Map 22/D1–23/C1)

A combination of the Atnarko and the Talchako Rivers, the Bella Coola has excellent fishing for cutthroat trout during the March fry migration. The river is also a hot bed of activity during the salmon runs. Chinook begin to appear in the river in late May and run through July. Bar fishing with a heavy weight and a Spin-N-Glo is the preferred method for large fish that reach Tyee status of 13.5 kg (30 lbs). The other runs include Coho (September to November), pink and sockeye (August and September) and chum salmon (late July through October). There is also a small winter steelhead run. Popular holes include most stream mouths (including Thorsen Creek and Salloomi River) as well as the ever popular Airport Hole and McCall Flats. Most of the property surrounding this river is private and access is limited. Floating the large river in a row boat or (less preferred) a canoe is a popular method of fishing the river. Consult the regulations before heading out as there are many restrictions on this big river.

Big Creek (Map 3/E4–16/C2)

This is indeed a big creek as it flows from Elbow Mountain all the way north to the Chilcotin River. The creek contains wild rainbow that are best caught by fly-fishing or with small spincasting gear from July through October. The creek also contains Dolly Varden in its upper reaches, which can be accessed by trail.

Blackwater [West Road] River (Maps 38, 39, 53–56)

The Blackwater River is one of the premier rainbow trout rivers in BC; it flows hundreds of kilometres through several lakes to finally join with the Fraser. The river is gentle and can be drifted in a canoe (with a few notable exceptions). The river contains rainbow, whitefish and pike minnow and is a great fly-fishing river, with trout averaging 35 cm (14 in). The best angling is early in the season as the water levels allow the trout to roam freely between all the neighbouring lakes and streams. Fly anglers should note the stonefly and caddis hatches. Access is limited in the upper regions (above Kluskoil Lake Provincial Park) and there are only a few places where bridges span the river.

Bonaparte River (Map 6/C7–7/C2)

The Bonaparte is a salmon-bearing river, but like a lot of the rivers this far upstream, there is no salmon fishing allowed. Instead, you can try your luck for the wild rainbow, which are plentiful along the 145 km (90 mi) course. It is a small shallow river with clear water that can make the fish skittish. The river is heavily regulated including no fish under 25 cm (10 in) and a daily limit of two that can only be taken on a single barbless hook with no bait.

Bowron River (Map 57/F1–58/D7)

Flowing from the mountains in Bowron Lake Park northwest to the Fraser River, there is good access to most of this river. You will find bull trout, kokanee, rainbow and lake trout. Fly-fishing, spincasting and using bait in any of the numerous pools can produce fish that reach 1 kg (2 lbs) on occasion.

Braden River (Map 35/A4–B6)

All but inaccessible to most anglers, this river offers great fishing for resident cutthroat trout. If you are in the Ocean Falls area, this stream is found by boat from Link Lake.

> Steelhead are the most highly prized sportfish in BC due to their acrobatic fighting ability. They are a sea-run version of rainbow trout that can get as large as 9 kg (20 lbs). Winter steelhead usually run from December through April, peaking in March, while summer steelhead runs begin in late May and peak anywhere between June and late July. Note that steelhead are heavily regulated and regulations are subject to change on short notice.

Canim River (Map 19/D1–E1)

This short river is a catch-and-release stream that connects Canim Lake with Mahood Lake. The river offers good fly-fishing for rainbow that can reach 2 kg (4.5 lbs). The best fishing is after spring runoff in some of the deeper pools. This river is catch-and-release only (pay attention to yearly bait bans). Boaters should be wary of the dangerous waterfalls and rapids.

Cariboo River (Map 43/F5–44/B4; 44/C3–59/D7)

There are two sections to this river. The section north of Cariboo Lake is quite remote and the water can be silty. The section between Cariboo Lake and Quesnel River has much better access and cleaner water. Rainbow are usually small at approximately 20 cm (18 in), while the bull trout average 30 cm (12 in). Bigger fish are best taken from July to September by fly-fishing, spincasting or using bait.

Chilako [Mud] River (Map 54/C2–55/F1)

The Chilako drains Tatuk Lake, crossing a number of forest service roads, and continues north of our maps to the Nechako River (see Northern BC Mapbook). The Chilako offers decent fly-fishing for rainbow using Adams, midges, caddis, stoneflies and muddler patterns. Due to the dark muddy waters, anglers should use flies with attractants or spinners. Consult the regulations before heading out.

Chilcotin River (Maps 15, 16, 26, 27, 39)

A major tributary of the Fraser, the Chilcotin has resident stocks of wild rainbow and dollies. The fish can be found throughout the river year round and average about 1 kg (2 lbs) in size. But most anglers visit this stream for the strong runs of winter and summer steelhead and fall Chinook that run as far upstream as the Chilko River. Check the regulations before heading out as there are several restrictions on different parts of the river.

Chilko River (Map 14/B5–27/B5)

Flowing out of Chilko Lake and into the Chilcotin River, the wild waters of the Chilko can produce great fishing for rainbow, dollies, steelhead and Chinook. The best fishing for rainbow and dollies is the first 20 km (12 mi) below Chilko Lake. The river is heavily regulated to protect the fishery. Check the regulations before heading out as there are several restrictions on different parts of the river.

Churn Creek (Map 4/C3–16/G6)

A waterfall 19 km (12 mi) upstream of Churn Creek's confluence with the Fraser creates an effective barrier, dividing the creek in two. Above the falls, the creek contains rainbow and bull trout. Below the falls, the creek plays host to migrating Chinook and pink salmon. West Churn Creek also contains both rainbow trout and bull trout, although the bull trout are only found in the lower reaches, as they are unable to get beyond a series of waterfalls. Access into this remote system is very limited.

Coglistiko Rivers (Map 39/E3–40/F1)

The Coglistiko River is a major tributary of the Blackwater. There are a few access points off logging roads west of Nazko, but the most popular place to access the river is near its confluence with the Blackwater, north of Nazko. The Coglistiko is known for offering excellent fly-fishing for wild rainbow averaging 2 kg (4.5 lbs) and bull trout to over 4.5 kg (10 lbs).

Dash Creek (Map 3/G3–4/C2)

Dash Creek contains rainbow and bull trout. These are important populations as they are isolated from the rest of the Fraser River drainage by falls on Churn Creek.

Deadman River (Map 6/G7–7/E3)

The Deadman River has two distinct sections. Above the impressive Deadman Falls, it is a wild, beautiful river offering good fishing for rainbow to 35 cm (14 in) by fly or bait fishing. Below the falls, the river flows through dry ranch country and the trout fishing is marginal. Although steelhead, Coho and Chinook salmon run the lower reaches, these fragile runs are closed to fishing.

Dean River (Maps 24, 25, 36, 37, 38)

Natives originally called the Dean River the Salmon River. It flows out of Nimpo Lake, through Anahim Lake and then on to Tweedsmuir Park and eventually down into the Pacific Ocean. The Lower Dean is one of the finest fishing destinations in the province during its summer steelhead run, which peaks in August. Steelhead range 9–13 kg (20–27 lbs) in size. Although access is limited to boat or plane, it still sees a lot of pressure for such a remote river. It also sees a strong Chinook run in June and a fair Coho run in August and September.

The Upper Dean River is a completely different river, offering fine fly-fishing for resident trout in early summer. The system has good hatches and is rich in aquatic life. The trout are usually 25–40 cm (20–16 in) in size. Access to the Upper Dean is easy, as the river even crosses Highway 20 between Nimpo and Anahim Lake. The Dean is a heavily regulated river; check the regulations before heading out.

Dore River (Map 59/F3–E6)

Surrounded by dynamic mountain scenery, the water flows quickly in the remote upper reaches of the Dore. Most of the fishing is found closer to McBride, where road access is good. Fishing is generally fair for small rainbow and bull trout after the high water has receded in July.

East Twin Creek (Map 59/E2–F1)

North of McBride, this small stream flows from the Rocky Mountains into the Fraser River. The creek is accessible via the Mountainview Road and offers good summer fishing for rainbow trout, bull trout and whitefish along the lower reaches.

Euchiniko River (Map 53/F2–55/B5)
Another tributary of the Blackwater, this river also drains a series of lakes and streams. The Batnuni Road provides fair access to the lower reaches, but it is the upper reaches that produce the better fly-fishing opportunities.

Fraser River (Maps 5, 16, 17, 28, 29, 42, 56, 59)
The mighty Fraser River stretches from the Continental Divide in the Rocky Mountains almost 1,450 kilometres (900 mi) to the Pacific Ocean. During the summer and fall salmon runs the river thrives with activity. Look for Chinook starting in June, sockeye in August, Coho and pink in September, and chum in October. There are also resident rainbow trout, bull trout and whitefish along this stretch of river. The best places to fish are usually where streams enter the river. There are special restrictions on the river, so be sure to watch for closures.

Chinook salmon are the largest of the Pacific salmon and have been known to reach up to 27 kg (60 lbs) in size. Although they can be in some streams as early as May, they typically run from late August to November. Coho are another prized salmon that look similar to, but are much smaller than Chinook. Coho typically run from September to November and range from 2.5 to 4.5 kg (5 to 10 lbs).

Goat River (Map 58/F4–59/C1)
Highway 16 crosses the Goat River north of McBride, while the Goat River Forest Road provides access to the upper reaches. Fishing in the river is good after the spring runoff period for small rainbow trout, whitefish and bull trout. Try where the feeder streams flow into the river for best results.

Homathko River (Map 1/A2–13/F7)
While the Homathko is most certainly fishable south of Tatlayoko Lake, access is fairly difficult. The river is renowned for its steelhead, cutthroat, rainbow and Dolly Varden, along with bull trout recorded up to 12 kg (27 lbs). The lower reaches of the river near Bute Inlet have salmon return in the fall. There is no fishing on this lake from April 1 to June 30.

Horsefly River (Map 30/B1–31/D1)
The Horsefly River system is 98 km (60 mi) in length and offers a unique race of trophy size rainbow trout along with Chinook, Coho and sockeye salmon. In the fall, anglers can find big trout that enter the river from Quesnel Lake to spawn. It is a catch and release fishery for rainbow, while Chinook and Coho salmon are closed year round. Check the regulations before heading out, as there are several restrictions on different parts of the river.

Kilbella River (Map 9/E3–22/B6)
The Kilbella River is another stream that drains into Kilbella Bay before flowing into River's Inlet and the Queen Charlotte Sound. You will find trout and salmon along this remote river. Make sure to check the regulations and restrictions here, as there are closures and special mandatory stamps for fishing licenses.

Klinaklini River (Map 11/G7–25/C7)
Fly-in access only, the Klinaklini River meanders its way through lonely, secluded landscapes in the northern basins of the Pantheon Range to the north of Mount Waddington. It loops northeast onto the Chilcotin Plateau before bending south to reach its mouth at the head of Knight Inlet some 200 km (124 mi) later. The main species are rainbow and bull trout. There is a no-fishing ban from April 1 to June 30.

Koeye River (Map 8/F1–9/C1)
Partly due to the difficult access, the 22 km (14 mi) long Koeye is one of the best salmon streams in the Mid-Coast Region. Some anglers take advantage of the lodge at the mouth of the river, where most of the fishing action takes place. In addition to salmon, the river is home to resident populations of cutthroat, Dolly Varden and rainbow trout, the latter to 2.5 kg (5.5 lbs).

Lone Cabin Creek (Map 4/F2–5/A1)
There is a set of impassable falls a mere 200 metres up from Lone Cabin Creek's confluence with the Fraser. Below the falls the river contains rainbow and Chinook salmon. Above the falls, the creek and its tributaries contain bull trout.

Mahood River (Map 31/G7)
Only 5 km (3 mi) long, the Mahood River drains into the Clearwater River. It is possible to navigate the river on boat from Mahood Lake to the waterfalls or by trail. Fishing can be good for generally small rainbow by fly-fishing, spincasting lures or using bait. Fly anglers should try bigger stonefly patterns in June.

Martin River (Map 21/A1–35/B7)
Located near Ocean Falls, this remote west coast stream is known more for its cutthroat trout fishing than salmon fishing. The stream does support small runs of chum, Coho and pink salmon, as well as steelhead. The river is accessed by boat or float plane to Ocean Falls, then a hike along an old road and trail.

McClinchy Creek (Map 24/C6–25/A7)
Highway 20 parallels this stream for a few kilometers and provides the best access to this fast moving creek. The pristine stream is rarely visited and boasts of wild rainbow trout that have a lot of energy.

McKale River (Map 59/F2)
Also known as the Blackwater, the McKale River is located northwest of McBride via Mountainview Road. The river offers fair to good fishing for rainbow trout, whitefish and bull trout. Fishing is best well after the spring runoff period.

Mitchell River (Map 45/A3–4)
Meandering approximately 30 km (19 mi), this tributary of the Quesnel River originates in the glaciers in the northern Columbia Mountains and flows southwest through Mitchell Lake and into Quesnel Lake. Beautiful bright coloured rainbow in the 1 kg (2 lb) range and huge bull trout to 4.5 kg (10 lbs) call this river home. Be sure to check regulations for fishing restrictions in various spots.

Nazko River (Map 27/A3–55/A6)
This slow moving river is best fished after spring runoff when it is possible to work around the bush that lines the banks. There are plenty of good access points to the river, as the Nazko and Honolulu Roads parallel the lower and mid-sections of the river. The river and its tributaries hold wild rainbow, whitefish and the odd big bull trout to 4.5 kg (10 lbs). Notable tributaries include Clisbako River, Snaking River and Wentworth Creek.

Quesnel River (Map 42/E1–44/A6)
This large river flows from Quesnel Lake to the Fraser River. Although most of the river has good road access, there are a few stretches that rarely see an angler. The deeper pools hold fish up to 4.5 kg (10 lbs), but the rainbow and bull trout are usually much smaller. Fishing is best between July and October. Check the regulations before heading out as there are several restrictions on different parts of the river.

Swift River (Map 43/B1–E2)
Average sized rainbow and bull trout can be found throughout this river. Where access is better (closer to Highway 26) the fishing is slower. The upper and especially the middle reaches see fewer anglers, and the fishing can be quite good on occasion.

West Twin Creek (Map 59/C4–D2)
Within the West Twin Provincial Park, this scenic creek can be reached via old logging roads off the south side of Highway 16. The creek holds generally small rainbow trout, bull trout and whitefish. After high water some big bull trout migrate into the stream. Try minnow imitation lures and streamers for the bigger bull trout.

Willow River (Map 57/B1–G7)
Flowing north from Wells towards the Fraser River, the Willow River has good road access along most of its length. After the spring runoff, good fishing can be found for small but plentiful rainbow trout. Fly-fishing and spincasting are the best methods for stream trout.

Ocean Fishing

Central Coast Ocean Fishing

Anglers come from around the world to test their luck in the waters of BC's beautiful mid-coast. The myriad of small islands, inlets and coves make this an amazing fishing destination. The area includes Hakai Pass and Rivers Inlet, two of BC's most popular fishing hot spots.

This area has maintained good returns on most salmon species. The fishing season really kicks off in June, when the first runs of Chinook appear. These are usually smaller fish than the later runs, although the odd fish reaches 15 kg (35 lbs).

A few weeks after the Chinook appear, Sockeye descend on the area from up and down the coast. This is typically around mid-June. Sockeye are one of the smaller salmon species, but what they lack in size, they make up for in taste.

Shortly after the sockeye, the Coho start to appear, usually towards the end of June. The height of their run is in late July and August, which is when fishing in the area is at its best. In addition to Coho, chum and pink salmon thrive in these waters as well. Most people who come here in late July and August are looking for the trophy-sized Chinook. Catching Tyee in excess of 25 kg (55 lbs) is fairly common, but fish half that size are more typical.

Next to salmon, halibut is probably the next most popular catch. These bottom feeders prefer sandbanks and can be caught throughout the year. Fish in excess of 90 kg (200 lbs) are pulled from time to time, although the chickens (less than 14 kg/30 lbs) are more common and much better to eat.

Burke and Dean Channels (Map 20/F5–36/A2)

Burke and Dean Channels have sheer vertical walls that plunge hundreds of feet down. This means that there are very few points where salmon will congregate, making it hard to find fish. Furthermore, winds can play havoc with small boats. The area sees some use when the feeder Chinook are in the area (winter and spring), since the weather at this time keeps people further inland (closer to Bella Coola).

Hakai Pass (Map 8/D2)

The area around Hakai Pass is world renowned for both the beauty of its scenery and the intensity of its fishing. An angler's paradise, this area is home to fish of legendary sizes, including a 38.78 kg (85.5 lb) Chinook caught in 1987 and the famed 57 kg (126 lb) Chinook off Cape Calvert that was landed by a commercial fisherman.

The lodges open in June and stay open until September and offer unbelievable fishing for all five species of salmon and ground fish like halibut, rock cod and red snapper. Chinook are by far the largest and most popular catch, but there have been some impressive Coho caught in these waters as well.

Finding hot spots in the Hakai Pass area is very easy. Salmon can be found at almost any point of headland along the passage. Alternatively, watch where the guides are going. Three places worth noting are Odlum Point, on Calvert Island, The Gap and Barney Bay. The standard set-up is a large cut plug in tandem hook arrangement, with 4 oz. banana weights. The lodges are in the area supply bait.

The first summer runs are sockeye, which show up in June. You will also still find feeder Chinook in the area, but the big Tyee (13.5 kg/30 lb+ Chinook) don't show up until July, which is also when anglers start appearing in large numbers. The Tyee peak in the third week of August. Coho begin appearing in June, but peak (in both size and numbers) in August and September. Come August, pink and chum can also be found in the area. From October to May, the feeder Chinook pile into the Pass, but few people are around to catch them due to the weather.

Red snapper are ridiculously easy to catch, especially around West Bay, Airocobra and Dublin Point. Halibut over 50 kg (100 lbs) can be found around West Bay and in the open waters outside the Pass.

Namu (Map 8/F1–20/F7)

Located across Fitz Hugh Sound from Hakai Pass, Namu lacks the same recognition as Hakai. The main focus here is the Koeye River, which sees a tremendous congregation of Coho in late August. There are also a number of small inlets and river mouths to fish just south of the mouth of Burke Channel.

Rivers Inlet (Map 8/G6–9/E3)

Rivers Inlet is sacred ground for anglers from around the world. While you will find bigger fish out in the Hakai Pass, this area yields 25 to 30 kg (50 to 60 lb) Tyee with more regularity. The big fish, the sheer beauty of the area and the glassy smooth waters make this one of BC's top three ocean fishing destinations. The inlet is 30 km (18 miles) long and has a number of popular resorts along its shores.

Nearly two decades ago, the lodges in the area constructed a Chinook hatchery at Shotbolt Bay to ensure strong returns. It is a strategy that appears to be working. There are two runs each year. The first run, destined for the Kilbella and Chuckwalla Rivers appear in early June. They peak at the end of the month when they are joined by fish from the Wannock River. The really big ones show up in late July to mid-August, destined for the Wannock and Neechanz Rivers and the Owikeno Lake system. In winter (October to May), fishing for feeder Chinook is said to be amazing in Rivers Inlet. Unfortunately, the area is exposed to prevailing winds and few people bother to fish at this time.

While all five species of salmon can be found here, chum salmon are not common, heading instead towards Smith Inlet, farther south. Furthermore, the sockeye population suffered radical declines in the 90's and fishing will be closed for the foreseeable future. However, the area sees good returns on pink to 3.5 kg (7 lbs) and Coho up to 9 kg (20 lbs).

The Inlet is home to ground fish like halibut and lingcod, but only near the mouth of the inlet, west of Goose Bay. Salmon can also be caught near the mouth of the inlet, with anglers focusing on the Wall, Rouse Reef and Wadhams Pass. Higher up the inlet, you will find great fishing around McPhee Bay, Rutherford Point, Whale Rock, Baker's Hole, and the most popular spot of them all, Marker 16.

Because navigating the inlets and channels can be difficult, and the area is so remote, we recommend going with an experienced guide or staying with one of the many lodges operating in Hakai Pass and Rivers Inlet.

Shearwater (Map 20/E4)

Found near Bella Bella, the resort at Shearwater is open year-round. There is also a year-round marina, an airstrip and BC Ferries lands here from Port Hardy. Despite the easier access and protected waters, few people come in the off season.

The protected waters of Hunter Channel, Lama Pass and the more popular Seaforth Channel offer great fishing without a lot of exposure. The best place on the inside is Idle Point. The outside islands can also produce well with the best fishing being around Ivory Island and Cape Swaine. Other great areas to name include: Tinky Island, Cape Swaine, Spider Island, Barba Point and Dryad Point. Bottom fishers can try Purple Bluff, Seaforth Channel and Cultus Sound.

While cut plugging is the most common way of luring the big Chinook, hootchies, large Tomic and dark green plugs also work. For the smaller pink and sockeye, try small red Hotspot flashers. This area is unique, as there is a strong annual pink run from early July to early August, as opposed to every two years elsewhere in the province.

Smith Inlet (Map 9/B7–G6)

The Inlet sees little fishing pressure. This is partly due to the (somewhat) smaller fish and partly due to no lodges or marinas in the area. Only boats with enough fuel to make it here from Rivers Inlet and back again make the trip. Add to that the possibility of getting stranded in bad weather and you will see why few people venture here.

In addition to steady fishing for Chinook and Coho salmon, there are also some great crabbing areas here. The area is closed to sockeye fishing and there is a rockfish conservation area at the mouth of the inlet.

Hunting
Adventures

The Cariboo Chilcotin Coast encompasses a colourful range of habitats. From the dewy rainforest of the Pacific Coast, to frosty mountain peaks from east to west, to the whispering forests and grasslands of the interior wet belt and gently rolling plateaus, the land is a study in contrasts. In addition to creating spectacular scenery, the diverse habitats of this region lend themselves to exciting hunting opportunities.

Hunters flock to the Cariboo Chilcotin Coast for big game — most notably moose and mule deer. Moose appear in wet meadows, river valleys and around the sites of recent logging and forest fires. Mule deer also frequent forest openings, but they prefer drier and steeper country. In addition to these ungulates, you will find mountain sheep, mountain goat, white-tailed deer and caribou. Uncommon for southern BC, woodland caribou are open for hunting in Wildlife Management Unit 5–12 in the west Chilcotin.

Black bear inhabit most management units, and grizzlies can be found near the Pacific coast. Towards the centre of the region, hunters commonly pursue wolves. Game bird hunters are bound to have success, especially near the Fraser River. Choose from four species of grouse, including the readily available ruffed grouse. Big or small, there is game here for everyone.

Because most of the population falls within three central Wildlife Management Units (5–2, 5–13 and 5–14), the majority of the deer, moose and grouse harvest occurs here. Hunters concentrate within a north-south band that follows the Fraser River and Cariboo Highway (Highway 97). For more isolated hunting opportunities, move farther away from the highway.

Note that in order to hunt in BC, you must have a Hunter Number. You can acquire this by completing the Conservation and Outdoor Recreation Education course at www.bcwf.bc.ca. BC residents (those living in BC for a minimum of six months) also need a hunting license and species tag for each big game animal hunted. Find details at www.env.gov.bc.ca/fw/wildlife/hunting/regulations. Non-residents must be accompanied by a licensed guide when hunting big game in BC.

Note also that vulnerable or high-demand species may be subject to Limited Entry Hunting (LEH). See www.env.gov.bc.ca/fw/wildlife/hunting/resident/leh.html for more information. Waterfowl hunters need a federal Migratory Game Bird Hunting Permit, which is available when you purchase your hunting license. Please also check the regulations for bow hunting restrictions.

Lone Butte Sporting Goods

GATEWAY TO THE FISHING HIGHWAY

www.lbsportinggoods.com
Email: lbgun@hotmail.com

YOUR STORE FOR HUNTING,
FISHING & ARCHERY

250-395-2217
Box 40, 6051 Hwy 24, Lone Butte, B.C., V0K1X

Game Species

Black Bear

Black bear are the most common carnivore in central BC and can be found in good numbers in almost any habitat from river flat to mountaintop. Adult male black bear can weigh up to 300 kg (660 lbs) and females as much as 200 kg (440 lbs). They get to that size by eating almost anything, from grasses, roots and berries to freshly killed meat and carrion – but they especially like to eat spawning salmon. Despite the animal's name, the colour of their long fur ranges from deep black to light blonde.

There are both spring and fall hunting seasons for bear. In spring, the right habitat is just about anywhere that there is new green growth. Logged openings, recent wildfires and utility corridors are good areas to start in. The south-facing slopes of major river valleys green up quickly and are a prime choice for hunting bear in the early season. By fall, bear are working hard to fatten up for winter hibernation and can be found anywhere that there is an abundance of food. Good places to start a fall bear hunt are wild berry patches or along streams, particularly those with spawning salmon.

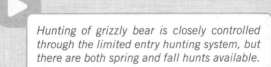

Wildlife Management Units 5–2 and 5–13 are the most productive areas for bear hunters in the Cariboo Region.

Bighorn Sheep

Home to California bighorn, the Cariboo Region has an open season for full curl rams in Wildlife Management Unit 5–2, and part of 5–4. Bighorn sheep are medium-sized ungulates, with a stocky body that in adult males (rams) may weigh 100 kg (220 lbs); females (ewes) reach weights of 60–75 kg (130–165 lbs), depending on the sub-species. Both sexes of both sub-species sport a brown coat, a white belly and muzzle, and a large, conspicuous white rump patch.

Bighorn are so named for good reason. The horns of both sexes start as outgrowths of the frontal bone of the skull above the eye socket, then curve up and gently back as the animal grows. A ram's horns are much larger and longer than those of a ewe, sweeping back, down and forward so that by age five, they may make a full curl. Often the horn tips are broken off or "broomed" back, so that the horns of a trophy ram can be much shorter than full curl. Ewe's horns look similar to those of a very young ram, being up to 30 cm (12 inches) long, and curving slightly back.

Bighorn are primarily grazing animals and so are found in the grasslands and open forest habitat of the southern parts of this region – particularly along the Fraser River. They are challenging to hunt, and good optics (binoculars and spotting scope) will help to find game. Bighorn have excellent eyesight and live in open country, so a hunter must take advantage of optics and stalk carefully.

Caribou

Caribou are a moderately large, deer-like ungulate found in two widely separated mountainous areas in the Cariboo Region. Bulls weigh about 250 kg (550 lbs) and cows about 150 kg (330 lbs). You will recognize these hearty, medium-sized members of the deer family by their curved antlers. Unlike most other species of deer, both the males and the females carry them. In profile, the main beam of caribou antlers resembles a forward-facing "C" with small palms and clusters of points at either end. Caribou are covered with brown to grey hair, with a lighter coloured mane that is more pronounced on the bull.

In the Cariboo Region, caribou are found east in the Cariboo Mountains and in the Itcha and Ilgachuz Mountain areas of the western Chilcotin. Currently, only the western area (WMU 5–12) is open for caribou hunting under a general season for 5-point bulls.

Cougar

British Columbia is home to one of the largest subspecies of cougar in North America. Also known as the mountain lion, the cougar is the largest wildcat found on the continent (the title of heaviest, however, goes to the jaguar). Adult males range from 60 to 70 kg (130 to 160 lbs) and females from 40 to 50 kg (90 to 110 lbs). From nose to tip of tail, a large cougar can reach 3 metres (10 ft) in length. Its long tail comprises a third of that total. The adult cougar typically appears a tan yellow in colour, although its fur graduates from a reddish-brown to grey, with a light belly, chin and throat. These wildcats have short black ears and a long, rounded, black-tipped tail.

People rarely spot cougars as they are very secretive animals. They hunt at night and rarely stray from the cover of dense trees. Cougars are predators, and they feed primarily on deer. Often they will hunt other large game animals, as well as rodents, hares and birds. Rarely will they attack humans. Conflicts usually happen in late spring and summer, when young cougars begin searching for their own territory. Attacks during hunting season are even rarer.

These wildcats are more abundant in the southern regions where deer – typically mule deer – are found. Hunters will have luck in Wildlife Management Units 3–17, 3–29 and 3–31.

Grizzly Bear

This animal is a big predator. Males weigh as much as 450 kg (990 lbs), with females about two-thirds that size. Grizzly bear fur is usually brown, but can vary from tan to black. The white tips of individual hairs give the "grizzly" appearance. Most of these bear have a pronounced hump on their shoulders, one of the features distinguishing them from black bear.

These large and powerful animals prey on almost any other animal in the bush, from moose to ground squirrels. They are omnivorous, however, and most of their diet consists of vegetation and berries. In the fall they feed on spawning salmon, making the coastal Wildlife Management Units a bountiful spot for hunters.

Hunting of grizzly bear is closely controlled through the limited entry hunting system, but there are both spring and fall hunts available.

Grouse

Grouse are a popular game bird in BC. On a still autumn morning, while sneaking through the forest watching and listening for the slightest hint of movement, you can nearly step on one of these birds before they take off in a chaotic explosion of feathers. Once in the air, grouse fly quickly and randomly, making them difficult to hit.

Grouse inhabit dense young forest or transition zones near the edges of streams. Because they often reside in thick brush, flushing and shooting prove difficult. The four game species of BC grouse are: ruffed, spruce, sharp-tailed and blue. You can spot ruffed grouse by the ruff of black features around their neck. They are about 43 cm (17 inches) long. The smaller spruce grouse, at 38 cm (15 inches) long, appears a mottled grey, brown and black with a red patch under its eye. The sharp-tailed resembles a larger spruce – however, spruce grouse fly a short distance and hide in the trees when flushed, while sharp-tailed grouse will flee farther. Contrary to its name, the blue grouse is actually a slate grey colour with a solid black tail. At 53 cm (21 inches) long, it is the largest of the four subspecies.

Ruffed grouse inhabit the expanse of BC, from sea level to alpine. They prefer lower elevations and brushy areas in the moist forests of major river valleys and in forests of mixed conifers and aspens. They can often be found in forest areas disturbed by fire, logging or petroleum exploration. Spruce grouse, true to their name, inhabit spruce forests across central BC east of the Coast Range. They typically live in coniferous forests where they eat conifer needles and buds. The sharp-tailed subspecies is widely distributed in western

Canada, except in south central BC. You will typically encounter these birds in grasslands, prairies, clear cuts and burned forest, as they prefer open country. Look for blue grouse in open, dry Douglas fir forests or in old logging blocks when hunting earlier in the season; in the late fall, follow them into the higher elevation spruce, balsam and pine forests.

Currently, all moose hunting in the Cariboo Region is controlled by limited entry hunting, and there is no general open season. However, there is a large number of LEH authorizations available, often separated into two or three week time periods to reduce the concentration of hunting pressure.

Moose

The largest member of the deer family and the largest ungulate in North America, moose top the list of most prized animals to hunt in BC. A full-sized moose can stand at 2.75 metres (9.25 ft) tall. Because of their size they have few predators, although wolves sometimes attack young or weakened moose. Moose look quite distinct with their long legs, large, drooping snouts, and bell-shaped flap of skin under their throat. These dark brown to black animals have broad hooves. The males sport large, broad antlers, highly prized among hunters.

The highest harvest of moose in the Cariboo Region comes from Wildlife Management Units 5–2 and 5–13, but these animals can be found in pretty much any management unit east of the Coast Mountains. Early in the hunting season, look for moose near lakes and swamps. However, as summer wanes and the weather cools, moose can be found in forest openings such as those created by logging and forest fires. Lucky hunters may encounter a moose just by driving on logging roads, but other hunters increase their odds by using cow or bull calls, which can be especially effective during the rut (mid-October).

Management Units 5–2, 5–13 and 5–14 are particularly productive for mule deer. When hunting these deer, hunters should be walking or driving slowly and constantly glass with binoculars any openings on the hillsides, particularly at dawn and dusk and during the rut in November.

Mountain Goat

In the Cariboo Region, mountain goat are found in parts of the Coast Range, the south Chilcotin and in the Cariboo Mountains. Despite its name, this muscular, plodding beast is not really a goat. Due to its white pelage that blends with the snow, and its extreme habitat, often halfway up sheer mountain slopes, the mountain goat is one of the least observed and least hunted animals in the province. With a massive front end and a compact rear, the sure-footed mountain goat is built for rocky terrain. Billies weigh between 70 and 120 kg (150 and 250 lbs), and nannies from 55 to 75 kg (120 to 160 lbs).

This species' success is attributable to its ability to digest a wide variety of plants, to tolerate deep snow for short periods and to live on steep and rocky slopes where there are few predators and little competition for food.

Mule Deer and Coastal Black-tailed Deer

Deer in British Columbia are either white-tailed or black-tailed. The two sub-species are related, but carry differences in appearance, habitat and habits. Hybrids of the two can occur where their ranges overlap, such as east of the Bella Coola Valley. When hunting mule and black-tailed deer, hunters should constantly glass the hillsides with binoculars.

Mule Deer take their name from their large, mule-like ears. They have a grey/brown coat and a light cream-coloured rump patch with a narrow, black-tipped tail. Bucks weigh about 100 kg (220 lbs), with does about two-thirds that weight. These deer have excellent senses of smell, sight and hearing, but they are curious creatures that will stop even when fleeing to take one last look. When startled, they will "strot" away, bounding forward with all four feet. Mules prefer mixed-wood forests, hilly areas and the edges of coniferous forests. They inhabit open country like the alpine and burned forest areas. You will find them scattered throughout the region east of the Coast Mountains, with the numbers peaking in the dry forests and grassland near the Fraser River.

The black-tailed deer has no rump patch, but a wide, black tail. This smaller subspecies weighs around 90 kg (200 lbs), with some females as small as 40 kg (90 lbs). What they lack in size, however, they make up for in cunning. These deer can be elusive as they navigate the farmland of the Fraser Valley and get lost in the underbrush of the coastal mountains. Black-tailed deer, when startled, will sneak away into heavy cover. In the Cariboo Region, limited access in the black-tailed deer range means a relatively small harvest from the coastal WMUs.

Be sure to check the BC Hunting Regulations (www.env.gov.bc.ca/fw/wildlife/hunting/regulations) for updated rules and regulations regarding bag limits and season opening and closing dates.

Wolf

The range of wolves in BC includes virtually all of the Cariboo Region. They look like large grey or black German shepherd dogs, with long legs and an oversized head. They prey on pretty much any animal in the forest and often hunt in packs of four to eight, generally following the distribution of key prey such as deer and moose. Adult wolves weigh 35–40 kg (75–85 lbs), but can eat almost a quarter of that weight in one feeding. In the Cariboo Region, most wolves are killed by hunters in the management units with strong game numbers, such as 5–2, 5–13, 5–14. Although not a popular species to hunt, wolves have a generous hunting season, closed only for a couple of months in the summer during pup season. Most hunters take wolves incidentally during a deer or moose hunt, but some specifically hunt these animals in the winter.

Wildlife Management Unit Highlights

WMU 5–1
This is a small management unit that includes the rolling forest land east of 100 Mile House and south of Canim Lake. It is characterized by Douglas fir forests and many lakes. It is a good choice for hunters because access is easy and camping opportunities are numerous. Mule deer are the most commonly sought big game animal, but there are decent numbers of moose and black bear taken every year. This is one of the few areas in the Cariboo Region where you can hunt white-tailed deer. This WMU is also a good choice for upland bird hunters, with respectable numbers of spruce, blue and ruffed grouse taken each year.

WMU 5–2
This is a huge management unit covering the Cariboo Plateau, east of the Fraser River, and includes the major population centres of Williams Lake and Quesnel. There are some upland areas in the south and east, but this WMU is primarily rolling forest of Douglas fir, lodgepole pine and aspen, interspersed with grasslands and many lakes and meadows. Access is plentiful and combined with the highest density of people in the region; it is not surprising that this WMU also has the highest harvest of most of the Cariboo game animals and game birds. Actually, just under half of the mule deer and moose taken in the entire region come from this WMU alone, and it also supports the highest harvest of Cariboo Region black bear. Upland bird hunting can be spectacular, with ruffed grouse being particularly bountiful. Sharp-tailed grouse also are found in this area and provide relatively productive hunting as well.

WMU 5–3
A relatively dry climate dominates a variety of ecosystems in this management unit, from the grasslands along the Fraser River to the Camels Foot Mountain Range. Typical forests are Douglas fir on the lower elevations that change to lodgepole pine and Engelmann spruce with increasing elevation. This is not a bad choice for a mule deer hunt and there are modest numbers of moose and black bear taken by hunters each season. There is limited upland bird hunting, with a decent harvest of blue grouse.

WMU 5–4
About two thirds of this management unit are Chilcotin Plateau while the southern third is very mountainous, occasionally topped by glaciers. Forest types are equally varied, from Douglas fir and pine on the gentle land to pine, Engelmann spruce and sub-alpine fir on the mountain slopes and treeless alpine at the highest elevation. Much of the high land is contained in parks, and hunting success is limited. The lower elevations have some mule deer, the eastern fringe produces some moose and the mountains give up a few mountain goat.

WMU 5–5
There is a small area of Chilcotin Plateau country north and east of Tatlyoko Lake, but otherwise this is a very rugged and mountainous management unit. The scenery is spectacular, but access is limited. Regardless, there is a fair harvest of mule deer by dedicated hunters, and a few mountain goat are taken each year. This WMU offers limited interest for other species.

WMU 5–6
This management unit is dominated by the high, rugged, snow-covered Coast Mountains with a piece of Chilcotin Plateau in the northeast. Access is difficult and game numbers relatively low, but determined hunters take a small number of mule deer and moose from this area.

WMU 5–7, 5–8, 5–9
Wet coastal forests and wet, cold Coast Mountains do not provide the kind of habitats favourable to most game species. Adding to this, access in these management units can be challenging because of the mountains and the long inlets of the ocean. However, grizzly bear are attracted to the river valleys for the spawning salmon runs, and these WMUs are the best choice in the region for hunting this big predator.

WMU 5–10, 5–11
These two management units make up the spectacular mountain scenery of Tweedsmuir Provincial Park, but much of the park is closed to hunting. The areas open to hunters produce a small number of moose and mule deer, but the limited access and mountainous terrain otherwise limit the interest of this area to hunters.

WMU 5–12
The Chilcotin Plateau, with its forests of lodgepole pine and spruce, surrounds the isolated Itcha and Ilgachuz Mountains in this management unit. The climate is mostly cool and dry in the rainshadow of the Coast Mountains. Hunting for moose, mule deer, black bear and grouse produces fair, but not spectacular results. However, this management unit is notable because it is the only area in the Cariboo Region for hunting woodland caribou. The current season is a general open season for 5-point bulls.

WMU 5–13
In this management unit, the land gradually increases in elevation from the eastern lowlands along the Fraser River near Quesnel to the uplands of the Fraser Plateau. Logging access is plentiful throughout the lodgepole pine and white spruce forests, and moose habitat is widespread in the logged openings and wet meadows. This WMU is an excellent choice for a moose or black bear hunt and a good choice for mule deer hunters as well. For upland game birds, like ruffed and spruce grouse, this area is second only to WMU 5–2 in terms of hunter harvest in the region.

WMU 5–14
For hunters, this is a relatively small but productive management unit west of the Fraser River near Williams Lake. Gentle terrain and abundant logging access make this area attractive to hunters. There is a modest harvest of moose and a small harvest of black bear from this WMU, but this is mule deer country – likely the best choice in the region for hunting this deer species. In addition, all four species of grouse reside here in decent numbers, providing good sport for bird hunters.

WMU 5–15
This management unit captures the uplands of the Quesnel Highlands and the western edge of the Cariboo Mountains. It is within the interior wet belt and supports forests of spruce, hemlock and cedar, similar to coastal rainforest, but much more productive for game animals. Logging has opened the access, and the new logging blocks provide very good moose habitat. Hunters also take decent numbers of mule deer and black bear here. In addition, this is the most productive area in the Cariboo for mountain goat hunting. Upland bird hunters can do well in this WMU, hunting for spruce, ruffed and blue grouse.

WMU 5–16
This area covers Bowron Lakes Provincial Park and there is no open hunting season in the park.

Surrounding Regions

WMUs 3–17, 3–28, 3–29, 3–30, 3–31, 3–32, 3–33
Region 3 spans a diverse range of habitats, with good opportunities for mule deer across all management units. Bighorn sheep appear in WMUs 3-17, 3-29, 3-31, 3-32 and 3-33 (the latter two through limited entry), and there are high harvests of black bear in WMUs 3-17, 3-28, 3-29 and 3-31. Bird hunters will find a variety of game in the dry grasslands and forests of WMU 3-29 and in the slopes of WMUs 3-30, 3-32 and 3-33. For moose, try WMUs 3-28 and 3-30. Cougar can be pursued in WMUs 3-17, 3-29 and 3-31.

WMUs 6–1, 6–2, 6–4
The geography of this area is relatively gentle, and the climate is relatively dry. Large lakes fill many valley bottoms, and the uplands support forests of lodgepole pine and spruce. Moose range is widespread, and WMUs 6–1 and 6–4 are the hunter's best bets for this species. Mule deer and black bear can be found in good numbers in WMU 6–4, and upland bird hunters take ruffed grouse and spruce grouse here as well.

WMUs 7–4, 7–5, 7–6, 7–7, 7–8, 7–9, 7–10, 7–11, 7–12
This area contains a variety of forest types, including cedar, hemlock, spruce, fir, lodgepole pine, cottonwood and aspen. The region is prime territory for moose, as well as mule deer and black bear – especially in WMU 7-7. Bird hunters will discover ruffed grouse across all management units, with spruce grouse appearing in WMUs 7-11 and 7-12. These two WMUs also boast opportunities for wolf hunting. For elk, white-tailed deer and grizzly bear, try WMUs 7-4, 7-5, 7-6 and 7-7. Please respect private land, most notably in WMUs 7-8, 7-9 and 7-10.

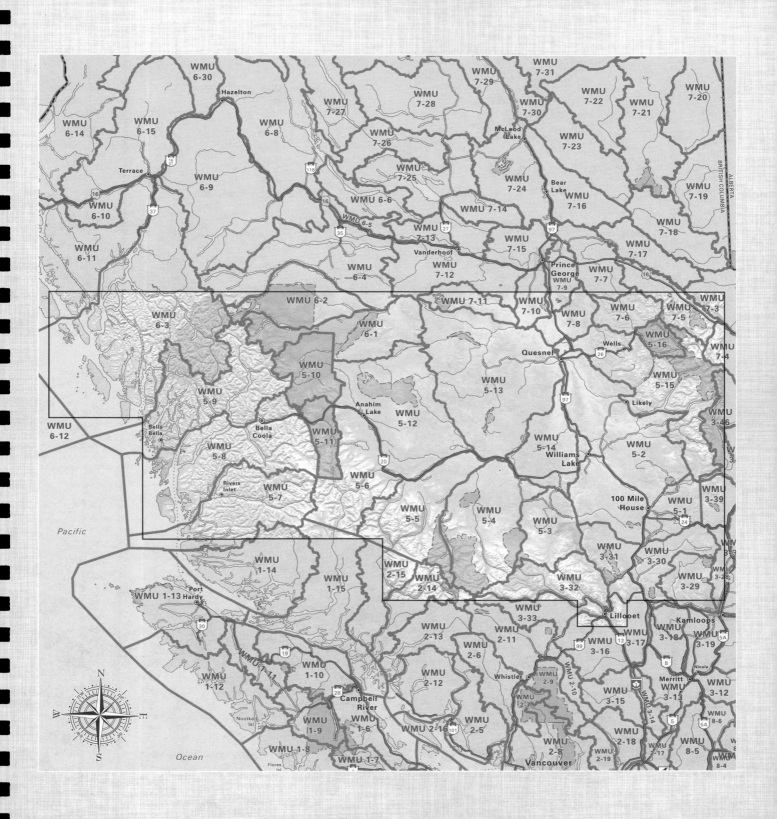

Paddling
Adventures

Alexander Mackenzie came to the Bella Coola area in 1793, making his way primarily by water across the country. Simon Fraser followed the river that bears his name in 1808. Even before the early explorers, the First Nations people used the rivers of the Cariboo Chilcotin Coast as their highways.

Today, paddlers can retrace many of these river routes or choose from a virtually endless array of options. From the world-famous Bowron Lakes, to the lesser known but even more inspiring Hakai Conservancy, there are endless paddling adventures waiting to be discovered. Even if you are only out for the day, there are many fine lakes and streams to dip a paddle into in this part of BC.

Flatwater or lake paddling enthusiasts have literally thousands of lakes to choose from. We have limited our descriptions to canoe routes and multi-day destinations. This region of BC offers numerous fantastic routes, including the popular Bowron Lakes and the exhilarating Turner Lakes Chain. For smaller and more easily accessed lakes, check out the Parks and Recreation Sites section of this book.

Since this book covers the mid-coast region of BC, we have added an ocean paddling section. The Cariboo Chilcotin is an area of steep, narrow fjords, rocky islands and dense forest. Although this creates stunning scenery, it also makes for risky kayaking since there are few landing spots. There are exceptions, however, including the Hakai Conservancy — which has become one of the province's great kayaking destinations, with its protected beaches and amazing scenery.

Cariboo Chilcotin Coast rivers offer a bit of everything. From easy floats to hair-raising descents, the variety is thrilling. If you are a serious whitewater paddler, the rivers are at their best in the late spring run-off. The summer sees lower water levels and is therefore a good time to fine-tune your skills on bigger rivers or leisurely paddle those small, low-flow streams.

On the following pages, we list a few of the best-known areas for all three types of paddling opportunities. Please note that the descriptions given are limited, and may not contain enough detail for you to navigate certain routes safely — especially those rivers with higher gradings. We recommend that you check current conditions with local canoeists/kayakers or outdoor stores before heading out. Some local clubs include Northwest Brigade Paddling Club (paddlepg.blogspot.com) and Quesnel Paddlers (quesnelpaddlers.com). Lastly, it is always essential to scout rivers, since conditions can change daily.

Paddling Adventures

Lake Paddling

Bowron Lakes Canoe Routes (Map 58/B5–59/A7)

The Bowron Lakes are one of the best wilderness canoeing destinations in all of North America. With a fantastic mix of river and lake paddling amongst the towering Cariboo Mountains, there is plenty to see and do. There are two main paddling routes available. The Full Circuit route encompasses the entire 108 kilometre loop, while the West Side Route includes only the lakes along the western part of the park. The canoe circuit is open from May 15th to September 30th. The campsites and portages are well-maintained and marked. Bears are common in the area and food caches are available at all campsites. A canoe cart is recommended for the long portages.

Bowron Lake itself allows motor boats, so be prepared for this as you start out. As trippers head along the Cariboo River, extra attention needs to be paid as sweepers, deadheads and other natural hazards will present themselves. There is no cell phone service around the entire route but the park has placed six two-way radios at strategic locations for emergency use only. Note also that paddlers should leave their four legged friends at home, as dogs are not allowed on the canoe circuit.

Reservations are recommended as only a limited number of paddlers are allowed each day. If you do not plan to make reservations or want to avoid the crowds on the route, mid-week or off-season (May, June and September) departures are recommended. The registration centre for the park is found at the end of the Bowron Lake Road near the campground. Reservations for groups of four or more canoes are mandatory. Call 1-800-435-5622 to book or find out more information.

Full Circuit

Beginning at Bowron Lake, this clockwise 108 km (67 mi) route can be done in six to eight days. From the northeast end of Bowron Lake, the circuit begins with a challenging 2,400 metre portage to Kibbee Lake. From Kibbee Lake there is another 2,000 metre portage to Indianpoint Lake. There are two camping areas on Kibbee Lake and another six as well as a cooking shelter on Indianpoint. Next is a short paddle along a creek and pond to the 1,600 metre portage to Isaac Lake. Isaac Lake is jammed between the scenic mountains of the park and spans over 38 km. To break up the long paddle, there are 21 camping areas with over 100 sites available as well as two cabins and two shelters on a first come, first served basis.

The longest portage in the park is the 2,800 metre trek that takes you from Isaac Lake to a navigable portion of the Isaac River. The next portage, found on the western shore is a 1,000 metre portage that traverses past the picturesque Isaac River Falls and to the northern end of McLeary Lake. McLeary Lake is one of the smaller lakes along the circuit and offers two camping areas with eight campsites. The circuit continues from the southern end of McLeary Lake along the Cariboo River. This portion is slow and marshy, the perfect area to spot moose or waterfowl. The river flows into the second largest lake on the route, Lanezi Lake, then onto Sandy Lake to the west. Both Lanezi and Sandy Lake offer some of the best views in the park. Lanezi Lake has six camping areas with 20 campsites and a cabin on the northeastern shore, while Sandy Lake offers three areas with about 20 campsites. From Sandy Lake, the 108 km (67 mi) circuit finishes by tracing the West Side Route back to Bowron Lake.

West Side Route

The West Side Route travels in a counter-clockwise direction starting on Bowron Lake. This route usually takes three or four days depending on your experience, conditioning and weather. There are no campsites available on Bowron Lake so give yourself enough time to paddle the lazy Bowron River to Swan Lake, which is part of the Spectacle Lakes. You will find 10 separate camping areas with over 40 campsites scattered along the shoreline of these lakes. Basic shelters are also available near the north end and southwest shore of Swan Lake. From the southern end of the Spectacle Lakes, a short 400 metre portage leads to Skoi Lake. The smaller lake connects with another short portage leading to Babcock Lake. A secluded two site camping area sits along the southern shore of the lake.

The last leg of the route begins with a 1,400 metre portage to the Cariboo River. Once in the river, it is a short paddle to Unna and Rum Lakes. (It is not possible to travel Sandy Lake due to the current along the river). Unna and the smaller Rum Lake are home to three camping areas, while a short hike from Unna Lake to the spectacular Cariboo Falls. The return trip follows the same route back to Bowron Lake.

Chilko Lake (Maps 2, 14)

Chilko Lake, located within Ts'yl-os Provincial Park, is not recommended for open canoes, but for folks in closed boats, especially touring kayaks. This is a marvelous destination. The often windy lake is much like a fjord, although it is actually well above sea level. As you paddle farther south, the mountains get bigger and more impressive. There are rustic camping spots at various creek mouths along the lake.

In June of 2014, the Supreme Court of Canada granted the Tsilhqot'in First Nation an area of aboriginal title land including the north end of Chilko Lake. If you wish to camp or kayak in the upper areas of the lake, it is recommended that you contact the Tsilhqot'in National Government for permission. You can find their contact information on their website at www.tsilhqotin.ca.

Clearwater Lake Route (Map 31/G4–G2)

The access point for this route is located in Wells Gray Park at the end of the Clearwater Valley Road. There is a registration station with a fee drop-off box at the launching site. The trip up Clearwater Lake takes about two days to cover the 21 km (13 mi) to the river mouth at the north end. There are 33 tent sites on the big lake that features forested slopes and the mountain peaks of Mount Ray and Azure Mountain.

At the Clearwater River, you can paddle about 3 km upstream to a 500 metre portage to Azure Lake. The portage is well established, but ladders make canoe carts useless. It should also be noted that during high water in June and July, the river current can be challenging. Azure Lake is 20 km (12.5 mi) long and the distance deters most people from visiting the picturesque Rainbow Falls at the eastern end of the lake (east of our maps). In all, there are 21 campsites in four separate areas available. A round trip to Rainbow Falls is around 96 km (58 mi) and will take at least four full days to complete. If you have the time, check out the Zodiak Peak or Huntley Column Trail. There is also a 15 km trail to Hobson Lake. Be sure to bring along your fishing rod and always keep your eyes open for wildlife. For more information call 604-828-4494.

Eleven Sisters Chain (Map 15/B2)

Remote and wild is the best way to describe these lakes. Other than Scum Lake, which has a recreation site, these lakes see few visitors. But the close proximity of the core lakes (Norma, Nancy, Lac LeLievre, Ruby and Roxanne) makes stringing these lakes together into a wilderness paddling route possible. There are no established portages, but the nice scenery and good fishing for small, wild rainbow should make up for the lack of development. Located approximately 90 km southwest of Williams Lake, this area was made into a provincial park by the BC Government in 2013.

Emar Lakes Canoe Route (Map 19/F6)

This is an easy route to access as it lies off the south side of Highway 24 west of Little Fort, about 2 km west of Taweel Road. There is a user-maintained campsite at the access point as well as a few rustic sites found along the western shore of the lake. This short, small lake route travels in a circle from Long Island Lake and back. The first and longest portage at 1,000 metres is located along the southeast shore of Long Island Lake and leads to Chub Lake. The route continues over five more portages and four waterbodies, including Boulder, Willowgrouse, Emar and Dytiscid Lakes. Rustic camping opportunities exist on all the waterbodies, and wildlife viewing and fishing are popular pursuits. The normal barriers like low water and fallen trees on the rustic, unmaintained portages are commonplace. The route can be done in a day, but it makes an ideal overnight trip.

Be sure to contact BC Parks at 250-371-6200 for current status as the route may be closed due to the mountain pine beetle infestation.

Flat Lake Provincial Park (Map 18/B6)

Southeast of 100 Mile House, the access to this park and canoe route can be found by taking the Davis Lake Road west off Highway 97. Signs point visitors to the second lake of the chain since Davis Lake is surrounded by private property. The quiet canoe route travels across several unnamed lakes all the way to Flat Lake in the western end of the park. From Flat Lake, the route traces itself back towards Davis Lake. A return trip covers about 20 km (12.5 mi) and can be done in two days. Although the lakes and portages are forested, a good portion of the surrounding terrain is made up of rangeland. There are rustic, unmarked campsites on each lake. The portages are easy, although they can be difficult to find due to lack of use. Fishing is limited, but for the explorer at heart there are a number of lakes that lie in the eastern portion of the park that are rarely visited and can extend the overnight trip.

Ghost Lake (Map 44/G2–45/A2)
It is a good haul by road to get to Ghost Lake, but once there, you can plan on having solitude. Leaving Likely, follow the Keithly Creek Road for 25 km and turn onto the Cariboo River Forest Service Road for another 65 km to the Ghost Main Forest Service Road. Visitors will find five campsites at the small campground and an unmarked trail that leads from the campground to the lake. There are also some wilderness campsites on the lake, which offers excellent views of the Cariboo Mountains. Other highlights include the two waterfalls, one near the entrance to the campground, and the other accessed from the campground. Cache food and be aware that there are active cougar and bear populations in the area. The lake offers great fishing for various species of salmon and trout so bring your rod and license.

Lupin Lakes Canoe Route (Map 7/F2)
This canoe route involves a six hour paddle through six small interconnecting wilderness lakes. You will be required to pack your canoe over four short portages, with the last portage being uphill. The main access to the lake system requires a portage off the Bonaparte Forest Service Road to the south near the Spruce Grove Lodge.

Moose Valley Canoe Route (Map 17/F4–18/A4)
The main access area for this route is Marks Lake, which is found in the western end of the Moose Valley Park. Look for the access road at the 1117 km mark of the Gustafsen Lake Forest Service Road (1100 Rd). The 10 to 14 km long canoe route has up to 17 portages as travels through the low-lying marshland area connecting eleven small waterbodies. Allow at least two days for this rustic route. There are established campsites on Marks, Maitland and Long Lakes, while Marks offers a shelter on its large island.

Beginning at Marks Lake the route heads east towards Long Lake crossing five waterbodies and six short portages along the way. The 400 metre portage between Kirkland Lake and the first Beaverlodge Lake is nicknamed the "Boulder Portage" for good reason. The portages between the Beaverlodge Lakes and Long Lake are passable by canoe during high water. Once you arrive at Long Lake, the route circles across Moose Lake, Grebe Lake and Canoe Lake before returning to Long Lake. It is possible to end your trip on Long Lake, as there is a trail from the south end of the lake to a short access road that branches off Dog Creek Road (the western extension of 1100 Road).

Note that fishing is not permitted in the park and when water levels are low, portages must be used as the area is home to very sensitive moss beds which will be damaged by dragging a canoe. For more information, call 250-398-4414.

Nazko Lakes Canoe Route (Map 27/A2–41/B7)
Although these lakes can be paddled in one very long day, we recommend an overnight trip to really get a feel for the area. The magic of these lakes comes when you slow down and watch the eagles circling in the air or watch the fish jump to catch insects in the evening. Lucky visitors may even be graced with a flight of giant pelicans passing overhead. The 20 km (12.5 mi) route travels through Deerpelt, Nazko, Tanikul, Nastachi, Tzazati and Tchusiniltil Lakes. The portages are short and easy and there are four designated campsites. One campsite can be found at the north end of Nazko Lake, two are on Tanikul Lake at the north and south ends, and the fourth campsite is at the south end of Tzazati Lake. Because of the delicate ecosystem, paddlers are asked to only camp at these locations. Go early in the year when the water is high. During summer a couple of the lakes are very shallow and weed choked, making passage difficult.

Nechako Reservoir Circuit (Maps 50–53)
BC Parks say don't do it, but people do anyway. These are big, windy lakes and you will have to paddle though a flooded forest with lots of snags in a very remote part of BC. But the area offers some remarkable scenery and quite frankly, poses a challenge that many avid adventurers can't pass up. Expect to take a week to make your way around the circuit.

There are a few places to launch since Knewstubb Lake, Intata Reach, Ootsa Lake and Whitesail Lake are all accessed by logging road from the north (see our Northern BC edition). There are portages joining Whitesail Lake and St Thomas Bay of Eutsuk Lake as well as linking Eutsuk Lake with Tetachuck Lake. The remote area offers endless areas to pull up on shore and camp, but please stick to the designated campsites (marked on the maps) when travelling through Tweedsmuir Park. Many people rig their canoes with sails to help pass the many miles. We aren't recommending this trip, as it is for experienced wilderness travellers only.

Quesnel Lake to Horsefly Lake (Maps 30, 31, 44, 45)
There are a number of different access points to this large lake, although the preferred access area is from the Quesnel Lake Public Landing (Map 36/E7). The public landing can be found not far off the Hen Ingram Lake Road northeast of Horsefly. From the landing, it is recommended to travel east along the shoreline of Quesnel Lake. This way the lake quickly opens into two arms, the North Arm and the East Arm. Both arms offer fine paddling opportunities with forested shorelines and spectacular views. Although there are no official campsites, you can pitch a tent almost anywhere along the shore. For the more adventurous, it is possible to link with Horsefly Lake to the south. The portage can be found in Slate Bay and traverses past the small Suey Lake. The area also affords plenty of opportunities for wildlife viewing, with black and grizzly bear, caribou, coyote and wolverine being spotted on occasion. Along the Eastern Arm of Quesnel Lake, mountain goat can also be seen on the steep cliffs.

Although traffic is relatively low, it is recommended to be aware of boat traffic on both big lakes. Afternoon winds and storms can also cause havoc for paddlers on both these lakes.

> As a general rule, smaller lakes are easier to paddle since they are not subject to the same winds that bigger lakes are. Bigger lakes, like Chilko, Quesnel and Taseko Lakes should be left to experienced paddlers, preferably in closed crafts.

Schoolhouse Lake Provincial Park (Map 18/G1)
The main access route to this park and paddling area is by following the Bradley Creek Road west of Canim Lake to the Berlichingen Creek Road. This road travels north to Dor Lake in Schoolhouse Lake Park. The undeveloped park encompasses a number of small lakes that can all be found a short distance from each other. The area is quite rustic and there are very few if any portages established between lakes. With a compass and good navigational skills, adventurous canoeists could have a fantastic time exploring lakes that are rarely visited.

Turner Lake Canoe Route (Map 23/G3–F4)
One of the most celebrated lake circuits in the province, this superlative-laden trip is nearly impossible to oversell. The trip is second in popularity only to the Bowron Lakes and only because access to this circuit is limited by a 16.4 km portage along the Hunlen Falls Trail from the parking lot or by flying in. For those not interested in carrying a canoe that far, there are rentals available at Turner Lake. The lakes are located in the high mountains of Tweedsmuir Park and cut through virgin forest set beneath towering, snow-capped peaks. There are beautiful white sand beaches, backcountry campsites and very good fishing along the way. The route begins at Turner Lake and travels through Cutthroat, Vista, Junker, Widgeon and Kidney Lakes. Portages between the lakes are short, well-marked and supplied with canoe rests. Those feeling energetic at this point can also hike to Sunshine Lake.

Note that winds can be strong at times, especially on Junker, Widgeon and Kidney Lakes, as they are channelled through the mountains. Also, lining canoes is not allowed as it disturbs the gravel creek bed that is important habitat for spawning fish.

Tuwut Lake Canoe Route (Map 7/E3)
While it is possible to cram all ten (or more, depending on your route) lakes of this circuit into one day, most people spread their enjoyment out over two or three days. This is not a developed paddle, and access to Tuwut Lake is through an old clearcut off the Windy Lake Road. The carry down to the lake will take about twenty minutes and is by far the most difficult portage of the entire journey. There is no established circuit, although there are well-beaten animal/angler trails between the lakes. The close proximity of lakes makes it possible to shorten or lengthen the trip.

Paddling Adventures

River Paddling

Baezaeko River (Map 40/F1–55/A6)

From the put-in near Coglistiko Lake to where it joins the Blackwater, the Baezaeko is a fast-moving, low flow river with lots of rocks and corners. Do not take a boat that you love, as you will probably hit lots of rocks on your way down. The river is probably a Grade II+, but is more exciting in higher water levels that occur just after spring run-off. The river banks are prone to erosion and large trees frequently fall into the water, creating dangerous hazards; even if you are familiar with the river, keep an eye out ahead. It is about 45 km (28 mi) to the take-out at the bridge on the Nazko Road. Allow about 10 hours to complete this section.

Baker Creek (Map 41/G2–42/E1)

Extreme kayakers in the central interior stick to a short section of Baker Creek that features a 2 metre high waterfall and a pair of rapids, rated Class IV and Class V. But there are 55 km (34 mi) of much milder, Grade II water featuring some Class III sections on the creek. The big rapids come at the 15 km (9 mi) mark below the put-in at the bridge over Baker on Tibbles Road. To access this section, drive 30 km along the Nazko Road from Highway 97 and watch for the gravel pit on your left. Portage trails developed by folks running this section can also be used to portage around the rapids. Below these rapids, the river continues on to its confluence with the Fraser. The take-out is in Quesnel, behind the West Park Mall.

> We use a modified version of the international scale to grade rivers. The Grade of a run tells you how difficult a particular stretch of river is overall. Class rates individual rapids, chutes and other features. For example, a run might be rated Grade II overall, but one section might feature a Class IV drop.

Bella Coola River – East (Map 23/A1–C1)

The 70 km Bella Coola River is a beautiful, rarely paddled river west of Tweedsmuir Park. The river has enough features to keep paddlers on their toes, while still giving them lots of time to enjoy the stunning scenery. The river can be divided into eastern and western sections. To access the eastern end of the Bella Coola River, use the old Steep Roof Launch just south of Highway 20 as the highway exits the west end of Tweedsmuir Park. This section of the Bella Coola River takes paddlers on a mostly easy, three hour paddle from the boat launch to the bridge. This trip is mostly Grade I/II paddling, but the river is big and should not be underestimated. Only confident river paddlers should attempt to run this section in a canoe. While there are few rapids here, paddlers need to keep their eyes open for sweepers, log jams and other hazards, including plenty of grizzly bear – especially during salmon season. A good location for taking your boat out of the water is where the Highway 20 Bridge crosses over the river.

Note due to winter flood damage, the Steep Roof Boat Launch may be closed.

Bella Coola River – West (Map 22/E1–23/A1)

You can continue on your route from the eastern point or simply start here at the Highway 20 Bridge. Like the eastern section of the Bella Coola, this section is mostly Grade I/II, with the occasional sweeper and log jam to keep paddlers on their toes. Paddling in the early morning is not recommended, as this is when the grizzly bear are most active around the river. This section of river passes through the mid to lower section of the Bella Coola Valley and is known more for its stunning scenery than for its exciting paddling. There are, however, a couple of standing waves that play boaters will find to be a nice diversion from an otherwise easy paddle. The river is big and pushy and should only be paddled by those with river experience, especially in a canoe. The route ends at the Bailey Bridge Campsite, just north of Highway 20.

Blackwater River [West Road River] – West (Map 38/D1–55/A6)

The Blackwater River originates northwest of Quesnel in the Ilgachuz Range and carves its way through black volcanic rock. Also known as the West Road, this river was the main route west for fur traders in the 1800s. In late summer and fall, the river runs low and you may need to get out and line through shallow sections, but one of the nicest times to go is after the leaves change in the fall. There are very few alternate take-outs on the river, so travellers need to be self-sufficient. The river features a series of rapids and canyons, dropping 900 metres (2,950 ft) over its 280 km (175 mi) length and ending at the confluence of the Fraser River.

Access to western section of the river is via a long (very long) carry-in along the Alexander Mackenzie Trail, or by floatplane. Do yourself a favour: choose the latter. From Eliguk Lake, follow Ulgako Creek to its junction with the Blackwater. You will probably have to carry for this first 2 km section. Below the junction, the Blackwater is little more than a creek, with narrow rapids, logjams and sweepers, as well as waterfalls interspersed with some sections that can actually be paddled. The river flows into Tsasha Lake, then out again, through a portagable canyon and over the 4 metre (13 ft) high Kusyuko Falls (2.5 km upstream of Euchinko Lakes). Below Euchinko, the river moves quickly (Grade II), but keep your eyes out for Chinee Falls below Kluskoil Lake. Past the falls, the river continues to a good take-out area at the Nazko Bridge and the West Road River Recreation Site.

Blackwater River [West Road River] – Nazko Section (Map 55/A6–B5)

The Nazko Section of the Blackwater begins at the Nazko Bridge. It is one of the easiest sections of the river, with small riffles followed by shallow pools. This is a great paddle for beginners! For the true beginner, take-out at Gilles Crossing, which can be accessed by paddling a short way up the Euchinko (which enters river left). As the river begins to pass through rapids in the last 1.5 km to the Batnuni Bridge, the section becomes very difficult. It includes a Class III+ canyon that is very difficult to scout, let alone portage. This section is recommended only for expert paddlers with properly equipped canoes or kayaks. After this section, a good area to take-out is the Batnuni Bridge.

Blackwater River [West Road River] – Canyon Section (Map 55/B5–E4)

The Canyon Section begins from the Batnuni Bridge. The river is a mix of easy Class I sections with a fair number of Class III or higher features to keep you on your toes. Kayakers might find the long sections of flatwater boring. Conversely, inexperienced paddlers hoping they can get around the rapids will find themselves in trouble quite quickly. For the experienced open canoeist, this is a great section. Remember to scout all rapids! One of the most interesting sections is the second canyon, where the river narrows to a mere four feet of calm water. At high water levels, this section becomes a lot harder and should only be attempted by experienced paddlers. A good point to stop is at the Blackwater Road Bridge.

> Ranging from wild whitewater to gentle floats, this vast area of BC provides a lot of variety for river paddlers.

Blackwater River [West Road River] – East (Map 55/E4–56/A4)

The East Section of the Blackwater begins from the Blackwater Road Bridge and heads east to the Fraser River. This section of the Blackwater is Class II and III+, with a variety of Grade III and higher features. It is one of the best open craft paddles in the area, but experienced kayakers can find some good play area with steep walls, headwalls and ledges. There are some lengthy mild stretches between these rapids. As with the previous sections, there are a number of difficult technical sections that are nearly impossible to portage around, and inexperienced or ill-equipped paddlers will find themselves in trouble quite quickly. There are a lot of things to keep your eyes open for: fast rapids, plenty of boulders, standing waves, holes and ledges. Fortunately, there are a lot of eddies, too. The take-out is reached by paddling up the Fraser River for 2 km to an old logging landing. At last report, the current is a lot easier to paddle against on river left (across the river).

Bowron River (Map 58/B5–57/F1)

To canoe from Bowron Lake all the way to the Fraser River north of Highway 16 (and our maps) can take anywhere from seven to 12 days. However, covering 175 km (109 mi), this would require a very long shuttle. Although in the Cariboo region the river is rarely travelled, it would be regarded as a Grade II type river with several leisurely sections. As with most rivers in BC, the Bowron can be very dangerous during the spring and early summer runoff. Advanced scouting is essential, as various obstacles may need to be portaged around. The first section of the river, from the outflow from Bowron Lake to the Beaver Road Bridge (north of these maps), is a fairly easy Grade I/II paddle, with several take-out locations along the road found river right. Watch out for private property alongside the river, log jams in it and, in the fall, grizzly bears. The main take-out for this route is at the bridge on Highway 16. Between this bridge and Beaver Road Bridge (24 km/7 hours) is mostly Grade II water with one Grade II canyon that can be very pushy in high water. This canyon can be portaged around.

Cariboo River – North (Map 58/D7–44/E1)

The Cariboo River links Bowron Lake Provincial Park with Cariboo Lake, providing paddlers with two distinct sections to explore. If you plan to travel the Bowron Lake Park stretch of the Cariboo River, you must first travel across five lakes in the south part of the park to Unna Lake along the Bowron Lakes West Side Route. This section of the Cariboo River is a challenging, remote route that is only suitable for advanced paddlers. Although most of the route is only Grade II-III, there are a few areas that are rated as high as Grade IV, especially in higher water levels. The Cariboo Falls, an impressive 24 metre (79 ft) cascade, is an obstacle that must be portaged around regardless of your skill. After the falls, be sure to take-out before the Matthew River junction where the logging road crosses the river. You do not want to miss the take-out since there is a dangerous 5 km long gorge just past the Matthew River estuary.

Cariboo River – South (Map 44/D2–C4)

Beginning at Kimball Lake, the Cariboo River continues south towards Cariboo Lake, covering just over 20 km (12.5 mi). Two days are recommended for the trip. Much of this portion of the river is regarded as Grade I or II, as it winds its way south through a lush wetland region. Chances of spotting a moose as well as the abundant waterfowl are quite good, while campsites are few and far between. You can take-out at a number of areas along Cariboo Lake. The Ladies Creek Recreation Site is near the north end of the lake. It is also possible to paddle the river downstream past the lake and into the Quesnel River, and eventually Quesnel Lake. There is little information on this last section, so be sure to scout ahead.

Chilcotin River (Map 15/F1–16/G6)

The Chilcotin is one of the major tributaries of the Fraser River. The most popular section of the river is from Hanceville to Farwell Canyon Bridge, although this is a difficult take-out up the steep-walled canyon. An easier alternative is to take-out at the Durell Ranch, if you can get permission from the owners. The Chilcotin is mostly Grade I, with a pair of canyons and rapids up to Class III (Big Creek Rapid). The trip from Hanceville to Big Creek can take up to eight hours to complete. The route starts in an open valley, drops into a canyon and rapids, and then travels along a flat section before hitting the Grade III rapids just past Big Creek.

A much less-tested route is to continue on past the Chilcotin/Fraser Confluence and take-out at the Gang Ranch Bridge, which is a multi-day trip through very remote country. If you get into trouble, there is little chance of outside help. Big John Canyon, just above the Fraser Confluence, is one of the most difficult sections of the trip, and is rated Class III+ or higher. The Fraser section is mostly flatwater, but it is a big river and should not be underestimated.

Chilko River – Chilko Lake to Henry's Crossing (Map 14/B5–C3)

The Chilko River is 75 km (47 mi) in length flowing northeast out of Chilko Lake to the Chilcotin River. The section starting at Chilko Lake makes a great rafting and kayaking trip before entering the Chilcotin River at Bull Canyon. From the put-in at Chilko Lake, an easy Grade I/II paddle offers canoes a wide, slow moving river with great views of the surrounding mountains. The river picks up speed at Henry's Crossing, which is a good place to take-out.

Chilko River – Henry's Crossing to Taseko Junction (Map 14/C3–26/G7)

The Chilko picks up steam below Henry's Crossing, as it passes into a canyon with small rapids (up to Class III) and some big standing waves. Kayakers often put in just above Bidwell Rapid and the famous White Mile, a mile-long stretch of continual Class IV rapids. A popular take-out is just after the Eagle Claw Rapid, the last major feature on the river. Alternatively, continue to the Taseko Junction Recreation Site.

Chilko River – Taseko Junction to Bull Canyon (Map 26/G7–27/C6)

From the Taseko Junction, this last section of river is rated Grade II/III+, with one hazardous spot at Siwash Bridge. The river funnels into a narrow opening between the bridge piers, which is essential to scout ahead (as wood can block the opening). Not a challenging section, but lots of little play features. A good take-out spot is at the Bull Canyon Provincial Park.

Dean River – Nimpo Lake to Boy Lake (Map 38/D7–37/E2)

The Dean River starts at Nimpo Lake, but most people start at Anahim Lake. One option is to arrange for a fly-out at Boy Lake. This section is fairly easy; in fact, the upper section can be drifted comfortably in a canoe. There are, however, a few rapids that may need to be portaged around and a couple of shallow sections that may need to be lined. Give yourself about five days to get to Boy Lake, as the river wanders across the high country into Tweedsmuir Park.

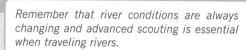

> Remember that river conditions are always changing and advanced scouting is essential when traveling rivers.

Dean River – Boy Lake to Dean Channel (Map 37/E2–36/B3)

Below Boy, the Dean begins its descent from the Chilcotin Plateau down to the ocean. This section is most famous for its world-class steelhead fishing, but it is also a classic Class V whitewater adventure through remote wilderness. Don't underestimate the difficulty of this section, as you will face many rapids, waterfalls, constricted canyons and maybe some logjams.

Dore River – South Fork (Map 59/F5–F4)

The Dore River is a wild, fast flowing river that creates some fascinating whitewater. From the first bridge along the South Dore Forest Service Road to the take-out about 4 km (2.5 mi) north along the South Dore FSR, the South Fork of the Dore River is a fast, glacial-fed run that is Grade IV-V depending on water levels. There are plenty of Class III-V rapids throughout the run, suitable only for expert paddlers. With everything from large outcrops to narrow channels and hidden logs or sweepers, this river run is not for the faint of heart. The most treacherous of all the rapids is known as the Sucker Punch, which is found near the end of the run. There really is no sign of the take-out. You should scout the entire run before you decide on your take-out area. There are a number of tricky Class V rapids further down the river that most recreational paddlers should not run. Wherever you decide to take-out, be sure to mark the area well.

Dore River – West Fork (Map 59/F4)

Linking the second or third bridge on the Dore River Forest Service Road with the take-out on Highway 16, the West Fork of the Dore River is regarded as a Grade IV-V whitewater run depending on the water level. From the get-go, the river rarely gives you a chance to catch your breath as it winds through sharp channels and over countless boulders. Around the second access point at the second bridge, the Dore River is much tamer, ranging from Grade II to Grade III in high water. The last section of the run stretches through a narrow canyon and ends with a spectacular Class V-VI cascade. Before the canyon, ensure you do not miss the take-out, which can be challenging to get to due to the flow of the water approaching it. Needless to say, anyone attempting this run should be an experienced paddler that has scouted the river for dangerous log jams. This action-packed, 6 km (3.8 mi) trip takes about two hours to complete.

Entiako River/Fawnie Creek (Map 52/G6–53/B1)

This is a wilderness route that passes through a number of lakes, many of them sporting lodges. The best time to go is just after spring runoff, as the water levels get too low in summer. Upstream of Fawnie Creek, the river is little more than a trickle, which is fine since the creek is also the farthest road-accessible point in the area. Fawnie can be a rough ride; it's not difficult, just shallow. If you treasure the bottom of your boat, you might want to line. More adventurous paddlers can put-in at the bridge over Matthews Creek and ride this constantly moving, rocky stream. The take-out is at Kenney Dam and requires a 30 km (18 mi) paddle along the often windy, snag-riddled Nechako Reservoir. (The wind is usually a tail wind; set up a sail and coast home.) The route is rated at Grade I/II. Watch for sweepers around some of the corners.

Fraser River – Quesnel to Highway 20 (Map 42/E1–28/G7)

The Fraser is a big river, with more sections and more features than can be accurately described. It ranges from a slow, meandering behemoth to a thundering man-killer. The Fraser from Quesnel to the take-out at Highway 20 offers a fast, mostly flatwater route. However, there are few access points; and the sheer volume of water should not be underestimated, especially in spring. This section of the river is best left to the fall, when the water levels are lower and the current isn't quite so pushy.

Fraser River – Highway 20 to Dog Creek Road (Map 28/G7–16/G6)

From below Highway 20 to Dog Creek Road, the mighty Fraser River enters some dynamic canyons and rapids that need to be scouted and should only be run by the experienced kayaker. The Dog Creek Road put-in marks the beginning of a popular commercial rafting area. If you want to sample this river, we recommend going with a rafting company. Take-out at the Dog Creek Road.

Goat and Milk River (Map 59/B3)

Both rivers lie in a picturesque valley nestled between high mountains and wilderness terrain. They are glacier-fed streams that provide a good challenge for intermediate paddlers, with a few sections that should only be run by experts. The Goat River Forest Service Road travels parallel to the rivers and provides good access to help scout the river or even emergency take-out points if needed. From the put-in at the first bridge crossing of the Milk River on Goat River Forest Service Road, the Milk River run ranges from Grade II to III whitewater runs, depending on water levels. Along the route, you will experience a variety of rock gardens and small ledges, coupled with a few tricky corners. However, it should be noted that there is a Class IV-V drop along the river found about halfway along the route. Unless you are an expert paddler, this rapid should be avoided. The take-out is at the confluence of the Goat and Milk Rivers.

Goat River Canyon (Map 59/B3–C2)

Starting at the confluence of the Goat and Milk Rivers, paddlers should be prepared for a challenging canyon section. During low water levels, the Goat River run is a Grade II-III river, but in higher water the river can get as challenging as a Grade IV. The majority of the rapids along the route are Class II-III. However, there is a constricted canyon that even at low water is a Class IV run; when the water is high, the canyon is a difficult Class V. There are also some other challenging rapids that should not be underestimated. The take-out is at the Highway 16 Bridge. To get to the put-in, from the take-out, drive 4 km east to the top of the hill, and turn south onto a good gravel road. Drive about 13 km, and then turn right and downhill to the new forestry bridge. Put-in just downstream of the bridge.

> *Always bring dry clothing along in waterproof bags or containers – especially in spring and fall when air and water temperatures are usually cooler.*

Horsefly River (Map 30/B1)

The access area to this part of the Horsefly River is off the Mitchell Bay East Road at a site known as Rocky Bar. The short 5 km (3 mi) stretch to the main take-out at the Horsefly River Flats (formerly Squaw Flats) Recreation Site is a Grade II-III run ideal for day paddlers in kayaks. This stretch of river offers the chance to paddle through a series of fast flowing rock gardens, which are best run after the high runoff period in the late spring and early summer. Beyond the flats, the river tames and is an easy paddle to Quesnel Lake, despite the logjams that may impede travel.

McKale River (Map 59/F2)

The McKale River is a wild, glacial-fed river that flows through a narrow valley with views of the Rocky Mountains. The put-in is found about 5 km up the McKale River Road, while the take-out is found at the Mountainview Road Bridge. This challenging run is regarded as a Grade III-IV run, depending on water levels, with non-stop rapids that are sure to test your physical endurance. There are plenty of Class III-IV rapids throughout the run, with one particularly difficult Class IV-V drop about three quarters of the way along the route. If you arrive early, you may easily complete a few runs during the day.

Nazko River (Map 41/C5–55/B5)

From the 35 km bridge on Honolulu Road, it is a five hour, Grade II/III trip down the Nazko to the 13 km bridge. This section of the river is faster moving than the lower Nazko and should only be attempted by folks with some experience on moving water. Below the 13 km bridge, the Nazko is an easy (Grade I) float down to the Blackwater. Most people continue up to the Euchinko River and the Gilles Crossing take-out. These routes include the four to five hour trip from 13 km on the Honolulu Road to the Nazko Valley Lodge, the eight hour trip from the Nazko Valley Lodge to the Snaking River Bridge, and the eight hour trip from the Snaking River Bridge to Gillies Crossing. It may be possible to canoe the river from the end of the Nazko Lake Chain, but the river moves very little water and goes over a number of waterfalls that will be difficult to get around.

Quesnel River (Map 42/G2–F1)

The Quesnel River is a large river that flows northwest from Quesnel Lake to the Fraser River near the city of Quesnel. Most of the paddling takes place around the canyon west of town. Access to the put-in location is off Blue Road, which in turn is accessed off Highway 26. This road and the road along the canyon are extremely rough and should only be attempted with a high-clearance four-wheel drive vehicle.

The first 5 km (3 mi) portion of the river is a challenging stretch that takes paddlers through the canyon to the take-out further down the river. The take-out at the end of the canyon run is found on river right. The canyon has a multitude of drops, boulders and boiling eddies, and is regarded as a Grade III run with Class IV rapids in low water. In high water, the route is classed as Grade IV. Regardless of season, this route is recommended for expert paddlers only.

Some people opt to put-in below the canyon and paddle the lower section of the river, although it is a very long, rough shuttle to get here. The lower section of the river is a much gentler ride that offers some mild, rolling Grade II water that eventually tames to a leisurely Grade I paddle into Quesnel. Watch for the take-out a few metres below the trail bridge that crosses the Quesnel River just before it flows into the Fraser. It is a short walk from here back to your vehicle, parked at Ceal Tingly Park.

Taseko River (Map 3/A1–26/G7)

From Taseko Lake, the Taseko River follows a road for about a third of its length, before heading through a mostly untracked wilderness. The river is mostly Grade II/III, but there are some Class IV features, including Taseko Falls. Expect to take three days from Taseko Lake to the confluence of the Taseko and the Chilko. The entire route, including the lakes (Upper Taseko, Taseko and Lower Taseko) is about 140 km (88 mi) in length. During July and August, Chinook and sockeye salmon run the river, meaning that grizzly bear numbers increase along with good viewing opportunities. It also means choosing safe campsites with food hung well up and away from camp.

West Twin Creek (Map 59/C3–D2)

This Grade IV-V creek flows through a tight valley as it shoots towards the Fraser River. From the put-in off Legrand Road, the run begins with a long series of Class III rapids and tests your skill with a few Class IV spots before reaching a tight canyon. The canyon portion is very difficult as it presents a series of Class IV-V type drops. Steep banks restrict the possibility of portaging around the canyon, and advance scouting is essential. This section should not be run in high water.

After the creek reaches Highway 16 and the first take-out, it slows considerably to a Grade III type run. Regardless of the water conditions, the most challenging rapid you will encounter in this portion of the creek is Class III. The second take-out is found east of Highway 16 at the first bridge over the creek off Lamco Road. For those that plan to tackle the more difficult upper section, the short lower portion is the perfect warm-up for the tougher run.

Willow River (Map 57/C3–B1)

The Willow River Route is a moderate trip over meandering Grade I-II water that flows over 50 km (31 mi) north of this book to Highway 16 east of Prince George. The gentle paddle is interrupted by the occasional Class II rapid, frequent logjams and a tricky canyon section found shortly after you pass the bridge before the Willow Bend Recreation Site north of our maps (see Northern BC Backroad Mapbook). The canyon can be portaged around or run by

more experienced paddlers who have done some advance scouting. The best time to travel this route is after the spring flood levels recede, usually in June and July. Later in the summer, water levels can be too low and hinder travel. There are a number of recreation sites available for camping, and the road is always nearby in case of trouble.

The furthest common put-in along this route is the put-in near Stony Lake off Naver-Ahbau Forest Service Road (700 Rd). To shorten your trip there are several other places where you can put in or take out, including off the Willow South Forest Service Road near the inflow of the Jerry Creek. Be sure not to miss the take-out at the Willow North Recreation Site (marked in the Northern BC Backroad Mapbook). Class III-V whitewater is found after the site.

People have been known to put into the Willow River upstream of Stony Lake, as far upstream as Wells, but this is not recommended. It is a beautiful section of river, but it is totally clogged with downed trees, deadheads and sweepers. In some places, the debris is up to several hundred metres long and you will find yourself bushwhacking more than paddling.

> Weather information can be picked up on VHF Channel 21B (151.65 MHz). Be sure to bring along the appropriate marine charts as well.

Ocean Paddling

Bella Bella Area (Map 20/D3)

Located along a sheltered channel between Denny and Campbell Islands, this small town is one of the most remote settlements in BC with a fair-sized population. While Hunter Channel is protected, it can sport brisk riptides. Some popular destinations in the immediate area are Seaforth Channel and the lagoons on Athlone and Hunter Islands. For the more adventurous, there are thousands of tiny Islands in Queens Sound, as well as an 8.5 km (5 mi) open water crossing to the Goose Island Group. The end result is access to a pure white beach at the north end of Goose Island.

Another difficult but rewarding 80 km (50 mi) route takes experienced paddlers on four or five days of good paddling to circumnavigate Swindle Island. This route offers a mix of inside channel paddling and fairly exposed paddling on the outer coast. Beaches are rare and should be treasured when found. Part of the route follows the exposed west coast of Price Island, with its many small bays hidden behind protective islets, and involves a challenging crossing of Milbanke Sound.

In addition to the outside islands, there are plenty of channels in the Bella Bella area to explore, all offering great scenery. A few of the more exceptional channels include Spiller up and into Ellerslie Bay, Roscoe Inlet and the Troupe Passage. Those making the trip to Ellerslie Bay should visit Ellerslie Falls. In addition, a trail, which can be portaged, leads up and into Ellerslie Lake, a large body of water surrounded by cliffs and mountains. Alternatively, Troupe Passage offers many small islands for exploration while other channels in the area such as Return, Gunboat and Bullock Channels, make very scenic alternative routes. It is best to avoid Fisher Channel as it is the main channel used by commercial boats in the area.

Dean Channel [Bella Bella to Bella Coola] (Map 20/D3–22/D2)

Although a heavily travelled commercial route, the trip up or down the Dean Channel offers great scenery and historical highlights. Mackenzie Rock, Eucott Bay Hot Springs, the ruins of Ocean Falls – featuring a seven-story concrete hotel with trees growing out of the lobby –, pictographs and another ghost town near Port John are just some of the noteworthy places to visit. This is also one of the few coastal areas that can be accessed by vehicle; although the Bella Coola Valley is a long drive from Highway 97, the drive is quite interesting and avoids taking the ferry.

Hakai Luxvbalis Conservancy Area (Map 8/D2-20/C6)

This is one of the premier paddling destinations of the province. It is also one of the hardest to get to, and as a result, you can often have the area all to yourself. The area is located 130 km north of Port Hardy on Vancouver Island, which is where many people catch a ferry from. The Discovery Passage ferry stops at Bella Bella, but the ferry will do wet launches for kayakers in the Hakai area. You can also catch a charter out of Bella Coola.

The area offers many sheltered bays and straits, as well as its share of exposed coast and difficult open water crossings of Queen Charlotte Sound. More cautious paddlers can explore the more sheltered McNaughton Group, Spider Island and Kildidt Sound. Wolf Beach, a popular destination at Hakai, often shows wolf prints on the beach when you land. Further afield, the Goose Group features the ghost town of Namu and its cannery ruins. The Koeye River is a grizzly habitat, and these amazing creatures can be seen near the estuary on occasion. Adding to the mix, BC Ferries will let kayakers out at the sheltered entrance to Kwaksua Channel, a narrow channel between Calvert and Hecate Islands. From here, a popular and challenging trip is to circumnavigate Calvert Island.

> The mid-coast is remote and paddlers need to be self-sufficient and prepared for layovers. Sea fog is common, currents can be strong and campsites are scattered. There are also long crossings of open sounds, and wind can funnel down the steep-sided channels.

Princess Royal Island (Map 33, 34, 47)

Starting from Klemtu, it is a 12 km (7 mi) paddle to Princess Royal Island, home of the Kermode (Spirit or White) Bear. Sightings of these beautiful creatures are rare. Also hard to find here are: campsites, freshwater and places to land. Cagey paddlers can circumnavigate the island—the third largest in BC—although this is a difficult trip. Paddlers with poor timing can run into trouble as they make their way from one beach to the next. The area features white sand beaches leading to 1,000 metre (3,280 ft) high granite cliffs. If you travel the inside passage here, plan a stop at Butedale. The folks here are working to reclaim their village from nature and are very friendly and accommodating. If you want to see wolves, the Princess Royal Island will offer plenty of these animals; they even come up near your tent during the night!

Park
Adventures

The provincial parks of the Cariboo Chilcotin Coast offer an excellent way to explore the heart of BC. They range from wilderness retreats to roadside campgrounds and picnic areas. Whether you are the most hardened outdoor enthusiast or someone new to the world of camping, these parks will dazzle you with spectacular scenery, easy access to recreational activities, and the least amount of human impact on the environment.

While it can be difficult to find a spot to truly call your own, once you get away from the main travel corridors, this becomes easier. The Cariboo Chilcotin is a sprawling and wild landscape, encompassing both the arid interior and the rainforests of the Coast Mountains. In general, the farther west you travel, the more rugged and less populated the landscape becomes.

This is one of the least populated areas in the province and is home to some of the largest parks in BC. Parks like Tweedsmuir (the largest) and Wells Gray (fourth largest) feature upgraded amenities, but they also contain vast areas of untracked and untouched wilderness that are rarely, if ever, visited. There are many other parks in the region that offer little in the way of amenities and can be difficult to access. At these locations you will be rewarded with remote and beautiful locations. Many of these wilderness areas are not regularly serviced or patrolled, and visitors must be self-sufficient.

Some parks have more of a recreational focus, while others are set aside to protect unique landscapes, sensitive habitats or representative ecosystems. There are multiple park designations depending on what the focus is, ranging from ecological reserves (which have almost no recreational value) to recreation areas, which are set aside for recreational use.

Outdoor adventurers can pursue every imaginable activity through the provincial park system. To make things easier for you when planning a trip, we have added recreational symbols beside each park name. The symbols show you some of the more popular activities pursued in the area, and the description gives you the basics for your trip. Please be sure to practice no-trace camping in the backcountry!

Many roadside parks offer full camping services; these are a great way for families and those new to the outdoors to experience the Cariboo Chilcotin Coast. These parks can be quite busy. You can make reservations through Discover Camping (discovercamping.ca or 1-800-689-9025). For more information, visit www.bcparks.ca. We have also included a sampling of the many conservancies that grace the mid-coast area of the province.

With over 1000 provincial parks to explore,

You'll never be lost for adventure.

Find yourself in BC Parks.

www.bcparks.ca

BRITISH COLUMBIA | BCParks

Arrowstone Provincial Park (Map 6/D7)
Northeast of Cache Creek, this wilderness park preserves the Arrowstone Creek drainage as well as the Cache Creek Hills, and offers no facilities or developed trails. The 6,203 hectare (15,326 ac) park offers hiking and backcountry camping in the remote and pristine valley, with access off Highway 97 near Cache Creek. There is also a forestry road that follows a section of the park's boundary, providing opportunities to enter the park from various spots. Fishing and hunting are other main park activities. Snowmobiling is not permitted, but visitors can snowshoe in winter.

Barkerville Campgrounds (Map 58/A7)
Next to the historic Barkerville townsite, the former provincial park is now managed by the townsite. There are three campgrounds here. The rustic 23 site Government Hill Campground has pit toilets and is within walking distance of the townsite. It is not suitable for RVs or larger units. Lowhee Campground is 3 km east of Barkerville and offers 87 sites, showers with flush toilets and a playground. The 54 site Forest Rose Campground is 3 km down Bowron Lake Road and offers showers with flush toilets, a group picnic shelter and horse paddocks. In addition to exploring Barkerville, enjoy the scenic views, mountain creeks, and walking and biking trails, or spend your time fishing for rainbow trout. To make reservations, call 1-866-994-3297 or visit www.barkervillecampgrounds.ca.

Big Bar Lake Prov Park (Map 5/E1)
A popular destination in the south Cariboo, this park is home to a scenic beach and 46 campsites (20 of which are reservable) spread over two different areas overlooking Big Bar Lake. There is a nice 3.5 km self-guided trail that leads from the north end of the park to Otter Marsh, where a variety of wildlife can sometimes be spotted. Big Bar Lake makes a great summer or day-trip destination. There is a day-use area complete with picnic tables and pit toilets near the beach and swimming areas. There is a paved boat launch for anglers looking for that trophy trout, and the playground and 'Big Toy' are popular with families.

Big Creek Provincial Park (Maps 3, 15)
From the dramatic, mountainous terrain in the south to the flat, forested Chilcotin Plateau and gentler volcanic hills in the north, this is a magnificent 65,982 hectare (163,045 ac) park. The southern part of the park is popular for backpacking, fishing, horseback riding, hunting, mountaineering and wildlife viewing. The park is also home to many wildlife species, from bighorn sheep and moose to wolves and bears, both grizzly and black. Backcountry camping is permitted in the park, but there are no facilities.

Bishop River Provincial Park (Map 2/C6)
This remote park protects the headwaters of the Bishop River, just south of Ts'il-os Park. Access is a challenge, but backcountry hiking and hunting are permitted. The park can be accessed by air or by boat up Bute Inlet to Waddington Harbour. There is a forest service road to the south of the harbour that follows up along the Southgate River and ends close to the western boundary of the park. Wildlife viewing is another possible activity here.

Bonaparte Provincial Park (Map 7/E3)
Found in the highlands of the Bonaparte Plateau and accessed by Jamieson Creek Forest Service Road, northwest of Kamloops, this park can be accessed by floatplane, horse or on foot. Snowmobiling is allowed in the southern portion of the 11,811 hectare (29,186 ac) park; there are two cabins maintained by the Kamloops Snowmobile Association along with several private lodges to service visitors. Within the park are numerous fishing lakes, including four fly-in fishing resorts; several hiking trails that can also be skied or snowshoed; a canoe route; and backcountry campsites. There are some unique geological features here, including the volcanic plug of Skoatl Point and Stockton Hill. Horseback riding is possible, with permission. There is a walk-in campground in the southern end of the park with picnic tables and pit toilets. There are also several lakeside user-maintained sites.

Bowron Lake Provincial Park (Maps 44, 45, 58, 59)
Bowron Lake Park is a large wilderness area situated on the western slopes of the imposing Cariboo Mountain Range. Home to the world-renowned Bowron Lake Canoe Circuit, the 116 km chain of lakes, waterways and connecting portages is extremely popular. In addition to the famous canoe route, popular activities here include fishing, hiking, swimming from beautiful sandy beaches, and wildlife viewing. In winter, backcountry skiing and snowshoeing are popular. Along the

canoe circuit there are 54 wilderness campsites with pit toilets, as well as some group sites. In case of emergency, six cabins are strategically spread out along the route, although these are not intended for camping. Near the Registration Centre at the north end of Bowron Lake there is a nice 25 unit drive-in campground, which offers nine reservable sites and a boat launch. Note that there are no backcountry campsites and powerboats are not permitted on Bowron Lake.

Bridge Lake Prov Park (Map 19/C6)
Located just off Highway 24, 51 km east of 100 Mile House, this small, 405 hectare (1,001 ac) park protects a scenic point at the southern end of Bridge Lake. The park is home to 13 drive-in campsites and three walk-in sites, which are all first-come, first-served. There is a boat launch, pit toilets, a day-use area with picnic tables, and a short trail that circles the park. The main attraction is the fabulous fishing in Bridge Lake, and visitors can also enjoy canoeing, swimming and waterskiing.

Bull Canyon Provincial Park (Map 27/C6)
One of the few developed campgrounds in the area, this park is found in a beautiful canyon between the cool, colourful Chilcotin River and Highway 20, just 6 km west of Alexis Creek. There is a short walking trail next to the river, and the surrounding area supports excellent fishing lakes, bird watching and wildlife viewing opportunities. There are 20 campsites available on a first-come, first-served basis, with a day-use area and pit toilets, one of which is wheelchair accessible. Bull Canyon Park is a great spot to use as a base for exploring the Chilcotin region.

Calvert Island Conservancy (Map 8/E4)
Located 55 km southwest of Bella Bella in Fitz Hugh Sound, this area sees a lot of recreational use due to its proximity to Hakai Pass. Calvert Island offers beautiful stretches of white sandy beaches and recreational activities like boating and sea kayaking, fishing, scuba diving, whale watching and wilderness camping. Protected anchorages are found in Pruth Bay and Safety Cove. There is great fishing for cod, halibut, rockfish and red snapper, but please note the restrictions within the Rockfish Conservation Area, which is located in this park.

Canim Beach Provincial Park (Map 19/A2)
This small, 6 hectare (15 ac) park provides access to the western shore of the lake and offers splendid views of the surrounding Cariboo Mountains. The park sports a cartop boat launch and picnic tables for day visitors to the beach. It is located 43 km northeast of 100 Mile House via the Canim Lake Road. Popular park activities include fishing, paddling, swimming and waterskiing.

Cariboo Mountains Provincial Park (Maps 44, 45)
The 113,469 hectare (280,388 ac) park is located 70 km, or about 1.5 hours, from Barkerville on the Cunningham Pass Forest Service Road (3100 Rd). The main activities include backcountry camping, fishing, hiking, hunting and wildlife viewing. The main access to this park is via Ghost Lake, where visitors will find five rustic, user-maintained campsites with views to the adjacent Matthew River Falls. The campsites include a pit toilet, and are available on a first-come, first-served basis. There is also a rough cartop boat launch for those willing to carry their boat.

Cariboo Nature Provincial Park (Map 17/G1)
As part of the Cariboo basin, this small, undeveloped 98 hectare (242 ac) park lies 40 km north of 100 Mile House, or 15 km north of Lac La Hache off Highway 97. The park encompasses the quiet Wood Frog Lake and a portion of the San Jose River, and is great bird watching site for waterfowl and shorebirds.

Cariboo River Prov Park (Map 44/D3)
This park protects the river corridor from Cariboo Lake to the smaller Kimball Lake, northeast of Likely. The primary recreational use of the 3,211 hectare (7,935 ac) park is paddling and backcountry camping. Hunting is also permitted. Many wildlife species, including moose and waterfowl, frequent the area. The waterfalls, old-growth trees and estuaries at this park can be accessed via canoe or powerboat. The park sits 90 km from the town of Likely on 6400 Road, or 70 km from the town of Barkerville on 3100 Road.

Castle Rock Hoodoos Provincial Park (Map 7/A4)
This area was set aside to protect the titular rock formation in the Deadman Valley, 75 km northwest of Kamloops along the Deadman Valley-Vidette Lake Road. The hoodoos are fragile, so visitors are asked not to walk or hike the area. Hunting is permitted in the park.

Cedar Point Prov Park (Map 44/A6)

This small, year-round, 8 hectare (20 ac) park has a fantastic beach and a playground, along with 40 vehicle-accessible campsites available on a first-come, first-served basis. Visitors will find a group campsite, pit toilets, sanistation dump and a day-use area with an outdoor mining museum. There is a boat launch next to the park allowing boaters to explore Quesnel Lake, with its spectacular scenery, excellent swimming, boating, waterskiing and fishing. The park is just 6 km from Likely.

Charlotte Alplands Protected Area (Maps 12, 24)

The Charlotte Alplands is an area protected from logging that has been set aside for backcountry recreation. The area lays claim to the largest concentration of alpine lakes in BC, many of which are home to rainbow trout and kokanee that rarely, if ever, see a hook. In addition to housing rare alpine wildflowers, the area is rich in wildlife, including caribou, bear, mule deer, mountain goat and wolf, as well as bald eagles and peregrine falcons. Access is best through the many lodges and outfitters that operate out of this area. A few informal trails also cut through the area, although many of the lower elevation routes are very old and overgrown. Horseback riding and backcountry camping are permitted.

Chasm Provincial Park (Map 6/B3)

Chasm Provincial Park is one of the most geologically unique parks in the Cariboo, protecting a picturesque and colourful chasm that was carved out of the Fraser Plateau. The fantastic natural colours of the chasm have long fascinated travelers. Explorers are free to venture into the park; however, there are steep cliffs throughout the area. It can be accessed by taking Highway 97, 16 km north of Clinton and then driving 4 km to the park on a paved road east of the highway. There is a day-use area with a viewpoint and pit toilet. Park activities include hiking, horseback riding and hunting.

Churn Creek Protected Area (Maps 4, 5, 16, 17)

Hike or ride through this rare bunchgrass landscape that lies 60 km southeast of Williams Lake on the western bank of the Fraser River. The remote area has difficult access, and the roads can become dangerously slick when wet. A four-wheel drive vehicle is recommended. There is a small camping area with pit toilets at the Empire Valley Ranch near the calving barn. Alternatively, camping is possible off the side of various roads and in the backcountry. Please camp at existing sites to limit vegetation impact. There is also a cabin to rent at the ranch as well as a day-use picnic area. Hunting is permitted in the park, and winter activities include snowmobiling on marked trails, cross-country skiing and snowshoeing.

> To reserve your campsite, visit Discover Camping at discovercamping.ca or call 1-800-689-9025. Note that not all parks in the Cariboo Chilcotin BC regions operate within the reservation system.

Codville Lagoon Marine Prov Park (Map 20/G5)

This small park is located on King Island, 80 km west of Bella Coola in Fitz Hugh Sound. The area offers a protected anchorage and a short but challenging trail to Sager Lake, which has a unique red sand beach, swimming and rainbow trout in its waters. Note that a landslide into the lagoon, along with logs and deadheads, has rendered most charts of the area out of date. Backcountry campers can find some lovely spots near Sager Lake. Paddling and hunting are two popular activities in this park.

Cottonwood River Provincial Park (Map 56/E6)

North of Quesnel, you can find the small Cottonwood River Provincial Park off the Old Prince George Highway. Set along the Cottonwood River, this small park offers a few user-maintained campsites and access to the river.

Dante's Inferno Provincial Park (Map 16/B1)

Located about 56 km southwest of Williams Lake, this 376 hectare (930 acre) park is named after the canyon, which can get quite hot in the summer. There is a scenic, recreational lake amidst the basalt cliffs where anglers go for early season fishing, and a 5 km (3 mi) hiking trail starting from Beaumont Road. Bird and wildlife enthusiasts will appreciate the presence of several species of bats here, along with pikas, flammulated owls and poorwills.

Downing Prov Park (Map 5/F5)

This 100 hectare (247 ac) park lies in the northwest shore of windy Kelly Lake and is home to a fine day-use picnic area, a splendid beach and walk-in campsites with pit toilets. The 18 lakeside campsites are spread out over a grassy field adjacent to the parking lot with fine views of mountains, including the 2,243 metre Mount Bowman. There is a rough boat launch available. The park is located 18 km southwest of Clinton along the Clinton Pavilion Road, a scenic alternative to Highway 99 that is unpaved, narrow and switch-backed. Kelly Lake is popular with swimmers and with anglers for its rainbow trout.

Dragon Mountain Park (Map 42/G3)

Located 14 km south of Quesnel, this park is 1,773 hectares (4,381 ac) in size. Established in 2013 as a result of the Cariboo-Chilcotin Land-Use Plan Goal 2 process, the park protects the viewscape of the area. It encompasses conifer, deciduous and old forests, as well as a mule deer winter range. There is a series of trails in the park that can be used by hikers and mountain bikers.

Eakin Creek Canyon Provincial Park (Map 19/G6)

Found west of Little Fort off the south side of Highway 24, this small, 10 hectare (25 ac) canyon site offers a short, unmaintained trail to a scenic 8 metre (26 ft) waterfall.

Eakin Creek Floodplain Provincial Park (Map 19/G6)

This 126 hectare (311 ac) undeveloped floodplain site features ancient cedar and cottonwood trees. Bird watching is a popular activity in summer, and ice cave exploration is possible during the winter. Fishing is also permitted. The park is accessed by a gravel road off Highway 24, 15 km west of Little Fort.

Edge Hills Provincial Park (Map 5/E5)

This wild, 11,850 hectare (29,282 ac) park is a fantastic place to explore on foot, bike or horse, with a maze of established but unmarked trails woven throughout. The diverse landscape provides habitat for a wide range of wildlife species and is accessed off of rough four-wheel drive roads. The High Bar Road enters from Jesmond Road, but visitor use of this road is not recommended beyond the lookout at Cougar Point because the road is extremely steep. The Cavanagh Creek Road enters from Pear Lake and is extremely rough, providing limited motorized access only. Visitors should bring water and be self-sufficient, especially when backcountry camping.

Emar Lakes Provincial Park (Map 19/F6)

Accessed from Long Island (Janice) Lake off the south side of Highway 24, there is a chain of lakes with wetlands within a forested setting in the Emar Creek watershed. There are small and rustic, user-maintained campsites with pit toilets here, as well as a cartop boat launch at the campsite on Long/Janice Lake. Paddlers can follow a canoe loop route to Emar Lake and back. Other park activities include hunting, fishing and hiking. The 1,604 hectare (3,964 ac) wilderness park is found 22 km west of Little Fort on Highway 24. Note that at the time of publication, the Emar Lakes canoe route and backcountry trail system is closed until further notice, due to a Mountain Pine Beetle infestation. For updates and information, call BC Parks at 250-371-6200.

Entiako Prov Park and Protected Area (Maps 38, 51, 52)

At 121,529 hectares (300,305 ac), this park is quite large. It protects the gentle rolling woodlands and old pine trees of the region as well as a diverse selection of larger mammals, including woodland caribou, moose, bear and wolves. Found 150 km southeast of Houston, access by boat is possible through the Nechako Reservoir to the north. In 2014, a large wildfire consumed a major portion of the park, so use caution in those areas. Backcountry camping, hunting, paddling and fishing are permitted.

Park Adventures

Erg Mountain Provincial Park (Map 58/G1)

Erg Mountain has historically been a hiking and backcountry camping destination. It offers an excellent viewpoint of the Upper Fraser River Valley and the surrounding mountains. However, access is currently very difficult since the Ptarmigan Creek Forest Service Road is washed out at the 3 and 12 km marks, and the foot bridges crossing the Ptarmigan Creek have been washed away. The trailhead is 8 km in from Highway 16, about 5 km west of Crescent Spur, or about 165 km east of Prince George. Park wildlife includes caribou, grizzly bear and mountain goat. Winter activities include backcountry skiing.

Finger Tatuk Provincial Park (Map 54/B2)

Located 80 km south of Vanderhoof, Finger Lake and the west end of Tatuk Lake can be accessed off the Kluskus Forest Service Road. You can access the east end of Tatuk Lake via Pelican or Bobtail Forest Service Road. There are abundant populations of rainbow trout and kokanee that are the main attraction for anglers, and the diverse habitat in the 17,151 hectare (42,381 ac) park allows for a range of animal species, including grizzly and black bear, waterfowl, shorebirds and eagles. There are two resorts within the park: the Finger Lake Wilderness Resort is located at the west end of Finger Lake, and the Tatuk Lake Outfitters & Wilderness Resort can be found on the northwest shore of Tatuk Lake. Alternatively, former recreation sites on Finger and Tatuk Lake offer campsites with a boat launch and pit toilets, but no potable water. Backcountry camping is an option, as are paddling, swimming, windsurfing, hiking and hunting. Winter activities include cross-country skiing, snowmobiling, snowshoeing and skating.

Flat Lake Provincial Park (Map 18/B6)

A popular canoeing area, Flat Lake Park can be found 20 km southwest of 100 Mile House by following Davis Lake Road off the west side of Highway 97. Portages have been established between a number of the lakes, and there are rustic backcountry campsite areas along the canoe route. In winter, skiers, snowshoers and snowmobilers visit the area.

Fraser River Provincial Park (Map 56/C2)

Located on the west bank of the Fraser River, this 4,899 hectare (12,106 ac) park was created to protect a piece of one of BC's greatest rivers. There are no developed facilities at the park, and access is challenging. Horseback riding and hunting are permitted.

Fred Antoine Provincial Park (Map 5/B7)

Combining the Fred Creek and Antoine Creek watersheds, this 2,230 hectare (5,510 ac) park rests north of the Bridge River Road, near Moha. Home to old growth Douglas fir, the area is also an important wildlife wintering range for goats and deer. Grizzly bear, wolves, cougar, California bighorn sheep, fisher, rubber boa and peregrine falcon are all seen here on occasion. Visitors may also find numerous signs and artifacts of past First Nations use.

French Bar Creek Provincial Park (Map 5/B2)

This 1,159 hectare (2,864 ac) park is located 60 km north of Lillooet. Established in 2010 as a result of the Lillooet Land and Resource Management Plan, this park protects under-represented dry forests and grasslands and a small frontage on the Fraser River. The area is a migration route for bighorn sheep.

Green Inlet Marine Prov Park (Map 34/A1; 48/A7)

Located in a scenic fjord, this 37 hectare (91 ac) park offers sheltered anchorage for boaters on the east side of Tolmie Channel across from Princess Royal Island. It is 196 km south of Prince Rupert and accessible by boat only. The tidal lagoon of Green Inlet features reversing, but unnavigable, rapids at Baffle Point. Park activities include paddling, fishing for rockfish and salmon, swimming in the cold water and hunting.

Green Lake Provincial Park (Map 18/E7)

Green Lake is a popular recreational lake named for its brilliant colour. Popular picnic sites and beaches are scattered around the lake, and there are boat launches at Sunset View Campground and Little Arrowhead Day-Use Area. Park activities include cycling, guided horseback riding (at Emerald Bay), hiking, paddling, powerboating, swimming and waterskiing. The lake is restocked annually to help the fishery.

For campers, there are 121 vehicle-accessible campsites that are found at three separate park areas: Emerald Bay, Arrowhead and Sunset View. Arrowhead Campground is the smallest, with 16 sites. Emerald Bay is a treed campground with 51 sites, a playground and a nearby store. Sunset View is the largest of the three, housing 54 sites and four large-group areas. Both Sunset View and Emerald Bay offer day-use picnic areas, pit toilets, playgrounds and sani-dump stations. All three sites are wheelchair-accessible and can be reserved via Discover Camping (discovercamping.ca).

High Lakes Basin Provincial Park (Map 19/F7)

This remote park lies north of Bonaparte Lake, 16 km west of Little Fort, covering three high elevation lakes that contain wild trout. There is no access into the park, but it is possible to bushwhack in on foot or by horseback from the logging roads north of Caverhill Lake. There are some rustic, user-maintained camping areas in the park. Other park activities include hunting, paddling and wildlife viewing.

Homathko Estuary Provincial Park (Map 1/B6)

Because of its location and the fact that water access is hindered by extensive mud flats, this park offers few recreational opportunities. It is possible to explore the beach area at low tide or observe grizzly bears from a distance. Possible activities include paddling and tidal fishing outside of the Rockfish Conservation Area.

Homathko River-Tatlayoko Protected Area (Maps 1, 12, 13)

Protecting the Homathko River and Mosley Creek Valleys, this remote park protects low-elevation coastal rainforests and wetlands about 30 km south of Tatla Lake. Boating is popular, and consistent afternoon winds create good windsurfing conditions – although the lake is rather chilly for swimmers. Anglers will find wild, indigenous bull trout in Dumbell Lake, Homathko River and Mosely Creek. Hunters can use horses for transportation in the park, and backcountry camping is also permitted.

Horsefly Lake Provincial Park (Map 30/C2)

This park is quite popular during summer months, with 23 lake-view campsites (12 of which are reservable), and seven hike-in campsites. Other features include a boat launch, a children's play area with a basketball hoop, a day-use picnic area and sandy beach, a horseshoe pitch and featherball court, pit toilets and showers. Angling enthusiasts can try their luck in Horsefly Lake or at one of the many nearby lakes, and hikers can enjoy the short trek to a natural lookout over Horseshoe Lake. Other lake activities here include paddling, scuba diving, swimming, waterskiing and windsurfing. The closest community is Horsefly, located 13 km southwest of the park.

Huchsduwachsdu Nuyem Jees/Kitlope Heritage Conservancy (Maps 34, 35, 48, 49)

Located 50 km northwest of Bella Coola, this 322,020 hectare (795,729 ac) park protects the world's largest intact coastal temperate rainforest, which is home to giant old-growth trees over 800 years old. There are many rustic backcountry campsites with pit toilets and campfire rings, and a couple of cabins. All campsites are available on a first-come, first-served basis only. The Kemano Cabin, on the north bank of the Kitlope River, offers pit toilets, and the cabin sleeps four. Fishing, hiking, hunting, paddling and swimming are all possible activities here.

Itcha Ilgachuz Prov Park (Maps 38, 39)

The Itcha and Ilgachuz Ranges, which are examples of isolated shield volcanoes, rise up to 2,400 metres (7,800 ft) above sea level and are home to the largest herd of woodland caribou in southern BC. Bighorn sheep and moose are also seen here. Access to this 111,977 hectare (276,701 ac) park is along maintained, but long riding trails that can be hiked or ridden on horseback. Backcountry camping, fishing and hunting are permitted in the park, and snowmobiling is a popular winter activity. There are two public-use cabins at Itcha Lake that hold six people each, along with some pit toilets.

Jackson Narrows Marine Prov Park (Map 34/C5)

This small 71 hectare (175 ac) park, located in a small bay about 236 km south of Prince Rupert, features a small beach and good anchorage. The narrows should only be attempted at high slack by small boats.

Junction Sheep Range Provincial Park (Map 16/F2)

Overlooking the confluence of the Chilcotin and Fraser Rivers, the Junction Sheep Range Park is only accessible via a rough four-wheel drive road through private ranch land. The road in doubles as a great mountain bike ride, and there are other trails/old roads to explore on foot, by bike or on horseback, if hunting. The scenery is spectacular, with deep gullies, cliffs and hoodoos breaking the arid grassland. The park is also home to one of the largest herds of California bighorn sheep in the province. Facilities are limited.

K'Distsausk/Turtle Point Conserv (Map 47/A2)

K'Distsausk/Turtle Point Conservancy is only accessible by boat, located at the north tip of Gil Island. The 142 hectare (345 ac) conservancy protects an area of high cultural and historical value to the Gitga'at First Nation. The sandy beach of Fisherman Cove makes it a popular spot for boaters and anglers.

Kitasoo Spirit Bear Conserv (Map 33/E2)

Kitasoo Spirit Bear Conservancy is located on Princess Royal Island, 15 km west of Klemtu and 130 km south of Kitimat. Visitors can explore the hiking trails on Swindle Island, go backcountry camping or try river and ocean fishing. Kayaking and canoeing are also popular pastimes here. With hundreds of reefs, pocket beaches, tiny sheltered bays and rich intertidal marine life, exploration is seemingly endless on the shorelines of the islands.

K'Lgaan/Klekane Conservancy (Map 47/G3)

K'Lgaan/Klekane Conservancy is only accessible by boat or floatplane. The protected anchorage sits adjacent to the main Inside Passage Route, and visitors can spend the night to rest, fish or relax in the small hot springs. There is a small bath house and pool to help visitors enjoy the springs.

Kluskoil Lake Prov Park (Map 54/E5)

It is a long walk down the Alexander Mackenzie Heritage Trail, a slow float on the Blackwater River, or a bumpy ride on the four-wheel drive road leading to the eastern boundary of the park. If you want to drive, then a high clearance four-wheel drive vehicle or ATV is needed. Follow the Batnuni Road and turn off at the 108 km mark. This trail will lead to the crossing of the Euchiniko River, which can be several feet deep most of the year and even higher during spring runoff. From here, travel 18 km to Kluskoil Lake Campsite on the Alexander Mackenzie Heritage Trail. The rustic campsite offers three sites set in the trees, an information shelter and pit toilets. There are other informal campsites along with several good fishing lakes in the 15,548 hectare (38,420 ac) wilderness park. Hiking, horseback riding, hunting and swimming are popular park activities.

K'Ootz/Khutze Conservancy (Map 48/C5)

Only accessible by boat or floatplane, this conservancy is located about 65 km southeast of Hartley Bay and 110 km south of Kitimat. K'Ootz/Khutze Conservancy provides a protected anchorage adjacent to the main Inside Passage Route where visitors can camp, fish, hunt, kayak or take in the scenic waterfalls and abundant wildlife.

Kt'li/Racey Conservancy (Map 33/C1)

Located on the west side of Princess Royal Island, 130 km southwest of Kitimat, this conservancy can only be accessed by air or boat. At 1,261 hectares (43,509 ac), the area features scenic waterfalls and good hiking opportunities, such as the trail leading to the waterfall-draining Archie Lake. Other popular pursuits in the area include camping, fishing, kayaking and wildlife viewing.

Ktisgaidz/Macdonald Bay Conserv (Map 46/G3)

At 482 hectares (1,191 ac), this conservancy is located on the west side of Gil Island on Squally Channel. MacDonald Bay is a snug, sheltered anchorage on the west side of Gil Island, and is ideally situated for small boats heading for the outer coast. A stream in the bay also provides a good source of drinking water for boaters. Other activities here include camping, fishing, hunting and wildlife viewing.

Lac du Bois Grasslands Protected Area (Map 7/F7)

Lac du Bois has open grasslands, dry forests and grand cliffs and canyons. The 15,712 hectare (38,825 ac) park is bisected by the Lac du Bois Road and preserves a series of small lakes in addition to the grassland. There are few facilities in the area, but there are a variety of trails to explore on foot or bike, along with fishing for trout in Deep Lake and hunting. Winter activities include cross-country skiing and snowshoeing. California bighorn sheep, moose, mule deer and waterfowl are common residents and visitors to the park, while the flammulated owl, sharp-tailed grouse and western rattlesnake lead more reclusive lives within the park boundaries. Historically, this region was grazing land for cattle, horses and sheep, and there is also archaeological evidence of First Nations use. Backcountry camping is permitted and there are rustic user-maintained campsites at Watching Creek.

Lac La Hache Provincial Park (Map 17/G2)

Along Highway 97, this popular lakeshore provincial park offers 83 vehicle-accessible campsites, 30 of which are reservable. Visitors can enjoy a variety of activities such as boating, cycling, fishing, swimming, waterskiing and other watersports. A self-guided nature trail is located within the park as well as a boat launch, day-use picnic area with a playground and sandy beach, pit toilets and a sani-dump station. This area is rich in tales of fur traders, gold seekers and cattle ranchers. The 24 hectare (59 ac) park lies 13 km north of the community of Lac La Hache.

Lax Ka'Gaas/Campania Conserv (Map 46/F5)

Located 120 km southwest of Kitimat and 135 km southeast of Prince Rupert, access to this 20,504 hectares (50,666 ac) conservancy is primarily by boat, with a number of sheltered inlets suitable for anchoring. Mount Pender, which rises to 740 m (2,427 ft), is the central feature here.

Lax Kwil Dziidz/Fin Conserv (Map 46/G3)

This 1,902 hectare (4,699 ac) conservancy is only accessible by boat. It is found about 17 km southwest of Hartley Bay and 100 km southwest of Kitimat. The island has three sheltered bays (Brant, Curlew, and Hawk), which are used by boaters and anglers for anchorage. Visitors will also find great swimming, paddling, fishing and hunting.

Marble Canyon Prov Park (Map 5/G7)

Covering 355 hectares (877 ac), this park is found just east of Pavilion on Highway 99, about 40 km northwest of Cache Creek. Marble Canyon is set at the base of 1,000 metre (3,250 ft) high limestone cliffs. It contains a trio of lakes: Crown, Pavilion and Turquoise, with a 30 unit campsite at the south end of Pavilion Lake that has pit toilets and a day-use area. The limestone canyon is a rather rare geological formation in British Columbia, which makes picnicking here an unusual experience and mountain climbing a popular activity. A waterfall on the far side of Turquoise Lake reminds you of the power of the elements that have shaped this park. Visitors can fish, scuba dive and bird watch as well.

> Be bear aware, and never leave food or coolers unattended. If tenting, be sure to store your food, toothpaste and any scented items in your vehicle or in a bear cache.

Marble Range Provincial Park (Map 5/E3)

West of Clinton, this 12,236 hectare (30,236 ac) park received its name due to the predominant limestone topography featured throughout its mountain ranges. The traditional territory of the Shuswap People, this park is home to a large herd of California bighorn sheep as well as a good population of mule deer. There are no facilities provided, but wilderness camping is permitted; please practice no-trace camping and bring your own water. Horseback riding, hiking and hunting are permitted in the park.

Maxtaktsm'Aa/Union Passage Conservancy (Map 46/F1)

This 2,519 hectare (6,224 ac) conservancy (only accessible by boat or float plane) features excellent camping, paddling, fishing, hunting and wildlife viewing. The conservancy is located approximately 15 km southwest of Hartley Bay and 90 km southwest of Kitimat, between Grenville Channel and Squally.

Moksgm'Ol/Chapple—Cornwall Conservancy (Map 47/C5)

Only accessible by boat, floatplane or helicopter, this 29,116 hectares (71,947 ac) conservancy is located about 35 km south of Hartley Bay and 105 km southwest of Kitimat. Floating lodges, fishing (fresh and saltwater), heli-hiking, bear viewing and safe boat anchorages are some of the recreational uses.

Park Adventures

Monckton Nii Luutiksm Conserv (Map 46/D2) 🔱⚓🏕🏊🛶🎣🚶🏕
This conservancy is only accessible by boat, floatplane or helicopter. Camping, fishing, paddling and wildlife viewing are some of the main activities at this 24,775 hectare (61,220 ac) conservancy. There are safe boat anchorages. Visitors will find diverse fish and wildlife habitats, including marine, intertidal areas, small lakes, streams, estuaries, wetlands, forests and salmon spawning habitats.

Moose Valley Provincial Park (Map 17/G4–18/A4)
🎿🏕⚓🛶🏊🚶🏃🎿🚶🎣🏕
A popular destination for canoeing enthusiasts, the park comprises 2,500 hectares (6,178 ac) of rolling landscape scattered with lakes and wetlands. There are three vehicle-accessible units available at Marks Lake, and rustic interior campsite areas with pit toilets are available along the chain of 12 small lakes throughout the park. For wildlife enthusiasts, the surrounding marshes bring in moose, waterfowl and other species. Although the Gustafsen Lake Forest Service (1100) Road is unmaintained during the winter, the area is still a haven for cross-country skiing and snowshoeing. Local outfits offer dog sled tours in the winter and guided canoe trips in the summer. There is also a short hike to Maitland Lake, where there is a cabin. Moose Valley Provincial Park is located 31 km west of 100 Mile House. Hunting is permitted.

Nazko Lake Prov Park (Map 27/A2–41/B7) 🎿🏕⚓🏊🛶🎣🏃🐾🛶🎣🏕
Best known for the Nazko Lakes Canoe Route, this park has two-wheel drive accessible campsites with pit toilets at Loomis, Deerpelt and Summit Lakes and informal camping along the canoe route. Nazko Lake is a popular fishing lake, but the real draw to the area is the wildlife, most notably the white pelicans that feed here. The 12,419 hectare (30,688 ac) park is located in the northern part of the Chilcotin Plateau, 60 km northwest of Alexis Creek.

Nunsti Provincial Park (Map 14/F3) 🏕🐾🎣🚶🎣🏕
Located northeast of Chilko Lake in the Chilcotin Plateau, south of the junction of the Taseko and Chilko Rivers, this 20,898 hectare (51,640 ac) park protects valuable moose habitat. It encompasses abundant wetlands and small lakes. The area is open to hunting, trapping and cattle grazing, but many trails remain closed after a fire in 2004. As of June 26, 2014, the park may only be used with permission of the Tsilhqot'in Nation as per the Supreme Court of Canada's aboriginal title declaration. Visit www.tsilhqotin.ca for information.

Oliver Cove Marine Prov Park (Map 20/B1) 🔱🏊🏕⚓🛶🎣🏕
Also known as Port Blackney, this small park protects 74 hectares (183 ac) of marine and land area that is home to orcas, dolphins, sea lions and whales. There is also an impressive intertidal area where you will find all manner of sea life. This makes the park popular for scuba diving. The excellent all-weather anchorage and sheltered inside route provide protection for small boats, although there are no landing docks or other facilities. The closest communities for supplies are Bella Bella and Shearwater. Hunting is also permitted in the park.

Penrose Isl Marine Prov Park (Map 8/G5 – 9/A5) 🏕⚓🔱🏊🏕⚓🛶🎣🏕
Located 86 km north of Port Hardy, at the entrance to Rivers Inlet and the south end of Fitz Hugh Sound, this area is a great place for kayaking, with a series of islands, small coves and narrow channels to explore. There is a network of narrow channels with sand and white shell beaches along the southwest shoreline. Fishing, kayaking and scuba diving are popular pursuits. The beach at Clam Bay is the most popular camping area, but most visitors prefer to sleep onboard their boats. Hunting is also permitted in the park. Enter from Klaquek Channel into sheltered anchorages on the east side.

Pinnacles Provincial Park (Map 42/D1) 🏃🏕
This day-use only park is 128 hectares (316 ac) in size and is found 8 km west of Quesnel on Pinnacles Road. A short 1 km trail leads through the forest to the edge of a basaltic cliff, where you will find a great view of the rock formations. You will find pit toilets at the viewpoint. The park is open year-round for day use and sightseeing.

Pooley Conservancy (Map 34/D3) 🏕🔱🏊🏕🏃🛶🎣🏕
Located 45 km north of Bella Bella, this 3,000 hectare (7,413 ac) conservancy can only be accessed by boat via Mathieson Channel or via Finlayson Channel and Sheep Passage. The elusive white Kermode bear frequents the estuaries of Pooley Island, and salmon use the main creeks at James and Windy Bays.

Porcupine Meadows Provincial Park (Map 7/E5) 🏃🐾🚶🎣🚶🏕
This park is comprised mostly of wetlands, with some patches of old growth forest. The area is designated for conservation, and recreation is limited. There are no roads, camping or day-use facilities, but there are a few trails within the 2,704

hectare (6,682 ac) park, including an old pack trail leading past several small lakes to Porcupine Ridge and an old forestry lookout. The trail can be used for hiking and horseback riding, or snowmobiling and snowshoeing in winter.

Ptarmigan Creek Provincial Park and Protected Area (Map 58/G2)
🏕🏃🎿🏂🎿🎣🚶🏕
The narrow, steep-sided valley at the north end of the Cariboo Mountains has been set aside to protect caribou and grizzly bear. Covering 4,633 hectares (11,448 ac), it is found northwest of McBride and is accessible via trail from a gated area near the Ptarmigan Creek Recreation Site. Backcountry skiing and camping are popular in this park, and adventurers can also fish, hunt and snowshoe. The trailhead is 8 km in from Highway 16, about 5 km west of Crescent Spur, or about 165 km east of Prince George. However, access is currently very difficult since the Ptarmigan Creek Forest Service Road is washed out at the 3 and 12 km marks, and both foot bridges crossing the Ptarmigan Creek have been washed away.

Puntchesakut Lake ProvPark (Map 42/A1) 🍽🏊🏄🏊🛶🏊🚴🎣
Located on the east side of Puntchesakut Lake, this day-use park has picnic tables, a beautiful stretch of sandy beach, several pit toilets and two change rooms. There is no potable water. Activities here include boating, canoeing, swimming, waterskiing and fishing for trout year-round. The park comprises of 38 hectares (94 ac) of gently rolling forest, and is accessible off the paved Nazko Road, 40 km west of Quesnel.

Q'Altanaas/Aaltanhash Conserv (Map 48/A4) 🏕🔱🏊🏕🚶🏃🎣🏕
This is another boat or floatplane access conservancy located on the east side of Princess Royal Channel. This area shares its northwestern boundary with K'Igaan/Klekane and its southern boundary with K'Ootz/Khutze Conservancy. Found along the Inside Passage Route, Q'Altanaas/Aaltanhash provides a protected anchorage where visitors can camp, fish, hike, kayak or watch wildlife.

Ruth Lake Provincial Park (Map 18/F2) 🍽🏊🏕🏊🏕🛶🎣
Ruth Lake Park can be found off the Eagle Creek Road, 30 km northeast of 100 Mile House. The park is perfect for a summer family outing, as visitors can enjoy a picnic on the grassy area that overlooks a small beach and floating dock. Along with basic outhouses, the park sports a boat launch. Popular lake activities include paddling, swimming and waterskiing, along with fishing for trout.

Schoolhouse Lake Provincial Park (Map 18/F1) 🏕🏃🎣🚶🏕
Encircling a number of picturesque, rarely visited lakes, this park is best accessed by a floatplane, 50 km northeast of 100 Mile House. The roads that do reach the park boundary are quite rough and can be impassable even with a four-wheel drive vehicle. Backcountry camping, fishing, hiking and hunting opportunities exist at the 5,106 hectare (12,617 ac) park.

Shearwater Hot Springs Conserv (Map 48/A1) 🏕🔱🏊🏕🏊🎣🚶🏕
Also known as Europa Hot Springs, this conservancy protects popular hot springs and a sheltered boat anchorage along Gardner Canal. Other activities here include swimming, paddling, fishing and hunting, as well as camping and picnicking. The springs are only accessible by boat or floatplane and are located approximately 45 km east of Hartley Bay and 65 km south of Kitimat.

Sir Alexander Mackenzie Prov Park (Map 21/D1) 🔱🏊🏕🏃🐾🎣🚶🏕
"From Canada by Land." These immortal words were inscribed on a rock on July 22, 1793 by Alexander Mackenzie, the first European to cross North America. Today, this park marks the end of an extensive backcountry hiking or horseback riding journey along the Alexander Mackenzie Heritage (Grease) Trail. Note, however, that in order to reach the park, hikers must still travel the last segment of the journey by boat, as did Sir Alexander Mackenzie. The 5 hectare (12 ac) historical site is located near Elcho Harbour on Dean Channel, 65 km northwest of Bella Coola. Anchorage at the actual rock is poor and exposed to high winds; better protection is found at the head of Elcho Harbour. There are also campsites a short distance northeast of the point that are not in the park.

South Chilcotin [Spruce Lake] Provincial Park (Maps 3, 4)
🏕🏊🏃🎣🐾🏂🚵🎿🏇🎣🚶🏕
This beautiful area offers world-class hiking and backpacking, horse packing, mountain biking and mountaineering. Visitors can also fish and hunt, or heli-ski, backcountry ski, snowmobile and snowshoe in winter. There are 164 km of wilderness trails, traversing gentle mountain passes and meandering through lush alpine grasslands and flowers to destination trout lakes. Six designated wilderness campsites with pit toilets have been established to help

visitors explore the area. These sites can be found at Jewel Bridge, Gun Creek Grasslands (aka Cowboy Camp), Hummingbird Lake, Spruce Lake North & South and Trigger Lake. The park is 56,796 hectares (140,346 ac) in size and lies 95 km west of Lillooet off the Carpenter Lake Road, off Highway 40. Many roads around the park require a four-wheel drive vehicle.

Taweel Provincial Park (Map 19/F4)

This 4,558 hectare (11,263 ac) park has no day-use or camping facilities, but there are private resorts in the area that offer services and cabins. The resorts can be reached by rough four-wheel drive roads, but there is no access directly into the park by road or trail for the general public. (Other roads in the area have been deactivated, resulting in limited access.) This area is noted for fishing, hiking and the beautiful wilderness setting. Park visitors can also canoe, kayak, horseback ride and hunt.

Ten Mile Lake Provincial Park (Map 56/F7)

Located 11 km north of Quesnel, off Highway 97, this popular 260 hectare (642 ac) park offers a good variety of activities. There are two separate campgrounds, Lakeside and Touring, totaling 107 campsites. The 61 sites at Lakeside are reservable. Amenities include a playground, washrooms with showers and sani-dump station. There are a series of trails in and around the park that can be used year-round. The boat launch, large picnic area, three sandy beaches and great fishing are some of the attractions to the park.

Three Sisters Lake Provincial Park (Map 56/E1)

There are no established facilities available within this park, but nearby recreation sites provide a good base from which to explore. The 968 hectare (2,392 ac) park is located 35 km southeast of Prince George, and includes three small lakes and unique canyon features on Government Creek. Activities include fishing, hiking, hunting and paddling.

Tsintsunko Lakes Provincial Park (Map 7/E4)

Located on the Bonaparte Plateau, 40 km northwest of Kamloops, this 333 hectare (823 ac) day-use only park protects a series of interconnected lakes and wetlands. Angler trails lead to the lakes, and can be snowshoed in the winter. In addition to rainbow trout in the lakes, wildlife enthusiasts should note that the park provides calving and summer habitat for moose and is also home to a variety of waterfowl.

Ts'yl-os Provincial Park (Maps 1, 2, 3, 14)

In June 2014, the Supreme Court of Canada declared this region a Tsilhqot'in First Nation aboriginal title land. In order to use the park, visitors must obtain permission from the Nation; visit www.tsilhqotin.ca for information. Ts'il-os (pronounced "sigh-loss") Park encompasses 233,240 hectares (576,349 ac) of rugged mountains, clear blue lakes, glaciers, alpine meadows and waterfalls. It is bordered by the rugged peaks of the Coast Mountains to the west and the dry Interior Plateau to the east. The heart of the park is the turquoise-coloured Chilko Lake, the largest high elevation freshwater lake in Canada. The lake is popular with anglers, boaters and kayakers. In addition to watersports, the park is home to great backcountry camping and hiking. There are two main vehicle-access routes into the park, both of which take four to six hours from Williams Lake, and two campgrounds, one at the end of each route. Nu Chugh Beniz Campground is the main site, with 16 sites on the eastern shores of the lake, while Gwa Da Ts'ih Campground is a small, rustic campground with space for eight groups at the north end of the lake.

Tweedsmuir Provincial Park - North and Tweedsmuir Corridor Protected Area (Maps 49, 50, 51)

Tweedsmuir Park is the largest park in the province, and is divided into North and South. The North has Pandosy Lake and Eustuk Lake, which provide paddling opportunities, with a portage system at Chikamin Bay Rail Portage connecting Eustuk to Whitesail Lake. Permits are required, so please inquire ahead of time. Guided fishing is available from both Redfern River Lodge and Pondosy Bay Resort, and the Lake District Air Services provide lodging and access to Tesla Lake. Visitors will find several trails for hiking and hunting, along with backcountry camping and wildlife viewing opportunities in this massive, 446,107 hectare (1,102,354 ac) portion of the park.

Tweedsmuir Provincial Park - South (Maps 12, 23, 24, 36, 37)

The southern portion of the park is 989,616 hectares (2,445,394 ac) in size. Set along Highway 20, the Atnarko Campground and Fisheries Pool Campground total 36 non-reservable sites. There are also four picnic areas with pit toilets and picnic tables close to the highway, with nearby hiking opportunities, including the Alexander Mackenzie Heritage Trail. Further afield, there is backcountry camping as well. For those that prefer a roof, the Rainbow Cabin and the Tweedsmuir Ski Club operate a reservable cabin close to the ski area. Home to the Turner Lakes Canoe Circuit, one of the premier canoe routes in the province, the park also holds dozens of trails, ranging from short day hikes to week-long backcountry treks. There is good fishing and the incredible Hunlen Falls to view. Other park activities include downhill skiing, fishing, horseback riding, hunting, mountain biking and swimming. Trail conditions and routes can change due to flood damage, so check ahead before entering the park.

Wells Gray Provincial Park (Maps 19, 31, 45)

From massive glacial-fed lakes to towering mountain alpine peaks, Wells Gray offers visitors the chance to experience a truly wild part of the province. The park is home to a variety of large mammals, such as black bear, deer, moose, and in alpine areas, caribou, grizzly bear and mountain goat. There is a multitude of hiking trails, maintained and rustic camping, and a number of excellent paddling routes. On the maps in this book, the Mahood Lake Campground offers 39 campsites that can be reserved from mid-May to late September. This is a beautiful and quiet campground that is popular with anglers, as it sits on the shore of Mahood Lake. There is also a day-use area with picnic facilities, a playground and grassy field, and a paved boat launch. The other campsites are found along the popular corridor area that is covered in the Thompson Okanagan BC Backroad Mapbook. Outdoor enthusiasts can pursue pretty much every activity in this park, including, but not limited to: boating, fishing and hunting, guided horseback riding, paddling and river rafting, as well as wildlife viewing and birding. There are even historical opportunities based on early BC settlement history.

Wendle Park (Map 58/A6)

This Barkerville park was named after conservationist, avid hunter and fisherman Joseph Wendle, who with his wife Elizabeth Wendle, played a large part in the park's development. There are a number of nearby trails in the area.

West Twin Provincial Park and Protected Area (Map 59/C3)

This diverse area is home to an abundance of wildlife and is a popular backcountry destination, with great views of the Robson Valley. There are a number of trails in the 22,317 hectare (55,147 ac) park and a cabin at the West Dore River (which can be booked through the Ozalenka Alpine Club). Visitors can partake in backcountry camping year-round, backcountry skiing, hiking, hunting and snowshoeing. The park is located 180 km southeast of Prince George off Highway 16, where there is a pull-out with day-use area and a Forestry Interpretation Trail.

White Pelican Provincial Park (Map 27/G3)

This 2,763 hectare (6,828 ac) park was created to protect important nesting habitat for White Pelicans on Stum Lake. This is the only nesting habitat in the province for this rare bird. As these creatures are very sensitive to disturbance, there are several restrictions to protect the lake. The lake is closed to the public from March 1 to August 31. In summer, the birds feed in nearby lakes, including those of Nazko Lake Park. The park is 60 km northwest of Williams Lake.

Yalakom Provincial Park (Map 4/F4)

Located about 60 km northwest of Lillooet, this 8,941 hectare (22,094 ac) park protects the undeveloped basin of Yalakom Creek and much of Nine Mile Ridge. It contains diverse habitats, including old growth forest, high elevation aspen stands, wetlands and krumholz forest, and it houses California bighorn sheep, mountain goat and mule deer. Hunting is permitted here, and there are a number of backcountry trails in the area. Note that at the time of printing, the western access to the park via Yalakom Forest Service Road is compromised until further notice due to a First Nations blockade. For alternative access, take West Pavilion Forest Service Road.

Recsite
Adventures

Scattered across the Cariboo Chilcotin Coast are a series of campgrounds and day-use sites known as recreation sites. Established by the forest service, in conjunction with local forest companies, these sites are located on Crown land to provide recreational opportunities in a forest setting.

Recreation sites offer a nice balance between the developed, but often crowded provincial parks and a completely undeveloped patch of Crown land. The sites are usually small and rustic, but offer access to some of the best fishing lakes, paddling routes and scenery to be found outside of a park. They are not as busy as parks or commercial campgrounds, especially during mid-week.

Formerly known as Forest Recreation Sites, many of the sites were originally developed by workers at forestry companies who wanted access to a good fishing lake or were interested in hunting, hiking, paddling or a similar type of recreational activity on their days off. As a result, many of the sites are found in remote locations, well away from any paved road. Almost all are located along logging roads, some of which are very rough and others which may have active logging take place. Take care when travelling on these roads, especially if hauling a boat or a trailer.

The sites are currently looked after by the Ministry of Tourism, Sports and the Arts, but are often maintained by local recreation groups, forest companies, First Nations or private contractors. Some of these sites are enhanced, and fees are collected (usually around $12/night). The level of services offered at these enhanced sites can rival provincial parks, although many are quite rustic. Local user groups maintain these sites simply because they have a vested interest in keeping them open. The rustic sites do not charge any fees and users are responsible for collecting their trash, getting their own firewood and providing their own toilet paper. All are available on a first-come, first-served basis. Those looking to visit during the weekend had best get there early.

Most recreation sites have a camping area, although some are day-use only. Visitors will usually find pit toilets and at least one or two picnic tables and fire rings. The larger sites will have developed trails, provide firewood, and even have a caretaker for on-site supervision and maintenance. Although boat launches are often provided on the lakes, these launches range from hand launch sites to paved ramps suitable for trailered boats. Visit www.sitesandtrailsbc.ca for more information.

B.C.'s Backcountry Playground

With over 1300 sites and 800 trails for you to explore.

Check out our website for information on locations, activities, and facilites.
www.sitesandtrailsbc.ca

BRITISH COLUMBIA | Recreation Sites and Trails BC

Recsite Adventures

Abbott Creek Rec Site (Map 44/D7)
Near Bean Point on Quesnel Lake, this is an open, eight-unit site with a beautiful beach. Found off Spanish Lake Road, the last stretch of access road to the site is very steep and can be challenging for larger units. The boat launch is across the beach; four-wheel drive might be necessary.

Ahbau Lake Rec Site (Map 57/B4)
Located on the north end of Ahbau Lake, this extensive, recently upgraded site includes over 20 campsites and plenty of room. There are pit toilets, tables, fire rings and designated camping pads. A concrete boat launch is available, and the site can be easily accessed by two-wheel drive vehicles. South of Hixon, turn left onto 700 Road; turn left again at the 734 km marker and you will find the site at the 1038 km mark.

Alexis Lakes Rec Site (Map 27/B3)
A semi-open site on the shores of the lake, this quiet, family-friendly site has five units, and a small beach for swimming. This is a popular fishing destination, but you will need to carry your boat to the water here! Access can be found via Alexis Creek Nazko Road (aka Alexis Lakes Road) off of Highway 20.

Allan Lake Rec Site (Map 7/G2)
With 15 campsites along with a cartop boat launch, this is a popular site for anglers throughout the ice-free season. The high elevation makes it a nice place to escape the heat in summer. Space here can be limited, especially on weekends. From Kamloops, the site can be reached by taking Westsyde Road and then taking the turn-off to the Jamieson Creek Forest Service Road and continuing for roughly 45 km.

Arthur Lake Rec Site (Map 53/G1)
This small, single-unit site sits on the south end of Arthur Lake. To reach it, drive south on Kluskus Forest Service Road to 59.5 km and turn left onto the Gold Road. You will find the site access road after 3.3 km.

Atan Lake Rec Site (Map 58/B6)
Given this site's rough two-wheel drive access off the 2900 Road, it sees very few visitors throughout the year. The secluded site is home to a rough boat launch and a few picnic tables.

Barton Lake Rec Site (Map 55/C2)
Featuring two, small recently upgraded sites with access points 300 metres apart, this site makes a fine camping destination. There is good two-wheel drive access for people wishing to bring in small RVs.

Batnuni Lake East Rec Site (Map 54/D4)
Located on the east shore of Batnuni Lake, this site has five designated campsites. It sits on an open grassy area on the beach and there is a narrow boat launch available. The site includes tables and toilets, and campers will find opportunities for canoeing and fishing in the lake. To reach the site, take Blackwater Road to about the 155 km mark and turn east of the Batnuni Road. It is another 65.5 km or so to the recreation site on this logging road.

Batnuni Lake West Rec Site (Map 54/D3)
This four-unit, moderately-sized, site sits on the west side of Batnuni Lake. To reach it, take Blackwater Road to about the 155 km mark and turn east of the Batnuni Road. It is another 73 km or so to the recreation site on this logging road. Set amidst the trees at lake level, this site is subject to spring flooding. For alternative options, try the camping areas just off the main road or the Batnuni Lake East site.

Beaverdam Creek Rec Site (Map 4/G5)
Beaverdam Creek is a small, grassy site set in an opening next to the creek. There are five spots here, including enough space for RVs to park. Access can be found northwest of Lillooet via Highway 99 and Yalakon River Forest Service Road.

Beaverdam Lake Rec Site (Map 6/A2)
Seven units are spread along an open grassy area on the eastern shore of the lake. The good road access enables larger vehicles like RVs to access the site; hence both the lake and the site can be busy during the summer months.

Beavermouth Rec Site (Map 43/B5)
This is a large two-section site with multiple campsites. The upper section is a large open area with several campsites and the second is just a few campsites along the river complete with toilet facilities. The waterfall area is ideal for swimming, and a rustic boat launch provides access to the river.

Becher's Pond Rec Site (Map 28/E7)
Located on the western shore of Becher's Pond, this three-unit site is a popular camping spot for hunters. The campground can be accessed west of Williams Lake via Highway 20. Once past Riske Creek, Becher's Pond will be along the left side of the highway down a short and bumpy side road.

Big Lake Rec Site (Map 14/F6)
This Big Lake is situated in the low, rolling, forested hills of the Chilcotin plateau and offers great views of the nearby Coast Mountains. It is one of the few developed campsites in the area and remains a popular summer destination. Fees apply from May 15th to October 31st.

Big Stick Lake Rec Site (Map 24/G6)
There are three campsites at Big Stick Lake. With a boat launch and a sandy beach Big Stick Lake is a popular boating and camping site. To access the site from Highway 20, turn west onto the Big Stick Forest Service Road. After 200 metres, turn left and continue for approximately 10 km to the site.

Blackwater River Crossing Rec Site (Map 55/F4)
Blackwater River Crossing is a six-unit site on the shores of the Blackwater River. The treed site is on the north side of the river and is RV accessible. The historic Alexander Mackenzie Trail crosses through and there are walking trails along the river in both directions. The site offers recently upgraded toilets, tables and fire rings.

Blue Jay Lake Rec Site (Map 22/B3)
Blue Jay Lake is a great staging area for a variety of activities in the Coast Mountains southwest of Bella Coola. There are five campsites on the shores of the lake and scenic trails leading past small lakes to an impressive viewpoint over the Bentinck Arms. Access is via a steep, sometimes rough forestry service road.

Blue Lake North Rec Site (Map 29/A2)
This small, three-unit site can be found between the gas line and Blue Lake. When the campsites are full, many folks camp on the gas line. The actual site includes tables and toilets, and there are opportunities for fishing and swimming in the lake. For access, turn east onto Blue Lake Road from Highway 97, and after 3 km, turn south onto the gas line for 500 metres.

Blue Lake West Rec Site (Map 29/A2)
This beautiful site lies amidst mature fir trees on the high shoreline of Blue Lake. Closed to vehicle traffic, the site is walk-in only. Boat access is also possible via a private resort 400 metres west of the site. There are four campsites here with table and toilets.

Bluff Lake Rec Site (Map 13/D3)
This popular fishing site is limited to day-use only. The stunning mountain views, the scenic Bluff Lake-Pioneer Trail and abundant rainbow and bull trout make this a hot spot for recreation. Access can be found from Highway 20 by turning south on Tatlayoko Lake Road and then taking a right on Bluff Lake Road (aka West Branch Road) and continuing for 17 km.

Boar Lake Rec Site (Map 17/G6)
Just northwest of Flat Lake Park, this small three-unit site is situated along the eastern shore of Boar Lake. Access to the site is very rough at times and four-wheel drive is recommended. A rough boat launch is available.

Boat Lake Rec Site (Map 54/F4)
Another in a series of lakes strung along the Euchinko River. The site features a mix of sites in an open meadow or in the forest at the edge of the lake. Fishing is popular in both the lake and the river.

Bog Lake Rec Site (Map 7/A2)
Located just southwest of Bonaparte Lake, this is a popular destination for campers and anglers. There are several access roads that lead into the three-unit site (most notably from North Bonaparte Road and Bog Lake North Road), and there is a boat launch, picnic tables and toilets.

Bonaparte Lake Rec Site (Map 7/C2)
Situated on the west side of the lake, this site is open and grassy and has four campsites with a good gravel boat launch. Primarily used as a hunting camp, this site is RV and trailer accessible and is accessed off the 3700 Road.

Bonaparte River Bridge Rec Site (Map 6/D2)

This is a scenic, two-unit site on the Bonaparte River. It is suitable for small RVs and trailers, and there are toilets available. Visitors will find fishing opportunities in the river. Traveling east, the site appears north off of Clinton Loon Lake Forest Service Road (3400 Rd) before the bridge.

Bonaparte River Suicide Crossing Rec Site (Map 6/F2)

This single-unit site rests in a quiet and scenic spot on the Bonaparte River. There are tables and toilets available, and opportunities for fishing and picnicking. Traveling north on Mount Grant Forest Service Road, take the northeast branch after 3.5 km, travel for 4 km, turn east and follow the road into the site.

Boot Lake Rec Site (Map 55/D5)

This is a small site set in the forest next to Boot Lake. There is a cartop boat launch and two or three campsites, not suitable for larger trailers.

Bootjack Lake Rec Site (Map 43/F7)

Southwest of the town of Likely, this heavily used site offers nine semi-open campsites, but only two are along the lakeshore. Use caution as the access road is an active mine access road.

Bosk Lake Rec Site (Map 31/B4)

A sandy beach along the shore makes this site an ideal family attraction. The site is located along the eastern shore of the lake and is home to four vehicle units, which are trailer accessible. The boat launch is across the beach; four-wheel drive might be necessary.

Boundary Lake Rec Site (Map 19/D3)

Boundary Lake is a small marshy lake found off Road 7, west of Clearwater. The site is small with about three campsites equipped with picnic tables. There is a gravel boat launch enabling small boats, canoes and kayaks onto the lake.

Bowers Lake Rec Site (Map 19/C3)

Access to this quiet, lakeside site is via a very rough four-wheel drive access road. The site lies along the east side of the lake and is home to four campsites and a cartop boat launch. There is a nice beach and good access to the lake for paddling and fishing.

Brewster Lake Rec Site (Map 53/F3)

There's space for two vehicle units at this small site on the shores of Brewster Lake. As you might expect, fishing is the prime pursuit here. To access the site, turn west off Kluskus Forest Service Road onto Marten Road. The site access road will be 1 km from here.

Brigham Springs Rec Site (Map 17/C5)

The mineral springs are the main attraction to this small five-unit campsite, which is furnished with picnic tables for the benefit of both day-use and overnight visitors. The site is popular with equestrian riders and hunters and is easily accessed off the Upper Dog Creek Road.

Cariboo Island North Rec Site (Map 44/C7)

This beautiful beach site rests on the north side of Cariboo Island in Quesnel Lake. It has two units with tables and toilets, and there are opportunities for boating, fishing and beach activities. Visitors will find gorgeous views of the lake and the Cariboo Mountains. The site can be accessed by boat, with launches available at Abbott Creek, Horsefly Bay and Likely.

Cariboo Island South Rec Site (Map 44/C7)

This two-unit site can be found along the beach on the south tip of Cariboo Island in Quesnel Lake. It is a great spot for canoers and kayakers. There are tables and toilets, and opportunities for fishing and beach activities in the lake. A primitive hiking trail follows the island shore. This site can be accessed by boat, with launches available at Abbott Creek, Horsefly Bay and Likely.

Carol Lake Rec Site (Map 4/F7)

Carol Lake is a small, popular fishing lake, just north of Carpenter Lake. There are eight RV friendly campsites and a cartop boat launch onto the lake. There is an extensive trail network accessible from the site. Access can be found off of the Marshall Lake Road from Highway 40.

Charlotte Lake Rec Site (Map 24/E4)

Charlotte Lake is a big lake that provides good swimming and canoeing in the summer. The ten-unit campsite is easily accessed from Highway 20. As a result, campsites are at a premium on summer weekends.

Chaunigan Lake Rec Site (Map 14/E5)

Offering scenic views of the Coast Mountains, there are six campsites and a cartop boat launch on the west side of this often-windy lake. There is also a lodge found on the east side of the lake. Windsurfing is popular here.

Chilko-Taseko Junction Rec Site (Map 26/G7)

This site is primarily used as a put-in or take-out for kayakers and rafters on the Chilko River. There are five sites with a boat launch at the site. Anglers and hunters also use the open, grassy site above the confluence of the two rivers.

Chimney Lake Centre Rec Site (Map 17/D1)

This large, open and grassy site has been recently upgraded. It boasts 11 units, with tables, toilets and a boat launch. This launch is the best choice for ski boats accessing Chimney Lake. In addition to boating, there are opportunities for fishing and swimming. Easily accessed off the Chimney Valley Road, there is a fee to camp here from April to November.

Chimney Lake North Rec Site (Map 17/D1)

This 25-unit, vehicle-accessible site offers opportunities for boating, fishing, swimming and waterskiing. The large, recently upgraded units sit in an open grassland area with a large beach and day-use area. There is also a boat launch available. Easily accessed off the Chimney Valley Road, there is a fee to camp here from April to November.

Chisel Lake Rec Site (Map 58/C6)

Due to the challenging road conditions, this site is not heavily used and can often be found vacant. It lies along the scenic Chisel Lake shore and contains a rough boat launch and three campsites with picnic tables.

Choelquoit Lake Rec Site (Map 14/B4)

Better known as a day-use destination, there is space for two vehicle units behind the sand dunes at the east end of the lake. A sandy beach, lots of Chilcotin sun plus a phenomenal view of the Niut Range in the background make this a great place to stay during the summer.

Christmas Lake Rec Site (Map 19/B1)

This lakeside site has two nice units set amidst heavy forest cover. Unfortunately, they lie within close proximity to the Canim-Hendrix Lake Road, which is an active haul road. The site is equipped with a boat launch. Access can be found via Canim-Hendrix Lake Road. When this road becomes the gravel 6000 Road, continue past the 60-07 km marker and make a right onto the Christmas Lake access road.

Chubb Lake Rec Site (Map 56/D5)

Situated on the north end of Chubb Lake, this regularly maintained and recently upgraded site is open year round. It offers a boat launch, with opportunities for swimming, fishing and ice fishing. The site is accessible by two-wheel drive vehicles. Follow the Chubb Lake Bible Camp sign about 9 km south of Hixon. At 100 metres, turn left, travel to the "Y" in the road, keep right, and turn right at 7 km.

Chutanli Lake Rec Site (Map 53/G4)

Chutanli means, "Where the trout swim under the spruce trees" in the language of the Carrier people. Not surprisingly, there is good fishing in the lake. There are 13 campsites at this site as well as a boat launch onto the lake. An old prospector's cabin is also found in the area.

Clearwater Lake Rec Site (Map 25/A6)

Found alongside the graveled section of Highway 20, this small site offers space for only two parties. It is found in an open spruce forest and also sports a cartop boat launch.

Cleswuncut Lake Rec Site (Map 55/F4)

This small site is located next to the Blackwater Road south of Prince George. It is a single-unit site with day-use amenities along the Alexander Mackenzie Trail. A small car topper boat launch is available.

Cochin Lake Rec Site (Map 13/F2)

There are six campsites amid the open pine and aspen forest on the shores of the lake. Also home to a boat launch, the site is located on the southern shore off the Tatlayoko Lake Road. To the north is a series of cross-country ski trails that make for fine hiking or biking in summer. This site is also a popular destination for anglers.

Recsite Adventures

Coldscaur Lake North Rec Site (Map 19/E3) 🦶🏕️🪑🚤🚶🛶⛵🎣🚗🚩
Located on the north end of Coldscaur Lake, this well-developed, 13-unit site offers opportunities for fishing, picnicking, hunting and boating. The vehicle-accessible site includes tables, toilets and a boat launch. To reach it, take TFL 18 Road 2 north of Clearwater for 28 km. While in the area, be sure to visit the nearby trail that leads from the western end of the lake to an impressive rock bridge.

Coldscaur Lake South Rec Site (Map 19/F3) 🦶🏕️🪑🚤🚶🛶⛵🎣🚗🚩
This medium-sized campsite lies on the south end of Coldscaur Lake. It offers two separate areas, with basic facilities including a boat launch, tables and toilets. There are opportunities for picnicking and fishing here. While in the area, be sure to visit the nearby trail that leads from the western end of the lake to an impressive rock bridge.

Cougar Lake Rec Site (Map 19/C3) 🦶🏕️🪑🚤🛶🎣🚗🚩
South of Canim Lake, this site sits on the northern shore of the small lake and is a popular spot with anglers. There are three campsites available along with a cartop boat launch. Access is off the Bowers Lake Forest Service Road, which can be reached via the Mahood Lake Road.

Crater Lake Rec Site (Map 40/G3) ⛺🚶🎣🚗
This small recreation site can be challenging to access due to the steep hiking trail that leads into the area. The site has two tenting sites and a toilet located next to the lake. Access to the trail that leads into the site can be found from Nazko via the Michelle Bazekeo Road.

Crescent Lake Rec Site (Map 57/D5) 🦶🏕️🪑🎣🚗🚩
This site has good two-wheel drive access along with a cartop boat launch and a basic shelter. There are only three campsites here, which are usually full during hunting season.

Crooked Lake North Rec Site (Map 31/B3) 🦶🏕️🪑🚤🚶🎣🚩
This site lies in a large and open space, suitable for large groups. With five camping areas scattered from the shoreline to the trees, there are opportunities for boating, fishing and hiking up to the nearby alpine. There is a boat launch available, as well as tables and toilets. The site can be accessed from Crooked Lake Road; follow the signs for Crooked Lake Resort.

Crooked Lake South Rec Site (Map 31/B3) 🦶🏕️🪑🚤🛶🎣🚗🚩
This scenic, two-unit site on the west shore of Crooked Lake is the perfect beach camping spot. There is a boat launch available, with opportunities for fishing, kayaking and beach activities. Facilities here include tables and toilets. The site is vehicle accessible, although access may be limited to those with large trailers. Access is off Crooked Lake Road north of Hendrix Lake.

Crystal Lake Rec Site (Map 19/B6) 🦶🏕️🪑🚤🎣🚗🚩
Not far from Highway 24 via the North Bonaparte Road, this site is situated along the northern shore of the lake. The 12 vehicle units along with a cartop boat launch can be used as a base to explore the many lakes in the area.

Davidson Bridge Rec Site (Map 14/G5) 🦶🏕️🪑🎣🚗🚩
Found about 73 km down the Taseko Lake Road (900 Rd), there are two RV friendly campsites at this site, which is a popular launching point for rafters and kayakers heading out onto the Taseko River. Anglers also use the site.

Deadman Lake Rec Site (Map 7/A4) 🦶🏕️🪑🚤🎣🚗🚩🚻
Deadman Lake is found in the eerily named valley north of Kamloops Lake. The site is off the Vidette Road, 47 km north of Highway 1, and has four treed campsites together with tables and a cartop boat launch.

Dean River [Fish Trap] Rec Site (Map 24/F2) 🦶🏕️🪑🎣🚗🚩🚻
This site is found north of a historical site and offers three well-spaced campsites along the river. The meandering river is a nice place to canoe, but most come for the fabled trout fishing.

Dewar Lake Rec Site (Map 29/E4) 🦶🏕️🪑🎣🚗🚩
Northeast of Williams Lake, off Spokin Lake Road, this small, five-unit campsite is primarily used by anglers. A steep and rough cartop boat launch is also available at the lake; four-wheel drive is recommended. To access the site, take Horsefly Road east from Highway 97 and make a right onto Spokin Lake Forest Service Road. The site will be on the right after 400 metres.

Dorsey Lake Rec Site (Map 29/E1) 🦶🚶🎣🚗🚩
Set amid the UBC Alex Fraser Research Forest, Dorsey Lake is a seldom-visited spot due to the rough four-wheel drive access. This small three-unit site is rarely used and trailers are not suggested. There is a small cartop boat launch at the lake.

Double Lakes Rec Site (Map 19/E2) 🦶🏕️🪑🚤🛶🎣🚗🚩
Northwest of Clearwater off Road 20, this site is quite popular with anglers as there are three shoreline campsites, along with picnic tables and a rough boat launch onto the lake.

Drewry Lake East Rec Site (Map 19/B3) 🦶🏕️🪑🎣
This three-unit site on the northeastern shore of Drewry Lake provides opportunities for fishing and boating. It offers a boat launch as well as picnic tables and toilets. The site can be easily accessed off of Mahood Lake Road (8000 Rd).

Drewry Lake West Rec Site (Map 19/A3) 🦶🏕️🪑🎣
Situated on the western shore of Drewry Lake, southeast of Forest Grove, this five-unit site provides opportunities for fishing and boating. The site can be accessed off of 201 Road at 22.5 km. The rough access road is rocky and may not be suitable for large trailers.

Dugan Lake Rec Site (Map 29/D5) 🦶🏕️🪑🎣🚗🚩
The lake can be found off the Horsefly Road and is a favourite destination of local anglers for its abundant trout. There are two parts of the site; the first has 11 large and level gravel pads, ideal for RVs. The second is a treed area along the lake shore for smaller truck campers and tenting. In total there are 23 sites with a boat launch and small dock.

Dunsapie Lake Rec Site (Map 7/G3) 🦶🏕️🪑🚤🎣🚗🚩🚻
This site is located on the Jamieson Creek Forest Service Road and receives heavy use throughout the summer months. It has three camping units as well as a cartop boat launch.

Eagle Lake Rec Site (Map 13/F1) 🦶🏕️🪑🚤🎣🚗🚩
Although the lake is not far from the highway, this site is not very busy. Perhaps it is the open meadow setting, which can get rather hot in the summer. Maybe it is the fluctuating water levels that make boat access difficult. No matter the reason, visitors should find space to camp and good fishing.

East Maury Lake Rec Site (Map 19/G1) 🦶🏕️🪑🚤🛶🎣🚗🚩
This site lies on the north end of the lake, providing three campsites along with a gravel boat launch and picnic tables. An alternative to this popular area are the less developed campsites found at Maury Lake to the west.

Ejas Lake Rec Site (Map 19/F1) 🦶🏕️🪑🚤🛶🎣🚗🚩
There are three camping units at this site, which is set along the western shore of Ejas Lake. Picnic tables and a cartop boat launch are also available at the lake.

Elbow Lake Rec Site (Map 31/A4) 🦶🏕️🪑🚤🛶🎣🚗🚩
This multi-level recreation site has several campsites along the shoreline of Elbow Lake. There are treed sites further from the lake. There is no designated boat launch; however, small boats can be hand launched from the shore.

Elk [Island] Lake Rec Site (Map 29/C1) 🦶🏕️🪑🎣🚗🚩
Elk Lake is located off the north side of the Beaver Lake Road, east of McLeese Lake. The site has two camping areas; first a large open pasture area, and the second has two spots closer to the lake. Boat access is limited; however, a small dock gives improved access.

Felker Lake Rec Site (Map 29/C7) 🦶🏕️🪑🎣🚗🚩
Set along a lakeshore opening and sporting picnic tables and a boat launch, this 11 unit site was upgraded in 2010 with large, well-defined camping areas. Fees are in effect April to November. Access can be found off Highway 20 by turning west on Dog Creek Road. Continue for 7 km onto the Chimney Lake Road and proceed for another 15 km.

Fir Lake Rec Site (Map 28/B4) 🦶🏕️🪑🚤🚶🛶🎣🚗🚩
RVs will find plenty of room at this 12 unit, semi-open site, with large, well-defined camping areas. The site also has a large boat launch and parking area. The lake is known as a great fly-fishing destination and there is a hiking trail around the lake for all to enjoy.

Fish Lake Rec Site (Map 15/A7)
To access the lake, a four-wheel drive vehicle and lots of patience is necessary since sections of the road are in poor condition with downed trees and high water levels. Adding to the uncertainty is the possibility of the Taseko Gold Mine taking over the area. Fish Lake offers five campsites and a cartop boat launch with the beautiful backdrop of Anvil Mountain.

Fishpot Lake Rec Site (Map 40/F2)
There is a small, open site with space for five vehicle units on the shores of Fishpot Lake. The road in is steep, but manageable by two-wheel drive vehicle. There is a gravel boat launch onto the lake.

Fletcher Lake Rec Site (Map 15/F3)
A rough boat launch has been built at this open, grassy site with space for six camping units. The site is usually busy since the roads from Farwell Canyon and Hanceville are both good and there are some large trout in the lake. From Highway 20 at Lee's Corner, follow the Big Creek Road (700 Rd) for about 26 km to find the recreation site.

Fly Lake Rec Site (Map 18/C1)
Set below Timothy Mountain, Fly Lake is a small, scenic lake located north of Lac La Hache off the Timothy-Fly Lake Road (1600 Rd). With just one campsite the lake is also a popular picnicking area. The site offers a cartop boat launch.

Forest Lake Rec Site (Map 29/C3)
North of Williams Lake, Forest Lake is a popular angling and water sport destination. The site has 12 defined spots, but the open grassy area allows for more units to crowd in. There is a boat launch and basic facilities available.

> *Be careful when travelling to any site and watch out for industrial vehicles in active logging areas.*

Access can be found off of Highway 97 by turning right onto Lyne Creek Road, which leads to the Forest Lake Road and the recreation site some 5 km later.

French Lake Rec Site (Map 19/B5)
Despite the rough four-wheel drive access and lack of facilities, this site is a popular day-use area for anglers. There is a well-used boat launch area and room for a couple of campsites.

Friburg Rec Site (Map 4/B6)
Friburg is found on the western shore of the picturesque Tyaughton Lake. Natives named the lake Tyaughton or 'jumping fish' due to the incredible aerial display the trout in this lake like to perform. The open site has a cartop boat launch and room for about five campsites.

Gavin Lake Rec Site (Map 29/F1; 43/F7)
Southwest of Likely, Gavin Lake forms the hub of the UBC Alex Fraser Research Forest. The site offers five designated sites in an opening next to the east end of the lake. Enjoy canoeing or fishing or explore the fantastic research forest trail system throughout the year. To reach this RV accessible site, follow Gavin Lake Road to the Education Centre.

Genevieve Lake Rec Site (Map 56/G5)
Found about 13 km from Highway 97, this small, user-maintained site can be a challenge to access during wet weather. Access is found by taking a right of 1200 Road at 1222 km. There are three campsites, a rustic boat launch and decent fishing or canoeing on the lake.

Government Lake Rec Site (Map 56/E1)
Access from the south end of the lake is deactivated, while access from the north is reported to be washed out. Needless to say, this small, rustic site with a cartop boat launch is not that busy. In addition to fishing, there are trails in the area.

Greenlee Lake Rec Site (Map 19/A2)
Near Canim Lake, Greenlee Lake is accessible via a rough, steep two-wheel drive access road. The site offers two vehicle units and a rustic boat launch in a heavily wooded area along the northern shore of the smaller lake.

Greeny Lake North Rec Site (Map 18/C2)
The close proximity of the lake to Lac La Hache makes this lake a popular spot. The site is quite large with 16 recently upgraded campsites, a beach and boat launch along the northern shores of Greeny Lake. There is a good mix of both grassy open campsites and treed sites to choose from. Fees are in effect from May to November.

Groundhog Lake Rec Site (Map 44/A1)
Located on the shores of Groundhog Lake, this site is known as a great picnic spot for hikers, bikers, cross-country skiers and snowmobilers. The site is accessible via the Groundhog Lake Trail from the top end of the Main Street in Barkerville.

Gun Lake South Rec Site (Map 4/A7)
Easily accessed off the Gun Lake Road, this seven-unit site is suitable for RVs. There is a separate boat launch and a host of trails in the area for those not interested in boating, fishing or other watersports.

Hammer Lake North Rec Site (Map 7/C2)
This site is found off the Egan-Bonaparte Forest Service Road (3700 Rd) and offers 11 campsites with a boat launch. ATV and snowmobile trails are readily accessible in the area. Boaters should note the electric motor only restriction.

Hangman Springs Pit Rec Site (Map 42/C2)
This small, day-use only, site is a staging area that is maintained by the Quesnel Cross Country Motorcycle Association. ATVing is a popular activity in the area, in addition to horseback riding and snowshoeing. Access can be found about 20 km west from Quesnel on the Nazko Road. The site will be on the right side of the road.

Hanham Lake Rec Site (Map 54/E4)
This small, open site is found at the end of a narrow, winding access road. There is good fly-fishing along the Euchiniko River, which flows into and out of the lake. The two campsites are above the lake with no easy access to launch a boat.

Helena Lake Rec Site (Map 17/G2)
A popular recreation site, this recently upgraded site offers 13 well-defined campsites and is RV accessible. Fees are in effect from May to November. Access can be found off of Wright Station Road, southwest of Lac La Hache.

Hen Ingram Rec Site (Map 30/F1)
Hen Ingram Lake offers a medium-sized site that is accessible to larger RVs. There are nine well-defined campsites along the shoreline. With a good boat launch and lots of parking this site can get extremely busy.

Hihium Lake South Rec Site (Map 6/F5)
Easily accessed off the Clinton-Loon Lake Forest Service Road (3400 Rd), this 20 unit site is suitable for RVs and trailers. Fishing is the main attraction to the area and there is a boat launch at the site. Note the engine size restriction of 7.5 kW (10 hp) on the lake.

Hobson Lake Rec Site (Map 53/D1)
A narrow, winding road leads to this lake, which is named after cowboy author Rich Hobson. A small site with two campsites, there is a small cartop boat launch, suitable for small boats or canoes only. The site is accessed off the Kluskus-Hobson Forest Service Road.

Honolulu Indian Head Rec Site (Map 41/C4)
It's an exotic name, but don't expect a jungle full of orchids dripping dew here. This small two-unit campsite site is located on the Nazko River and is all about dry, arid, Chilcotin–style summer. The semi-open area is accessed about 23 km down the Honolulu Road (7000 Rd).

Horn Lake Rec Site (Map 13/D2)
The largest (and arguably nicest) site in the area, Horn Lake sports 14 park-like campsites spread along the waterfront. Despite easy access to the site, it is remote enough that the campsite is rarely full. Further south, Bluff Lake offers a day-use site with a boat launch and there is a nice trail up Butler Peak. Fees apply from May to October.

Recsite Adventures

Horsefly Bay Rec Site (Map 30/C1) 🥾🏕🛶🎣🚣🚶🛥🌲
There are three campsites in this very small site at the mouth of the Horsefly River. There is limited space for trailers and the site offers a boat launch for small cartoppers only. Access is via Horsefly Bay Road.

Horsefly River Flats Rec Site (Map 30/B2) 🥾🏕🛶🏍🎣🌲
Formerly Squaw Flats, this roadside site is often used as a day-use area to float down the river or watch the salmon spawn in fall. There are two campsites next to the Mitchell Bay Road and the Horsefly River north of Horsefly.

Horsefly River Rec Site (Map 30/F3) 🥾🏕🛶🎣🚣🏍🎣🌲
The small treed area lies along the north side of the river near the junction between the Black Creek Road and McKinley Lake Road (500 Rd). The river is a fine fishing destination and there are five large, open and level campsites that are a great location to make a basecamp. A boat launch is available.

Hotnarko Lake Rec Site (Map 24/B1) ⛺🚣🚶🚴🐴🎣
This three-unit campsite is limited to foot, bike or fly-in access making it a peaceful tenting area for people willing to trek in. Anglers are well advised to haul in a canoe or small boat as shore fishing is difficult and the lake is too windy for float tubes.

Howard Lake Rec Site (Map 19/B2) 🥾🏕🛶🚣🐴🛥🏍🎣🌲
On the western shore of Howard Lake, this popular site is home to 18 vehicle units complete with picnic tables and a cartop boat launch. Most campsites are set in an open area next to the lake, although there are a few secluded sites as well.

Howes Lake Rec Site (Map 29/B2) 🥾🏕🛶🏍🐴🎣🌲
You can find this eight-unit treed site off a rough road north of Williams Lake. All the campsites are scattered along the eastern shore of Howes Lake and are divided into distinct access points. This allows plenty of privacy between each site.

Irish Lake Rec Site (Map 18/E5) 🥾🏕🎣
This popular fishing lake has a very small recreation site with room for one camping party on its shores. With a cartop boat launch, the site is mostly used as a day-use site by 100 Mile House residents. The lake is stocked and aerated.

Isobel Lake Rec Site (Map 7/F7) 🥾🛶🚣🚶♿🎣🛶🛥♿
Part of the Isobel Lake Interpretive Forest, this site is wheelchair accessible with 19 campsites. There is also a group camping area that can be reserved as well as a cartop boat launch and a well-developed cross-country ski trail system in the area. There is a fee to camp here from June through October.

Italia Lake Rec Site (Map 19/F2) 🥾🏕🛶🚣🏍🐴🎣🌲
Italia Lake is one of the bigger lakes in the area and is easily accessed off the busy Road 20. There two-units available at the south end of the lake as well as picnic tables and a gravel boat launch.

Jacksons Hole Rec Site (Map 29/B1) 🥾🛶🚣🏍🐴🎣🌲
East of McCleese Lake, you can find this seven-unit site off the rough two-wheel drive Jackson Lake Road. The site has one large open area around the recently improved boat launch as well as some treed sites along the lake shore.

Jacobie Lake Rec Site (Map 43/E7) 🥾🛶🚣🎣🌲
Off the Likely Road, this is a popular site with easy access. With level sites along the shoreline there is room to group together as the sites are primarily open. Technically, there are seven designated sites and a boat launch suitable for trailers.

Jacques Lake Rec Site (Map 30/E1) 🥾🏕🛶🚣🛥🏍🐴🎣🌲
Easily accessed off the Haggens Point Road (Z Rd), northeast of Horsefly, Jacques Lake offers seven campsites along the northern shore of the good fishing lake. The first three sites are in a large open area that is suitable for a large group. There is a small trailer-accessible boat launch.

Jim Creek [Windy Mountain Road] Rec Site (Map 19/C4) 🥾🏕🎣
This single-unit recreation site sits north of Bridge Lake between Bowers and Needa Lakes, near Jim Creek. Amenities include a fire ring, toilet and table. The site is accessible to smaller RV's willing to drive down the Windy Mountain Forest Service Road. Look for the site just past the bridge crossing over Jim Creek.

Jones Creek Rec Site (Map 4/F7) 🥾🏕🛶🚶🛥🎣
Jones Creek is a small three-unit site on Carpenter Lake, where Jones Creek flows into the man-made lake. The semi-open site has good road access, and larger units should have no trouble getting to the area.

Kappan Lake East Rec Site (Map 24/C2) 🥾🏕🛶🚣🛥🎣🖼
Situated on the eastern shore of Kappan Lake, this popular six-unit site provides a lovely view of Kappan Mountain. Visitors will find opportunities for fishing, boating and beach activities, and amenities including a boat launch, picnic tables and toilets. The rough and narrow access road can be found off of Kappan Mountain Road; four-wheel drive is recommended.

Kappan Lake West Rec Site (Map 24/C2) 🥾🏕🛶🚣🎣🌲
This is a popular two-unit site located on the western shore of Kappan Lake. There are great opportunities for boating and fishing, and the site includes a boat launch, tables and toilets. The rough and narrow access road can be found off of Kappan Mountain Road; four-wheel drive is recommended.

Keno Lake Rec Site (Map 44/E7) 🥾🛶🚣🎣🌲
Keno Lake is a popular stocked fishing lake found near Horsefly along the Haggens Point Road. This small two-section site has a large level site in the trees and a more open area beside the boat launch.

Kitty Ann Lake Rec Site (Map 19/E2) 🥾🏕🛶🚣🛥🐴🎣🌲🖼
Just off Road 231, this site sits on the eastern shore of Kitty Lake. The lake is quite small and is situated next to the scenic Rioux Mountain. There are five campsites available with picnic tables and a cartop boat launch.

Klinne Lake Rec Site (Map 44/E7) 🥾🏕🎣🌲
Klinne Lake is a small lake just south of the much larger Quesnel Lake. Most of the people who come to stay at this five vehicle site are anglers or overflow campers from the site on Quesnel Lake. There is no developed boat launch; however, it is possible to launch a cartop boat here.

Knewstubb Lake Rec Site (Map 53/B1) 🥾🛶🚶🐴🎣🌲
Overlooking the Knewstubb Lake portion of the Nechako Reservoir, this eight-unit site is located just east of Kenney Dam. It has good road access and a boat launch, and is an ideal base for day trips in the area.

Kuyakuz Lake Rec Site (Map 53/E6) 🥾🛶🚣🚶🐴🐴🎣🌲
The name of this lake means, "Fish come here." Not surprisingly, the seven unit campsite sees heavy use from anglers. It is also near the Messue Ford, an alternate access to the Alexander Mackenzie Trail for off-road enthusiasts.

Ladies Creek Rec Site (Map 44/C4) 🥾🏕🛶🚣🛥🎣🌲
Visitors can choose from six spots at this site, which lies along the eastern shore of Cariboo. There is a pebble beach and a steep, long boat launch that may require a four-wheel drive vehicle. Access the site from 6400 Road across the Cariboo River from Likely; there is a sign on the left.

Lake of the Trees Rec Site (Map 18/E2) 🥾🏕🚣🎣
This three-unit site sits on the eastern shore of Lake of the Trees, facing west into the sunset. Although there is no boat launch here, it is possible to hand launch small cartop boats or kayaks. Lake of the Trees lies north of 100 Mile House, off the Wilcox-Dempsey Forest Service Road.

Lake La Mare Rec Site (Map 4/G6) ⛺🚣🚶🐴🛥🐴🎣🌲
A deteriorating road leads to this small, three-unit camping area; four-wheel drive is recommended. There is a rustic launching site and access to trails leading to Buckholder or Carol Lake. Access the site via Yalakom Road off of Highway 40, west of Lillooet.

La Salle Lakes [West] Rec Site (Map 59/B1) 🥾🏕🛶🚣🚶🎣🛶
Just off Highway 16, northwest of McBride, La Salle Lake (sometimes called Lasalle West) offers a camping area complete with picnic tables, a small beach area and a boat launch. Little La Salle Lake can be accessed via a short trail from La Salle Lake and offers a small wharf and a 20 site tenting area.

Lastcourse Lake Rec Site (Map 7/B2) 🥾🏕🛶🚣🎣🛶
Located southwest of Bonaparte Lake, this rec site has room for one unit. To reach it, turn east onto 70 Mile-Green Lake/North Bonaparte Road off Highway 97. At the 3240 km marker, turn right onto the Eagan-Bonaparte Forest Service Road. Stay on this road for a while until you reach the Clinton Upper Loon Lake Road (3300 Rd), which leads to the short access trail.

Latremouille Lake Rec Site (Map 19/G6) 🥾🏕🛶🚣🎣🛶
This rustic, treed site sits on a popular fishing lake. It consists of nine campsites spread along the water's edge with some above, away from the water. There is a rough, cartop boat launch and two outhouses. Traveling west from Little Fort on Highway 24, the access road to the lake appears at about 16 km.

Lavoie Lake Rec Site (Map 54/A2)
A small, treed site lies on the eastern shore of this well-known fishing lake. It contains five campsites, tables, toilets and a boat launch. The main pursuits are boating and fishing. The site is accessible by two-wheel drive and can be reached via Gold Road, 16 km off of Kluskus Forest Service Road.

Lawrence Lake East Rec Site (Map 19/E2)
This small, two-unit site on the east end of Lawrence Lake provides a gravel boat launch, tables and toilets, with opportunities for fishing and boating in the lake. To reach the site, take Road 20 off of TFL 18 Road 2 from Clearwater.

Lawrence Lake West Rec Site (Map 19/E2)
Located on the west end of Lawrence Lake, this site has one unit set amongst the trees. The site offers tables, toilets and a boat launch, with opportunities for fishing in the lake. The site can be found at about 14.5 km down the Road 20, off of TFL 18 Road 2 from Clearwater.

Leon Creek Rec Site (Map 5/D6)
As of 2015, this small recreation site is closed due to a landslide blocking access.

Lightning Creek Rec Site (Map 43/B1)
A mid-sized site just east of Quesnel, this site has two camping areas along the creek with several more along the access road. The small site lies next to the Lightning Creek and is the perfect getaway for weary travellers. From Quesnel, take Highway 26 towards Wells and turn right onto 1300 Road.

Lintz Lake Rec Site (Map 55/A2)
Lintz Lake is small and stocked with rainbow trout. Located just off the Pelican Lake Forest Service Road on the north side of the lake, the recently-updated site has 10 units and a gravel boat launch. It is accessible by two-wheel drive.

Little Big Bar Lake Rec Site (Map 5/D1)
Access to this popular site is via a rough two-wheel drive road that branches off the Big Bar Lake Road off Highway 97. The site lies along the southern shore of the lake and offers six campsites in a semi-open setting. Picnic tables are available at the campsites as well as a steep cartop boat launch.

Little Scot Lake Rec Site (Map 7/B2)
The small recreation site is located on the north end of a small, popular fishing lake next to the Eagan-Bonaparte Forest Service Road (3700 Rd). Access to the site is good, and small RVs often fill the three spaces available.

Lorin Lake Rec Site (Map 19/C3)
Suitable for small RVs, this site has 11 campsites and a boat launch in an opening along the shoreline. Canoeing, fishing and hunting are the main attractions to the lake, and ATV and snowmobile trails are found in the area. The site can be found off the Bowers-Lorin Forest Service Road.

Lost Horse Lake Rec Site (Map 19/E5)
Lost Horse Lake lies southwest of Clearwater. The site is used mainly by anglers; there are four campsites with tables and a pit toilet. The access road to the lake branches off from Taweel Forest Service Road, which can be reached via Highway 24.

Lower Chilako River Rec Site (Map 55/F1)
Southwest of Prince George, the Pelican Lake Forest Service Road leads to a number of recreational sites. The Chilako Bridge and Chilako River Recreation Sites are no longer maintained. You may still camp there if you do not mind the steady rumble of logging trucks going by. There is a recreation site called Lower Chilako River at the junction of the Chilako River and Lower Mud Road (west side of bridge).

Lower Lake Rec Site (Map 18/E3)
On the eastern shore of Lower Lake, a rough road provides access to two campsites set amid a grassy area next to the water. There is a small boat launch at the lake and trails in the area. To reach the site, take Archie Meadow Road for 4 km off Canim Hendrix Lake Road (past Buffalo Creek).

MacKenzie Lake East Rec Site (Map 44/A1)
This small, recently upgraded site is located on the eastern of the MacKenzie Lakes. There is a boat launch, picnic tables, fire rings and a pit toilet, with opportunities for boating and canoeing and fishing. The site can be easily accessed by two-wheel drive. To reach it, take Blackwater Road to the Baldy Hughes community, where the highway turns to gravel. 6.5 km from this point, turn left, and then right at 1.5 km.

MacKenzie Lake West Rec Site (Map 44/A1)
This small rec site can be found on the western MacKenzie Lake. The site offers recently upgraded amenities, including a boat launch, tables, fire rings and one pit toilet. The lake is a good spot for fishing, canoeing and boating. Although usually accessible by two-wheel drive, this site may be difficult to access during springtime or after heavy rains. For site access, take Blackwater Road to the Baldy Hughes community, where the highway turns to gravel. At 8 km, the site appears on your left.

Mackill Lake Rec Site (Map 27/D3)
Mackill Lake is found southwest of Palmer Lake along the Lt. Palmer Route, a short walk from the road. The popular lake has lots of stocked rainbow and it is possible to tent here or camp at roadside where the outhouses are located.

Marshall Creek Rec Site (Map 4/E6)
Located just below where Marshall Creek flows out of Marshall Lake, this is a small, treed site, with space enough for three groups. There is a cartop boat launch at the site that has good road access. You can access the site from Marshall Lake Road South, off Marshall Lake Road, north of Carpenter Lake.

Marshall Lake North Rec Site (Map 4/D6)
This is a fairly open site on the northeastern shores of Marshall Lake. There are seven campsites for anglers and those looking for a nice place to camp. Trail enthusiasts will be amazed at the number of trails to choose from in the area. The site is split into two sections, which can be found off Marshall Lake Road North/Mud Creek Main.

Maude Lake Rec Site (Map 43/D4)
This medium-sized site is a popular spot, especially with anglers. The four campsites are set in a forested area next to the lake and are equipped with picnic tables. A rough boat launch is also available at the lake. The site can be found off the M Road, which branches off the 4900 Road.

Mayson Lake Rec Site (Map 7/F2)
Mayson Lake is a large, scenic lake just south of Bonaparte Lake. The site has four camping units and a cartop boat launch. Access is off the Jamieson Creek Road (rough two-wheel drive). There is a series of horseback trails along with ATVing and snowmobiling in the area.

Be sure to visit www.sitesandtrailsbc.ca for the latest information on fees, closures and upgrades to the recreation site you plan to visit.

McCall Flats Rec Site (Map 23/C1)
This site is a popular destination for bears, both grizzly and black, and the occasional angler or camper. Most locals avoid the flats because of the aforementioned bruins. There are five sites next to the Bella Coola River. The site can be accessed from the Talchako/Noomst Forest Service Road.

McIntyre Lake Rec Site (Map 28/G7)
Set in a small open area next to the lake, this site is easily reached via the Meldrum Creek Road (1100 Rd). Split into four camping areas each with its own entrance, the site has no defined boat launch. There are cattle at large in the vicinity, and the area gets busy during hunting season.

McKinley Lake Rec Site (Map 30/G3)
The beach area and fishing opportunities make this recreation area a great place to visit. The site lies along the west side of the lake and is home to five small, forested campsites. Facilities include a rough boat launch and space for RVs. The site can be found off of 500 Road, which branches off of the Black Creek Road (100 Rd).

Meadow Lake Rec Site (Map 55/B3)

If you are looking for a small, out-of-the-way campsite, this is the place to go. The three-unit site has limited access to the small lake, with a short trail leading to swampy edges for those with a canoe or float tube. Access can be found off 56 Road from the Pelican Forest Service Road.

Miner Lake Rec Site (Map 13/A1)

This small, remote site doesn't see much use during most of the year, except for hunting season. There are three campsites with picnic tables located on the southwest shores of the lake. The site can be accessed off the Miner Lake Forest Service Road, west of Tatla Lake.

Mitchell Bay Rec Site (Map 44/B7)

Both boats and vehicles can reach this scenic site, which is set in an opening next to the lake. The large, open grassy area along the banks of Quesnel Lake has space for about three groups. The boat launch is steep and may require four-wheel drive. Access can be found from Ditch Road, off of Mitchell Bay Road.

Moffat Lakes Rec Site (Map 30/F5)

Used primarily as a hunting base, this site offers three, well-defined rustic campsites near the western end of the first Moffat Lake. During wet periods, be prepared for a rough and slippery trek. To reach the site, take the Redeau Lake Road (2300 Rd) to the Moffat Lakes Forest Service Road, and follow this road for 86 km.

Moose Lake Rec Site (Map 7/A1)

This small recreation site is located on the Egan-Bonaparte Forest Service Road (3700 Rd) at the northwest end of the lake. It has a boat launch as well as space for about three vehicles.

Moose Lake Rec Site (Map 19/F3)

Not far down Road 10 west of Clearwater, a side road branches to the small lake and the single unit campsite. Visitors will find picnic tables, an outhouse and a gravel boat launch.

Mowson Pond Rec Site (Map 4/C7)

Mowson Pond was severely altered after the wildfire in 2009. Most of the trees around the seven-unit campsite are burned out and may be removed, and the lake is much lower than it was in the past. Still, the mountains fill the background, and the cartop boat launch allows easy access for anglers and canoeists. The site supports a number of recreational activities.

Mud Lake North Rec Site (Map 4/C4)

This five-unit site makes a popular spot for motorized use and hunters in the fall. It offers tables and toilets, and there are great opportunities for fishing in the lake. The site can be accessed via Mud Creek Forest Service Road, off of Tyaughton Lake Road. The rough and narrow road may not be suitable for two-wheel drive vehicles. Please note that motorized users must stay on existing trails and out of the alpine meadows, wetlands and the South Chilcotin Provincial Park.

Mud Lake South Rec Site (Map 4/C4)

This two-unit site offers opportunities for canoeing, hunting and motorized trail riding. There are tables and toilets available. The site can be accessed via Mud Creek Forest Service Road, off of Tyaughton Lake Road. The rough and narrow road may not be suitable for two-wheel drive vehicles. Please note that motorized users must stay on existing trails and out of the alpine meadows, wetlands and the South Chilcotin Provincial Park.

Naver Creek Rec Site (Map 57/A4)

This small, three-unit site on Naver Creek offers basic amenities, with opportunities for canoeing and fishing in the creek. The site is located past the left arm of the "Y" intersection on 700 Road, east of Dunkley Lumber. Please note this site is currently closed due to the impact of the mountain pine beetle.

Needa Lake Rec Site (Map 19/C4)

At about the 1,960 km mark of the Windy Mountain Forest Service Road (1900 Rd), a branch road leads to this site. The site has six campsites, ideal for small trailers or campers, and a steep cartop boat launch. The site provides opportunities for fishing, camping and boating.

No Name Lake Rec Site (Map 31/D6)

This site is home to four nice sites set in a grassy opening next to the lake. A trail leads from the campsite to the more secluded second lake and beyond. Found 3 km down the No Name Branch of the Spanish Creek Rd (7000 Rd), the site is RV accessible and offers a boat launch.

Nyland Lake Rec Site (Map 43/C4)

Found about 19 km down the Nyland Lake Road (2700 Rd) southeast of Quesnel, this popular site lies along the eastern shore of the lake. A cartop boat launch is also available at the site, which has room for several groups.

Odegaard Falls Rec Site (Map 23/B3)

Odegaard is a spectacular waterfall that cascades into the Nusatsum Valley. There are three campsites and a great view of the falls from the parking lot on the Nusatsum Forest Service Road. The scenic Nusatsum River site is used more as a staging ground to the Odegaard Falls Trail.

One Eye Lake Rec Site (Map 25/B7)

Due to the good access from Highway 20, this four-unit site is fairly busy throughout the year. Most of the use comes from anglers chasing rainbow and Dolly Varden. There is a boat launch at the site. From Highway 20, turn north onto Holm Road, travel 200 metres and turn right; the site appears 900 metres down this road.

Paddy Lake Rec Site (Map 19/B1)

Found at the southeast end of Paddy Lake, this is more of a parking lot than a campsite, with one unit. A short 100 metre trail leads down to the lake. The access road appears off of Canim-Hendrix Lake Road.

Palmer Lake Rec Site (Map 27/E2)

Found about 65 km from Highway 20, the last several kilometres into this popular fishing lake are very rough and the lake can be windy at times. Regardless, the nine unit site is often full. The site rests next to the historical Lt. Palmer Route. From the highway, take 1300 Road to 1700 Road; the access road appears at 8 km.

Pass Lake Rec Site (Map 7/E7)

Recently upgraded, this scenic site offers visitors a more formal camping area next to a good fly-fishing lake. There are 13 campsites set in the forest next to the lake. There is a fee to camp here from May 1st to October 12th. The access road appears off of the Lac Du Bois Road.

Pelican Lake Rec Site (Map 55/A4)

Easily accessed on the Pelican Lake Forest Service Road, this is a popular, RV friendly site. There are two sections with only the lower lake sections being used at this time. The 10 campsites have been cleared of the pine beetle killed trees, which opens up the site for larger groups. The lake is a fine fishing destination.

Pendleton Lake Rec Site (Map 31/E7)

North of Mahood Lake, this site is accessible by a rough road that is not suitable for RVs. Visitors will find three private, forested campsites and a steep rustic boat launch next to Pendleton Lake. The access road into the site branches off from the Spanish Creek Forest Service Road (7000 Rd).

Phinetta Lake Rec Site (Map 19/E6)

On Highway 24 west of Little Fort, Phinetta Lake makes a great stopover for weary travellers and ambitious anglers. There are two separate areas totalling four campsites; the northern site offers camping, and the southern site has camping and a boat launch. The sites rest along Eakin Creek Road.

Pinto Lake Rec Site (Map 13/F1)

This small, highway-side recreation site is a popular picnic site or road stop. There is space for two camping units. Larger units appreciate the pull through, and there is a nice view. The site is located off Highway 20, about 5.5 km east of the community of Tatla Lake.

Poison Lake Rec Site (Map 38/C6)

There is space for six groups at this site, which sits just north of Anahim Lake on the Upper Dean River Road. Despite the name, the lake is known for its good fishing. There are trails to explore and the famous Dean River to fish in this scenic area.

Recsite Adventures

Polley Lake Rec Site (Map 43/G7)
The Polley Lake Recreation Site has been closed due to a breach of the Mount Polley Mine tailings pond, near Likely, BC. The flood that resulted from the breach of the tailings pond has washed out the Ditch Road, which is used to access the site, and there is a complete water use ban in effect in the area. The site will remain closed until more information becomes available. A public information line has been established at 250-398-5581.

Prairie Creek Rec Site (Map 30/F1)
Set along the southern shore of Horsefly Lake, this recreation site has three small sites at lake level and more sites along the bench above the lake. The boat launch is suitable for trailered boats; however, the turnaround area may be full of campers. The site appears at the end of 6500 Road.

Pressy Lake Rec Site (Map 18/F7)
This is a small campsite, with space for three vehicles, located on the northeast end of this long and narrow lake. The access is good enough for small RVs and there is a boat launch on the lake. The site is found off the North Bonaparte Road (3200 Rd). Note the engine size restriction of 7.5 kW (10 hp) on the lake.

Punchaw Lake Rec Site (Map 55/G3)
Suitable for individual or group camping, this RV-accessible site is a popular destination for anglers. There are five well-maintained and recently updated campsites. The Alexander Mackenzie Trail also passes by the south end of the lake. The site rests at 24 km on the gravel portion of Blackwater Road.

Make sure your fire is completely out and cool to the touch before moving on.

Puntzi Lake Rec Site (Map 26/C4)
Puntzi Lake is a popular destination for anglers, but most visitors prefer to stay at one of the lake's many resorts. This means that this six-unit open site is often quiet. The site appears off of Puntzi Lake Road and is also home to a series of cross-country ski trails.

Pyper Lake Rec Site (Map 26/B6)
Offering a great view of the Coast Mountains, there are three campsites in a clearing at the east end of the lake. The site is a few minutes off Highway 20 and is a popular swimming hole with a cartop boat launch. The access road branches off from Pyper Lake Road.

Quesnel Forks Rec Site (Map 43/F5)
At the junction of the Quesnel and Cariboo Rivers, this medium-sized site has 11 vehicle units, and is set near a ghost town built during the gold rush years. There is also a hatchery in the area for visitors to view. You can reach the site from Quesnel Forks Road; note that there is a steep hill before the site.

Quesnel Lake Public Landing Rec Site (Map 44/E7)
Found off the Haggens Point Road on the south shore of the big lake, there are three campsites on the beach with an amazing view to the north. The boat launch crosses the sandy beach, so a four-wheel drive vehicle may be necessary when lake levels drop. For access, look for the sign post for Elysia Resort on the Z Road.

Raft Creek Rec Site (Map 44/A7)
This site is closed due to the breach of the Mount Polley Mine tailings pond, near Likely, BC. The flood that resulted from the breach of the tailings pond has washed out the Ditch Road, which is used to access the site, and there is a complete water use ban in effect in the area. The site will remain closed until more information becomes available. A public information line has been established at 250-398-5581.

Rail Lake Rec Site (Map 30/B7)
Found next to the often busy Spout Lake Road (1500 Rd), there are two treed campsites available along the northern shore of Rail Lake. A cartop boat launch provides lake access.

Raven Lake Rec Site (Map 28/A6)
There are about 19 vehicle units strung along between the shores of the lake and the often-busy 3600 Road, including space for RVs. There are two separate sections with separate entrances and two boat launches allowing small boat trailers.

Riley Dam Rec Site (Map 5/D1)
Riley Lake was formed by a dam on Big Bar Creek. Due to the good road access, it is a fairly popular four-unit site complete with picnic tables and a cartop boat launch. The site can be accessed from Big Bar Road (3600 Rd).

Roberts Lake Rec Site (Map 29/G2)
Next to the Beaver Valley Road (100 Rd), this site provides good access to the lake. It is a small grassy site with several campsites along the shoreline and a small boat launch that is suitable for trailers. The valley is especially beautiful during autumn.

Sapeye Lake Rec Site (Map 13/C2)
There are six developed campsites at this pretty site, found above the road at the base of Horn Bluff. There is also a small boat launch at the site. The access road is in good condition, but very narrow, and trailers are not recommended. A fee is in effect from May to October.

Schraeder Lake Rec Site (Map 4/G3)
The small, semi-open site on the shores of Schraeder Lake has space for two vehicle units. Fishing is a popular pastime and the site sports a cartop boat launch. Hunters also frequent the area in fall. The site can be accessed via the Big Bar Ferry, or from West Pavillion Road.

Scot Lake North Rec Site (Map 7/C2)
A popular fishing spot, Scot Lake is easily accessed off the Egan-Bonaparte Forest Service Road. The site provides four campsites and a boat launch at the north end of the lake. There is also a small, sandy beach on the lake.

Scum Lake Rec Site (Map 15/A3)
The lake doesn't live down its name, and it isn't the most popular destination. This is partly due to the rough access and the spotty fishing. Visitors will find a single-unit campsite and a cartop boat launch that doubles as a launch for canoeists interested in exploring the Eleven Sisters chain of lakes.

Sharpe Lake West Rec Site (Map 7/B1)
Sharpe Lake is found on Sharpe Lake Road, off of the Egan-Bonaparte Forest Service Road. The site offers space for two vehicles. A cartop boat launch provides access to the lake. This is a popular spot for fishing, boating and camping.

Sicily Lake Rec Site (Map 19/E2)
Easily accessed from Road 20, there is an undeveloped site at the north end of the lake and a fully developed site along the southern shore. The southern site also offers a gravel boat launch and six treed campsites. To reach the southern site, take TFL 18 Road 2 from Clearwater, turn right onto Road 20, and travel about 11 km to the site.

Sisters Creek Rec Site (Map 42/F3)
Found in the community of Kersley south of Quesnel, this rural site offers a short, wheelchair accessible trail and a nice picnic area. The 850 metre trail winds through the fir forest to a viewing platform overlooking the Fraser River. To reach the site, take Ardnolus Road from Highway 97.

Snag Lake Rec Site (Map 17/F4)
Accessed off the Tatton-Snag Road (1300 Rd) west of 100 Mile House, there are four campsites on the northwest side of the lake. Mainly used by anglers and hunters, there is a boat launch onto the lake.

Snag Lake Rec Site (Map 54/E4)
This is a small lake just east of Batnuni Lake, about 135 km from Quesnel. The lake outflow is a popular place to fish and the small lake warms up enough to swim in during summer. There are a few campsites on the bench above the lake. The site appears along the Swede Creek Forest Service Road.

Snaking River Rec Site (Map 55/A7)
At this point, the once wild Snaking River mellows to a gentle, warm river that is a great place to canoe or swim in. The site offers space for two units in a treed area on the banks of the river. To reach it, take Snaking River Forest Service Road, which branches off from Nazko Road at the 22 km mark.

Recsite Adventures

Snohoosh Lake Rec Site (Map 7/A4) 🍴🏕🚤🛶🎣
At the north end of Snohoosh Lake lies this small and rustic, two-unit recreation site with cartop boat launch. Site access can be found west of Kamloops off Highway 1 at km 43 on the Deadman Vidette Road.

South French Bar Creek Rec Site (Map 5/A3) 🍴🏕🏍🛶⛺
This small campsite has space for three vehicle units and sees heavy use in the fall. The site lies within the newly created French Bar Creek Provincial Park and sees a migration of bighorn sheep at times.

Spanish Lake Rec Site (Map 44/B6) 🍴🏕🚤🏊🛶🎣🛶⛺
This unique, seven-unit campsite rests on a spit of land jutting out from the south shore of Spanish Lake. The scenic sites fill up quickly despite the steep access down from the main road. There is a small boat launch suitable for boat trailers. The access road branches off from Spanish Lake Road.

Stony Lake East Rec Site (Map 57/D3) 🍴🏕🚤🏊🛶🛶🚤🛶
This recreation site can be found on the far eastern tip of Stony Lake. It is flat and open, with three campsites and a wide pebble shoreline with great opportunities for swimming, fishing, boating and canoeing. The site offers basic amenities, including a boat launch, picnic tables and toilets. The site is accessible by two-wheel drive along a rough road off the Willow Cale Forest Service Road at 112.5 km. Access may be blocked due to washouts; alternatively, try Highway 28 and the Ketchum Forest Service Road.

Stony Lake North Rec Site (Map 57/D3) 🍴🏕🚤🏊🛶🛶🚤🛶
This is a four-unit recreation site on the north shore of Stony Lake with great opportunities for boating, beach activities, canoeing and fishing. There is a 100 metre wide pebble beach, gravel boat launch, picnic tables and toilets. The site is usually accessible via the Willow Cale Forest Service Road; however, access may be blocked due to washouts. For alternative access, try Highway 28 and the Ketchum Forest Service Road.

Stony Lake South Rec Site (Map 57/D3) 🍴🏕🛶🏊🛶🛶
This small, rustic four-unit site appears on the southwestern end of Stony Lake. The site offers a gravel boat launch, tables, fire rings and a pit toilet, with opportunities for boating, canoeing, fishing and swimming in the lake. The site can be accessed via 700 Road at the 754 km marker east of Dunkley Lumber, or from the Willow Cale Forest Service Road to the north.

Stony Lake West Rec Site (Map 57/D2) 🍴🏕🚤🏊🛶🛶🚤🛶
Located on the northwestern shore of Stony Lake, this open four-unit site provides great opportunities for boating, fishing, swimming, canoeing and beach activities. There is a small pebble beach and boat launch available on the lake, as well as picnic tables and toilets. The rough road into the site can be found off of the Willow Cale Forest Service Road at 121 km. Access may be blocked due to washouts; alternatively, try Highway 28 and the Ketchum Forest Service Road.

Succour Lake Rec Site (Map 19/A1) 🍴🏕🚤🏊🛶🎣
Succour Lake can be reached via a rough four-wheel drive spur road off the Lang Lake Forest Service Road (610 Rd). Located on the northeast side of the lake, the site has two treed campsites available with picnic tables and a cartop boat launch.

Susan Lake Rec Site (Map 30/G7) 🍴🚤🏊🏍🎣🛶
North of Canim Lake on an old sawmill site, this single-unit site makes a fine fishing destination. Access is about 12 km down the Lang Lake Forest Service Road (610 Rd) north from the Canim Hendrix Lake Road. Continue past Succour Lake and then south of Boomerang Lake to eventually find Susan Lake.

Suscha Lake Rec Site (Map 53/G5) 🍴🏕🛶🏊🛶🛶
In the language of the Carrier First Nation, the name of this lake means "and big black bears, too." We think this is warning enough. The site is located in an open pine forest, with space for five groups. Just north of the camping area is a boat launch and picnic area. The site can be reached from Suscha-Blue Forest Service Road (6000 Rd).

Swartz Lake Rec Site (Map 4/C3) 🍴🥾🚤🏍🎣⛺
Despite (or maybe because of) the four-wheel drive access, this tiny lake remains a fairly popular destination with off-road enthusiasts and anglers. There is space for four vehicles at the lake, but there is no launch.

Tagai Lake Rec Site (Map 55/A2) 🍴🚤🛶🛶🎣🛶
Access into this site off the Pelican Lake Forest Service Road can be challenging when wet. However, the semi-open site was recently upgraded and now features a nice gravel boat launch. The eight sites see plenty of activity from anglers.

Tanli Lake Rec Site (Map 53/G4) 🍴🛶🛶🛶🎣
There is a silviculture camp on this small lake that is open to the public when not required by reforestation crews in the spring and early summer. The single-unit site is located at 6 km on the Kluskus-Blue Forest Service Road.

Tasse Lake Rec Site (Map 44/E6) 🍴🚤🛶🛶
This site is located on the southwest shore of Tasse Lake to the north of Quesnel Lake. The two-wheel drive accessible lake has one campsite and a rough launch. The remote site sees little use. The access road branches off from 1300 Road, which can be accessed from the Spanish Lake Road.

Tatla Lake Rec Site (Map 25/F7) 🍴🏕🚤🛶🛶🚤🎣⛺
Located in an open aspen forest on the slopes above Tatla Lake, this scenic spot is popular with kokanee anglers (and perhaps beer drinkers). The five-unit site is easily accessed off Highway 20 and is maintained by a campground host. There is a steep gravel boat launch onto the lake.

Tatlayoko Lake Rec Site (Map 13/G5) 🍴🚤🛶🥾🐴🛶🚤🎣⛺🛶
This site falls within a declared Tsilhqot'in First Nation area. Set alongside a turquoise lake in a mature stand of fir trees across from a dramatic mountain ridge, it is a wonderful camping spot. Although it can be windy, trees protect the seven large, well-spaced campsites. There is a boat launch onto the lake. Permits are required for hunting and fishing. Visit www.tsilhqotin.ca for more information.

Teapot Lake Rec Site (Map 57/C2) 🍴🚤🛶🛶🎣
Found 5.5 km down the Teapot Lake Road, this serene, out-of-the-way site offers two campsites tucked beneath a mature spruce canopy. There is a cartop boat launch and wharf on the lake.

Till Lake North Rec Site (Map 28/G6) 🍴🏕🚤🛶🛶🛶🎣
You can find this popular site via a rough two-wheel drive road that branches west off the 14 km mark of the Meldrum Creek Road (1100 Rd). This site sits in two sections; the first is a few sites along the lakeshore with the rest above the road, and the second section is found beyond the boat launch. The boat launch is good for boat trailers.

Tisdall Lake South Rec Site (Map 30/F4) 🍴🚤🛶🛶🛶🎣♿
This popular site is often quite busy during the summer due to the quality fishing opportunities that exist in the lake. There are 12 treed campsites available at the site, which is found along the eastern shore of the lake via a rough access road. A good trailer boat launch, fishing platform and wheelchair-accessible toilets are also found here.

Titetown Crossing Rec Site (Map 54/G4) ⛺🥾🐴🚴🛶🎣
A small tenting site along the Alexander Mackenzie Trail, this site sits just across the narrows from the Batnuni Lake Forest Service Road, on the east side of Titetown Lake.

Top Lake South Rec Site (Map 53/A5) 🍴🏕🛶🛶🎣
This is a small, two-unit site on a small roadside lake located in a low pass in the Fawnie Range. The site is just off the Kluskus-Ootsa Forest Service Road, at 140 km, and access is usually quite good.

Tory Lake Rec Site (Map 55/C2) 🍴🚤🛶🛶🎣
Appearing at the 41 km mark of the Pelican Forest Service Road, this small site can be a little loud when logging trucks are hauling. The three sites are set in an open area overlooking the small lake to the south. It is possible to hand launch canoes or small boats onto the lake.

Tranquille Crossing & Meadow Rec Sites (Map 7/D7) 🍴🏕🛶🎣⛺🎣
One of the bigger sites in the area, Tranquille Meadow offers about 50 RV friendly campsites next to the river. Tranquille Crossing is a much quieter destination with room for only two vehicles. Visitors can test their luck fishing or spend a few quiet moments looking for the wildlife that frequent the area.

Tsuniah Lake Bay Rec Site (Map 14/C5)

This site falls within a declared Tsilhqot'in First Nation area. The road access off of the Chilko Lake Forest Service Road can be a bit rough, but the excellent fishing and cartop launch attract a lot of anglers. There is space for about ten units at this scenic site. Permits are required for hunting and fishing. Visit www.tsilhqotin.ca for more information.

Twan Lake Rec Site (Map 28/D2)

This small, remote site is tucked in a maze of roads west of the Fraser. Access is best off the 100 C Road from the south, which can be picked up at the 65 km mark of the Tzenzaicut-Garner Road. There are three campsites that are mainly used by anglers and hunters.

Twin Lakes Rec Site (Map 56/A6)

Northwest of Quesnel, you will find this small three-unit campsite off the Blackwater Road. Set amid a thick forest, the steep bank down to the lakes makes launching heavier boats all but impossible. The Collins Overland Telegraph Trail also passes through the area.

Two Lake Rec Site (Map 27/B3)

A small three-unit site is set in a sandy, semi-open area next to the lake. In the fall, hunters are the main visitors to the area and ice fishing is common in the winter. The historical Lt. Palmer Route also runs through the area. Take Alexis Lakes Road to reach the access road into the lake.

Tyaughton Creek Rec Site (Map 4/C5)

This four-unit rec site rests within a popular area for horseback riding, camping, hunting and scenic viewing. Access is via Tyaughton Lake Road followed by the Mud Creek Forest Service Road.

Tyee Lake East Rec Site (Map 29/B2)

Accessed from the south along the Lyne Creek Rd (1700 Rd), this lakeside site offers a rough boat launch and a few picnic tables. Fishing is the main activity at the lake, while water sports are also frequently enjoyed during summer months. There are 11 campsites amongst the fir trees and a large open area next to the lake shore.

Keep the wilderness wild and pack out all your trash!

Tzenzaicut Lake North Rec Site (Map 42/A5)

Featuring 21 mostly lakefront campsites, this is a popular site. There is a good, large boat launch, ample parking and decent road access. The access road appears at 58 km on the Tzenzaicut Lake Forest Service Road. ATV users are asked to stick to main roads when leaving the site.

Upper Chilako River Rec Site (Map 54/C2)

This three-unit site is located next to Expansion Lake, a widening of the Chilako River near Finger Tatuk Provincial Park.

Valentine Lake Rec Site (Map 18/B5)

Valentine Lake is a popular fishing lake west of 100 Mile House. There are nine forested campsites suitable for campers and small trailers, along with picnic tables, outhouses and a cartop boat launch. Access is found about 9.5 km down the 800 Road.

Vedan Lake North Rec Site (Map 14/F5)

This scenic site appears along the Elkin-Taseko Forest Service Road and falls within a declared Tsilhqot'in First Nation area. There is a nice gravel boat launch and space for two units. The lake is quite windy, so canoeing is not recommended. Permits are required for hunting and fishing. Visit www.tsilhqotin.ca for more information.

Vidette Lake Rec Site (Map 7/A3)

Just north of Deadman Lake, Vidette Lake is a narrow waterbody offering anglers a chance to test their luck. The small site has two campsites and a cartop boat launch. Access can be found at 52.7 km on the Deadman Vidette Road off the Trans-Canada Highway, west of Savona.

Warttig Lake Rec Site (Map 45/C6)

Although the site is fairly remote, logging trucks may rumble down the access road on weekdays. Visitors will find a small, scenic spot along the southern shore of the lake. There are a few campsites and a small boat launch. The site appears at 18 km along Bouldery Creek Road (6100 Rd), which branches off of 100 Road.

Westroad River Rec Site (Map 55/A6)

Visitors to this site will see why the river is called the Blackwater. The two-unit site sees a lot of use by paddling groups as well as a few anglers and hunters. It is a tenting only site. To reach it, head north from Nazko on the Nazko Road. The site appears at about 26 km.

Whale Lake Rec Site (Map 17/G5) 6

The small Whale Lake can be found via a rough, four-wheel drive access road, just off the Gustafsen South Forest Service Road (1000 Rd). The site has two units with picnic tables and a steep boat launch.

Whiskey Flats Rec Site (Map 44/B1)

Not far from Barkerville, this small, three-unit site sits next to Antler Creek at 14 km on the Cunningham Pass Forest Service Road (3100 Rd). The site is often used as a staging area for snowmobilers and hunters exploring the area. Resting at the base of Antler Mountain, it is quite scenic.

White Lake Rec Site (Map 19/E3)

This site is located at the northwest end of the lake and is home to two small campsites and a boat launch. Nearby Road 10 can be busy with logging activity on weekdays. Access to the lake is by a steep foot trail. The site is located at about 12 km on Road 10.

Whitewood Lake Rec Site (Map 7/G4)

Accessed at 27 km on the Jamieson Creek Forest Service Road north of Kamloops, this five-unit site allows visitors to haul in a small RV. In addition to a cartop boat launch, visitors have a choice of either camping in the open or under the trees.

Winkley Creek Rec Site (Map 44/B7)

This large, open site has space for about nine groups. It sees heavy use in the summer since there is boat access and a sandy beach. You can choose sites along the shoreline or further back into the treed area. The site is access out of Likely off the Cedar Creek and Winkley Creek Roads.

Windfall Lake Rec Site (Map 7/F2)

This small lake lies along the Jamieson Creek Forest Service Road not far from Bonaparte Lake. The high-elevation, forested recreation site offers three campsites as well as a cartop boat launch for anglers and paddlers. There is a series of horseback trails along with ATVing and snowmobiling in the area.

Windy Lake Rec Site (Map 7/F4)

Found on the Bonaparte Plateau, Windy Lake can live up to its name. Luckily, the five-unit campsite is set in a dense forest. Skoatl Point Trail and Tuwut Lake Paddling Route are found nearby. Access can be found along the Windy Lake Road off the Jamieson Creek Forest Service Road.

Windy Lake Rec Site (Map 19/E3)

The rough road access deters most people from visiting this lake. There is room for a couple of vehicles at the site, and there is a short trail that accesses the lake. The site lies along Road 10, which can be reached from TFL 18 Road 2.

Wolverine Lake Rec Site (Map 44/A5)

This small, two-unit site is set next to Wolverine Lake north of Likely. Despite the rough road access, the lake is a favourite spot for local and visiting anglers. There is a rough cartop boat launch. The site appears at 8 km on the Kangaroo Forest Service Road.

Woodcock Lake Rec Site (Map 55/A1)

This remote site sits on the northeast shore of the small Woodcock Lake. There are three campsites plus a boat launch, tables and toilets. The lake offers opportunities for canoeing and fishing. To reach the site, take Grizzly 25 Road off of Grizzly Road for 4.8 km, and turn onto the rough access road.

Yalakom Rec Site (Map 5/A6)

Located next to the Yalakom River, this open five-unit site is easily accessed by RVs. Fishing, hunting and exploring the endless trail system are popular pastimes in this dry, often hot landscape. Access is via gravel road from the Yalakom River Forest Service Road. Note that during high water, the site is prone to flooding.

Trail
Adventures

The Coast Mountains, the Chilcotin Plateau and the Cariboo Mountains make up a vast area steeped in history. This is the land that explorer Alexander MacKenzie walked (and paddled through) back in 1793, following footpaths that had already been carved for thousands of years.

Other historical trails have fallen out of memory, but there remain endless routes to explore on the plateau and in the Cariboo forests. In the mountains, you will find the region's most dramatic hiking landscapes. Tweedsmuir and Wells Gray Parks top the list, and there are many other spectacular trails to be found.

To help you select the trail that best suits your abilities, we have included information on elevation gain, return distance and special features wherever possible. Unless otherwise noted, distances and times are for round-trip hikes. Also included in each listing are symbols to indicate what the trail is used for—mountain biking, hiking, horseback riding, etc. Multi-use trail descriptions are written from a hiker's point of view.

Although many ATV trails are multi-use, there are some formal ATV trail systems worth highlighting in the Cariboo Chilcotin Coast. You will find these trails listed in their own, separate section later in this book.

Due to the hot, dry climate of this region, it is highly recommended to bring plenty of water. We should also note that higher elevation trails and routes (above 1,000 metres/3,000 feet) may have a limited season due to late season snow. Trail users should leave these for late summer and early fall (from July to October).

Sometimes, finding the trailhead is half the fun – and half the work! Refer to the appropriate map in this book to determine where each trail begins. Note that our maps are designed only as a general access guide and are not intended to navigate you through a hidden mountain pass or across an expansive ridge network. If you are traveling on unmarked trails, we recommend that you have mountaineering knowledge and be equipped with a topographic map and compass. A BC Backroad GPS Map may also be invaluable to help mark trails you have taken.

The wealth of trails listed on the following pages still only represents a fraction of the outdoor opportunities available in the Cariboo Chilcotin Coast. Adventurers can follow old game trails or logging roads to places that few others know about. Remember: if you plan to go off the beaten path, be careful and always let someone know where you plan to go.

Backroad Mapbooks **BRMB** backroadmapbooks.com

MAKING TRACKS...

British Columbia
Backroad GPS Maps

ADVENTURE

Fishing | Hunting | Paddling | Parks & Campsites | Trails | & more

GARMIN

Not getting to the right places?
Let us show you the way with the most detailed GPS maps for BC.

1-877-520-5670 | www.gpsmaps.ca

99 Mile Trails (Map 18/C4)
Located only 2 km south of 100 Mile House, there are close to 40 km (25 mi) of ski/bike trails of varying difficulty here. The trails include an Adventure Trail for families, featuring special lighting effects and cartoon characters, and a wheelchair-accessible trail that travels through lush forests. Viewpoints, picnic tables and benches as well as warming huts such as the Nordic Beanstalk Cabin are found throughout the system.

108 Mile Trails (Map 18/C3)
Beginning at the rest area at the 108 Mile Heritage Site, follow the underpass tunnel under the highway to access the maze of interconnecting trails. Stay to the right and you will soon find an easy 5 km (3 mi) trail to 108 Mile Lookout. The 11 km (6.8 mi) Long Lake Trail continues straight, eventually looping back to the main road. The Sucker Lake Trail is an easy 9 km (5.6 mi) loop that also follows an old road from the underpass before skirting the eastern shore of the lake and looping back. The Sepa Lake Trail is a 9.2 km (5.7 mi) loop that takes rest area visitors around the northern shore of 108 Mile Lake, around Sepa Lake and past the golf course. The Hills Health Resort also provides access to a variety of trails including the Express Meadows Trails, which skirts open meadows and various ponds.

1861 Pack Trail (Map 58/A7–44/B4)
From Barkerville, follow the Cariboo Wagon Road south to just past the Richfield Courthouse. The 1861 Pack Trail leaves the Wagon Road to the east and begins with a crossing of Williams Creek. The trail is 37.7 km (23.5 mi) in length and gains about 600 m (1,970 ft) over its length. This trail is maintained by the Friends of Barkerville and is marked with plastic yellow markers.

Alexander MacKenzie Heritage Trail (Maps 23, 37, 38, 39, 53 - 56)
Alexander MacKenzie was the first European to cross North America, reaching the Pacific in 1793. This 420 km (260 mi) route, originally called the Nuxalk-Carrier Grease Trail, has been mostly preserved as it cuts an east-west path across the landscape. The trail includes a variety of roads and trails and is best done in late summer or early fall on foot, by bike, on a horse or on an ATV. Beyond the crossing of the Euchiniko River the route becomes very remote and should only be attempted by well-prepared backpackers. In the east, most start next to the Blackwater Road, but the actual Kilometre 0 is found further east on the banks of the Fraser River. The difficult 80 km (50 mi), or five to seven day stretch of the trail in Tweedsmuir Park is perhaps the most scenic. The trailhead is found on Highway 20. In between are some fabulous views, endless fishing holes and the odd lodge to pamper yourself before heading back into the wild. It is strongly recommended to pick up a copy of the trail guidebook In the Steps of Alexander MacKenzie before venturing out.

Alex Fraser Research Forest Trails (Map 29/E6; F1)
The Alex Fraser Research Forest is subdivided into two blocks with the Knife Creek block found southeast of Williams Lake and the Gavin Lake block resting in the Beaver Valley northeast of town. Covering 10,000 hectares (24,700 ac) of Crown land there are 15 signed, interpretive trails in the forests totalling 21 km (13 mi) in length. Many of the trails have brochures, so it can be an educational outing as well. You can also discover what the University of BC students are working on in different areas of the forest.

Alexis Creek Ski Trails (Map 27/E6)
There are four looping trails totaling approximately 10 km (6 mi) near Alexis Creek. You will climb about 200 m (655 ft) to the highest point of the system. The trails are used year round and located 2 km north of Alexis Creek on Stum Lake Road.

Avalanche Pass Trail (Map 59/E6)
This challenging backcountry trek covers about 26 km (16 mi) return, climbing over 940 m (3,085 ft). The trailhead is located at the end of the South Dore Forest Service Road. The route traverses into the sub-alpine then over Avalanche Pass before descending down to Cariboo Lake. At the pass, be prepared for snow any time before mid-August.

Baezaeko River Trail (Map 39/D4–40/E2)
Providing access to the west side of the dramatic Itcha Ilgatchuz Range Park, this scenic trail is horse and snowmobile friendly. The trail stretches over 80 km (50 mi) to the cabins in the park and there are ample camping spots en route. The trail has little elevation gain and crosses alternate seismic line trails (often used by ATVers and snowmobilers). From the cabins, trails lead up to the Itcha Plateau and beyond.

Baldy Mountain Trail (Map 56/F1)
Depending on how far you can drive up the rough Baldy Mountain Road and how far you ramble when in the alpine, this trail is at least 5 km (3 mi) long. The higher you can drive, the less elevation there is to climb.

Beaverpass Trail (Map 57/D7)
Located at Beaver Pass House, a small locale on Highway 26 west of Wells, is this 16.5 km (10 mi) loop trail. The trail runs from the highway to Four Mile Lake and back, following along Beaverpass Creek.

Beece Creek Trail (Map 3/C2)
This long pack trail can be used to connect Ts'il?os Provincial Park with Big Creek Provincial Park. At the Big Creek end, the trail hooks up with the Tosh Creek Trail. At its northwestern end, it hooks up with a rough road east of Taseko Lake. Once you've figured out a way across the Taseko River, there are a number of trails, marked and unmarked, into Ts'il?os, including the Yohetta Valley Trail. Expect a 30 km (18.5 mi) journey, with an elevation gain of 750 m (2,460 ft).

Beef Trail Route (Map 38/B5–37/F5)
Located in South Tweedsmuir Provincial Park, this 38 km (23.5 mi) trail provides access to the popular Rainbow Range from the Anahim area. It is shared with hikers, bikers and horseback riders in summer, and snowmobilers in winter. The trail travels along a good logging road and into the scenic backcountry, gaining 955 m (3,135 ft) in elevation along its course.

Belle Mountain Trails (Map 59/F4)
Belle Mountain is a popular multi-use recreational area west of McBride. From the parking area and cabin, at the 5 km (3 mi) mark, there are two options. To access the scenic alpine area around the summit, continue along the road. The complete route is about 25 km (15.5 mi) in length. The other option is to hike or ski the extensive, lower elevation trail system. The trail system offers over 18 km (11 mi) of easier trails. The system traverses through a mix of wooded and open areas, with a number of fine viewpoints of the valley below.

Big Bar Ski Trails (Map 6/A3)
These cross-country ski trails offer seemingly endless hiking and biking in the summer. There are over 50 km (31 mi) of easy to difficult routes to explore. There are route maps as well as shelters with fire pits and outhouses scattered strategically around the system. The main parking area is found 6 km down Big Bar Road.

Big Creek Provincial Park (Maps 3, 15)
This sprawling, scenic park is a popular destination for horseback riding, backpacking, hunting, wildlife viewing and mountaineering. As the area is very remote, visitors should be comfortable with backcountry travel. There are a number of trails in the area, including a handful of routes that are popular with mountain bikers. The 12 km (7.5 mi) Big Creek Trail has an elevation gain of 700 m (2,290 ft) and can be ridden in both directions. A challenging 13 km (8 mi) route, the Tosh Creek Trail involves a 470 m (1,540 ft) climb. Other trails include the 13 km (8 mi) multi-use Fish Lake/Big Creek Cutoff Trail, the 7.8 km (4.8 mi) one-way Dil Dil Nadila Trail across the Dil-Dil Plateau, and the 5.3 km (3.3 mi) Elbow Pass Trail, which makes for a challenging ride.

Big Cedar Trail (Map 22/B3)
This is a 6 km (3.7 mi) round trip off of the very difficult, four-wheel drive Clayton Falls Road.

Big Timothy Mountain Trail (Map 30/G5)
From the gate at the old Hendrix Lake Mine site, follow the trail signed 'to the volcano' that skirts around the open pit mines. The moderate trail ascends over 490 m (1,605 ft) to the extinct volcano complete with lava flows, a small crater lake and superb scenery.

Blackwater Canyon Trail (Map 55/F5)
A short and easy 3.2 km (2 mi) return trail leads from the Blackwater Crossing Recreation Site to the 60 m (200 ft) high cliffs above the canyon. You will pass beautiful pines and flowers and several viewpoints and picnic sites along the way. Also in the area is a maze of game and angler trails, as well as the Collins Overland Telegraph Trail leading south.

Blackwater Wagon Rd/Panhandle Phillips Horse Trail (Map 38/E7–39/A1)

Starting from the Stampede Grounds in Anahim Lake, this historic route is the main access into the Itcha Mountains region of the remote park. It spans 55 km (34 mi), gaining 640 m (2,100 ft) along the way. The route crosses several roads and creeks on its way up into this wild and rugged area before eventually dropping down to the Blackwater River Valley to join up with the Alexander MacKenzie Trail.

Bluff Lake Pioneer Trail (Map 13/D3)

Part of the historical route to Bute Inlet, this short trail climbs the hillside east of Bluff Lake for a fine view of the area. It is about 2 km return.

Bobbs Lake Project Road (Map 18/G2–19/A2)

This 10 km (6 mi) trail/old road system leads to the south end of Bobbs Lake to the west side of Canim Lake. The trailhead is off Canim Lake Road.

Boulder Mountain Trail (Map 59/C2)

This moderate trail begins by following the old lookout tower access road through some old growth cedar and hemlock. The route turns to a footpath that passes by an old forestry cabin before breaking through the tree line to a scenic open area. The difficult hike covers 7.5 km (4.6 mi) and gains about 1,200 m (3,935 ft) along the way.

Brett-Hog Creek Trails (Map 4/E7)

Accessed off of Marshall Lake Road, a series of 35 km (22 mi) of trails takes you around Carol Lake along Hog and Brett Creeks and beyond. There really is no limit to the distance you can travel.

Bridge Creek Trails (Map 18/D4)

Near the eastern end of 100 Mile House you can access this easy trail system from Centennial Park, off Cedar Avenue. The trail system follows old roads on the southern side of the creek. After veering north to an old ski cabin, the trail then loops back to Canim Lake Road and Highway 97. You can return via the same route or follow the highway back to the parking area. The total trip is just over 10 km (6 mi) in length. For a shorter trip, a 4 km (2.5 mi) loop climbs up to the old ski hill for a good view of 100 Mile House and area. People also venture to the falls and back.

Browntop Mountain Trail (Map 44/C5)

From the end of the road, the trail ascends over 490 m (1,605 ft) to the fantastic alpine area of Browntop Mountain. You can literally hike for days in this alpine region as the interconnecting ridges make a perfect mountaintop pathway. Depending on where you park, the trek from the road is at least 4 km (2.5 mi) in length and travels over difficult and remote terrain.

Bonaparte Provincial Park Trails (Map 7/E3)

Bonaparte Provincial Park makes a great wilderness location with a number of outdoor recreation opportunities. A number of multi-use trails travel throughout the park, including the epic 24.5 km (15 mi) Masters Subalpine Trek. The Deadman Trail is a popular route, with Shelly Lake being a good stop en route for anglers. The Heller Lake Circuit, accessible from Deadman Creek Road, offers several days' worth of exploring with many lakes along the way. Traveling to Mollimarn Lake is a 4.6 km (2.8 mi) one-way trail while the Skoatl Point Trail spans 12 km (7.5 mi) leading to a dramatic volcanic cone with a panoramic view of the surrounding lakes and forest. The latter route will take about four hours.

Bull Mountain Ski Trails (Map 29/B4)

The Bull Mountain ski area lies 16 km north of Williams Lake to the west side of Highway 97. There are 28 km (17 mi) of trails that are available for hiking during non-winter months. A posted trail map at the parking area helps you choose which trail to travel.

Burkholder Lake Trail (Map 4/G6)

From the Lac La Mare Recreation Site, anglers use this 10 km (6 mi) trail to access Burkholder Lake. The trail extends into the Schulaps Range to join up with a seemingly endless trail system above Carpenter Lake. This is a great destination for hikers or horseback riders. Further north, the trail joins up with the Noaxe Lake/Quartz Mountain system.

Burnt Creek Trail (Map 13/B3)

Beginning off the Mosley Creek Forest Service Road, this 4.8 km (3 mi) trail follows an old road for part of the way up into the alpine above Sapeye Lake, climbing 740 m (2,430 ft) along its course. Last report the route is in good condition as livestock frequent the area.

Butler Peak Trail (Map 13/D3)

This developed mineral exploration trail follows an old south of Butler Creek before branching east to eventually meet tiny Butler Lake. Located in the alpine northwest of Nuit Mountain, this is a very scenic area. The signed trailhead is found about 1.5 km south of Horn Lake on the Bluff Lake Road. Follow the steep four-wheel drive road for about 3 km to the trailhead. The difficult trail ends at a giant cairn and gorgeous viewpoint over the valley with the Chilcotin Mountains looming in the background. It is about 14.5 km (9 mi) to the lake, with an overall elevation gain of 1,200 m (3,935 ft).

Calvert Island Trails (Map 8/D3)

There are a number of short trails on the northwest corner of Calvert Island, including a trail to the microwave station and linking trails between the beaches. There is a fishing lodge on the island where you can ask for specific directions.

Cameron Creek Trail (Map 45/A3)

The trail follows an old logging road that is quite overgrown, although it is passable on foot or by bike. This 10 km (6 mi) moderate trek ascends into the mountains above Cameron Creek. At the top of the trail, you will be rewarded with great views of Quesnel Lake to the south and Mitchell Lake to the east.

Cameron Ridge Trails (Map 44/G3–45/A4)

A series of trails are found off an old mining road north of Maeford Lake on the Cariboo Lake Road. The first trail leaves the mining road at the 6 km mark and winds its way through an open sub-alpine forest to the Cameron Ridge Viewpoint overlooking Mitchell Lake and the Penfold Valley. This trail climbs 600 m (1,968 ft) in elevation. The second trail begins near the end of the mining road at about the 12 km (7.5 mi) mark. The trail treks through sub-alpine forest and wetland areas before intersecting the first trail below the viewpoint. The third route leaves the mining road near the second trail and travels straight into the alpine and on to the Goose Range where ample hiking opportunities can be found. Overall, there are at least 20 km (12.5 mi) of moderate trails to explore in this area.

Canim River Trail (Map 19/D1)

Just before the Mahood Lake Campground, look for a logging road off the north side of the main road. Follow this logging access road for about 300 metres and look for a sign reading 'Fishing Trail'. This is the Canim River Trail, which is a 4 km (2.5 mi) return hike to the remains of an early homestead along the river. The Scott family established the homestead in the early 1900s.

> Proper footwear, such as quality hiking boots, can be the difference between a great hike and a painful adventure.

Canyon Mountain Trail (Map 40/D6)

In the heart of the Chilcotin, Canyon Mountain rises 1,465 m (4,805 ft) above sea level. And where there is a mountain, people will climb it. This informal trail leads about 14.5 km (9 mi) and climbs 165 m (540 ft) from the end of Scotty Meadows Forest Service Road.

Capoose Summer Trail (Map 23/B1–37/D6)

This historic pack trail rises sharply from the Bella Coola Valley to connect with the Alexander MacKenzie Trail south of Fish Lake. The difficult route is 14 km (8.7 mi) one-way to the intersection with the heritage trail, climbing 1,405 m (4,600 ft) along the way. The trail continues into Tweedsmuir Park as the Capoose Trail.

Cat Trail (Map 38/D1–52/C7)

The Chilcotin is riddled with old trails that may or may not be there. This is another such trail that links the Kluskus-Malaput Forest Service Road with the Alexander MacKenzie Heritage Trail. The moderate trail follows an old road for 15 km (9 mi) climbing about 160 m (525 ft).

Charlotte Lake Trail (Map 24/D4)
This 16 km (10 mi) trail runs along the south shores of Charlotte Lake to Little Charlotte. In spring and early summer, Whitton Creek can be impassable. The trail starts at Rimarto Ranch and crosses private land.

Chaunigan Mountain Trail (Map 14/E5)
Located near Chaunigan Lake in the midst of untouched wilderness and alpine meadows is this moderate hike up 1,780 m (5,840 ft) to the top of Chaunigan Mountain. The trail is about 4.8 km (3 mi) return and it rewards you with panoramic views. Also in the area are short trails to Lily or Mainguy Lakes as well as the longer Konni Mountain Trail. Chaunigan Lake Lodge offers guided horseback trips.

Chilko Lake Trail (Map 14/B5)
This trail follows the west side of Chilko Lake to the Ch'a Biny Big Lagoon. A rough route heads west from here through Stikela Pass to Tatlayoko Lake. This trail falls in the Tsilhqot'in First Nation area. Visit www.tsilhqotin.ca for more information on access.

Chilko-Tsuniah Trail (Map 14/C4)
This easy, 8 km (5 mi) trail starts along the rough road just north of Tsuniah Lake and cuts west across country to hook up with the East Chilko River Trail. The second half of the route travels through Ts'il'os Provincial Park before reaching Chilko Lake. The trail climbs 240 m (785 ft) along the way. Part of this route runs along an old road. This trail falls in the Tsilhqot'in First Nation area. Visit www.tsilhqotin.ca for more information on access.

Choelquoit Lake Trail (Map 14/B3)
This flat, open trail passes through grasslands and open forest as it travels the south side of Choelquoit Lake. The trail is 13 km (8 mi) long and links up the recreation sites on either end of the lake. This trail falls in the Tsilhqot'in First Nation area. Visit www.tsilhqotin.ca for more information on access.

Christensen Creek Trail (Map 38/E6)
This old wagon road can be picked up just north of the Christensen Creek Bridge and Clesspocket Ranch on the Upper Dean River Road. The route breaks away from Christensen Creek and provides the main access into the Ilgachuz Mountains around the alpine and sub-alpine of Mount Scot. Routes continue north, east and west in the park.

Churn Creek Trails (Maps 4, 5, 16, 17)
The sprawling Churn Creek Protected Area is a unique and fragile landscape filled with rare flora and fauna. With the creation of the protected area, the Churn Creek area has been divided into two recreation sub-zones. The motorized sub-zone (a small area in the north and a large area in the south) allows motorized travel along old roads and cart tracks. The large non-motorized zone has a number of old logging roads, ranch roads and cattle trails that are open to hiking, biking and horseback riding. The trails are unmarked and unmaintained, and ATV use is prohibited. Some of the trails in the area include the Churn Flats Trail, the Clyde Mountain Trail, the Coal Pit Trail, the Koster Lake Trail, the 13 km (8 mi) Little Churn Creek-Big Basin Trail, with an elevation gain of 655 m (2,150 ft), and the Sheep Point Trail. Please respect the private land of the Empire Valley Ranch in the area.

Coleman Flyshacker Trail (Map 13/A2)
This trail accesses the alpine above Sapeye Lake. It is an extension of the former Glacier Valley Trail that hooks up with both the Burnt Creek and Sapeye Creek Trails. The 11.5 km (7 mi) trail gains 200 m (655 ft) over its course.

Collins Overland Telegraph Trail (Map 55/C1–56/C7)
The Telegraph Trail is part of a historically significant route that ultimately failed to establish telegraph communications between New Westminster and the Yukon during the early 1900s. The best section of the route for trail enthusiasts is the 33 km (20.5 mi) section from Pantage Creek in the west to Whittler Creek in the east. Further north, after crossing the Blackwater River, the route follows a series of roads northwest past Bobtail Lake and towards Fraser Lake.

Corkscrew Creek Trail (Map 38/E7–39/A5)
Starting at Bryant Road in Anahim Lake, this trailhead starts near the trailhead for the Blackwater Wagon Road/ Panhandle Phillips Horse Trail. The route heads northeast from Anahim Lake to the south end of Itcha Ilgachuz Range Provincial Park, 36 km (22 mi) one-way.

Cornish Mountain Recreation Area (Map 57/G6)
Located just north of Wells, this area has 25 km (15.5 mi) of trails open to hikers, bikers and skiers. The shortest trail is a 4 km (2.5 mi) trail that heads to One Mile Lake. The longest, the moderate 17 km (10.5 mi) Cornish Mountain Loop, is a bit more scenic. Another named trail in the area is the 7 km (4.3 mi) Coronado Loop.

Corsica Mahood Trail (Map 19/E1)
This multi-use trail leads from the north end of Corsica Lake to the south side of Mahood Lake. Depending on the route, it is over 8 km (5 mi) from the Corsica Lake to Mahood Lake. Trails and roads lead in all directions for extended riding.

Crater Lake Trail (Map 40/G3)
The 1.3 km one-way trail leads to the small hike-in lake. The hill up to the site can be challenging, but it is worth it to access your own private lake. The trailhead is located approximately 21 km southwest of Nazko, off the Michelle Bazekeo Road.

Crazy Creek Trail (Map 13/F3)
Maintained by locals, this trail follows Crazy Creek to the beautiful alpine north of Niut Mountain. There are a series of small lakes here, including Butler Lake. To access the trail, drive 2 km up the driveway of Snoring Horse Ranch, off Tatlayoko Road. The trail begins from a small parking lot before the bridge over the creek. To the left is a smaller horse trail; head right on the ATV trail. The route climbs for 8.5 km (5 mi) to Fox Rock and then heads down to a guide cabin (not available for public use). Continuing past Niut Mountain is a steep scree climb that leads to loops along Valleau Creek and Jamison Creek.

Crooked Lake Trail (Map 31/C3)
The moderate 11 km (6.8 mi) trail ascends along an old mining road to an alpine ridge presenting excellent views of the surrounding mountains. From the alpine ridge, the route eventually leads down to a sub-alpine forest and past several small, picturesque lakes. You can find the trailhead in an open area off the Crooked Lake Road just north of Crooked Lake, from the Crooked Lake Recreation Site.

Crystal Lake Trail (Map 19/B6)
This easy 12 km (7.5 mi) trail begins on the west side of the lake at the Crystal Waters Guest Ranch. Be sure to check in with the ranch before heading out. The circle route travels around the lake through mixed timber and past a few other smaller lakes. The trail eventually reaches the North Bonaparte Road on the east side of the lake. You can return the way you came or continue along the road.

Cutoff Butte Trail (Map 53/C1)
The hike to Cutoff Butte is a short, 1.2 km trek that packs a punch, with a steep incline to the peak climbing 160 m (525 ft). The trail switchbacks through the volcanic rock to the peak and offers great views of the surrounding area. There is a log book hidden in the peak cairn with quotes from those who have completed the climb. The trailhead is found about 11 km east of the Kenny Dam.

Dante's Inferno Trail (Map 16/B1)
Now protected by a provincial park, Dante's Inferno is named after the canyon that can get quite hot in summer. A trail leads about 5 km (3 mi) from Beaumont Road, south of Highway 20, to a small lake called Crater Lake. This lake offers a good early season trout fishery, and the scenic basalt cliffs are home to bats. Some of the other wildlife seen in the area includes pikas, flammulated owls and poorwills.

Deserters Creek Falls Trail (Map 42/E4)
Also known as the Deep Creek Falls Trail, this moderate, 2.6 km one-way trail is located off the West Fraser Road south of Quesnel. The route travels along the Narcosli Creek and Deserters Creek to the site of a scenic 61 m (200 ft) high waterfall.

Dick Brunt Trail (Map 18/F7)
This relatively flat 5 km (3.2 mi) round-trip has less than 20 m (65 ft) in elevation gain. Access can be found via Green Lake Road North, south of Highway 24.

Dome Trail (Map 28/D6)
Found in the heart of the Chilcotin Military Training area, access to this trail may or may not be possible, depending on the day and whether anything is happening at the site. This round volcanic rock is fairly easy to get to via a 5.5 km (3.4 mi) trail, gaining 325 m (1,055 ft) to the top. The views of the surrounding plateau are impressive.

Donnely Lake Trail (Map 19/C3)
This easy 3 km trail travels from the Bowers Lake-Canim Forest Service Road through the timber to the shore of Donnely Lake. The lake is very picturesque, as its waters are remarkably clear.

Dragon Mountain Trails (Map 42/F3)
The Dragon Mountain Trail network is a very unique mountain bike experience just south of Quesnel. This area is home to large Douglas fir and some of the only slick rock riding in the Cariboo. There are over 13 trails ranging from cross-country to downhill, easy to advanced. Catch a ride to the top and enjoy the single track downhill with lots of jumps and drops.

Eagle Valley Trail (Map 59/F5)
At the 14 km mark of the South Dore Forest Service Road, a deactivated logging road branches east to the Eagle Valley Trailhead. It is a moderate 12 km (7.5 mi) return trip gaining 485 m (1,590 ft). In addition to providing access to a moraine and glacier area, there is a backcountry hut available for overnight use. Cabin bookings are possible through the Ozalenko Alpine Club at 250-569-2596.

East Chilko River Trail (Map 14/B4)
This 11 km (6.8 mi) trail is found along the east side of the Chilko River, from Henry's Bridge to the lake. At its south end, it links up with the Chilko-Tsuniah Trail. There is an overall elevation gain of 280 m (920 ft). This trail falls in the Tsilhqot'in First Nation area. Visit www.tsilhqotin.ca for more information on access.

Entiako Trail (Map 52/C3–38/A1)
There are no developed trails in Entiako Provincial Park, however, there is a former pack trail leading from the north section of the park south towards the Dean River. A 38.5 km (24 mi) route starts near the mouth of Aslin Creek. It runs for 24 km (15 mi) to the Entiako River. South of the river, a portion of the trail travels south for 21 km (13 mi). There is an overall elevation change of 160 m (525 ft) over the course of the trail. Alternately, the old wagon road leading north from the Upper Dean River Road is used to access the Alexander MacKenzie Trail as well as this route. The trail is not maintained and likely not easy to follow.

Erg Mountain Trail (Map 58/G1)
Erg Mountain has historically been a hiking destination, and it offers an excellent viewpoint of the Upper Fraser River Valley and the surrounding mountains. The trail is 8.5 km long (5.3 mi), with an elevation gain of 1,400 m (4,595 ft). Access is currently very difficult since the Ptarmigan Creek Forest Service Road is washed out at the 3 and 12 km marks, and the foot bridges crossing the Ptarmigan Creek have been washed away. The trailhead is 8 km in from Highway 16.

Eureka Bowl Trail (Map 31/C3)
Good navigational skills and a four-wheel drive vehicle will help make this interesting hike fairly easy. From the end of the road, a narrow and steep access road drops about 150 m (500 ft) in elevation down to the bowl below Eureka Peak. The bowl is home to two scenic lakes and is quite interesting to visit, as there are remnants of an old mining camp and mining shafts to explore. Depending on how far you can drive on the MacKay River Road, the trail is about 2-3 km to the bowl.

Eureka Rim Trail (Map 31/B2)
Look for a series of logging roads off the south side of Black Creek Road (100 Rd) about 6 km east of the junction with the Crooked Lake Road. After navigating your way through a maze of spur roads, the trailhead to the Eureka Rim Trail is marked by a picnic table. The trek begins in the forest, climbing through sub-alpine forest before opening up into the alpine. Once in the alpine, the route traverses along the ridges and eventually leads to the base of Eureka Mountain. The moderate 10 km (6 mi) hike gains 610 m (2,000 ft) in elevation. An overnight hike is recommended for those that wish to further explore the area.

Fawn Lake Trail (Map 19/A5)
This easy 26 km (16 mi) out-and-back trail is used mostly by mountain bikers and horseback riders in the summer. The elevation change is only about 70 m (230 ft). Look for the trailhead about 2 km along Fawn Creek Road.

Fish Lake Trail (Map 24/D5)
This old hunting trail heads south past the Cowboy Lakes to Fish Lake from the Rimarto Ranch on Charlotte Lake. It hooks up with the McClinchy Creek Trail. Heading east will bring you back to a logging road along McClinchy Creek, which will eventually bring you back to Charlotte Lake. West brings you along the Stewart Lake Trail to Crazy Bear Lake.

Gavin Lake Trail (Map 29/F1)
Located in UBC's Alex Fraser Research Forest northeast of Williams Lake, this 6.7 km (4 mi) trail is an easy interpretive hike along the shore of Gavin Lake. It leads through old growth forest, with an elevation gain of 25 m (80 ft). A boardwalk and viewing platform at Gavin Creek are accessible to low-mobility trail users. The trail is accessible from Gavin Lake Road and is marked by signs.

Goat River Trail (Map 59/B3–58/E4)
The historic Goat River Trail spans over 95 km (60 mi) from the Fraser River to Kruger Lake near the northwest boundary of Bowron Lake Park, with an overall elevation gain of about 440 m (1,445 ft). The trail was originally established in 1886 as a pack trail for prospectors wishing to travel from the town of Barkerville to the Fraser River. Today, the trail provides glimpses of old mining activity, the odd old cabin and a cable car crossing of the Goat River near Whitehorse Creek. In the east, the trail can be accessed from a number of different areas, with the Goat River Forest Service Road providing the main access point. In the west, the main access is from the Littlefield-Kruger Forest Service Road.

Grasslands Community Trail (Map 7/F7)
Best accessed from the north trailhead off McQueen Lake Road in Lac Du Bois Provincial Park, this trail links with the trails around Deep Lake and the trailhead off Westsyde Road at the end of Ida Lane. All told, you lose 540 m (1,770 ft) over 12.6 km (7.8 mi), if travelling south.

Gray Jay Lake Trail (Map 22/B3)
Found high above Bella Coola along a rough forestry road, this short, easy 2 km hike starts behind the campsite at Blue Jay Lake. It traverses some sensitive wetlands to a spectacular viewpoint overlooking the fjord-like coast of the Bentinck Arms.

Gullchuk Lake Trail (Map 8/F1)
This 10 km (6 mi) boat access trail takes hikers to Gullchuk Lake. There is good fishing at nearby Namu Lake.

Haller Trail (Map 5/C3)
The Haller Trail is found near Jesmond to the west of Clinton. There are many trails in the area for ATV and snowmobiles, but this trail is special for horse riders. You can ride the 23 km (14.5 mi) loop or just get lost for a while amongst the surrounding trail systems.

Hallis Lake Ski Trails (Map 42/F2)
The well-maintained, multi-use Hallis Lake Ski Trails are located just east of Quesnel via the Quesnel Hydraulic Road. There are multiple loops to choose from ranging from 2.5 km (1.5 mi) to 16 km (10 mi). In the winter, these trails are used for Nordic skiing, cross-country skiing and snowshoeing. In summer months, these trails are great for family hiking or biking. Full details about the trails and the club can be found on their website at www.caribooski.ca.

Hammer Lakes/Ape Lake Trail (Map 23/A4–C5)
From about the 28.5 km mark on the road, this trail is only 6 km (3.7 mi) one-way to the Iroquois Ridge Lookout near Hammer Lake, which overlooks the rugged, ice-capped Coast Mountains that Ape Lake is located in. There is a 430 m (1,410 ft) elevation gain to Hammer Lake, and another 500 m (1,640 ft) to the viewpoint. This first part of the route is moderately challenging. Beyond the viewpoint, a rough route extends southeast another 14 km (8.7 mi) to Ape Lake. Although it is easier in the winter, we cannot overstate how difficult this hike is. In addition to creek crossings, there is a daunting 750 metre high by 2 km wide avalanche slope to pass before getting to the glacial lake.

Hangman Springs Trails (Map 42/C2)
A network of over 20 km (12.5 mi) of easy to moderate riding trails wind their way through the bush. They are located west of Quesnel off the Nazko Road.

Harman Lake Horse Trails (Map 5/F6)
This 24.4 km (15 mi) network of equestrian-friendly trails is located north of Lillooet. Access can be found via Pavilion-Clinton Road to the south of Kelly Lake/Downing Provincial Park.

Hidden Valley Trail (Map 24/F7) 🥾🏔️
This rough route can be accessed from either the west or the east and takes people into the alpine east of the Klinaklini Valley.

Hogback Trail (Map 5/B5) 🥾🏔️
Beginning near the end of the Leon Creek Forest Service Road, this 6 km (3.7 mi) hike leads to the alpine meadows of Hog Mountain. Allow about 3 hours for this hike.

Horsefly Mountain Trail (Map 30/E2) 🥾🚵🐎🚴🏔️
A series of logging spur roads provide access to the top of Horsefly Mountain. It is recommended to park much further down in order to experience the route on foot or by bike. Once at the top, a moderate trail continues by skirting around the summit and opens up fantastic views along the way. Depending where you park, expect about a 10.5 km (6.5 mi) trek gaining 680 m (2,230 ft) to the summit.

Horseshoe Bend Trail (Map 5/B7) 🥾🏔️
This scenic, but short 1.2 km round trip leads to a geocache on Bridge River. Access can be found off of Bridge River Road. Expect to climb over 100 m (330 ft) in elevation on the way back.

Isobel Lake Trails (Map 7/F7) 🥾🚵⛷️🎿🛶🧗
It's an easy 3 km walk around Isobel Lake with interpretive signs describing the ecology of region. If you wish for a longer trip, you can continue on the 10 km (6 mi) of cross-country ski trails in the area. Another alternative is to bike down the roads next to Dairy Creek from Isobel Lake to Westsyde Road. Along the way, you will cross several trails and roads (stay right at all intersections). This moderate ride is 14.5 km (8.8 mi) long.

Jubilee Creek Trail (Map 58/A6) 🏕️🥾🎿🏔️
The Jubilee Creek Trail is one of the routes to the Mount Murray area. The trailhead can be found at 6.3 km on the Bowron Lake Road. The moderate trail follows an old logging spur to a small creek where a rough, unmaintained route continues into the alpine. In total, the Jubilee Trail treks across 9 km (5.6 mi) round-trip and climbs over 620 m (2,035 ft) in elevation. For an alternative journey back from the summit, you can take the Yellowhawk Trail back down to the road.

Junction Sheep Range (Map 16/F2) 🥾🚵🐎🚴🏔️
The long, hot trails through open grassland are better suited for mountain biking or horseback. Big, open, rolling grassland mean fast, fun riding. (Watch out for saddle spilling rocks!) As an added bonus, this area is home to the largest herd of California bighorn sheep in North America. The main cart track is open to four-wheel drive vehicles and ATVs.

Kappan Mountain Trail (Map 24/C2) 🏕️🥾🛶🏔️
From the south end of Kappan Lake, a trail makes its way up to Kappan Mountain and beyond. The trail is also known as the Floyd Mecham Trail, after the pioneer who discovered the route.

Khutze Inlet Trail (Map 48/C5) 🥾🏔️
It is about 5 km (3 mi) from the beautiful waterfall at the head of the river valley to an abandoned gold mine along an old road. Boaters need to watch for a sunken barge near the waterfall by the trailhead.

Klinaklini River Trails (Map 24/F7–12/D2) 🥾🚵🐎🚴🏔️
From Highway 20, just north of Kleena Kleene, an old four-wheel drive/ATV road leads about 7 km (4.3 mi) to the Klinklini Falls. Further up the valley, the old road leads to a route that leads up Brussel Creek into the alpine area west of Tweedsmuir Park. It is a long, rugged haul into the remote Klinaklini Lake so be prepared for an overnight trip. The area is known for its abundant wildlife, including grizzly bears and trekkers are advised to follow bear safety guidelines.

Kluskus Trail (Map 54/A6–D7) 🥾🐎🚵
Not to be confused with the adventure book of the same name, this flat, 17.8 km (11 mi) trail is a former First Nations carrier route that linked to a remote village. Although a new road now services the area, pieces are still found and are often ridden by off-road enthusiasts and horseback riders.

Kristi Glacier/Cariboo Pass Trail (Map 59/E6) 🏕️🥾🏔️
Beginning from the end of the Middle Dore Forest Service Road, this moderate 18 km (11 mi) backcountry trail traverses some magnificent terrain. The trail quickly ascends into the alpine before reaching the Cariboo Pass and eventually the scenic Kristi Glacier Campsite, with an overall elevation gain of 700 m (2,300 ft).

Lang Lake Interpretive Trail (Map 30/G7) 🥾🧗
Also known as the Wet Belt Interpretive Trail, this 2.5 km trail is found east of Lang Lake along the Lang Lake North Road (610 Road). Look for the parking area about 17 km from the Canim-Hendrix Lake Road turnoff.

Lime Ridge Trails (Map 5/E4) 🥾🏔️
The northern access trail is actually an extension of the Mad Dog Trail that travels through the sub-alpine before ascending sharply to the ridge. The moderate trek is about 12 km (7.5 mi) return. From the south, look for a clearing off the east side of Jesmond Road where an old mining road can be seen. The trail travels along the old road to the base of the ridge, where there is no definitive trail to follow. Once atop the ridge, it offers seemingly endless hiking possibilities and beautiful views.

Lincoln Pass Trail (Map 13/G4–14/A4) 🥾🚵🐎🏔️
This trail passes through an old growth Douglas fir forest before breaking into the open grasslands. This is a heritage trail that is used mostly by horseback riders and hikers, although mountain bikers have been known to make their way up here. This trail falls in the Tsilhqot'in First Nation area. Visit www.tsilhqotin.ca for more information on access.

Lingfield Creek Trail (Map 14/B4) 🥾🏔️
This developed trail follows Lingfield Creek to connect up first with the Choelquoit Fire Road and then with the Potato Range Trails. This trail falls in the Tsilhqot'in First Nation area. Visit www.tsilhqotin.ca for more information on access.

Little McClinchy Creek Trail (Map 24/F6) 🥾🐎🏔️
This remote, 11.6 km (7.2 mi) trek gains 340 m (1,115 ft) over its course. Suitable for horseback riding or hiking, it takes you into the pristine high alpine where you will find diverse plant and animal life, including caribou, mule deer and birds. There are a number of camps in the area.

Liza Lake Trail (Map 4/D6) 🥾🏔️
Access can be found off Carpenter Lake Road via the Marshall Lake Trail. This is a 9.2 km (5.7 mi) return journey with 230 m (755 ft) elevation gain.

Lost Lake Trail (Map 22/G1) 🏕️🥾🏔️
Lost Lake is a tiny lake at the base of Saloomt Peak. The 2 km trail is fairly easy, although there are a few steep pitches as it winds up the southern toe of the mountain to the small lake. Allow an hour to soak in the views to the south and west.

Lt. Palmer Route (Maps 23, 24 - 28, 38, 42) 🏕️🥾🐎🚵🎿🛶🏔️
Stretching from the Coastal Mountains to the Fraser River near Alexandria, this historical route may be restored as a National Heritage Trail. The trail begins near the Precipice in Tweedsmuir Park (Map 19/G2) and joins up with Lunass Trail, which takes it across Highway 20 north of Nimpo Lake. The trail follows the highway south for a stretch before veering east past Aktaklin Lake. The route then intermixes stretches of trail with logging roads as it continues west of Puntzi Lake. The stretch from Puntzi towards the old fur trading fort at Alexandria (Map 34/F6) is not as defined, but it does pass by several lakes where camping is possible. Tracking the trail through the maze of logging roads is rather challenging.

Lucas Plateau Trail (Map 19/C6) 🥾🏔️
Located near the Lac Des Roches Resort at the west end of Lac Des Roches on Highway 24, this is a 2.2 km one-way trail with an elevation gain of 90 metres (295 ft). To access the route, turn right off of Highway 24, eastbound just before Little Lac Des Roches. The trailhead is located on private property. Call the Lac Des Roches Resort for access permission at 250-593-4141.

Lucille Mountain Trail (Map 59/G4) 🏕️🥾🐎🛶🎿🏔️
In McBride, Samson Road leads to the Lucille Mountain Forest Service Road, which eventually accesses an old logging area. The trailhead is located on the east side of the upper cut blocks. The moderate route travels 3.4 km (2 mi) one-way into the alpine area of Mount Lucille, gaining 560 m (1,835 ft) along the way.

M. Gurr Lake Trail (Map 22/C3) 🥾🎿🎿🏔️
Leading to a spectacular viewpoint, the most difficult part of this easy hike is the drive up from Bella Coola. The viewpoint of the fjord-like coast will astound even the most casual outdoorsperson. The moderate, 1.7 km one-way trail climbs about 215 m (705 ft) in elevation.

MacKill Lake Trail (Map 27/D3) 🏕️🥾🛶
This easy 3 km trail circles MacKill Lake and offers visitors a chance to try their luck fishing. Part of the trail follows the remnants of the old Lt. Palmer Route.

Mad Dog Mountain Trail (Map 5/E3)

The trailhead can be found off the east side of Jesmond Road, near an old home foundation. From here, the trail travels east along Foundation Creek for about 4 km (2.5 mi). It then branches north from the main trail towards Mad Dog Mountain. This last stretch of the trail can be challenging to follow and may require bush-whacking to reach the mountain. Overall, the moderate trail covers about 14 km (8.7 mi) return, with an overall elevation gain of 680 m (2,230 ft).

Marmot Lake (Map 41/A2)

This is an easy, 4 km (2.5 mi) hiking trail around Marmot Lake. The trail provides good shore access for anglers.

Marshall Lake Trail (Map 4/D6)

A 10 km (6 mi) scenic trail takes you up the hill from the east side of Marshall Lake down to Carpenter Lake. From here, you can arrange for a pickup or retrace your path. There are also several other trails in the area, including a nice ridge walk.

Marshall Ridge Trail (Map 4/D7)

This is a 6.4 km (4 mi) return trip just north of Carpenter Lake. There is a steep 650 m (2,135 ft) elevation gain over the course of this route. Access can be found via Carpenter Lake Road.

Martin Meadow Trail (Map 41/C5)

This trail follows an old wagon trail past a remote stretch of the Nazko River for about 20 km (12.5 mi) through Loomis Meadows to Martin Meadows. The trail starts at the 35 km mark of the Honolulu Road and is ATV friendly.

> The wealth of trails listed here only represents a fraction of the outdoor opportunities available in the Cariboo Chilcotin Coast. Adventurers can follow old game trails or logging roads to places that few others know about.

Masters Subalpine Trek (Map 7/D6–F2)

This difficult four to five day trek extends for 24.5 km (15 mi) through the sub-alpine terrain and past numerous wilderness lakes and meadows of the Bonaparte Plateau. The main access points are from the Tranquille Lake Resort to the south or from around the 63 km mark on the Jamieson Creek Road to the north. Along the route are several cabins, which you can overnight in, as well as many remote fishing lakes. There is an overall elevation gain of 420 m (1,380 ft). The trail is very isolated and wanders through vast stretches of unspoiled wilderness. Hikers should come prepared with topographic maps and compass and should also be bear aware.

Maydoe Creek Trail (Map 24/E5–B6)

The Maydoe Creek Trail starts at the south end of Charlotte Lake and skirts the north side of the creek before breaking out into the alpine area around Whitton and the aptly named Wilderness Lake. Sections of the trails may be boggy or tricky to negotiate due to rocky terrain. In addition to exploring the alpine, there are backcountry cabins and some fine summer fishing for rainbow available. Contact Nuk Tessli Alpine Experience for more information.

Mayson, Bogmar, Allan & Scott Lake Trails (Map 7/F2)

This network of eight trails is used to access a series of lakes just southeast of Bonaparte Lake. All told, there are about 31 km (19 mi) of trails here, ranging from half hour jaunts to overnighters. Best traveled from June to September, the trails are mostly easy and used by horseback riders and anglers. Some sections can be boggy. Note that there may be active logging in the area.

McClinchy Creek Trail (Map 24/E5)

From the end of the logging road west from Highway 20, a trail can be picked up on the north side of the creek. It is a long walk into the lake and most come here to fish.

Medby Rock Lookout/Nusatsum Mountain Route (Map 22/G1–23/A1)

Named after artist Carl Medby, who liked to come to this spot to paint, the Medby Rock Lookout is a moderate uphill climb through the forest to an old fire lookout. Allow two hours to enjoy the views of the Coast Mountains and Bella Coola Valley. Once at the lookout, mountaineers can follow the ridge route over to Nusatsum Mountain. This is a long, hard slog (give yourself at least eight hours) up the shoulder of the mountain to this lovely alpine summit.

Meldrum Creek Trail (Map 28/G6-G5)

Located just west of Williams Lake, this 27 km (17 mi) trail runs alongside the Fraser River. Access can be found off of Highway 20 via Meldrum Creek Road, or from the other end of the trail via Chilcotin-Meldrum Road. Over the course of the route there is a 240 m (785 ft) elevation gain.

Messue Horse & Wagon Trails (Map 53/E6–D5)

Tracking this seldom used historical route may be a challenge. Found north of the village of Kluskus, the trail links Tatelkuz Lake with the Alexander Mac-Kenzie Trail south of the Blackwater (West Road) River. The wagon road is about 26 km (16 mi) one-way. There is also the horse trail that adds a further 15.5 km (9.5 mi). Today, the short 4.7 km (3 mi) stretch between km 146 on the Blue Forest Service Road and the Alexander MacKenzie Trail is often used as an alternate for off-road enthusiasts. It requires crossing the Blackwater at the Messue Ford, which is best done later in the season.

Mill Creek Valley Route (Map 22/E1)

This is a difficult route and is only for folks with strong route finding skills or a guide. The trail initially starts out along an old logging road (after wading across Mill Creek), but you will need to veer north to gain the west shoulder of the creek. The route becomes more defined as there are some old blazes leading past an old trapper's cabin to the top of a prominent headwall. Strong route finders can do this trip in a day, but most people take a couple of days.

Mitchell River Trail (Map 45/A3)

From the end of Z Road, this trail actually follows a deteriorating road through a few plantation areas and eventually an old growth cedar forest. The trees along this part of the trail are quite large and eventually give way to the shore of the North Arm of Quesnel Lake. Overall, the trail is a moderate 10 km (6 mi) return hike.

Mosquito Pass Trail (Map 22/G2–23/A2)

Formerly called Cooks Trail, this steep route starts off the south side of the creek on the East Nusatsum Forest Service Road. You will need good route finding skills to follow the game trails up to the beautiful pass, and some bushwhacking may be required. The trail is marked by flagging tape. From the pass, there is access to a number of Coast Mountain peaks in the area.

Mount Bowman to Mount Kerr Trails (Map 5/E3)

This trail system begins at the Circle H Mountain Lodge off Jesmond Road. Be sure to check in at the office before heading out. Behind the lodge, look for a 'pipeline trail' sign, which marks the beginning of the forested trail that follows a small stream. About 5 km in, the Mount Bowman Trail veers north off the main trail towards the base of mountain. From the base, you can follow one of the many switchback trails to the mountain ridge and peak area for a moderate 14 km (8.7 mi) return trek. The moderate 18 km (11 mi) Wild Horse Ridge Trail continues along the creek valley to the ridge found in Marble Range Park. This section of the trail is well marked and is ideal for horseback riding. The Mount Kerr Trail is a 10 km (6 mi) return extension of the Wild Horse Ridge Trail. The route to Mount Kerr follows an alpine ridge trail that offers panoramic views along the way. Splitting the difficult trip into two days is recommended. Whichever route you take, there is an elevation gain of about 880 m (2,885 ft). Be sure to bring water.

Mount Brew Trail (Map 44/D6)

Follow the Spanish Lake Road (1300 Rd) east from the town of Likely and look for the 1324 km sign. At the sign, follow the four-wheel drive access road as it switchbacks up the mountain eventually reaching a large clearing, where a flagged trail can be found. The moderate 5 km (3 mi) trail travels through the timber to the top of Mount Brew for a panoramic view of Quesnel Lake.

Mount Patchett Trail (Map 58/C7)

Access to this moderate 6.5 km (4 mi) trail can be found off the Pleasant Valley Road (1600 Rd) to the east of Barkerville. Look for the side road just after the small lake and 1614 km marker. The trail climbs roughly 755 m (2,475 ft) up Mount Patchett and offers a fine view over the Bowron Lakes and Barkerville areas. This area is closed to snowmobiles.

Mount Stevenson Trail (Map 44/E5)
East of Likely, this mountain sits above Grain Creek and the North Arm of Quesnel Lake. A rough route runs 8.5 km (5 mi) up the south side of the mountain, climbing over 915 m (3,000 ft).

National Hiking Trail (Maps 22–24, 38, 39, 42-44, 53-56, 58, 59)
While the Trans Canada Trail down south has been getting all the publicity, the National Hiking Trail is a more traditional trail that should eventually cross the country. Most of the BC route is found in this book as it follows the Bella Coola Valley over to Anahim Lake and the Blackwater Wagon Road. This trail links with the Alexander MacKenzie Trail to the north, which stretches east to the Fraser River. From here it passes Quesnel en route to the 1861 Goldrush Pack Trail that has been blazed from Keithley Creek north to Barkerville. Eventually you will link with the Goat River Trail that takes you further east towards McBride and beyond the reaches of this book. For more information, contact the Federation of BC Mountain Clubs (www.mountainclubs.bc.ca) or the National Hiking Trail Committee (www.nationaltrail.ca).

Natsadalia Trail (Map 24/B1–38/D7–24/F2)
An original grease trail, this 52 km (32 mi) trail is the northern extension of the Lt. Palmer Route. The trail branches north from Hotnarko River and Precipice Creek and continues east to the Natsadalia Crossing of the Dean River north of Anahim Lake. This was once the site of a Hudson's Bay Post. The trail continues around the lake to the Dean River Road and along the northeast side of the river, which parallels the highway. The trail eventually joins the Lt. Palmer Route. There is an overall elevation gain of 400 m (1,310 ft). Note that the trail crosses private property around Anahim and Nimpo Lakes. Please ask permission to cross.

Noaxe Lake/Quartz Mountain Trails (Map 4/D4)
Between Noaxe Creek Road in the west, the Swartz Lake-Poison Mountain Road in the north and the Yalakom River to the east is an area dominated mostly by open grasslands and the high alpine of the Schulaps Range. This area is home to a number of backcountry horse or ATV trails that predominantly follow old logging roads. Away from the roads, there is a rat's nest of old cattle and game trails that often start at one place, braid, split and then end for no reason at all. Route finding through the open grassland isn't too difficult (especially with a compass or GPS unit), but don't trust the trail you're on to lead to where you want it to go. Popular destinations in this area include Yalakom River, Poison, Quartz and Big Sheep Mountains as well as Noaxe and the Mud Lakes. A new mine in the area may restrict access from the Yalakom/Blue Creek area.

No Name / Hidden Lake Trail (Map 31/D5)
A moderate 15 km (9.3 mi) trek links the No Name Lakes Recreation Site with Deception Lake. It is possible to shorten the trail since the Spanish-No Name Branch Road intersects the north and south sections of trail. This route is best travelled on foot, although bikers and horseback riders do venture up.

North Itcha Trails (Map 38/G3, 39/A3)
The North Itcha Trails run north of Itcha Igachuz Provincial Park. There are over 40 km (25 mi) of trails that follow old roads and game trails south into the park. Depending on the route, expect a 400 m (1,310 ft) elevation gain.

Obsidian Creek [Anahim Peak] Trail (Map 38/C4)
Beginning south of Obsidian Creek, you will have to cross the Dean River to access this trail. The trail then crosses the creek on its way up to Anahim Peak in Tweedsmuir Park. The reward is a fantastic view of the Coastal Mountains, the Dean River Valley and the Chilcotin Plateau.

Ocean Falls Area (Map 35/B1)
The now almost-deserted mill town of Ocean Falls is home to several trails that are falling into disuse. Still there are many trails or routes to explore if you happen in the area. Baldy Mountain Trail is a short 3 km round-trip with a viewing tower and ranger cabin at 600 metres. Goat Mountain, Mount Caro Marion and Sawmill Mountain are other flagged but difficult routes to follow that see few visitors. Martin Lake Trail is a fairly easy 10 km (6 mi) trail that takes hikers along the Martin River to the lake. It is possible to camp and fish at the lake. Roscoe Road follows the road for about 16 km (10 mi) to Shack Bay. Along the way at about the halfway point, you will pass the Twin Lakes, where you can find a rustic campsite next to a sandy beach.

Odegaard Falls Trail (Map 23/B3)
The Odegaard Falls Trail is a moderate 4 km (2.5 mi) return trail that begins at the nearby Nusatsum River Recreation Site. The trail begins by winding its way down through the beautiful forests next to the river that flows through a steep, narrow canyon. After about 30 minutes, the trail meets Odegaard Creek where a bridge marks the beginning of a steady climb up to the viewpoint of the 200 m (655 ft) high falls. For those looking for more of a challenge, a difficult, flagged route climbs to the wet meadow at the top of the falls. You are rewarded with views of glaciers and mountains before looping back down to the main trail.

Ozalenka Trail (Map 59/E4)
The trailhead to this backcountry hiking or skiing route can be found past the 19 km mark of the West Dore River Road. From the road, the trail is a moderate 12 km (7.5 mi) hike along the valley to the pass between Ozalenka and Clyde Creeks, with an elevation gain of 460 m (1,510 ft).

Paradise Trail (Map 59/G3)
This trail can be found off the north side of Mountainview Road north of McBride. Look for a small parking area that marks the trailhead to this moderate 14 km (8.7 mi) route. The trail provides great views of the Rocky Mountain Trench as it ascends 1,480 m (4,855 ft) up Mount Monroe.

Perkins Peak Trail (Map 12/G2-13/A2)
Perkins Peak is the first major peak heading south out of the Chilcotin and into the Coast Mountains. From the end of the four-wheel drive accessible Miner Forest Service Road (park as far up the road as you are willing to drive), an old road heads up to a lake basin near the base of the peak. The peak boasts amazing views of the bigger mountains to the south, the Kliniklini Icefield and the Niut, Pantheon and Waddington Ranges. To the north, the relatively flat Chilcotin stretches to the horizon.

Pete Kitchen Lake Trail (Map 18/C2)
You can find this easy 4.5 km (2.8 mi) trail off the north side of Spring Lake Road, off Highway 97. The trail follows an old logging road through some scenic meadows to the shore of Pete Kitchen Lake.

Peter Fuller Pack Trail (Map 38/C4)
Another route into the mountains of Itcha Ilgachuz Park, this trail requires crossing private property to access. Please ask permission from the folks at Kinto Ranch. The ranch and trailhead are found about 3 km off the Upper Dean Road.

Porcupine Creek Canyon Trail (Map 5/E4)
This is another scenic trail that starts from Jesmond Road. Most choose to park on the main road and hike the four-wheel drive road to the trailhead. This adds 4 km (2.5 mi) to the 10 km (6 mi) hike to the fabulous Porcupine Creek Canyon. The actual trailhead is found off the north side of the four-wheel drive road before the creek crossing. This trail travels through Marble Range Provincial Park to the canyon, making an easy, almost-loop with an overall elevation gain of 660 m (2,135 ft). It should take about three hours to complete. Along the way, hikers will discover beautiful wildflowers, deer, gorgeous alpine landscapes and, if they're lucky, migrating bighorn sheep.

Potato Range Trails (Map 13/G6–14/A5)
A number of trails have been developed in the area. The 15.3 km (9.4 mi) Crest Route is one of the most popular and can be found at the end of a rough four-wheel drive road near the north end of Tatlayoko Lake. It is an additional 6 km (3.7 mi) to hike up the road. The route ends at Bracewell's Wilderness Lodge, where it is possible to arrange for a shuttle back. Expect and elevation gain of around 360 m (1,180 ft). The Potato Trail begins at the lodge and follows the Cheshi Creek Valley for a few kilometres, before climbing steeply up to the Echo Lakes, where Bracewell's maintains a cabin. From the lakes, the trail continues north, below the ridge of the Potato Range, through Groundhog Basin and to the north trailhead, a distance of 9 km (5.6 mi) from the lakes. Allow for an overnight trip if you plan to do both trails. The full stretch of the Potato Trail sees an overall elevation gain of 1,000 m (3,280 ft). The Skinner Mountain Trail departs the Potato Trail a short way from the trailhead and climbs steeply up to Skinner Mountain. You can return the way you came or follow the trail to a cabin at Echo Lakes and return down the Potato Trail. These trails fall in the Tsilhqot'in First Nation area. Visit www.tsilhqotin.ca for more information on access.

Potts Farm Trail (Map 19/D6)

This easy 14 km (8.6 mi) round trip is located at the west end of Lac des Roches and leads past a large fir tree to a series of ponds and Grizzly Lake. The trailhead can be found on the north side of Highway 24, east of Gerald Crescent. The overall elevation gain is 75 m (245 ft). Visitors can enjoy hiking, or snowshoeing and cross-country skiing in winter. Be wary of thin ice in winter.

Powell Creek Trail (Map 3/C3)

The trail along Powell Creek takes travellers to the headwaters of Powell Creek and beyond, into an area of scenic lakes and meadows. The trail continues through Powell Pass to connect up with the Tosh Creek Trail into Big Creek Provincial Park. It also hooks up with the Beece Creek Trail, which could form a long loop trip.

Preacher Lake Trail (Map 19/C4)

The Preacher Lake trail is 2.2 km return with less than 50 m (165 ft) elevation gain. This relatively flat and easy route leads to the southwestern shore of Preacher Lake.

Ptarmigan Creek Trail (Map 58/G2)

Access is currently very difficult since the Ptarmigan Creek Forest Service Road is washed out at the 3 and 12 km marks and both foot bridges crossing the Ptarmigan Creek have been washed away. This will extend the route that once started at the gate and followed the creek to eventually climb to the first Hammel Lake, set in the sub-alpine below Mount Hammel. From the gate, the difficult route is about 12 km (7.5 mi) and hard to track.

Rainbow Creek Trail (Map 2/D3)

Access to this rough, steep trail is by boat along Chilko Lake. From a cabin on the lake, the trail climbs steeply over 6.5 km (4 mi) to Dorothy Lake, where the trail joins with the Yohetta Valley Trail and the Spectrum Pass Trail. Either return the way you came in or arrange for a (very long) shuttle in the Gunn Valley.

Rainbow Lake Trail (Map 38/C3)

This 29 km (18 mi) trail begins from a rough four-wheel drive road system west of the Upper Dean River Road. One option is to follow the old road north to the Alexander MacKenzie Trail. This is an easy trail with a minimal elevation gain of 80 m (260 ft). Another option is to follow the old trail that climbs past the lake into the mountains of Itcha Ilgachuz Park.

Rea Lake Circuit (Map 7/F4)

This 12 km (7 mi) trail will take around six hours to complete. It is a moderate wilderness circuit leading past several remote wilderness lakes. The trail is generally well-marked but can be tough to follow in places. The circuit also links up with the Tsintsunko Lake Trails. The trailhead is found at the end of Bob Lake Road or the Rea Lake Road.

Red Mountain Trails (Map 4/E3)

Red Mountain is an open peak that is easily walked to from a number of different access spots. Most venture in from the Poison Mountain Road. Be forewarned: there are a number of cattle and game trails in the area that may not lead to where you think they do. Since the ground is open and easy to cross, it might be easier to make your own way along the ridge.

Roaring Creek Trails (Map 44/G5)

Boaters exploring the North Arm of Quesnel Lake will find a designated recreation area on the south side of Roaring Creek. Although nothing formal is here, there are about 3 km of easy trails to explore. They run along the shoreline and up the creek. The trail leading up the creek gains about 150 m (490 ft) in elevation.

Round Lake Trail (Map 7/D4)

From the 8 km mark on the Deadman Creek Road, this 3 km (1.8 mi) one-way hike leads through a second growth Lodgepole pine stand with little elevation gain. While it is not a long trail, it is seldom used, and it can be quite difficult to follow the old blaze marks.

Saloompt Forest Trails (Map 22/F1)

There is a network of forest trails in the Saloompt Forest, ranging from 300 metres to 1 km in length. The network makes for a flat and easy trek with interpretive signs guiding you through the ancient forest. This ecologically diverse area is filled with treasures, from eagle nests to temperate rainforest undergrowth to spawning salmon in the Saloompt River. The trailhead can be found on the Saloompt River Road. Note that there are bears here during spawning season.

Saloompt Peak Route (Map 22/G1–36/G7)

This is a long, steep climb through second and old growth forests common to coastal rainforests. The trail gains an astounding 1,525 m (5,000 ft) over about six hours and there are some exposed sections near the end that should only be attempted by experienced mountaineers.

Sapeye Creek Trail (Map 13/C2)

This difficult trail takes hikers along Sapeye Creek to the alpine. From here a rough route connects to the Coleman Flyshacker Trail. Depending on how far you trek, the trail is about 13 km (8 mi) long, gaining over 1,000 m (3,280 ft).

Schoolhouse Mountain Falls Trails (Map 22/F1)

After an initial forest swamp stretch with a long boardwalk, there are two routes that you can take: the 1.5 km east trail, and the 2 km west trail. Both are moderate routes, with the east being more difficult. Both travel uphill to the cascading Schoolhouse Mountain Falls with an overall elevation gain of about 300 m (985 ft). At the falls you will encounter spectacular views of the surrounding valleys.

Written from a hiker's perspective, distances and times provided are for return hikes, unless otherwise noted.

Shaggy Top Trail (Map 18/G3–19/A3)

This 8 km (5 mi) round-trip trail has a 500 m (1,640 ft) elevation gain. Access can be found about 650 metres down Canim Lake South Road; take a right down the unnamed road that eventually leads to the trail.

Sheridan Lake Trails (Map 18/G5–19/D5)

At the west end of Sheridan Lake is a nest of old roads and multi-use trails. Access to these trails is off the Boulanger Road, which in turn is off West Sheridan Lake Road. These trails are used by snowmobilers in winter and by most everyone else in summer. There are over 200 km (130 mi) of trails here (in truth, mostly old roads), not all of which are worthwhile for hikers unless looking for exercise.

Shulaps Basin Trail (Map 4/F6)

Part of a series of trails in the Shulaps Range, this trail leads to the divide between the eastern and western parts of the Shulaps Range. The scenic trail stretches almost 19 km (11.8 mi) from the trailhead found west of the Lake La Mare Recreation Site to the Marshall Creek Forest Service Road near Brett Creek. Serpentine Lake makes a nice, 2.5 km one-way side trip. Please note that this trail is not ATV friendly.

Silviculture Trail (Map 29/B4)

You can find the Silviculture Trail not far off Highway 97 north of Williams Lake. The trail is located between the Bull Mountain Ski Trails and the Minton Creek Walk. The Silviculture Trail is an easy, self-guided interpretive trail that travels 3 km through a variety of forestry sites.

Snooka Creek Trails (Map 22/E2)

A trio of trails offers easy to moderate year round use. The three trails total 10.9 km (6.7 mi). One is a loop over the creek; the second is a popular bike trail that cuts through the old growth forest to private land; the Snooka West Trail is the most popular. It climbs 500 m (1,650 ft) to a viewpoint over the town of Bella Coola and out to the historic Talleo Cannery on North Bentinck Arm.

Beyond these trails is a challenging mountaineering route up to the headwaters of Snooka Creek, in the shadow of Noohalk Mountain. The trail cuts through some lush vegetation and is often overgrown. Once you reach the lakes, there are many ridges, peaks and summits to explore. Give yourself at least six hours to make it to the lakes, or bring a pack and spend a few days exploring this alpine wonderland.

South Chilcotin Mountains Park (Maps 3, 4)

The Spruce Lake area offers a world-class trail system open to all but ATVers. There are about 200 km (124 mi) of wilderness trails in the area, which travel over gentle mountain passes and meander through lush alpine grasslands and flowers to destination trout lakes. The main access points into the area are the Gun Creek, Mud Creek-Taylor Creek and the Slim Creek Forest Service Roads. Most of the trails have few or no signs and there are a number of rough routes that are only for experienced route finders. Also, due to snow accumulations, the trails are best hiked or biked in late summer/early fall. Here is a selection of the more active trails in the area:

B&F Creek Trail (Map 4/A6)
Located in the South Chilcotin Mountains, this challenging wilderness trail descends 698 m (2,295 ft) over 8.6 km (5.3 mi). It is a less-used trail on account of its steep access and lower maintenance. There are some wild sections, with blow down and alder whips. It is recommended to bring a folding saw. Note that the trail is used by packhorse trains; use caution.

Dash Cabin Hill/Dash-West Churn Trails (Map 4/A2)
The 15 km (9.3 mi) Dash-West Churn Trail is a motorized route that climbs about 180 m (590 ft). At its south end, it links up with the Dash Cabin Hill Trail. This trail spans 8.4 km (5.2 mi), climbing 620 m (2,035 ft) as it travels south into Big Creek Provincial Park. This portion of the trail is non-motorized.

Deer Pass Trail (Map 3/F5)
From the packer's cabin near Trigger Lake, this trail climbs 800 m (2,600 ft) in 4.5 km (2.8 mi) to Deer Pass. The trail continues north and loses 600 m (1,950 ft) in the next 5.5 km (3.4 mi) to Tyaughton Creek, where it joins the Tyaughton Creek Trail.

Gun Creek Trail (Map 4/A6–3/D5)
From the signed trailhead off Slim Creek Forest Service Road, this is the main trail into the heart of the Spruce Lake area. The trail crosses a footbridge (Jewel Bridge) and follows the north side of Gun Creek, eventually breaking from the pine forest (after a climb of 450 m/1,475 ft) to the open grasslands and aspen trees. The mountain views are tremendous. At the 11.5 km mark the trail branches. Heading north is the popular trail that climbs 200 m (655 ft) in 1 km to Spruce Lake, where there are campsites and a beach. Continuing west, the Gun Creek Trail passes Cowboy Camp, Hummingbird Lake and Trigger Lake (at 19 km) before climbing an additional 200 m (655 ft) over 12.5 km to the junction of Deer Pass and Warner Pass Trails. The Upper Gun Creek Trail continues southwest to Taylor Pass gaining 500 m (1,640 ft) over 12 km (7.5 mi). The northern section beyond Trigger Lake doesn't see a lot of use and is reportedly overgrown.

High Trail (Map 4/B6)
The trailhead for this scenic trail is near the south end of Tyaughton Lake. The trail passes through alpine meadows with nice mountain views before reaching the south end of Spruce Lake. The first 5 km of the trail comprise an old, four-wheel drive accessible mining road, which climbs quickly to the ridge between Eldorado Basin and Pearson Creek. Once over the steep hill of the ridge (this point is 1,000 m/3,280 ft higher than the trailhead), the trail drops into the Eldorado Basin and climbs another 450 m (1,475 ft) up to Windy Pass. Beyond Windy Pass, the trail drops to the Spruce Lake Trail. The High Trail is almost 21 km (13 mi) long, with an overall elevation gain of 1,140 m (3,740 ft).

Little Paradise Creek Trail (Map 3/G4)
This trail starts 27 km along the Tyaughton Creek Trail and heads north to a pass overlooking Little Paradise Valley. It is 4 km (2.5 mi) and 500 m (1,625 ft) up to the pass. At the pass, another route to Castle and Cardtable Mountains follows a ridge heading southeast. Beyond the pass, the trail follows Little Paradise Creek to its confluence with Relay Creek, another 8.3 km (5 mi) beyond and 600 m (1,950 ft) below the pass. There are no trail markers or signs.

Lorna Pass Trail (Map 3/F4)
This 7 km (4.3 mi) trail is a quick-access single-track trail that leaves from Lorna Lake in Big Creek Park. The wilderness trail is extremely technically and physically challenging, including a highly difficult climb of close to 320 m (1,050 ft) to the pass. Enjoy the great views before dropping 480 m (1,575 ft) to Tyaughton Creek Trail in South Chilcotin Mountains Park.

North Cinnabar Trail (Map 4/B6)
The North Cinnabar Trail spans 9.5 km (6 mi) with an overall elevation gain of 925 m (3,035 ft). Bikers prefer to ride this one downhill; expect a technically challenging run. The trail begins on the ridge, disappearing in the meadows and reappearing at the tree line before climbing up once again to the ridge. It finishes at the road crossing after a good run down.

Paradise Creek Trail (Map 3/G4-4/A4)
Located in the outskirts of South Chilcotin Mountains Provincial Park, this multi-use trail is primarily used by mountain bikers. There is a 300 m (985 ft) descent over the course of the difficult, 5 km (3 mi) single-track trail.

Relay Creek Trail (Map 3/G3)
The Relay Creek Trail is a 22 km (13.5 mi) route with an elevation gain of 580 m (1,900 ft) before dropping into the Big Creek Valley. The difficult, remote route runs from Tyaughton Creek Recreation Site to Big Creek near the Graveyard Cabin.

Sheba Ridge Trail (Map 3/G5–E5)
This 24 km (15 mi) hike-a-bike ridge route features great views to the west of Spruce Lake. It has an overall elevation gain of 715 m (2,345 ft), making it a very challenging route.

Slim Creek Trail (Map 3/F6–D6)
From the trailhead at the end of the rough Slim Creek Forest Service Road, it is 15 km or so to the pass. Expect to gain about 660 m (2,165 ft) in elevation. The multi-use trail is popular year round as it can be used by snowmobilers looking to access the Lillooet Icefield.

Spruce Lake Trail (Map 4/A5)
Also known as the Spruce Lake Main Trail, this trail leaves the Gun Creek Trail at the 11.5 km mark and climbs 200 m (655 ft) in 1 km. It then leads past the Grasslands and High Trail junctions as well as designated campsites at the southeast end and north end of Spruce Lake. The moderate 4 km (2.5 mi) trail has an elevation gain of 230 m (760 ft). Note that the west side of Spruce Lake is private property, as are the cabins at the north end of the lake.

Taylor Basin Trail (Map 4/B5)
This is one of the gentlest mountain routes you will ever encounter. It starts about 1.5 km down the Mud Creek-Taylor Creek Forest Service Road; however, with a four-wheel drive you may be able to drive quite a bit further. Depending on how far you can drive up the road, it may take you a few hours to walk to the cabin at Taylor Basin. The route follows an old road beyond the footbridge as it slowly climbs through a scenic valley with wildflowers, wildlife and fantastic mountain views. The route is extremely popular with mountain bikers and snowmobilers.

Tyaughton Creek Trail (Map 4/B6–3/F4)
One of the main routes in the Spruce Lake area, this trail has two trailheads along the Mud-Paradise Creek Forest Service Road. The moderate trail is about 35 km (21.5 mi) long to Elbow Pass, and then it splits, with the Lorna Lake Trail heading west to Big Creek (another 3.5 km/2.2 mi). Another route leads north along Graveyard Creek to Big Creek (another 7 km/4.3 mi). There is an overall elevation change of 600 m (1,970 ft), and great views over the valley. Other notable junctions include Spruce Creek and the northern access to Spruce Lake at 12 km (7.5 mi) and Lizard Creek Trail at 25 km (15.5 mi). Note that there is an unbridged crossing over Tyaughton Creek.

Warner Pass Trail (Map 3/F5)
This popular trail links the Spruce Lake area with the Taseko Lakes area. It starts from the end of the Gun Creek Trail just past the packer's cabin northwest of Trigger Lake and climbs along Warner Creek to Warner Lake. Past the lake, the trail climbs to the pass, then down to the end of the mining road at Battlement Creek. From the cabin to Battlement Creek is 21.5 km (13.5 mi). The actual Warner Pass Trail gains 750 m (2,460 ft) over 12 km (7.5 mi).

Spanish Lake Trail (Map 31/F5)
From the end of the Spanish Creek Forest Service Road, it is necessary to cross the creek and follow an overgrown road to the actual trailhead. From here, the easy trail leads about 5 km (3 mi) to the site of ancient lava beds and the extinct Flourmills Volcano.

Spectrum Pass Trail (Map 2/E3)

The Spectrum Pass Trail leads from the outfitters cabin on the Tchaikazan Valley Trail up and over the 2,287 m (7,500 ft) pass to hook up with the Yohetta Trail at the west end of Dorothy Lake.

Stewart Lake Trail (Map 24/B6–B5)

This trail starts near McClinchy Lake on the McClinchy Creek Trail and takes travellers past a number of Lakes in the Charlotte Alplands, including the titular Stewart Lake. From the end of Crazy Bear Lake, a rough route hooks up with the Charlotte Lake Trail. This route would be shorter, but trickier than returning the way you came.

Stupendous Mountain Route (Map 23/C1)

Stupendous Mountain is the monolith that rises across the river and above the Fisheries Pool Campsite in Tweedsmuir. The difficult route begins where the Noomst Forest Service Road crosses the creek. Climb above the old logging and go south through sections of slide alder and talus slopes. You will need at least seven hours to get to the top. For the explorer at heart, other lower summits are climbable from the Talchako Forest Service Road. Most offer fine views of the hanging glaciers and the north face of Stupendous.

Suey–Slate Bay Trail (Map 31/A1–45/A7)

This 5 km (3 mi) one-way trail connects Quesnel Lake and Horsefly Lake passing the much smaller Suey Lake en route. The easy trail can only be accessed by boat from either Quesnel Lake or Horsefly Lake. Due to the flat terrain the route traverses, the trail can double as a portage between the lakes.

Swan Lake Trail (Map 4/F2)

This 5.6 km (3.5 mi) trail climbs 140 m (460 ft) as it connects the Red Mountain Trail to Swan Lake. The trail continues past the lake along French Bar Creek.

Swift River Trail (Map 43/E4)

Hidden in the backcountry southeast of Quesnel, this 2.7 km one-way trail leads to the Swift River. There is minimal elevation gain (than 20 m/65 ft) making it fairly easy walk. However, lack of use may result in it being overgrown/hard to find. Look for it north of the Sundberg Forest Service Road.

Taseko Lake Trail (Map 3/A1–A3)

This old horseback route follows the east side of Taseko Lake, connecting two rough roads. Informal trails continue south, along Upper Taseko Lake and over to Fishem Lake. In total there are 21 km (13 mi) to travel, mostly flat, with an overall elevation gain of 160 m (525 ft).

> *Due to the hot, dry climate of this region, it is highly recommended to bring plenty of water.*

Tatla Lake Trails (Map 13/E1–25/E7)

A series of loop trails that total about 30 km (18.5 mi) in length are found between Tatla Lake and Martin Lake. While these trails are best known as ski trails, they are open in the summer for hiking, biking and horseback riding. Look for trailhead signs 1.5 km off the highway on Graham Road.

Tatlayoko Lake Trails (Map 13/G5)

There is very little elevation gain along the trail that has been developed along the east side of Tatlayoko Lake. The trail passes through a stand of old growth forest and there are frequent views of the big mountains on the west side of the lake. It is also possible to bushwhack around the south end to an old logging road that runs along the west side, to make an almost-loop of the lake. This trail falls in the Tsilhqot'in First Nation area. Visit www.tsilhqotin.ca for more information on access.

Tchaikazan Valley Trails (Map 2/G3–F4)

From the airstrip at Fishem Lake, a rough, maintained road branches west up the Tchaikazan River. From the end of the road, a trail follows the river to an outfitters cabin below Spectrum Pass. It is also possible to follow a rough route along the river to the Tchaikazan Glacier. This route is best left to mountaineers as there is a difficult creek crossing en route.

Teapot Mountain Trails (Map 31/B1)

A four-wheel drive vehicle is needed to access this moderate trail system, which climbs Mount Elsey or Teapot Mountain. The southernmost trail climbs about 885 m (2,904 ft) in elevation over 5 km (3 mi), while the shorter 2.4 km northern route climbs approximately 550 m (1,804 ft).

Teepee Lake Trail (Map 55/A6–54/F6)

This 20 km (12.5 mi) trail begins a kilometre north of the Blackwater Bridge on the Nazko Road. The route follows an old four-wheel drive road that can be ridden or walked. There's an old ranger cabin at the lake that is well kept, and fishing is rumoured to be great. The cabin makes a nice winter destination.

Tom Baptiste Wagon Trail (Map 39/B1)

This remote 5.5 km (3.4 mi) route connects to the historic Alexander MacKenzie Heritage Trail. Access can be found off the Kluskus Wolf Forest Service Road southwest of Vanderhoof. The route has a 60 m (195 ft) elevation gain and.

Tsintsunko Lake Trails (Map 7/E4)

From the 14 km mark on the Shelley Lake/Beaverhut Road, this 4 km (2.5 mi) easy walk follows a well-marked trail through second growth timber to the Tsintsunko Lake. At the north end of the lake, it is possible to join up with a few other trails in the area, including a rustic 3 km one-way route to Caribou Lake.

Tsuniah Lake & Ridge Trails (Map 14/C4)

A relatively flat, 8.7 km (5.4 mi) trail follows the eastern shore of Tsuniah Lake to the south end of the lake. Those looking for more of a challenge can track the route up onto Tsuniah Ridge. These trails fall in the Tsilhqot'in First Nation area. Visit www.tsilhqotin.ca for more information on access.

Tullin Mountain Trails (Map 14/B5)

From the north end of Chilko Lake (at the Gwa Da Ts'ih Campground), it will take six hours return to hike the 16.5 km (10 mi) Tullin Mountain Trail. This trail has an elevation gain of 820 m (2,690 ft). The glacier-fed Chilko Lake offers an inspiring view from the top. There are also a number of routes in the alpine above Chilko Lake, including the Tullin Ridge Route that links with the Potato Trail at Echo Lakes. This trail falls in the Tsilhqot'in First Nation area. Visit www.tsilhqotin.ca for more information on access.

Tweedsmuir Park Trails (Maps 11, 12, 23, 24, 36, 37, 38, 49, 50, 51)

From the low, coastal rainforest of the Atnarko Valley, to the high, colourful alpine of the Rainbow Range, Tweedsmuir is a land of contrasts and great beauty. It is also a huge area. Trails around Highway 20 are generally in good condition, but the trails in the north end are not maintained at all. Guide outfitters with lodges in a seemingly empty wilderness have created these routes and their status is not always known. Only visitors with lots of wilderness experience should venture far from the road.

Alexander MacKenzie Trail–Tweedsmuir Park (Map 23/C1–37/G2)

From the trailhead on Highway 20, this challenging 80 km (50 mi) or five to seven day trek leads through some remote, but spectacular alpine scenery. You climb up over the Rainbow Range, through the MacKenzie Valley, past the Tanya Lakes and over the Dean River before stepping out of the park and into another vast wilderness area. Along the way, there are rustic campsites and backcountry cabins to overnight in as well as some fine fishing holes.

Capoose Trail (Map 37/D6)

This moderate, 12 km (7.5 mi) return trail connects the Alexander MacKenzie Heritage Trail to the Tweedsmuir Trail near Octopus Lake. The trail crosses a beautiful sub-alpine valley and has minimal elevation change. Allow five to six hours.

Crystal Lake Trail (Map 37/F6)

Breaking off the Octopus Lake Trail, this moderately difficult trail climbs 1,000 m (3,280 ft) to the Rainbow Cabin and a junction with the Alexander MacKenzie Trail beneath Mount MacKenzie. The trail is 16.5 km (10 mi) long with an overall elevation gain of 360 m (1,180 ft). When linked with the Tweedsmuir Trail, this forms the northern stretch of the Crystal Lake Loop. This is prime caribou country and there is a good chance you will see some, especially in the alpine ridge around Crystal Lake. A side trip up Mount MacKenzie is certainly worth it, especially during wildflower season.

Hunlen Falls Trail (Map 23/G3)

From Turner Lake Campground, it is only a 30 minute walk to the spectacular Hunlen Falls. The falls drop some 401 metres (1,316 ft) below the sheer granite cliffs holding Turner Lake. From this trail, a short side trail leads to another lookout over Lonesome Lake.

Junker Lake Trail (Map 23/G3)

Looking to see the Turner Lake Chain, but don't want to canoe? This moderate trail passes by four of the six lakes in the chain, as it travels through rolling pine forests and meadows. The trail covers 21 km (13 mi) return and winds up at a sandy beach on the northeastern shores of Junker Lake.

Octopus Lake Trail (Map 37/F6)

The trail to Octopus Lake gains about 200 m (655 ft) in elevation over 14 km (8.7 mi) one-way from the Rainbow Range Trailhead. This is an easy introduction to longer hiking, but the trail does cross two branches of Young Creek. There is a tent pad and fishing for cutthroat at Octopus Lake. This trail can be linked up with the Crystal Lake Trail to form the Crystal Lake Loop.

Precipice [Hotnarko Canyon] Trail (Map 23/G2–24/C1)

A moderate hike gaining 400 m (1,300 ft) over 12 km (7.5 mi), the Precipice Trail is in variable condition. It once followed an old telegraph trail to 150 Mile House, but over time parts have been covered by slides and alder growth. The section in Tweedsmuir Park is fairly easy to follow as it follows an old road. Outside of the park, the route links with the Lt. Palmer Route near the Precipice, an area bounded by miles of sheer cliffs formed by basaltic rocks.

Ptarmigan & Panorama Lakes Trails (Map 23/F3)

West of Hunlen Falls, there is good alpine hiking to Whistler Pass along the 14 km (8.7 mi) Ptarmigan Lake Trail. The moderate trail breaks into the alpine and follows a series of cairns to a campsite on Sandy Ridge, at the northeast corner of Ptarmigan Lake. Beyond Ptarmigan, the Whistler Pass and Rosemary Pass Trails offer more challenging terrain to explore. Before Ptarmigan, the Panorama Lakes Trail loops south past Echo and Gem Lakes on its way to Molly Lake. It also hooks up with the Whistler Pass and Rosemary Pass Trails.

Rainbow Range Trail (Map 37/G6)

The Rainbow Range Trail is a moderate trail leading into an almost surreal alpine landscape of kaleidoscope-hued mountains. The 7 km (4.4 mi) trail starts out in a Lodgepole pine forest and climbs to the alpine. The trail ends at a small alpine lake, but there is so much open ground to explore up here that you could wander for days, even weeks. The sub-alpine forest in this area is home to one of BC's largest herds of mountain caribou and there is a campsite and bear locker at McCauley Lake.

Sugar Camp Trail (Map 23/G1–24/D1)

A historic First Nations trade route, this 12 km (7.5 mi) trail starts on the Tote Road. It is a part of the route that Lt. Palmer followed into the interior. Prior to the construction of Highway 20 in 1953, this was the lifeline between Anahim Lake and Bella Coola. Watch for the unmarked trailhead, about 100 metres past the Sugar Camp Creek Bridge. Similar to the Precipice Trail, this trail takes hikers out of the park through the upper Hotnarko River Valley, to the impressive Precipice.

Sunshine Lake Trail (Map 23/F5)

From the southern end of the Turner Canoe Circuit, this 2.5 km trail heads to Sunshine Lake. The 200 m (655 ft) climb makes lugging a canoe rather difficult, but there is camping and good fishing at the lake.

Turner Lake Trail (Map 23/G2)

Certainly one of the more popular destinations in the park, this trail is not for the faint of heart. You pass through prime grizzly bear habitat, will need to cross over blown down trees and ultimately climb 78 switchbacks and nearly 800 m (2,625 ft) over the 16.4 km (10 mi) one-way trek. Allow six to nine hours to reach the north end of Turner Lake, where there is a primitive campground. Once there, there are several other trails to discover including the short walk to the spectacular Hunlen Falls. The trailhead is about 12 km south of Highway 20 off Tote Road, which is four-wheel drive access only. Be wary as a large number of grizzly and black bears reside at the start of the trail, so travel between late morning and early afternoon to avoid them.

Tweedsmuir Trail (Map 23/E1–37/E6)

West of the park headquarters on Highway 20 (just east of the sani-station at Mosher Creek) is the start of the trail. This trail climbs to the top switchback before experienced hikers will need to pick a route to Deception Pass. Beyond the pass, the trail continues north past Octopus Lake and onto the old, unmaintained Rainbow Cabin on the Alexander MacKenzie Heritage Trail. This difficult trail is about 35 km (22 mi), with an overall elevation gain of 360 m (1,180 ft). It can be linked up with the Crystal Lake Trail to form the Crystal Lake Loop.

Valley View Loop/Burnt Bridge Trail (Map 23/C1)

Tweedsmuir is a big park full of big hikes. The Burnt Bridge Trail is a refreshing alternative to all of that. This is a short, fairly easy day hike. It does climb a bit, but it will take a mere two hours to complete. The trail heads north from the Alexander MacKenzie Heritage Trailhead along Burnt Bridge Creek to a small suspension bridge. It then loops back to the parking area. There is a great viewpoint over the Bella Coola Valley.

Whistler Pass/Molly Lake Trail (Map 23/E3)

From Ptarmigan Lake, this trail heads up through Whistler Pass to Molly Lake. The trail hooks up with the Panorama Lakes Trail and forms an 11 km (6.8 mi) circuit back to Ptarmigan Lake via Rosemary Pass.

Two Sisters Mountain Trail (Map 58/A5–57/G5)

The view from the top of Two Sisters Mountain is one of the best views in the area. On good days, you can see all the way to Mount Robson. The moderate, steep trail is 10 km (6 mi) return, with an elevation gain of 880 m (2,885 ft).

Tyaughton Lake Trails (Map 4/C6)

From Tyax Mountain Resort, a series of trails lead around the north end of the beautiful lake. These trails are used by guests on foot and horseback, and in winter on cross-country skis or snowshoes. To the south, an easy 2 km trail starts across from the Friburg Recreation Site and joins up with the High Trail leading to the Spruce Lake area.

Ulkatcho Trail (Map 38/A2)

This 7.5 km (4.6 mi) trail gains 120 m (395 ft) as it travels between the Upper Dean River Road and the Alexander MacKenzie Heritage Trail. The trail follows an old road along the eastern shore of Gatcho Lake.

Upper McClinchy Creek–Clearwater Creek Route (Map 24/E7)

This rough route connects to the McClinchy Creek Trail, passing into the subalpine and alpine around Mount McClinchy. This is a tough trail, but rewarding.

Valleau Creek Trail (Map 13/D3)

This moderately difficult, 20 km (12.5 mi) trail follows Valleau Creek all the way up to its headwaters and beyond. It accesses the alpine just east of Razorback Mountain. There is an overall elevation gain of 1,260 m (4,135 ft).

Viewland Mountain Trail (Map 30/E1)

This 3 km trail can be found off the Haggens Point Road (Z Rd) north of Horsefly Lake. The trailhead can be hard to find but the trek is rewarding. Overall, the moderate hike entails a 330 m (1,085 ft) climb to the top.

Waddington Traverse (Map 12/E7)

This 11 km (7 mi) trail is a challenging one-way trek recommended for experienced backcountry travelers only. Accessible by airplane only, this trail requires ice and rock climbing skills. The trip entails an ascent of 2,030 m (6,660 ft) and a descent of 1,620 m (5,310 ft).

Walker Island Park Trails (Map 22/E1)

Tucked up between Snootli Creek and the Bella Coola River, there is a handful of easy, short trails in Walker Island Regional Park. Most of the trails incorporate some road travel. For example, the Gazebo Loop is 3.6 km long, but only a portion of that is on actual trail. A definite highlight in the area is the big cedar trees near the parking lot and Beaver Pond.

Walker Valley Trails (Map 18/C3)

The Walker Valley lies between Watson Lake to the south and Lac La Hache to the north. To reach the trail system from the south, look for the South End Loop off Tatton Station Road opposite Watson Lake. The loop trail traverses through the open valley to a series of small ponds and a viewpoint for an easy 5 km (3 mi) return hike. The Walker Valley Trail continues north into the open valley. The route passes the 108 Mile Resort and over 111 Mile Road before ending around Ogden Road, south of Lac La Hache. The total distance for this easy trip is about 8 km (5 mi) one-way.

Waterlily Trail (Map 13/C2)

From the Sapeye Lake Recreation Site, the Waterlily Trail heads north, then counter-clockwise around Waterlily Lake to a rustic picnic area. The trail is 5 km (3 mi) long, although the truly adventurous can follow a rough route along Sapeye Creek into the alpine.

Wells/Barkerville Area Trails (Map 58/A7–44/A1)

The Wells/Barkerville area trails include hundreds of kilometres of multi-use trails weaving throughout the region. There is a vast selection here, most notably the 21.5 km (13.5 mi) Cariboo Waggon Road Trail, which travels from Barkerville to Stanley, the 38 km (24 mi) of multi-use trails in the Mount Agnes area, and the 37.7 km (23.5 mi) 1861 Pack Trail, maintained by the Friends of Barkerville. Other trails in the area range from easy boardwalk strolls to epic, wild expeditions. Some popular trails include the Grouse Creek Trail, the VanWinkle Trail and the Williams Creek Loop.

Cariboo Waggon Road Trail (Map 58/A7–43/F1)

One of the main routes in the Barkerville area, this 21.5 km (13.5 mi) trail travels from Barkerville to Stanley with an overall elevation gain of 440 m (1,445 ft). It can be used for hiking and biking in the summer, and skiing and snowshoeing in winter.

Cow Mountain Ditch Trail (Map 57/G7–44/A1)

This multi-use trail joins the Cariboo Wagon Road in the south to the town of Wells in the north. The trail leads you 12 km (7.5 mi) through the forested mountainside with several washout areas with bridges and steps installed in some places. The steps and steep sections can make cycling, skiing or snowshoeing challenging as you climb about 90 m (300 ft) in elevation.

Grouse Creek Trail (Map 58/B7–44/B1)

This trail goes from Barkerville to Racetrack Flats; it is about 13 km (8 mi) one-way climbing 90 m (300 ft). Much of the trail along the creek is the original trail used by miners to access gold claims, and there were several small towns located along the creek side. There are two campsites in Racetrack Flats.

Mount Agnes Area (Map 57/G6–44/A1)

The Jack of Clubs Forest Service Road leads to the base of Cow Mountain. From the road, about 38 km (24 mi) of multi-use trails in and around Mount Agnes are waiting to be discovered. Experienced backcountry travellers can follow the Bald Mountain-Prosperine Trail that begins at Groundhog Lake. It follows a rough, difficult trail climbing about 500 m (1,640 ft) in elevation through the sub-alpine to Bald Mountain. It is possible to continue over to Prosperine Mountain, onto the Conkin Gulch Road and Barkerville or south past Antler Mountain. Cooper's Cabin is a popular winter destination.

Wells Gray Provincial Park Trails (Maps 19, 31, 45)

From massive, glacial-fed lakes to towering mountain alpine peaks, Wells Gray offers visitors the chance to experience a truly wild part of the province. The park is home to a variety of large mammals and offers adventure seekers a multitude of trails to explore. The majority are found along the corridor and areas east of these maps, however. Here are a few to sample on the west side of the park:

Deception Falls Trail (Map 19/E1)

You can find this 4 km (2.5 mi) trail off the Mahood Lake North Road, just past the Mahood Lake Campground. There is a sign off the north side of the road that marks the trailhead. The trail is an easy uphill hike to the sight of this cascading 40 metre (131 ft) waterfall. In addition to a viewing area, there is a trail that leads down to the bottom of the falls.

Hobson Lake Trail (Map 31/F2)

This 15 km (9.3 mi) route is only accessible by boat from the river channel found near the north end of Clearwater Lake. The moderate trail is not well maintained and involves a 300 m (985 ft) elevation gain. Hobson Lake is a large, remote lake nestled in the heart of Wells Gray. If you are prepared to lug some sort of a watercraft, this wild lake would be a great place to explore.

Mahood River Trail (Map 31/G7)

Located in Wells Gray Provincial Park, this 4.7 km (3 mi) one-way trail leads to the east end of Mahood Lake and the campsite there. There is a 100 m (330 ft) elevation gain on the way to the lake.

Whale Lake Trail (Map 19/D1)

This moderate 10 km (6 mi) trail can be found near the Mahood Lake Campground, in the western end of Wells Gray Park. The trail follows the Canim River for a short distance before swinging north towards the lake. There is about a 300 m (984 ft) elevation gain en route to the lake, which is nestled between forested slopes just outside of the park.

Whitton Creek Trail (Map 24/C5)

An old trappers trail can be found on the south side of Charlotte Lake. It leads up Whitton Creek to the confluence just east of Whitton Lake. The trail is very overgrown and impossible to find in many places.

Wilderness Glacier Trail (Map 24/B7)

This fly-in trail in the Charlotte Alplands, east of Tweedsmuir South Provincial Park, makes for a stunning glacier experience. It is moderately challenging, and it travels 11 km (6.8 mi) round-trip. There is an elevation change of 315 m (1,035 ft).

Remember the golden rule of outdoor recreation: leave only footprints, and take only photographs.

Williams Lake Trails (Map 29/B5)

There are many trails in the Williams Lake area such as the Box, Desous Mountain, South Side and Westsyde Trails. They all have extensive trail systems that are designed for mountain biking, but make great hiking trails as well. Closer to town, the River Valley Trail leads along the river valley, spanning over 12 km (7.5 mi) from MacKenzie Avenue in the industrial area all the way to the banks of the Fraser. Off the Dog Creek Road, the Bond Lake Forest Walk offers about 12 km (7.5 mi) of informal walking on unmarked trails.

Willan Lake Trails (Map 15/D4)

South of Hanceville and Lees Corner, this series of cross-country trails explore the remote countryside around Willan Lake. There are over 30 km (18.5 mi) of easy trails/old roads to explore in this network. Access is found off the Big Creek-Willan Lake Forest Service Road.

Yellowhawk Trail (Map 58/A6)

The trailhead to this moderate backcountry route can be found just south of Wendle Park off the east side of the Bowron Lake Road, at 3.5 km. The 9.8 km (6 mi) round-trip route climbs to the alpine of Mount Murray and Mount Greenbury, offering panoramic views of the surrounding mountains and Barkerville. You will climb about 680 m (2,230 ft) in elevation gain. It is possible to link up with the Jubilee Creek Trail and loop back down to Bowron Lake Road. During winter, beware of avalanche conditions in the alpine areas. Note also that this is grizzly bear country; take necessary precautions.

Yohetta Valley Trail (Map 2/G2–E3)

From the South End of Tuzcha Lake, the route heads up an old road into Yohetta Valley along Yohetta Creek. Vehicles are only permitted up to the park boundary. The trail follows the north side of the creek to Yohetta Lake and continues around the north side of Dorothy Lake, to hook up with the Rainbow Creek Trail and down to Chilko Lake. South of Dorothy Lake, the Spectrum Pass Trail connects to Tchaikazan Valley for a longer loop.

Zinc Bay Mining Trail (Map 50/B2)

From Zinc Bay on Eutsuk Lake another water access only trail is found. This 4 km trail heads up from Zinc Bay along an old mining road, climbing 1,300 m, (4,225 ft) up the north side of the Chickamin Range.

ATV [OHV]
Adventures

The Cariboo Chilcotin Coast of BC bisects the province from the Pacific Ocean to the Rocky Mountains. Across the region, backcountry travelers discover a treasure trove of landscapes, from fields filled with wildflowers, to ancient hoodoo rock formations atop majestic limestone and sandstone canyons. What better way to explore all that the Cariboo Chilcotin Coast has to offer than from the saddle of an ATV?

Hop on your ATV and get rolling through the region's diverse terrain. Warm up by rambling along a quiet country road. Gear up to tackle those dramatic mountain switchbacks and be rewarded with breathtaking views across pristine valleys. Feel the wind as you tear along endless plateaus. Rattle across old railroad beds, and be amazed as you find yourself in the traditional hunting grounds and fishing holes of the area's First Nations. Visit tumbling waterfalls and towering viewpoints overlooking the coast or the Cariboo Mountains. Speed alongside rushing rivers, like the mighty Chilcotin or Fraser.

The Cariboo Chilcotin Coast pulses with history, from the historic gold rush town of Barkerville to scenic Gold Bridge. Step into the past as you ride through abandoned ghost towns and into old mining sites. Roads available for ATVing are plentiful, thanks to the mining and forestry industries. Many ATV trails overlap with multi-use or snowmobile routes. In the north, a network of gravel roads crawl across the landscape, taking you through hundreds of glistening lakes. Roads proliferate west of Williams Lake and around Anahim Lake on the Chilcotin Plateau in the heart of the Cariboo. Wherever you choose to ride, the roads and trails in this region will lead you somewhere new.

That being said, there are few formal ATV riding areas here. Unfortunately, the odd ATVer that rides irresponsibly attracts negative press, resulting in stricter rules for ATV use. For example, liability insurance is now required in order to ride on any forest service road. On the upside, such conflicts have inspired a growing number of ATV clubs to crop up across BC. These clubs are designed to promote positive ATV use and to protect riding areas. To help the sport of ATVing to grow and be enjoyed (or at least tolerated) by all, please respect the rules at all times and stick to designated trails. For a list of ATV clubs and more information, be sure to visit www.atvbc.ca.

Always be prepared for changing weather conditions, drive safe, and enjoy your epic ride across the Cariboo Chilcotin Coast.

Quad Riders ATV Association of British Columbia
Your voice working to protect our future.

ATV/BC
QUAD RIDERS ASSOCIATION OF BRITISH COLUMBIA

Make Your Voice Heard
Join or form a club in your area.

Help Us Promote
Family Sport
Environmental Stewardship
Safe & Responsible ATV Practices
Ethical Riding

Work With US
To maintain and develop existing and new riding areas and trails. As we work with other user groups for the benefit of all trail users.

Toll Free: 1.866.766.7823
E-mail: atvbc@telus.net
www.atvbc.com
Mail: #203 1139 12th Street
Kamloops, BC V2B 7Z2

100 Mile House Trails (Map 18)

The 100 Mile House area has hundreds of kilometres of trails, including snowmobile, multipurpose and seasonal; make sure to pay attention to the signage. One of the most epic trail networks in the region, the Gold Rush Trail extends south to 70 Mile House or north past Williams Lake. In addition to the numerous old roads in the area, there are routes leading east and west from town:

100 Mile Snowmobile Club House (Map 18/C4)

This is a great starting point to explore the areas on the west side of Highway 97. Trails head south to Valentine Lake or as far west as Dog Creek. About 40 km (25 mi) west, you will find a small memorial at the 1965 crash site of Flight 21.

Clearwater Route (Maps 18, 19)

Begin just east of the intersection of Evergreen Crescent and North Birch Avenue and travel about 127 km (79 mi) east of town to Clearwater. The trail passes by Deka, Needa and Coldscaur Lakes en route to the Clearwater airport. The terrain is suitable for ATVs and four-wheel drive vehicles; be wary during wet periods. There are many spots for backcountry camping. This is a remote trip, so bring extra fuel and supplies.

Alexander Mackenzie Heritage Trail (Maps 38, 39, 53, 54, 55, 56)

This difficult, historic trail has become a popular alternative for off-road enthusiasts and adventure ATV riders. The eastern stretch of the 420 km (260 mi) long corridor starts near the mouth of the Blackwater (West Road) River, west of Quesnel, and follows a series of roads and trails, crossing Kluskoil Lake Provincial Park. Elevation varies along the route from 455 m (1,490 ft) near Quesnel to around 1,225 m (4,015 ft) near Tweedsmuir Park. Alternative access points, like the Messue Wagon Trail or the rarely travelled trails from the Dean River end, are equally challenging. Beyond the Dean, the trail enters Tweedsmuir Park and leads to sensitive alpine areas that are best left to the hikers.

Barnett Perimeter Trail (Maps 6, 7, 18, 19)

This 400 km (240 mi) trail is also a popular snowmobile trail in winter. The long loop links 70 Mile House to 100 Mile House in the west with Bonaparte Lake and Bowers Lake in the east. The riding is mostly easy along developed trails. This is a key component to the Gold Rush Trail system because the loop provides access to other trail systems, such as the Green Lake Snowmobile and Interlakes Snowmobile trails.

Big Stick Lake Area (Map 24/G6)

Just west of Kleena Kleene, this 8.6 km (5.3 mi) long trail heads one way from the Clearwater Lake Recreation Site to Big Stick Lake. The trail starts 2 km south of the McClinchy Creek Bridge on Highway 20. Big Stick Lake has a small recreation site and offers excellent fishing and a nice beach. Roads and informal trails can be explored from here.

Cache Creek Trails (Map 6/E7)

North of Cache Creek, double-track trails meander up the Arrowstone Hills to the south end of Arrowstone Provincial Park. Access to this area can be found off Semlin Drive, Stage Road and Stanley Park Boulevard. The area north of town is great for novice riders, while more experienced riders can enjoy the many routes in the area between Lillooet, Lytton and Cache Creek (see our Vancouver Coast and Thompson Okanagan mapbooks). Adventurers can also search for old routes once called the Ashcroft Motorcycle Trails and explore south to the north end of Cornwall Hills Provincial Park. Most of these old routes are overgrown or have disappeared due to logging and private ranch lands.

Chilcotin Area (Maps 3–5, 15, 16, 27, 28)

ATVers in the Chilcotin region mainly explore old mining and logging roads and cattle trails used by ranchers. Popular areas include Big Bar, Big Creek, Bonaparte River, Churn Creek, Jesmond, Kelly Lake, Loon Lake, Nemaiah Valley and Pavilion. Travel past historic ranches and renowned areas such as Canoe Creek, Gang Ranch, Hat Creek and West Pavilion. Many backroads can lead south to the ATV haven, Gold Bridge, or west to the Nemaiah Valley.

Groundhog Creek Trail (Map 3/B1–15/E6)

This trail runs for almost 30 km (18.5 mi) just outside of the northwest boundary of Big Creek Provincial Park. Expect an elevation gain of 585 m (1,915 ft) and many side roads/trails to explore.

Junction Sheep Range Provincial Park (Map 16/E2)

An hour west of Williams Lake, turn south at Riske Creek; the site is 15 km south of Highway 20 on the Farwell Canyon Road. The park offers more than 400 hectares (1,000 ac) of rolling grasslands, with public off-road trails that lead to the confluence of the Fraser and Chilcotin Rivers. Check out beautiful Farwell Canyon and watch for sheep scaling the steep sandstone riverbanks.

Koster Lake Trails (Map 16/F7)

Near the Churn Creek Protected Area, this nice spot has relatively dry grasslands, slight elevation gains and many easy trails. Follow the Black Diamond Mine Road and look for a set of tracks heading north near the Perlite Road. Once at the lake, head west along the Koster-Clear Lakes Road to the Clear Lake Campsite.

Gold Bridge/Carpenter Lake Area (Map 4/D6–5/A6)

North of Carpenter Lake is the Shulaps Mountain Range, with multiple trails to explore. Access is via the Yalakom or Lac La Mare Recreation Sites, heading up to Burkholder Lake, or via Marshall Lake. Further north, the Noaxe Lake/Quartz Mountain system offers fine riding. Closer to Gold Bridge, trails run around Gun Lake and beyond.

Gun Lake Trails (Map 4/A7)

Gun Lake offers a good variety of trails at its north end that can lead you to Plateau Ponds, Downton Lake or up to the South Chilcotin Mountains Provincial Park. Be wary of the motorized closure area at the head of the well-traveled Slim Creek Forest Service Road. There are many old roads and ATV trails running throughout the Gold Bridge area.

Marshall Lake Area (Map 4/D7)

Marshall Lake is surrounded by trails connecting to very scenic areas. From the Marshall Creek Recreation Site, head north towards Shulaps Peak via the Jim Creek Road/Trail. This steep road climbs a stiff 2,135 m (7,000 ft). Around the 1,800 m (5,905 ft) level, look for the spur road that climbs through a meadow leading south towards Brett Creek. Other old roads/trails lead south of the lake and up to scenic Marshall Ridge.

Noaxe Lake/Quartz Mountain Trails (Map 4/D4)

Between Noaxe Creek Road in the west, the Swartz Lake-Poison Mountain Road in the north and the Yalakom River to the east is an area dominated by open grasslands and the high alpine of the Shulaps Range, with a number of multi-use trails. Riders should stick to the more developed trails.

Yalakom River Area (Map 4/G6–5/A6)

A route travels about 30 km (18.6 mi) between La Mare and Burkholder Lake in the Shulaps Range before looping south back to the Yalakom (Lillooet) Recreation Site. It is a mixture of remote and well-ridden roads and trails with some water crossings. Another route takes you to the abandoned Jade Mine at the top of Holbrook Creek, with lots of switchbacks. At 2,000 m (6,560 ft) there is a wonderful view.

New prohibitions under the Wildlife Act require off-road vehicles, including ATVs, to stay on existing paths or roads.

Gold Rush Snowmobile Trail (Maps 5, 6, 17, 18, 29, 44, 58)

The Gold Rush Trail is a 463 km (287 mi) trail heading north from Clinton to Wells. The trailhead starts at 70 Mile House; from here the 170 km (106 mi) section to Horsefly has been signed and maintained, but not all the trails have been developed just yet. The route follows unmaintained forest service roads, existing trail and even some new trail. Along the route, riders can explore mine sites and old ghost towns before settling in at a beautiful lake or at a resort in one of the many towns along the route. It is mostly a snowmobile route with some multi-use sections.

Green Lake ATV Trails (Map 6/D1–18/F7)

This area is loaded with multi-use trails that see most of their use by snow-mobilers in winter and ATVers in summer. Trails start from the snowmobile clubhouse on Green Lake South Road, about 14 km east of 70 Mile House. From Green Lake there are over 160 km (100 mi) of fantastic ATV trails to explore. Most are marked and run along logging roads, although connector trails have been cut to link road systems. Check out the Jeep Lake Lookout, which includes a river crossing at Rayfield River that can be fun to attempt.

Itcha Ilgachuz Seismic Line Trail (Maps 39, 40)

Found about 66 km from the Nazko Road along the Michelle Baezaeko Road, an ATV access corridor follows the seismic line to Kettle Cabin. ATVs are required to stay on the corridor with no riding permitted anywhere else. This popular ride is open from August 1st to 30th with just 30 trips permitted during that time. Permits are available on a first-come, first-served basis.

Klinaklini River Falls (Map 24/F7)

From Highway 20, just west of Kleena Kleene, there is a multi-use trail for hikers, ATVers and four-wheel drive enthusiasts that want to see the Klinaklini River Falls. The old, rough road is 12 km (7.5 mi) long and has a challenging grade of 25%. There is a parking area at the lookout above the falls as well as numerous lakes in the surrounding area to explore.

Kluskoil Lake Provincial Park (Map 54/F5–C5)

Located about 100 km northwest of Quesnel, access to this area is found south off the Batnuni Road at the 108 km mark. This track will lead to the upper crossing of the Euchiniko River (at the south end of Titetown Lake). This crossing is several feet deep most of the year, and may be inaccessible in the spring and early summer due to the high water levels. From here, it is 18 km (11 mi) via the historic Alexander Mackenzie Heritage Trail to Kluskoil Lake. Once at the park, please stay on the rough road through the park if travelling in a vehicle or ATV.

Mahood Lake Trails (Map 19/E2)

Although ATVs are banned from Wells Gray Provincial Park, there are plenty of trails south of Mahood Lake. The area is full of forest service roads and old roads and trails that lead to a lot of backcountry and small lakes. The trails are also enjoyed in winter by snowmobilers. Access is found about 7 km southeast of Mahood Falls along the Bowers Lake-Canim Forest Service Road (8200 Rd). The Corsica Mahood Trail leads south from Mahood Lake to Road 20 and also provides a good mix of forest roads and lakes to explore.

McBride Area (Map 59/F4–G2)

Off-highway riding is limited in the North Thompson area due to ranchland and concerns over caribou; however, the McBride area has a few areas to sample. These include Lucille Mountain, the Homes/Beaver River area and the McKale Forest Road leading into the alpine of Mount Renshaw. ATVs are not allowed in the alpine, but there are a number of roads/trails that can be ridden.

Beware of trucks and equipment transporting logs. Always pull over and let them pass in order to protect yourself from flying stones and dust clouds.

Old Bluff Lake Road (Map 13/D1)

About 3.5 km south of Tatla Lake off Tatlayoko Road, look for an old road/trail heading southwest. The moderate route leads between Suds Lake and Little Sapeye Lake before eventually reaching Waterlily Lake some 11.5 km (7 mi) later. There are multiple creek crossings that may be difficult to cross in spring or during wet periods. At Waterlily Lake, trails lead west to Sapeye Creek, but may be too wet to ride. Continue south to the main road or return the way you came.

Perkins Peak Trail (Map 13/A1–12/G2)

From the end of the four-wheel drive accessible Miner Forest Road, an old mining road heads up to Perkins Peak at about 2,819 m (9,250 ft). The road section of the route is easily accessible by ATV. The peak is in the northernmost part of the Pantheon Range, and the views of the bigger mountains to the south are amazing, especially in contrast to the relatively flat Chilcotin horizon stretching north. From Highway 20 west of Tatla Lake, it is almost 30 km (18.5 mi) to the peak.

Sheridan Lake Trails (Map 18/G5–19/D5)

While these trails are technically multi-use, they don't see a lot of use from hikers, as the old roads rarely lead to anywhere interesting. Instead, this area is left mostly to the ATVers, hungry for places to ride. There are over 200 km (130 mi) of mostly old roads in the area. Parking is available at a gravel pit on Little Green Lake Road at the west end of the E Snowmobile Trail.

Tchaikazan Valley Trails (Map 2/G3–F4)

From the airstrip at Fishem Lake, a rough, maintained road branches west up the Tchaikazan River. The trail is generally well-maintained, but can be a bit hard to follow in places. The trail offers viewpoints over the river at first, then it drops down to the valley and a possible camping area. This first stretch can get quite wet and muddy after heavy rains or during snowmelt. From here the trail stays quite close to the valley bottom, and tracking the trail can be quite difficult in places. The trail ends at Spectrum Creek, where an outfitters cabin is located. From here, there is a hiking trail leading further up the valley and another trail to Spectrum Pass and the Yohetta Valley. If it is late enough in the season, it is possible to fjord the Tchaikazan River when needed.

Veasy Lake Trails (Map 6/B6)

Found off a side road running parallel to Highway 97, between 20 Mile House and Carquile, these trails explore the area west around Veasy Lake. The inside loop is about 6 km (3.8 mi) long and the outside loop is 6.7 km (4 mi), for a combined 13 km (8 mi) of riding in the region.

Wells/Barkerville Trails (Maps 43, 44, 57, 58)

Barkerville was the centre of the Cariboo Gold Rush, dating back to 1862. Today, it is a fully preserved historic townsite with many abandoned mines and ghost towns to explore. Below is a sample of some of the rides in the area:

Jack O' Clubs Creek Road and Lake Road (Map 57/G7)

Following Jack O' Clubs Creek Road and creek south off Highway 26, it is possible to ride up to the peak of Richfield Mountain. This route is 5.5 km (3.4 mi) one-way, gaining about 200 m (655 ft) in elevation. Alternatively, begin at the south end of Gold Quartz Drive, cross the Lowhee Dike Trail and the creek, and head 6 km (3.8 mi) southwest to the shore of the lake. Expect about a 150 m (490 ft) elevation gain. This trail crosses two Placer Mining operations; if a mine is operational, access may be denied.

Old Cariboo Hudson Road / Proserpine Mining Road (Map 58/A7–44/C3)

This is a 29 km (18 mi) run gaining about 550 m (1,805 ft) to an old mining town. It begins directly behind the Barkerville Historic Town Offices. Cross the bridge over Williams Creek and follow the trail uphill; to the summit of Mount Proserpine at 1,879 m (6,164 ft) adds an additional 280 m (920 ft). There is tent camping and many trails further south.

Sugar Creek Loop (Map 57/G6)

This easy riding area runs north of Wells to create a 38.5 km (24 mi) loop. The route starts along Hardscrabble Road and leads over the Williams Creek Bridge before heading north to Sugar Creek and the loop east and south along Big Valley Creek. The route continues south past Nine Mile and Eight Mile Lakes to One Mile Road, which intersects with Highway 26. There is a 450 m (1,475 ft) elevation gain. Mining and logging activity may create detours.

Windy Mountain Trail (Map 19/B4)

From the Needa Lake Recreation Site, it is possible to ride north on the Windy Mountain Forest Service Road to the Windy-Preacher Lake Road (193 Rd) about 3.5 km later. Once on this branch road, look for tracks heading north and along the east side of Bowers Lake towards Cougar Lake. The ATV route is approximately 10 km (6 mi) long depending on where you want to go, and gains almost 550 m (1,805 ft) in elevation. It is possible to join up with the Barnett Perimeter Trail for extended riding.

Yanks Peak Trail (Map 44/B3)

Once called the Barkerville Wagon Road, the steep mountain terrain trip promises pristine meadows and scenery of old mines, awe-inspiring views and wildflowers in season. The designated ATV route follows a series of ridges and large alpine meadows below Yanks Peak. Access is found off the Antler Creek Road southeast of Barkerville or 18 km up the Keithley Creek Road from Likely (stay to the left at the top of the hill, and parking is found 300 metres up the road). ATVs need to stick to the trails, especially in the fragile alpine area, so watch the signage. Plan ahead, as snow can be present into July at the higher elevations.

Snowmobile
Adventures

The wide-open, snow-covered wilderness and frozen lakes of British Columbia make this province a snowmobiler's paradise. There is a wide variety of terrain, including groomed trails, massive glaciers and hillsides topped with snow. Adding to the appeal of snowmobiling in the Cariboo Chilcotin region are countless small lakes, old mine sites and backcountry cabins that serve as excellent rendezvous spots.

The Cariboo Chilcotin is a vast area that links the Vancouver Coast and Mountains and Thompson Okanagan regions in the south with Northern BC. Families and beginners can sled along many established routes through the forests and fields, while advanced riders can enjoy the steep and remote riding areas. Snowfall is quite generous in this region, resulting in lots of powder and a longer riding season.

BC has more than 70 local snowmobile clubs that maintain extensive trail networks and sledding areas. Visitors seeking good trails can often find knowledgeable guides and helpful club members in many of the snowmobile-friendly communities throughout the province. Snowmobile clubs like the 100 Mile (100milesnowmobile.com), Green Lake (greenlakesnowmobileclub.ca) and Williams Lake Powder Kings (wlpowderkings.com) have been very active in establishing more and more trails, most notably the Gold Rush Trail. For other clubs and more detailed season and route information, please contact the BC Snowmobile Federation at 1-877-537-8716, www.bcsf.org or www.abcsnow.ca.

The Gold Rush Trail cuts through the heart of the Cariboo and is part of the Trans Canada Snowmobile Trail, a project that will eventually stretch 10,000 km (6,213 mi) and will link all the provinces and territories. There are several other long distance routes and some fantastic destinations awaiting those who are willing to get out and explore.

When travelling in the backcountry, avalanches are always a danger. Visit www.avalanche.ca for current conditions and be prepared with both avalanche knowledge and safety equipment to ensure a safe trip to the mountains. Snowmobilers should also note that ecological reserves, private property and most provincial parks are off limits. There are also several areas that have been closed due to potential conflicts with mountain caribou. We show most of these on our maps (in light purple) or you can visit www.env.gov.bc.ca/fw/wildlife/snowmobile-closures. Another helpful site is www.snowmobile.gov.bc.ca. Stay informed and prepare for a safe and memorable winter adventure.

BRMB NAVIGATOR
Your Web and Smartphone Mapping Solution!

backroadmapbooks.com

Compatible

604.521.MAPS | www.BRMBnavigator.com

Snowmobile Adventures

100 Mile Area Snowmobile Trails (Maps 17, 18, 30)
With the Gold Rush and Barnett Perimeter Trails running through this area, there are some fine long distance routes to follow. Those looking for shorter day rides will find plenty of easily accessible routes on either side of Highway 97. Trails extend north past 108 Mile House to Spout Lake, west to Moose Valley Provincial Park and east to the Interlakes area and the Nehalliston Plateau around Taweel Lake.

Fawn Lake Trail (Map 18/G5–19/A5)
Found off Highway 24, about 25 km east of Highway 97, Fawn Lake offers a resort and access to some snowmobiling areas. The route is about 26 km long and goes from Fawn Lake Road, in the west, to the Windy Mountain Snowmobile Trails in the east. The Fawn Lake Trail is a level, easy graded route but opens up as you head east.

Allen Creek Snowmobile Trails (Map 6/A5)
Located 13 km south of Clinton, or 26.5 km north of Cache Creek, access is just off Highway 97 near the Carquile Rest Area. Experienced snowmobilers can ride the popular route into a vast alpine area.

Barnett Perimeter Trail (Maps 6, 7, 18, 19)
This trail is about 400 km (240 mi) long and is marked with black arrows on a yellow sign. Beginning at the 100 Mile House Clubhouse, the route heads south, following the Gold Rush Trail to 70 Mile House, where it crosses Highway 97 and hooks up with the Green Lake Trail system. It leads to Bonaparte Lake, and then climbs up to the Akehurst Lake region crossing under Highway 24 near Phinetta Lake. Veer west and north to the Wavey Lake Road, then down the rough creek trail to head up Windy Mountain and around the first bench to come down to the Mahood Lake Road. Going west to the north side of Drewry Lake, the trail heads southwest to the Horse Lake Road, which brings you to the top of the hill overlooking 100 Mile House.

Brown Creek Snowmobile Trail (Map 7/C2–19/E6)
The Brown Creek Trail refers to the portion of the Barnett Perimeter Trail north of Bonaparte Lake until it blends into the Windy Mountain Trail. The Brown Creek portion is 17 km (10.5 mi) long and starts at the Bonaparte Lake Recreation Site; there are no guarantees that access to the recreation site or the trail will be groomed.

Big Creek Trails (Maps 3, 15)
Linking to the Taseko Lake region, this trail runs along Groundhog Creek for almost 30 km (18.5 mi) just outside of the northwest boundary of Big Creek Provincial Park. Expect an elevation gain of 585 m (1,915 ft) and many side roads and trails to explore. Access is found off the Rocky Lake Forest Service Road south of Hanceville. There are lots of snowmobiling opportunities here including riding south around Anvil Mountain and down the Powell Creek Trail to Taylor Pass and the South Chilcotin Mountains Provincial Park.

Black Creek Area (Maps 30, 31)
The area south of Horsefly Lake, west to Wells Gray Park, and south to Canim Lake, is riddled with old roads and connector trails that offer seemingly endless riding opportunities. There is a good combination of easy riding on unploughed forest roads that lead past lakes and recreation sites to more challenging trails leading high into the alpine.

Blackwater Snowmobile Trails (Map 56/A1)
South of Prince George and west of Nadsilinich Lake is a well maintained series of snowmobile trails. They pass several smaller lakes, the Old Swanson Mill Site, and head up to Mount Baldy Hughes. Further south, MacKenzie Lakes are a popular destination for ice fishing.

Cariboo Lake East (Map 44/C4)
Found about 21 km (13 mi) northeast of Likely this route follows the 6400 Road along the east side of Cariboo Lake. The Ladies Creek Recreation Site is found 34 km (21 mi) from Likely and makes a decent base camp for the area. It is possible to continue to just past Maeford Lake where snowmobile closure areas exist to help protect caribou in the area. It is about a 50 km (30 mi) ride.

China Head Area (Map 4/G3–5/A3)
The China Head area is another riding area with limitless options. It is possible to string together a long ride up and over China Head Mountain and behind Poison Mountain. This route starts about 72 km north of Lillooet along the West Pavilion Road. Look for the China Head Forest Service Road leading northwest towards South French Bar Creek Recreation Site. The campsite is just past Moore Lake and marks the first stop on the roughly 96 km (60 mi) first leg. Continue westbound over China Head Mountain where it is possible to link up with the Yalakom River FSR, which, if unploughed, continues north behind Poison Mountain to the recreation sites along the Mud Creek FSR. Closer to South French Bar Creek, it is possible to ride the series of old roads and trails north to Schraeder Lake.

Churn Creek Trails (Maps 4, 5, 16)
Although most land in Churn Creek Protected Area is closed to motorized use, a designated snowmobile route runs through the park from the Empire Valley Road and Brown Lake along the Blackdome Mine Road. Please stick to designated routes and watch for signs.

Deacon Creek Trails (Map 42/G1–43/B2)
Look for the trailhead to the system off the south side of Highway 26 near Fifteen Mile Lake (about 15 km east of the Highway 97 junction). There are over 50 km (30 mi) of easy trails that can be explored, most of which follow logging road systems. There is a trail guide and picnic tables at the trailhead. Adding to the trails maintained by the Quesnel Snowmobile Club is the 20 km (12.5 mi) West Creek Trail. This is a family friendly ride that can be extended on any of the unplowed logging roads in the area.

Green Lake Snowmobile Trails (Map 6/D1–18/F7)
Beginning at the clubhouse on Green Lake, off Green Lake South Road, visitors can explore over 160 km (100 mi) of fantastic trails. Most of the marked route is along older logging roads, although connector trails have been cut to link road systems. The system connects to Gold Rush Trail, extending from 70 Mile House to Hammer Lake. The grasslands can only be used when covered with a good layer of snow.

Gold Bridge Area (Map 4/B7)
The Gold Bridge area features seemingly endless trails fit for snowmobilers of all skill levels. Riders will find hundreds of kilometres of logging roads, perfect for family snowmobile trips. Hurley River and Kingdom Lake Forest Service Roads are popular choices for snowmobilers. The Bridge River Valley Snowmobile Club is responsible for grooming and maintaining trails found on the Hurley River Forest Road, Lone Goat and Slim Creek Roads, making these exceptional routes for riding. North of Carpenter Lake, snowmobilers can look forward to great riding in the Shulaps Mountain Range. Access to this area is best via Yalakom or Lac La Mare Recreation Sites, heading up to Burkholder Lake, or via Marshall Lake. Please help by supporting the local clubs by purchasing a membership at the Mineshaft Pub, Morrow Chalets or Gold Bridge Hotel.

Bralorne Area (Map 4/B7)
The Kingdom Lake Forest Service Road is not ploughed and allows for easy riding past the small lakes in the area and over to the old Pioneer Mine. Those looking for a bigger challenge can access Sunshine Mountain. Home to the Bralorne Pioneer Ski Cabin, snowmobilers can follow a sled route that leads to a beginner ski run directly from Bralorne.

Bridge River FSR Snowmobile Trail (Map 3/D7–G7)
West of Gold Bridge and south of Downton Lake, snowmobilers will find 57 km (35 mi) of mostly easy snowmobile tracks to explore. This route stretches along the southern border of Bridge River Delta Provincial Park.

Grey Rock Mine Trail (Map 4/C7)
This is one of the many riding opportunities Gold Bridge has to offer. From town, head east along the Gray Rock Road for approximately 12 km (7.5 mi) then head south. From here, the route gets steep, climbing 600 m (1,970 ft) in a short 5 km (3 mi) stretch. The route runs along Truax Creek Forest Service Road for another 13 km (8 mi).

Gun Lake Area (Map 4/A7)
Gun Lake offers family friendly riding at the north end of the lake, by the airport. These trails lead to the Plateau Ponds, which is a great ice-fishing spot. At the south end, trails lead up Penrose Mountain and along Downton Lake. Riders can also access South Chilcotin Mountains Provincial Park along the Gun Creek Trail as well as the alpine area at the head of the well-traveled Slim Creek Forest Service Road. Be wary of motorized closure areas in both regions.

Gun Creek Trail (Map 4/B6–3/D6)

The Gun Creek Trail is open for riders from the Jewel Bridge to Taylor and Wolverine Pass. Considered part of the Trans Canadian Snowmobile Trail, this section of trail is over 40 km (25 mi) long and climbs some 1,150 m (3,775 ft). Riders should note that this is the only section of South Chilcotin Mountains Park open to snowmobiles. Riders are not permitted to descend into the Eldorado or Pearson Creek areas and avoid sledding into the protected mountain goat habitats. Pay attention to the signage.

Marshall Lake Area (Map 4/D7)

Marshall Lake is surrounded by trails connecting to very scenic areas. From the Marshall Creek Recreation Site, head north towards Shulaps Peak via the Jim Creek Road/Trail. This steep road climbs a stiff 2,135 m (7,000 ft). Around the 1,800 m (5,905 ft) level, look for the spur road that climbs through an open meadow leading south towards Brett Creek. Heading southeast will take snowmobilers to the beautiful Marshall Ridge. This riding area features over 12 km (7.5 mi) of snowmobile tracks. Similarly, the Marshall Lake Trail veers south from the Marshall Lake North Recreation Site and provides a great ride down to Carpenter Lake. The two can be combined for a nice loop ride.

Mount Penrose Snowmobile Trail (Map 4/A7)

Located west of Gun Lake, there are many possible routes up Mount Penrose for snowmobilers to explore. Most start at the southwest end of Gun Lake and follow the logging road west then north. There is easier riding around Lajoie Lake and the north side of Downton Lake, while more challenging routes follow the roads up the north side of Penrose.

Noaxe Lake/Quartz Mountain Trails (Map 4/D4)

Between Noaxe Creek Road in the west, the Swartz Lake-Poison Mountain Road in the north and the Yalakom River to the east is an area dominated by wide open snowmobiling terrain and the high alpine of the Shulaps Range, with a number of multi-use trails. Riders should stick to the more developed trails.

If you're looking for a local club, contact the BC Snowmobile Federation at 1-877-537-8716 or visit www.bcsf.org for more information.

Shulaps Range (Map 4/E7–5/A6)

The Shulaps Range is a high, narrow range of mountains running northwest between the Yalakom River and Carpenter Lake. Stretching almost 60 km (37 mi) long and 8 km (5 mi) wide, the area is rich in mining history. The dry, windblown mountains can be scarce of snow, but there are some nice bowls for snowmobilers to play in. Popular access points include the steep Jim Creek Road near Marshall Lake, the easier La Rochelle Creek or the Verbenkov Forest Service Road from the Yalakom (Lillooet) Recreation Site or from the Lake la Mare Recreation Site.

Slim Creek Snowmobile Area (Map 4/B6–3/D6)

Climbing as high as 2,700 m (9,000 ft), you can ride all day here without crossing your tracks. You can cover up to 200 km or more in a day, so bring extra gas. Be wary, this is an area for experienced riders only. It is also a terrible place to be in a snowstorm. It is easy to get lost in the wide open terrain, especially if you cannot follow your tracks back. From the north end of Gun Lake, 30 km (18.5 mi) of road riding will get you to the trailhead with a sign in box. From here, a trail follows Slim Creek for another 15 km (9 mi) or so until you get to the glaciers of the Lillooet Icefield. Make sure you have good visibility to travel the glaciers.

Taylor Basin (Map 4/B5)

Taylor Basin is an excellent alpine area for riding. In addition to a warming cabin at the 2,000 m (6,600 ft) level, there are two mountain slopes that climb up to 2,460 m (8,000 ft) in elevation. This area is open to all skill levels, but the higher slopes are best left to intermediate and expert riders.

Expect to put on up to 100 km (60 mi) as you play around on these open slopes. Access starts 5 km west of the Tyaughton Lake Road junction along the deteriorating Taylor Creek Forest Service Road.

Gold Rush Snowmobile Trail (Maps 5, 6, 17, 18, 29, 44, 58)

The Gold Rush Trail is a proposed 463 km (287 mi) trail that runs north from Clinton to Wells and will be part of the Trans Canada Snowmobile Trail. Currently, the 170 km (10 6 mi) section between 70 Mile House and Horsefly has been signed and maintained, but the stretches south and north are not well established. The route follows unmaintained forest service roads, existing trail, and even new trail. However, there are sections of the route that do follow public roads that are ploughed and includes one crossing of Highway 97. For current information, contact the BC Snowmobile Federation or the 100 Mile House Snowmobile Club.

Hendrix Ridge Snowmobile Area (Map 31/B5)

From Hendrix Lake, snowmobilers can ride west to Big Timothy Mountain, south to Weller Lake or north to Black Creek. The top of Big Timothy can be very wind-blown with hard snow pack so it is recommended to ride in the trees and some of the open areas. Better yet, stick to the forest roads heading north and south from the area.

Interlakes Snowmobile Area (Map 18/G6–19/B6)

Sheridan Lake is the centre of this multi-use area, with 208 km (130 mi) of signed and mapped trails. The system follows mostly old logging roads and animal trails. The routes can be accessed from the parking area on Boulanger Road at the entrance of the E Trail. Access and parking is also available at the gravel pit on Little Green Lake Road at the west end of the E Trail. The Barnett Perimeter Trail circles the area.

Itcha Ilgachuz Provincial Park (Maps 38, 39)

The local snowmobile club maintains a pair of cabins in the Itcha Ilgachuz, which can be used by all. This is big, wide-open country with lots of trails and alpine areas. However, the Ecological Management Zone in the park is not open to snowmobiling. Also, no snowmobiling is allowed before December 15th and after April 30th.

Jay Lakes Snowmobile Area (Map 22/C3)

The winter storms that bring rain to the Bella Coola Valley also bring tons of snow to the high country. The Jay (Blue & Gray) Lakes area is a popular local area for sub-alpine and alpine snowmobiling that can last until early summer.

Mahood Lake Trails (Map 19/E2)

Snowmobilers can enjoy plenty of trails just south of Mahood Lake. The area is full of forest service roads and old roads and trails that lead to a lot of backcountry and small lakes. Access is found about 7 km southeast of Mahood Falls along the Bowers Lake-Canim Forest Service Road (8200 Rd). The Corsica Mahood Trail leads south from Mahood Lake to Road 20 and also provides a good mix of forest roads and lakes to explore.

Corsica Mahood Trail (Map 19/E2)

This multi-use trail is perfect for snowmobiling during winter. The route leads from the north end of Corsica Lake to the south side of Mahood Lake. Depending on the route, it is over 8 km (5 mi) from Corsica Lake to Mahood Lake. Trails and roads lead in all directions for extended riding.

McBride Area (Map 59/G4)

Amid the beauty and splendor of the Rocky Mountains, the McBride area offers some of the best backcountry snowmobiling opportunities in the province. Using the town as a base area, you can explore deep powder in the mountains on either side of Highway 16. Forestry roads provide access. Some of the more popular snowmobiling areas include Bell and Lucille Mountains as well as the McKale Forest Service Road leading into the alpine of Mount Renshaw.

Belle Mountain Trails (Map 59/E4)

This family oriented riding area has around 15 km (9 mi) of groomed trails. A parking lot at the 5 km (3 mi) mark of the Bell Mountain Forest Service Road is shared with the Yellowhead Ski Club, while a cabin sits at the end of the groomed trail.

Lucille Mountain Trails (Map 59/G4)

This trail system features every type of riding experience, from groomed trails to extreme hill climbs. There is parking about 500 metres up the Lucille Mountain Forest Service Road, where there is a loading ramp and toilets. There is also a cabin at the end of the 12.5 km (8 mi) groomed trail.

Renshaw Trails (Map 59/G2)

Possibly the largest mapped riding area in BC, these trails are found just 15 minutes from McBride; follow Mountainview Road to the McKale River Forest Service Road. From here, there is a groomed trail that is 30 km long and leads to the remote riding areas. It is recommended that you carry beacons, shovels and extra gas when riding in this area.

Mica Mountain Trails (Map 31/F5)

The Mica Mountain Trails are found about 70 km east of 100 Mile House off the Spanish Creek Forest Service Road (7000 Rd). The trails provide great riding with over 10 km (6 mi) of trails and some great deep powder. The Mica Mountain Riders Association may be grooming trails in the area and if so, you must get a trail pass.

Milburn Mountain Snowmobile Area (Map 42/C1–56/C7)

Milburn Mountain, northwest of Quesnel, provides about 29 km (18 mi) of interconnecting trails through both forest cover and open areas. West of the mountain area, you can find a number of logging roads via the Nazko Road that also provide great backcountry snowmobiling opportunities. A parking area and trail guide is located off King Pit Road off the Blackwater Road.

Nehalliston Snowmobile Trails (Map 19/D5–F5)

North of Highway 24, between Bridge Lake and Taweel Lake is the Nehalliston Plateau. This high elevation area is riddled with small fishing lakes and old roads that make up a series of fine snowmobile trails. The Barrett Perimeter Trails also run through this area.

Windy Mountain Snowmobile Trails (Map 19/D4)

This 21 km (13 mi) trail links the 100 Mile area with the Nehalliston Snowmobile Trails. Access can be found via the Bowers Lake Forest Service Road. Alternatively, from the Needa Lake Recreation Site, it is possible to ride north on the Windy Mountain Forest Service Road to the Windy-Preacher Lake Road (193 Rd) about 3.5 km later. Once on this branch road, look for tracks heading north and along the east side of Bowers Lake towards Cougar Lake. This snowmobile route is approximately 10 km (6 mi) long depending on where you want to go, and gains almost 550 m (1,805 ft) in elevation. It is possible to join up with the Barnett Perimeter Trail for extended riding.

Pavilion Mountain Snowmobile Trails (Map 5/F6)

Pavilion Mountain sits 2,089 m (6,855 ft) above sea level to the west of Kelly Lake. Old logging roads lead up the peak from the west and south. Most venture in from the west off of the Clinton-Pavilion Road. In addition to road riding, there is informal riding in the alpine.

Rainbow Range Snowmobile Area (Map 37/F6)

This amazing riding area is the only chunk of Tweedsmuir Park that is open to snowmobiling. It covers the high country of Heckman Pass and parts of the Rainbow Range. The parking area is found off Highway 20 along the infamous Hill. It is possible to camp here or rent the nearby ski club cabin by calling 250-982-2231. The Rainbow Cabin is not maintained and is meant for emergency use only.

Thuya Lakes Snowmobile Trails (Map 19/F7)

West of the town of Little Fort, you can find the trailhead to this system off the Thuya Lake Road south of Eakin Creek Road. This collection of trails and roads connects a number of small lakes in the area and is usually well marked.

Tranquille/Sawmill Snowmobile Trails (Map 7)

This large riding area is accessed from the Kamloops Clubhouse at km 31.5 on the Sawmill Main Forest Service Road. There are plenty of groomed trails and unploughed roads to ride northeast of Tranquille Lake. Riders will find two shelters in the area, one just outside the Porcupine Meadows Park, as well as an old forest lookout at the height of land. Further north, riders can enjoy the trails around Bonaparte Provincial Park, while the Jamieson Creek Area is also known for its excellent snowmobile trails through beautiful meadows and lakes. Adding to the mix are a series of roads and trails leading further west to explore the plateau and connect up with the Deadman River. The main route leads past Gisborne Lake, over Criss Creek and past a series of lakes en route to Uren Lake. Continuing north from the Deadman River area trails lead past Hammer and Bonaparte Lake to eventually link with the Barnett Perimeter Trail.

Bonaparte Provincial Park (Map 7/E3)

Bonaparte Provincial Park is one of the few provincial parks that allow motorized use. The rolling, forested hills offer opportunities for a variety of trails, which are maintained by the Kamloops Snowmobile Associa-

tion. The well-established system runs through the southern portion of the park and includes public winter cabins. Currently, there is no park use permit or letter of permission required. Please note that snowmobiling is permissible in the Natural Environment Zone but not in the Wilderness Recreation Zone of the park. There are also trails northeast of the park that link to the Barnett Perimeter Trail.

Jamieson Creek Area (Map 7/G5)

Located just 30 minutes north of Kamloops, this area is loaded with unorganized trails. The Kamloops Snowmobile Association maintains some trails in the region and these, combined with the forestry roads allow riders to gain access to numerous meadows and lakes to ride.

Sawmill Snowmobile Connector (Map 7/B4)

Located northwest of Kamloops, snowmobile riders will find the 29 km (18 mi) Sawmill Snowmobile Connector off of Deadman Vidette Road. This snowmobile route connects the Deadman Valley to the Tranquille Plateau as well as to the trails around Bonaparte Park.

Tranquille Lake/Porcupine Meadows Snowmobile Trails (Map 7/E5)

Part of the Tranquille/Sawmill Trails north of Kamloops, Porcupine Meadows Snowmobile Trails are open from December 15th to April 15th, annually. Motorized access is not allowed outside of this timeframe. The Kamloops Snowmobile Associate maintains the trails throughout the Tranquille Lake area and a chalet at the 31 km (20 mi) mark on Sawmill Main Forest Service Road. However, the trails within the provincial park are not groomed. The trails around Tranquille Lake vary from unplowed forestry roads to actual marked trails. There is also an historic fire lookout tower at the highest elevation within the park boundary. Snowmobilers can use the trails to connect with Deadman River west of Porcupine Meadows Provincial Park.

> *Many of the alpine areas are prone to avalanches so proper equipment and training are essential. Be sure to leave your itinerary with a friend and stick to main routes to avoid any avalanche hazards or private property.*

Wells/Barkerville Snowmobile Trails (Maps 43, 44, 57, 58)

Covering a large area, this network stretches north from Cariboo Lake, past Barkerville and Wells, and beyond Stony and Narrow Lakes to meet the Prince George system. Snowmobile routes follow unploughed forest roads and connector trails taking in a host of sites including the Bowron Lakes, Yanks Peak and many old mine sites north and south of Highway 26. The Gold Rush Trail, Mount Agnes, Yanks Peak and Sugar Creek Loop are popular trails in area.

Jack O' Clubs Creek Road (Map 57/G7)

3.5 km (2 mi) west of the Wells Visitor Information Centre, the Jack O' Clubs Creek Road heads south from Highway 26. Here the trail follows the highway for about 100 metres then heads south again. The route follows the Jack O' Clubs Creek upstream to the 1,100 to 1,300 m (3,600 to 4,265 ft) level. After about 5.5 km (3.4 mi) the road turns sharply east where it is possible to link to the Richfield Mountain Route that leads steeply up to the peak of Richfield Mountain.

Mount Agnes Area (Map 57/G7–44/A1)

Accessed from the Jack O' Clubs Forest Service Road, the Wells Ski Area or Barkerville, there is an endless array of trail possibilities waiting to be discovered. You can enjoy the easier trails along the forest roads or, for the more adventurous; you can explore the alpine powder areas of Mount Agnes and beyond. In total, there are about 38 km (24 mi) of trails to explore and a warming cabin at Groundhog Lake. Please note; the south side of Bald Mountain is closed for Caribou habitat.

Old Cariboo Hudson Road (Map 58/A7–44/C3)

Found at the south end of Barkerville, right outside the park gate, this route starts from the bridge over Williams Creek, which is behind the

Snowmobile Adventures

Barkerville administration building. It is a multi-use path that runs about 29 km (18 mi) south with an elevation gain of 550 m (1,800 ft).

One Mile Lake Road (Map 58/A6)

Off Highway 26, about 2 km east of the town of Wells, look for One Mile Lake Road heading north. Park your vehicle here then start the 5.3 km (3.3 mi) route north to the Eight Mile Lake area. The moderate route gently slopes and reaches 1,300 m (4,265 ft) in elevation. From Eight Mile Lake it is possible to join the Sugar Creek Loop or the road leading to the Cornish Mountain Recreation Area for extended riding.

Proserpine Mining Road (Map 58/A7–44/A1)

This route also starts at the bridge over Williams Creek behind the Barkerville administration building. This is an 8 km (5 mi) trail that climbs steadily for about 500 m (1,640 ft). Follow the Old Cariboo Hudson Road for about 2 km to where the Proserpine Mining Road splits off to the south. Keep heading south to join the 4.5 km (2.8 mi) long Proserpine Multi-use Connector. This will link you up with the Bald Mountain Connector, the Powderhouse Trail and the VanWinkle Trail.

Richfield Mountain Route (Map 44/A1–58/A7)

Part of Wells area trails, this 8.5 km (5.3 mi) route goes up and over the Cow Mountain summit at about 1,800 m (5,905 ft). The trail begins off the Jack O' Clubs Creek Road, south of Highway 26. Shortly after the end of the road, the trail intersects the Cow Mountain Ditch Trail. Continue east to go over the summit and connect with the Nedis Connector. Access can also be found off the Cariboo Waggon Road about 1.8 km south of the Richfield Courthouse. This is in a region with Caribou closures so make sure to stay on the marked trail.

Sugar Creek Loop (Map 57/F5–G6)

The Sugar Creek Loop is considered the best all-ages riding location in the area. The 35 km (22 mi) loop starts and ends at Wells Meadow and climbs up through the Sugar Creek Pass. Both sides of the pass are closed for Caribou habitat and the pass itself holds a lot of wildlife to respect.

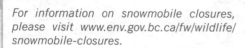

For information on snowmobile closures, please visit www.env.gov.bc.ca/fw/wildlife/snowmobile-closures.

Wells-Barkerville Winter Connector (Map 57/G7–58/A7)

This trail connects Wells to Barkerville in the winter. It is an easy and relatively flat route running about 7 km (4.5 mi) from the overflow parking lot west of Barkerville to the bridge near Blair Street and Baker Street in Wells. The route crosses the Bowron Lake Road approximately 2 km west of Barkerville; exercise caution here.

Williams Lake Area (Map 29)

The 150 Mile House/Williams Lake areas have a long reputation for being fantastic snowmobiling destinations. From open-field travel to forested routes, there is a great array of snowmobiling waiting to be discovered. Although the region is short on alpine, the area is perfect for long distance touring and family outings. Anglers at heart will also enjoy the numerous lakes that are available in the area for ice fishing.

Yanks Peak Snowmobile Trails (Map 44/B3)

The Williams Lake Powder Kings maintain the Yanks Peak area north of Likely near Keithley Creek. There are several trail options to sample. About 4 km (2.5 mi) from Keithley Creek along the Barkerville Road, the Shortcut Trail heads past the Yanks Peak Snowmobile Cabin. Next is the Snarlsburg Trail. This trail leads south of Yanks Peak from the 10 km (6 mi) mark of the Barkerville Road. Just about a kilometre up the road is the Hampton Trail, which leads up and over the 1,904 m (6,247 ft) peak. Last is the Little Snowshoe Route. Found approximately 14 km (8.7 mi) from Keithley Creek, this route goes behind Yanks Peak. All of the trails end up connecting with the Gold Rush Trail on the northeast side of the peak. This trail will lead you north into Barkerville.

BEFORE YOU GO OUT

- Check the weather forecast and trail conditions before you go out. In some areas, you may need to assess whether there is danger of an avalanche.

- Avoid snowmobiling on ice if you're not sure how thick it is or what condition it is in.

- It's helpful to know basic first aid including the signs of hypothermia and what to do if it happens.

HAVE THE RIGHT EQUIPMENT

- Wear well-insulated protective clothing including goggles, waterproof snowmobile suits and gloves, and rubber-bottomed boots.

- All drivers and passengers should wear helmets approved for snowmobiles (DOT or similar approved – not a bicycle helmet).

- Snowmobiles should have brightly coloured antenna flags mounted on rods that are 1.2 to 2.4 metres long located on the back of the snowmobile. This is especially important if you're driving in a hilly area so that others can see you.

- Carry a first-aid kit, an emergency tool kit (with spark plugs, and drive and fan belts), an extra key, and a survival kit that includes flares. A cellular phone is helpful if you're in an area with service.

DRIVE SAFELY

- Beginners should stick to groomed trails and drive during the day.

- Travel at safe speeds, especially on unfamiliar or rugged terrain where you might run into hazards you can't see, such as barbed wire or overhanging trees.

- Keep the headlights and tail lights on at all times to improve the visibility of your snowmobile to other vehicle operators.

- Travel in groups of two or more, and only on designated, marked trails away from roads, waterways, railroads and pedestrians. Do not carry more than one passenger.

- Don't pull people on saucers, skis, tubes, or toboggans behind a snowmobile.

- Never drink alcohol or use drugs before or while you're operating a snowmobile.

Wildlife
Adventures

The Chilcotin Plateau stretches over bountiful lands that thrive with some of the most amazing wildlife in the world. Witnessing these creatures roam in their natural habitats can provide some of the most thrilling experiences for outdoor adventurers.

Avid birdwatchers are always looking for new and unusual species to add to their lists, and the Cariboo is home to one of the largest populations of the rare American white pelican. The white pelican is a large bird that can be found feeding around many small lakes. It even has its own park, known simply as White Pelican Provincial Park.

The Chilcotin Plateau is also home to many other birds and large animals, including an impressive number of California bighorn sheep. The area is also home to the wild horse, one of BC's most controversial species. Horses are not native to North America. They were brought over by the Spanish people about 400 years ago and made their way into the interior about 200 years ago, before the arrival of European explorers. Considered a nuisance by some, there is a proposal to create a wild horse sanctuary in the Brittany Triangle area to help protect this unique form of wildlife.

Some creatures are easy to spot. Salmon viewing, for instance, is a matter of getting down to the right stream at the right time. On the other hand, many birds and animals tend to flee when they hear, see or smell humans. In order to improve your chances of spotting these elusive creatures, wear natural colours and unscented lotions. Bring along binoculars or scopes so you can observe from a distance, and move slowly but steadily. Keep pets on a leash, or better yet, leave them at home, as they will only decrease your chances to spot wildlife. Early mornings and late evenings are usually the best times to see most birds and animals.

Be aware of common wildlife food sources, but remember to stay well away from an animal's meal. Venturing too close may trigger aggressive behaviour, especially from bears. If you find yourself close to an animal, please remember not to feed it. This will keep both you and the wildlife safe.

Most wildlife watching is seasonal. Salmon spawn in fall. White pelican are seen primarily in the summer. Waterfowl are seen migrating in the spring and summer. Below we have included the most notable wildlife viewing areas in the region to guide you on your wilderness adventures. No matter which season you choose for your wildlife viewing adventure, the backcountry of the Cariboo Chilcotin Coast pulsates with life, making it a fantastic place to become one with nature.

Wildlife Adventures

100 Mile Marsh Wildlife Sanctuary (Map 18/D4)
In the spring and fall, the marsh sees trumpeter swans. From spring to fall, grebes, spotted sandpipers, sora, swallows, teals, Virginia rail and yellow-headed and common yellowthroat blackbirds use the area. The marsh is also home to beavers. The marsh is located in 100 Mile House proper; right behind the visitor's center.

130 Mile Marsh (Map 17/F1)
Located on the western side of Highway 97, this marsh has seen several habitat enhancing projects. The area is home to a wide variety of birds from May to September, including blue-winged teal, cinnamon teal, loons, osprey, sora, common snipe, belted kingfisher and yellow-headed blackbird.

Alkali Lake–Reidemann Wildlife Sanctuary (Map 16/G3–17/A3)
Alkali is a feeding spot for the American white pelican. This wildlife sanctuary protects these feeding grounds and is a good birdwatching spot. In the summer, watch for loon, teal and Barrow's goldeneye.

Anahim Lake (Map 38/E7)
Anahim Lake is used by the endangered American White Pelican as a feeding ground. The lake is also home to many species of waterfowl, like red-necked grebe, wood duck and green and blue-winged teal. In spring and summer, watch for muskrat and river otters, especially in the narrows between Anahim and Little Anahim Lakes.

Bella Coola Estuary (Map 22/D1)
This area is a great spot for birding. It is located right where the Bella Coola River flows into the North Bentinck Arm. The estuary is used by migrating waterfowl along with American widgeons, Barrow's goldeneye and trumpeter swans. Grizzly bear can be seen here with the salmon spawn, and the area is a wintering location for many animals, both big and small.

Big Bar Lake Provincial Park (Map 5/E1)
This easily accessible park features a 3.5 km self-guided trail that leads from the north end of the park to Otter Marsh. Wildlife viewers frequent this trail due to the high likelihood of spotting black bear, moose, mule deer, muskrat, river otter and beaver. The park is also excellent for bird watching as it is home to numerous species including bald eagle, Barrow's goldeneye, cinnamon and blue-winged teal, red-winged blackbird, ring-necked duck, bufflehead, song sparrow and northern harriers. The area is also well-known for its abundant rainbow trout that reside in the parks numerous lakes and ponds. Viewing platforms and interpretive signs are available.

Big Creek Provincial Park (Maps 3, 15)
Big Creek Park's southern region is home to a diverse population of wildlife. Often frequented for outdoor activities such as backpacking, hunting and mountaineering, the park is also known for its excellent wildlife viewing opportunities. Backpackers and wildlife viewers are likely to see large mammals such as California bighorn sheep and mountain goat. The presence of these large ungulates attracts numerous predators to the area including black and grizzly bear along with wolf.

Bishop River Provincial Park (Map 2/C6)
This remote park protects the headwaters of the Bishop River, just south of Ts'yl-os Park. Its proximity to the southern end of Ts'yl-os Provincial Park makes it see the same diverse range of birds and animals including bald eagle, black and grizzly bear, cougar, mule deer and peregrine falcon. With luck, it might also be possible to spot elusive wolverine within the park.

Bowron Lake Provincial Park (Maps 44, 45, 58, 59)
This large wilderness park is known for its canoe circuit and its wildlife. Sometimes, the wildlife encounters are not happy ones, as black bear are easily habituated to the presence of humans who do not cache their food properly. The area is also home to a wide variety of birds including bald eagle, osprey, song birds, trumpeter swan, waterfowl and woodpeckers. There is great bird watching in the Bowron Slough, and moose, along with beaver, muskrat and otter are often seen in marshy areas. In the lakes you will find bull, lake and rainbow trout along with kokanee and rocky mountain whitefish.

Bridge & Sheridan Lakes (Map 18/G6–19/C6)
The channel between Bridge Lake and Lesser Fish Lake is a great place to watch kokanee spawn in early fall. Also in the area is the Sheridan Lake Spawning Channel where some pretty large rainbow trout can be found spawning in late spring. In early fall, look for pink salmon to appear.

Brittany Triangle (Map 14/D4–26/G7)
The Chilcotin is only one of two places in Canada where wild horses can still be seen. As many as 200 wild horses roam the 155,000 hectare area defined by the Chilco River to the west, and the Taseko River to the east. The horses are believed to be descendants of the mustangs that spread into BC's Cariboo and Chilcotin region in the mid-1700s.

Bull Canyon Provincial Park (Map 27/C6)
Located just 6 km west of Alexis Creek, this park is found in a beautiful canyon between the Chilcotin River and Highway 20. There is a short walking trail next to the river, where visitors will see a large number of raptor species. Black bear are known to frequent the backcountry regions of this park, and pet-owners are advised not to take dogs into these areas. Bats are also a common sight here, as they rest inside the caves along the canyon walls.

Bull Mountain (Map 29/B4)
Located in the Cariboo Educational Woodlot north of Williams Lake, there are interpretive trails running through the area. While the focus of the trails is to teach people about small-scale forestry, the area is home to a variety of woodland creatures including moose and mule deer.

A good set of binoculars or spotting scopes will allow you to observe birds and animals more easily and from further distances.

Calvert Island Conservancy (Map 8/D3)
This conservancy protects a diverse wildlife habitat on Calvert Island. Located 55 km southwest of Bella Bella and 95 km north of Port Hardy, in Fitz Hugh Sound, the conservancy is a popular whale watching destination with humpback, gray and minke whales frequenting the nearby waters. Dolphins, harbour seals, porpoises, orcas and sea lions are some of the other sea-dwelling creatures that delight and amaze visitors at this location. Calvert Island's Hakai Pass is home to massive runs of all five species of Chinook, chum, Coho, pink and sockeye salmon, as well as halibut, lingcod and red snapper. On the island itself, visitors will have the chance to see mammas such as beaver, black bear, black-tailed deer, mink, river otter and wolf.

Canim Lake (Map 19/A2–C1)
Canim Lake, located 35 km northeast of 100 Mile House, is one of the top destinations for bald eagle enthusiasts. Visitors will also see American bittern, bobolink, marsh wren, swallows, warblers and waterfowl.

Cariboo Nature Park (Map 17/G1)
This undeveloped park protects Woodfrog Lake, just north of the town of Lac La Hache. It is a great bird watching site for shore birds and waterfowl. Other animals that might be seen here include black bear, coyote, fox, muskrat and hare.

Charlotte Alplands Protected Area (Maps 12, 24)
The Charlotte Alplands is an area protected from logging and is home to a massive concentration of lakes. In fact, the area lays claim to the largest concentration of alpine lakes in BC, many of which are home to rainbow trout and kokanee. The numerous waterbodies makes the area rich in wildlife, including black and grizzly bear, caribou, mountain goat, mule deer and wolf. Birdwatchers will find several birds of prey such as bald eagles and peregrine falcons. Access is best through the many lodges and outfitters that operate out of this area; a few informal trails cut through the area.

Chilanko & Puntzi Marshes (Map 26/B5–E4)
Located just off Highway 20, the Chilanko Marsh stretches along a rough, two-wheel drive accessible road. The area is best known for its waterfowl. In the winter, moose also feed in the area. Nearby, Puntzi Marshes contain similar species of shorebirds and waterfowl.

Chilcotin Lake & Marshes (Map 26/C2–E3)
This area is a popular birdwatching destination. Like many lakes in the area, Chilcotin Lake is used as a feeding spot from May to August for American white pelican. The Chilcotin Marshes are found between Chezacut Road and

the Chilcotin River. This lush wetland habitat is home to many nesting birds. The best time to view is from spring to fall. In winter, this is prime moose habitat. There is a 1.5 km trail leading to the marshes.

Chilko River (Map 14/B5)
Where Chilko Lake turns into the Chilko River is a great place to watch steelhead spawn in May. This is one of the largest steelhead spawning areas in the province.

Churn Creek Protected Area (Maps 4, 5, 16, 17)
If you cross the Fraser River over the Gang Ranch Bridge 100 km south of Williams Lake, you will find this expansive grassland park with a variety of bird species including bobolink, Brewer's sparrow, Lewis' woodpecker, per-egrine falcon, sage thrasher, sharp-tailed grouse and Swainson's hawk. Mam-mals include California bighorn sheep and mule deer, and gopher, racer and snake can also be seen. The viewing is best from April to October.

Dean River & Dean River Corridor Conservancy (Map 36/C3; 36/E4–37/A3)
In addition to linking the interior to the coast, the Dean River and Dean River Corridor area serve as an important habitat for spawning chum salmon. The river is also internationally famous for its steelhead fishing. With so much steelhead, and beaches that are ripe with spawning salmon and eggs, the river attracts a large amount of grizzly bear. Wildlife viewers should take cau-tion and maintain a significant distance when viewing these bears.

Dragon Lake (Map 42/F2)
Dragon Lake sees a fairly large migration of sandhill cranes in spring and fall. In the summer, the area is also home to waterfowl and shorebirds.

Dzawadi/Upper Klinaklini River Conservancy (Map 11/F4–12/B3)
Located 60 km southeast of Bella Coola, this remote conservancy is com-prised of a low-lying, valley bottom corridor and a portion of the Klinaklini Riv-er. Wildlife viewers will find that this corridor is used as a major travel route for grizzly bear. Migratory birds are known to fly through this area in large numbers as well. There are no established routes or trails in this conservancy, so wildlife viewers need to take the proper precautions for backcountry travel.

There are several resources to access prior to your adventures, including the Scout Is-land Nature Centre in Williams Lake, the 100 Mile Visitor Centre and the Nature Education and Resource Centre in Quesnel.

Eagle's Nest Marsh (Map 38/D7)
This viewing area is signed from the highway and starts near the Eagle's Nest Resort Sign. A gentle trail leads through the marsh, which is a good birdwatching area. There are also numerous beaver lodges along the trail.

Eakin Creek Floodplain Provincial Park (Map 19/G6)
Accessible by gravel road off Highway 24, 15 km west of Little Fort, this 115 hec-tare park is home to a significant stand of old growth trees. Wildlife viewers will find that these old growth stands provide a habitat for numerous winged wildlife including American dippers, bats and warblers. This has resulted in birdwatching becoming one of the most popular activities in the park during summer. Visitors will also find a healthy population of wild trout in Eakin Creek.

Edge Hills Provincial Park (Map 5/E5)
Located just west of Clinton, this wild 11,850 hectare park features a maze of established but unmarked trails. Wildlife viewers can use these trails to ac-cess the more interior regions of the park to spot some of the diverse wildlife that reside in the area. Black bear, California bighorn sheep, cougar, moose and mule deer are some of the notable species that inhabit the area.

Entiako Provincial Park and Protected Area (Maps 38, 51, 52)
Located 150 km southeast of Houston, this park is mainly accessible by boat from the Nechako Reservoir. The park features a cold and dry climate, making it abundant with lichens. Wildlife viewers will find that the presence of lichen at-tracts woodland caribou and moose. The abundance of large ungulates brings a number of predators to the area as well, including grizzly bear and wolf.

Erg Mountain Provincial Park (Map 58/G1)
Known as a great location for hiking and backcountry camping, Erg Moun-tain is also a fantastic wildlife viewing destination. The high elevation terrain makes it possible to see the elusive mountain goat. Other animals that are commonly seen include caribou and grizzly bear.

Exeter Lake Wetland (Map 18/C4)
Trumpeter swan stop at this extensive wetland area in spring and fall. The area also plays host to a variety of shorebirds and waterfowl over the sum-mer months, including blackbird, goldeneye, grebe, sandhill cranes, teal and tern. The wetland is 2.5 km west of 100 Mile House on Exeter Station Road.

Farwell Canyon & Junction Sheep Range (Map 16/D1–F3)
Farwell Canyon is a spectacular area of hoodoos and sand dunes along the Chilcotin River. Like the Deer Park Wildlife Reserve and Junction Sheep Range Park, it is home to California bighorn sheep. In fact, the herd in the park is the largest in North America. You may also see coyote and mule deer, as well as many smaller animals throughout the area. Please stay on the road corridors to avoid trespassing.

Finger Tatuk Provincial Park (Map 54/B2)
Located 80 km south of Vanderhoof, access to Finger Lake and the west end of Tatuk Lake is off the Kluskus Forest Service Road. This large 17,151 hectare park features a diverse habitat that sustains a wide range of animals. Wildlife viewers will find black and grizzly bear, deer, moose and small fur-bearing mammals. Birdwatchers will commonly see eagles, shorebirds and waterfowl.

Green Lake/Watch Lake (Map 18/D7–F6)
South of 100 Mile House, there are good birdwatching opportunities at the many lakes and ponds in this area, along with fish that spawn at certain times. From May to mid-June, rainbow trout spawn in Watch Creek. Kokanee spawn in late August to September. American white pelican and red-throated loon can be seen during migration at the west end of Green Lake. Other species include American dippers and belted kingfishers at Rayfield Creek and canyon.

Hakai Luxvbalis Conservancy (Map 8/D1, 20/C6)
Known for its spectacular ocean scenery, the conservancy also has a number of great places for watching wildlife. At Blenheim Island, just southwest of Hunter Island, watch for peregrine falcon in summer and northern sea lions in winter. In the Goose Island Group, black-tailed deer are fairly easy to spot. At Gosling Rocks, you can see a riot of seabirds and marine mammals like har-bour seals, northern sea lions and sea otters, especially in July and August. In Hakai Pass, there is great birding, as well as large marine mammals like orca and Pacific white-sided dolphins. Grey and humpback whales, porpoises, mink and over 100 species of birds can also be seen here.

High Lakes Basin Provincial Park (Map 19/F7)
This remote park lies north of Bonaparte Lake, 16 km west of Little Fort, and features high elevation lakes containing wild trout. There is no access into the park, but it is possible to bushwhack in on foot or by horseback from the logging roads north of Caverhill Lake. The park's close proximity to Bonaparte Provincial Park puts it in range of numerous wildlife species including black bear, fisher, marten, moose, mule deer and timber wolf.

Highway 26 (Maps 42, 43, 56–58)
Highway 26 connects Barkerville to the outside world. From Cottonwood to Stanley you stand a good chance of seeing moose. Drive carefully, especially in the early evening and at night.

Highway 97: 101 Mile to 108 Mile Ranch (Map 18/C3)
The stretch of Highway 97, starting 2 km north of 100 Mile House at 101 Mile Lake, has an abundance of waterfowl in the grassland ponds including sandhill cranes and trumpeter swans. Other birds to watch for include black-birds, black tern, killdeer, mountain bluebird, raptors, sora and Virginia rail. Black bear, coyote, mule deer, muskrat, red fox, river otter and yellow-bellied marmot are some of the other species found here.

Highway 97 (Maps 6, 17, 18, 28, 29, 42, 56)
The main north-south connector, Highway 97 is teeming with wildlife. Moose and mule deer can be found alongside and, too frequently, on the highway. Between 1982 and 2002, there were over three 100 animal-related accidents on this stretch of road, making it one of the most dangerous roads in the province.

Wildlife Adventures

Horsefly Bay (Map 30/B1)
Located on Quesnel Lake, this bay is a popular rest-over spot for migrating waterfowl. As you might expect, the best times to view are in spring and fall. The bay is found 10 km north of Horsefly.

Horsefly Lake & River (Map 30/B3)
The Horsefly River Spawning Channel is located along the Little Horsefly River within the community of Horsefly. This spawning channel is a popular place to watch kokanee spawn in the early fall. The best viewing is from a bridge over the river. The area around Horsefly Lake is also home to a large population of moose and mule deer.

Horse Lake (Map 18/E5)
Located just 10 km southeast of 100 Mile House, Horse Lake has American bittern, bald eagle, black swift, black tern, great blue heron, hummingbird, osprey, rufous warblers, sora and other waterfowl. At the west end of the lake, curlew and longbilled dowitcher are seen during spring migration.

Hot Springs–No Name Creek Conservancy (Map 22/B3)
This remote and difficult-to-access conservancy is mainly frequented by visitors who are on their way to Tallheo Hot Springs. The relatively low amount of human presence in the area makes it a good spot for wildlife viewing. Visitors that manage to access the conservancy will be rewarded with the chance to see grizzly bear and mountain goat.

Huchsduwachsdu Nuyem Jees/Kitlope Heritage Conservancy (Map 34, 35, 48, 49)
This massive park features the world's largest intact coastal temperate rainforest with enormous old-growth trees that are over 800 years old. Access is limited to boat or plane, making this a remote site that sees little human activity. This makes it a fantastic spot for intrepid wildlife viewers. Visitors will find a thriving habitat filled with large mammals such as black and grizzly bear, moose, mountain goat and wolf. Birdwatchers will find healthy populations of bald eagle, marbled murrelet and waterfowl.

Itcha Ilgachuz Provincial Park (Maps 38, 39)
This large park is in the rain shadow of the Coast Mountains. California bighorn sheep live here year-round, primarily in the Ilgachuz Range. Moose may be observed from May to September, and the largest southern BC herd of woodland caribou may be seen from June to December. Other species include cougar, mountain goat, mule deer and wolf. Access to the park is along maintained, but long riding trails.

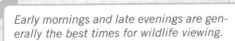

Early mornings and late evenings are generally the best times for wildlife viewing.

Kimsquit Estuary Conservancy (Map 36/A2)
This conservancy is located at the mouth of the Kimsquit River at the head of the Dean Channel. The estuary plays an important role in sustaining a healthy population of grizzly bear in the area. It is also an important habitat for juvenile salmon, and the estuary sees a lot of use for Coho salmon and cutthroat trout fishing. The thriving bear population has made grizzly bear viewing a popular pastime in this area.

Knife Creek UBC Alex Fraser Research Forest (Map 29/E6)
Just 21 km south of Williams Lake on Highway 97, this research forest has a 1 km interpretive forest trail that is located on the east end of Rodeo Drive. Interpretive signs describe the importance of this mule deer winter habitat, and deer can be seen here in spring.

Kwatna Estuary Conservancy (Map 21/E4)
The Kwatna River flows into Kwatna Inlet, creating a large estuary with meandering channels and prominent tidal flats. The estuary provides an important habitat for juvenile salmon, attracting a large number of grizzly bear. Wildlife viewers can often spot the grizzlies feasting on salmon along the water.

Lac Du Bois Grasslands Protected Area (Map 7/F7)
The Lac Du Bois Road divides this 15,712 hectare park in half, providing numerous access points. The open grasslands, dry forests, and grand cliffs and canyons of the park sustain a diverse range of wildlife. California bighorn sheep, moose and mule deer are commonly seen at the Dewdrop cliffs. Black bear and western rattlesnake also reside in the park. Birdwatchers will have the opportunity to spot the flammulated owl, sharp-tailed grouse and waterfowl within the park boundaries.

Loon Creek Hatchery (Map 6/B5)
The Loon Creek Hatchery produces kokanee and rainbow trout. Combined, these hatcheries populate about 1,200 lakes with between 10 and 12 million fish each year. The hatchery is located 20 km north of Cache Creek on the paved Loon Lake Road.

Marble Range Provincial Park (Map 5/E3)
Located west of Clinton, this 12,236 hectare park is comprised of a limestone riddled topography throughout its numerous mountain ranges. Wildlife viewers will find that the park is home to a large herd of California bighorn sheep as well as a large population of mule deer. The California bighorn sheep can be seen migrating between steep alpine ranges throughout the seasons. This is mainly for food and protection from predators.

Moose Valley Provincial Park (Map 17/G4–18/A4)
This provincial park is located 40 km west of 100 Mile House and provides winter habitat for moose. Bird enthusiasts will find Bonaparte gulls, nesting sandhill cranes, songbirds and a variety of waterfowl. Beaver, black bear, mule deer, river otter and muskrat call the park home as well. Due to the extensive marshy landscape, wildlife viewing is best done from a canoe or kayak.

Nazko Lake Provincial Park (Map 27/A2–41/B7)
Nazko Lake Provincial Park is located in the northern part of the Chilcotin Plateau, 60 km northwest of Alexis Creek. The chance to see American white pelican that feed in lakes of the park is one of the main highlights here. Visitors will find these rare and endangered birds feeding on fish, frogs, salamanders and crayfish, mainly during early mornings and evenings. The extensive wetland habitats sustain healthy populations of several other animals including beaver, moose, shorebirds and waterfowl.

Nunsti Provincial Park (Map 14/F3)
Located northeast of Chilko Lake in the Chilcotin Plateau, this 20,898 hectare park protects valuable moose habitat that encompasses abundant wetlands and small lakes. Wildlife viewers will find several other species in the area including beaver, black and grizzly bear, cougar, hare, martin, mule deer, muskrat and wolf. This park is now under the Tsilhqot'in Nation Aboriginal Title declaration as of June 26, 2014, which entitles the Nation to determine land use. Please seek the permission of the Nation prior to accessing the park.

Oliver Cove Marine Provincial Park (Map 20/B1)
This small park is also known as Port Blackney. Visitors will find a thriving habitat for spectacular sea-dwelling mammals such as orcas, Pacific white sided dolphins and sea lions. When the tide is low, a number of creatures are revealed along the shore, including chiton, mollusc, sea cucumber, sea star, urchin and multi-coloured algae. The wildlife continues on land as black bear, Columbia black-tailed deer, mink and wolf call this area home.

Pollywog Marshes (Map 13/F1–25/F7)
A variety of wildlife has been observed at the marshes, including birds and small mammals like beavers. The site is easily accessible off Highway 20 from the Pollywog Lake Rest Area.

Ptarmigan Creek Protected Area and Provincial Park (Map 58/G2)
The narrow, steep-sided valley at the north end of the Cariboo Mountains has been set aside to protect caribou and grizzly bear. Elusive mountain goats are also known to frequent the mountain ranges found within the park. The lower reaches of Ptarmigan Creek is home to Chinook salmon, rainbow trout and sculpin. The park is located northwest of McBride and is accessible via trail from a gated area near the Ptarmigan Creek Recreation Site. The trailhead is 8 km in from Highway 16, about 5 km west of Crescent Spur or about 165 km east of Prince George. However, access is currently very difficult since the Ptarmigan Creek Forest Service Road is washed out at the 3 km and 12 km mark, and both foot bridges crossing the Ptarmigan Creek have been washed away.

Scout Island Nature Park (Map 29/B5)

Located at the northwestern end of Williams Lake, this park offers great bird-watching opportunities. View a variety of birds, from raptors (bald eagle and osprey) and shorebirds (including great blue heron) to waterfowl (common loon, red-necked grebe and wood duck), either from the rooftop viewing platform or from the nature trails. Small animals can be seen in the forest, and beaver, mink, muskrat, river otter and the western painted turtle can be seen on and around the lakeshore.

Schoolhouse Lake Provincial Park (Map 18/G1)

This forest ecosystem supports habitat for a variety of wildlife including black bear, cougar, coyote, moose and mule deer. There are also songbirds, and it is possible to see hawks, even though they do not commonly frequent the area. The lakes support good populations of sportfish, as well as waterfowl and aquatic mammals like beaver, muskrat and otter.

Sheridan Creek (Map 28/G1)

Sheridan Creek is just north of the town of McLeese Lake. The highway passes over the creek, which is a good place to watch kokanee spawn in early fall. The stream is also home to large rainbow and brook trout, as well as a plethora of chironomids.

Snootli Creek Hatchery (Map 22/E1)

Established to enhance chum and Chinook salmon in the Bella Coola system, this hatchery also allows visitors to see steelhead and pink salmon in season. The facility is 4 km west of Hagensborg.

South Chilcotin Mountains Provincial Park (Maps 3, 4)

Wildlife viewing is popular in the park. Grizzly bear and mountain goat are commonly seen as are deer, grouse and birds of prey. Along with many types of songbirds, you may also see bighorn sheep, moose and, if you are very lucky, wolverine.

Tatla Lake Marshes (Map 13/E1–26/A6)

These marshes stretch along the southern shores of Tatla Lake just north of Highway 20. As a result, access to this area is good. Watch for nesting waterfowl, snipe and songbirds, including a couple of species of blackbird.

Taweel Provincial Park (Map 19/F4)

This remote park protects a representative sub-boreal spruce forest, with some old-growth and riparian areas at the north end of Taweel Lake. This creates an important habitat for fisher, marten, moose, timber wolf and birds, such as the barrow's goldeneye, common loon and the three-toed woodpecker. Wild rainbow trout are also found in the lakes.

Ten Mile Lake Provincial Park (Map 56/F7)

Walk the Beaver Pond Trail and view a beaver lodge and series of beaver dams. Ducks Unlimited has placed waterfowl nesting boxes and platforms around the pond. Black and grizzly bear are also known to frequent the back-country regions of the park.

Troup Passage Conservancy (Map 20/E2)

Protecting a narrow ocean passage between Chatfield and Cunningham Islands, the narrows here are rich in marine life. Many species that are typical to the region include harbour seal, orca, porpoise and sea lions. Paddlers and boaters can explore and see a variety of fish in the intricate shorelines, small bays and islets of this 2,617 hectare conservancy.

Ts'yl-os Provincial Park (Maps 1, 2, 3, 14)

A huge park in the southwestern Chilcotin, bordered by the rugged peaks of the Coast Mountains to the west and the dry Interior Plateau to the east, this area is home to a diversity of landscapes and habitat. Wildlife species include American beaver, black bear, mule deer, moose and mountain goat. Ecologically sensitive animal populations found in the area include bald eagle, California bighorn sheep, fisher, wolverine and a variety of amphibian species. Access is via rough two-wheel drive accessible logging roads.

Tsintsunko Lakes Provincial Park (Map 7/E4)

The park provides calving and summer habitat for moose and a variety of waterfowl. Wild rainbow trout are also found in the lakes and typically spawn from late May to early June.

Tweedsmuir Provincial Park (Maps 11, 12, 23, 24, 36–38, 49 - 51)

As the largest park in British Columbia, Tweedsmuir is host to an amazing range of birds and animals too large to list here. A few of the more easily accessed wildlife viewing areas are: Fisheries Pool (Map 19/D2), Lonesome Lake (Map 19/G3) and Rainbow Nature Conservancy Area (Map 29).

Upper Cariboo River (Map 44/C3–58/D7)

To access this wildlife viewing area visitors should take the gravel roads leading to Barkerville from Likely. Follow the 6400 Road system along Cariboo Lake over to Ghost Lake and the Matthew River before crossing the Cariboo River and the Cunningham Pass Forest Service Road north to Barkerville. You will find moose and waterfowl, and at the Antler Creek bridge in August, osprey and spawning Chinook salmon.

> *In order to improve your chances of spotting birds and animals, wear natural colours and unscented lotions.*

Upper Kimsquit River Conservancy (Map 49/F5)

Created in 2008, the highlight of this 10,588 hectare conservancy is its unique grizzly bear habitat. The area is an important feeding ground for these bear because adult sockeye salmon often freeze within Kwinquit Lake and then thaw during spring. The adult sockeye salmon carcasses provide a crucial source of early protein for the bears. This area is also one of the few coastal drainages that support a resident moose population. Black-tailed deer and mountain goat also reside in this area.

Wells Gray Provincial Park (Maps 19, 31, 45)

From massive glacial-fed lakes to towering mountain alpine peaks, Wells Gray offers visitors the chance to experience a truly wild part of the province. The wildlife viewing and birdwatching opportunities are abundant within the park. Wildlife viewers will find a variety of large mammals such as black bear, deer, moose and wolf. Venturing to higher alpine areas will reveal more elusive creatures such as caribou, cougar, grizzly bear and mountain goat. Smaller mammals include beaver, marten and weasel. Lucky visitors may even spot wolverine. Birdwatchers will also find several different bird species that reside within the park.

West Twin Provincial Park (Map 59/C3)

This diverse area is home to an abundance of wildlife and is a popular backcountry destination providing great views of the Robson Valley. The park is located 180 km southeast of Prince George off Highway 16 where there is a pull-out with day-use area and a Forestry Interpretation Trail. Wildlife viewers will find caribou and mountain goat in the higher elevation ranges of the park. Other large mammals include deer, moose and grizzly bear.

White Pelican Provincial Park (Map 27/G3)

Located 60 km northwest of Williams Lake, this 2,763 hectare park was created to protect important nesting habitat for white pelican on Stum Lake. This is the only nesting habitat in the province for this rare bird, which are very sensitive to disturbance, so there are several restrictions to protect the lake. The lake is closed to the public from March 1 to August 31. People looking to spot the birds in summer will find they feed in nearby lakes, including those of Nazko Lake Park. Other wildlife viewing opportunities within the park include moose and aquatic fur-bearing mammals such as beaver and otter.

Winter
Adventures

The Cariboo Chilcotin Coast is synonymous with winter fun. Each year the region is blessed with an abundance of clean, soft snow that offers incredible winter diversity and an opportunity to sample every imaginable outdoor activity.

The following section outlines only a few of the places where you can ski and snowshoe in the Cariboo Chilcotin region. They represent just the tip of a huge iceberg. For more adventures, check out the Trails section, where you will find a number of listings that make fine winter destinations when the snow falls. Some favourites with skiers include the Alexander MacKenzie Heritage Trail and the Wells/Barkerville Trails. Or simply pick a map and navigate the area's endless road systems. While some of the mainlines are ploughed, the rest make a wonderful playground for snowmobilers, skiers and snowshoers.

If you're looking for a different off-trail experience, try crossing a frozen lake. Although you will need to be cautious as some lakes never completely freeze solid, frozen lakes can provide great opportunities for winter recreation. Skiers, snowmobilers and snowshoers often cross these water bodies in order to reach areas that are mostly inaccessible during the summer. While these routes can get you into remote areas that few people ever see, there is always a risk of breaking through the ice. Please exercise extreme caution when traveling across any frozen water body.

South of Bella Coola, the Coast Mountains beckon backcountry skiers. Rarely traveled, these heavily glaciated peaks receive serious amounts of snow – in some places, the snowfall averages 20 metres (60 feet) or more! Areas like the Homathko Icefield and the Waddington Divide offer a number of difficult, multi-day (and even multi-week) routes that may see one or two groups every couple of years. For folks short on time and long on money, there are heli-skiing operations that can take you into some of the most remote backcountry in BC.

Visitors to all areas will find snow in the higher elevations by mid-November that can last until May and June in some areas. The low elevation season is from around December to April. Snowshoers in designated cross-country areas should stay off the track-set trails.

Note that when travelling in the backcountry, avalanches are always a danger. Visit www.avalanche.ca for current conditions, and be prepared with both avalanche knowledge and safety equipment to help make your visit to the mountains safe.

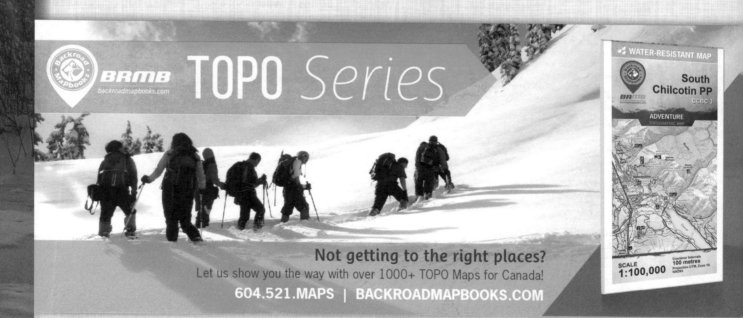

Backroad Mapbooks **BRMB**
backroadmapbooks.com

TOPO *Series*

WATER-RESISTANT MAP

South Chilcotin PP
CCBC 3

ADVENTURE
TOPOGRAPHIC MAP

SCALE
1:100,000

Contour Intervals
100 metres
Projection UTM, Zone 10,
NAD83

Not getting to the right places?
Let us show you the way with over 1000+ TOPO Maps for Canada!

604.521.MAPS | BACKROADMAPBOOKS.COM

99 Mile Ski Trails (Map 18/D4)

Just south of 100 Mile House, this area is home to a collection of multi-use trails that make excellent ski trails during winter. The 100 Mile Nordic Ski Society (100milenordics.com) grooms around 50 km (30 mi) of trails for use by all levels of experience. There are race trails in all different lengths from 1.5 km upwards to 20 km as well as more casual ski loops that range from 0.4 km to 11 km. This area truly has something for all levels, with steep climbs and tight corners, to long flat sections. For added fun, there are 5 km (3 mi) of trails lit for night skiing as well as a large log chalet that offers lessons and outdoor ice skating.

108 Mile Ski Trails (Map 18/C3)

You will find a fantastic array of groomed cross-country ski trails around the 108 Mile House Rest Area and Hills Health Ranch. In fact, this system is considered one of Canada's biggest and best Nordic ski resorts when combined with the 150 km (93 mi) trail network around 100 Mile House. The resort itself maintains 40 km (25 mi) of skate-set trails and a lit loop of trails for night skiing. The terrain ranges from broad, open flats to rolling hills to some challenging steep sections. There is a ski shop on-site offering lessons as well as a chance to explore the nearby Hills Health Ranch downhill ski park. The spa facilities at the ranch make a wonderful treat after a day's outing.

Alex Fraser Research Forest Trails (Map 29/E6)

The Alex Fraser Research Forest is located on 10,000 hectares (24,700 ac) of Crown land southeast of Williams Lake. There are 15 trails in the forest and they can be used to cross-country ski and snowshoe during winter months. Many of the trails have brochures adding to the experience.

Alexis Creek Cross-Country Ski Trails (Map 27/E5)

Near Alexis Creek, there are four looping trails totaling approximately 10 km (6 mi). You will climb about 200 metres (650 ft) to the highest point of the system. The two most popular loops are Gorby Killer and Schmidt, but there are a number of trails that loop and interweave, making this a great area to explore. These trails are usually track-set and cleared by community volunteers. Snowshoers, hikers and mountain bikers can also explore the area. The trails are located 2 km north of Alexis Creek on Stum Lake Road.

Bella Coola Area Trails (Map 22/D1)

The Bella Coola area offers some great hiking trails, many of which can be used for cross-country skiing and snowshoeing in winter months. Some of the trails include: Clayton Falls, Gray Jay/Blue Jay Lake, M. Gurr Lake, Medby Rock Lookout, Odegaard Falls/Nusatsum River Trail, Saloompt Forest, Schoolhouse Mountain Falls and the Snooka Creek Trail system. Most of these trails can be found with descriptions in the Trails section of this book.

Bell Mountain Ski Trails (Map 59/F4)

The main trailhead to the Bell Mountain Trails can be found by driving to Bell Mountain Road, which is 8 km west of McBride. Turn south off highway 16 and follow the road for 5 km. There is parking and trail signs with a ski cabin and maps nearby. The trail system is regularly groomed and track-set, and offers over 30 km (18.6 mi) of easy to difficult trails. The trails are colour-coded to indicate the level of difficulty. The system traverses a mix of wooded and open areas, with a number of fine viewpoints of the valley below. The cabin at the trailhead is also home to a firepit and outhouses. In addition, the Bell Mountain Trail, Dore River Trail, Eagle Valley Trail and Ozalenka Trail offer backcountry ski opportunities.

Big Bar Ski Trails (Map 6/A3)

Found northwest of Clinton, 6 km down the Big Bar Road, this large trail is utilized year-round. The well maintained trails lead through the forest and even offer views of the Mable Range in the southwest section. Sitting over 1,100 metres (3,600 ft) in elevation, snow is often more plentiful than on most other trails in the region. Volunteers from the Clinton Snow Jockey Club groom approximately 25 km (15.5 mi) of trails for cross-country skiing, plus there are 25 km of backcountry trails. Snowshoeing is possible here. There are route maps as well as shelters with fire pits and outhouses scattered around the system, and trail donations are requested.

Bouchie Lake Trails (Map 42/D1)

With money from Forest Renewal BC, the trails around Bouchie Lake have been upgraded. Located on the Nazko Road/Highway 59, northwest of Quesnel, the area offers both backcountry skiing and snowshoeing. The Claymine Trails are popular with snowshoers.

Bowron Lakes (Map 58/B5–59/A7)

If you want a challenge, you can traverse the 108 km (67 mi) circuit around the Bowron Lakes during winter. The frozen lakes and portage trails can be turned into a spectacular four or five day trip to Lynx Creek Cabin, or into a week and a half long trip around the entire canoe circuit. The area is rarely visited in the winter, and, while you will have to break trail for most if not all of the trip, it is worth it for the scenery and the solitude. The remote route has some dangerous thin sections, especially on Indianpoint Lake. A guide is recommended.

Bull Mountain Ski Trails (Map 29/B4)

You can find the Bull Mountain ski area 16 km north of Williams Lake off the west side of Highway 97. There is a posted trail map available at the parking area to help you choose which trail to travel. At Bull Mountain there are 28 km (17 mi) of trails that are groomed by snowcat for cross-country skiing (skate and classic) by the Williams Lake Cross-Country Ski Club. Two trail loops totalling 3.5 km are lighted for night skiing, and there are even designated dog trails. Visit the club website at www.bullmountain.ca for additional details.

> Note that when travelling in the backcountry, avalanches are always a danger. Visit www.avalanche.ca for current conditions, and be prepared with both avalanche knowledge and safety equipment to help make your visit to the mountains safe.

Canim Lake (Map 19/A1–C1)

Located 58 km west of 100 Mile House is Canim Lake. This popular summer fishing area offers great cross-country skiing in winter for those wanting to create their own path. Canim Lake is 37 km (23 mi) long and offers a large backcountry touring area. There are lodges at Canim Lake and at some of the nearby lakes that are open year-round.

Corner Lake Ski Trails (Map 30/C3)

Just south of the village of Horsefly, the Corner Lake Trails can be found off the Woodjam Road. From the parking area, the track-set trails meander 13.5 km (8.4 mi) through forest cover and along the Horsefly River.

Cornish Mountain Recreation Area (Map 57/G6)

Located next to the town of Wells, this popular recreation area has 25 km (15.5 mi) on groomed and ungroomed trails. The longest trail is the 17 km (10.5 mi) Cornish Mountain Loop, which has some long, sustained uphill sections, as well as some fast (and difficult) downhill sections. There are two other trails, the 4 km (2.4 mi) One Mile Lake Trail and the 7 km (4 mi) Coronado Loop Trail. For adventure seekers, the Sugar Creek Loop and Devil's Eyebrow are longer loops with fantastic views of the surrounding area.

Couchin Lake Ski Trails (Map 13/F2)

Not far from the town of Tatla Lake, volunteers maintain 30 km (18 mi) of groomed and signed trails. Turn south off of Highway 20 onto Tatlayoko Road and follow for approximately 17 km to the trailhead. The trails are located north of Cochin Lake and southeast of Lunch Lake. In the summer the trails can be used for hiking or mountain biking.

Dore River Ski Trails (Map 59/F4)

The Dore River Ski Trails encompass approximately 8 km (5 mi) of rustic trails just west of McBride. These trails are sometimes track-set as snow and weather permit. Found close to the Bell Mountain system, which offers an additional 30 km (18.6 mi) of groomed trails, there is no shortage of trails to explore in this scenic area. Both systems offer family-friendly terrain with easy access to the parking lots.

Hallis Lake Ski Trails (Map 42/F2)

The Hallis Lake Ski Trails are maintained by the Cariboo Ski Touring Club. These well-maintained multi-use trails are located just east of Quesnel via the Quesnel Hydraulic Road. There are multiple loops to choose from, ranging from 2.5 km (1.6 mi) to 16 km (10 mi) and more! There is also high quality Nordic skiing and a 3.5 km (2.2 mi) lit trail. Snowshoers can enjoy a 6 km (3.8 mi) and a 2.8 km (1.8 mi) loop as well. In the dry months, Hallis Lake is a great place for family hiking or biking. Full details about the trails and the club can be found on their website at www.caribooski.ca.

Homathko Icefield (Map 1/E4)

While a direct north-south crossing of the Homathko Icefield offers skiers the shortest possible crossing of the Coast Mountains, it is still a challenging two-week (minimum) trip. Other trips in the Homathko area are a two-day trip up Mount Tatlow and a weeklong trip alongside Chilko Lake. This is one of the largest icefields in the Coast Mountain Range, with an area of over 2,000 km^2 (770 mi^2). It is located between Chilko Lake and the Homathko River with an expanse of ice that stretches about 30 km (19 mi) across. Although this area is quite popular, it is very isolated and the difficult access makes it an expedition area for experienced mountaineers only.

Hush Lake Ski Trails (Map 56/F6)

The Hush Lake Trails are located 24 km north of Quesnel at the rest area off the west side of Highway 97. There is a collection of 25 km (15.5 mi) of trails that are regarded as moderate in difficulty. The track-set trails see regular use throughout the winter by both skiers and snowshoers.

Lower Lake Trails (Map 18/E3)

East of 100 Mile House on Back Valley Road, winter enthusiasts can explore 12 km (7.5 mi) of track-set trails. A trail map and warm up hut are found at the parking area. The relatively scenic trails pass through forest cover and along the shores of both Lillyleaf Lake and Lower Lake. Other recreational ski trails in the area include a 20 km marathon loop and a 5.5 km marathon and downtown connector both constructed by the 100 Mile Nordics Ski Society Volunteers. Depending on snow conditions the trails may be in use from early December through to the end of March.

Monarch Icefield (Map 23/A4–9/E2)

Partially inside Tweedsmuir Park, this large icefield can be accessed in about three days from the Ape Lake area to the north. South of this icefield is an even larger icefield, the Ha-iltzuk Icefield. Both are destinations for experienced backcountry skiers only. The Monarch Icefield is a heavily glaciated area, surrounded by deep canyons; it is also known to have some of the worst weather in the Coast Range, with almost 4 metres (13 ft) of rain a year. When that is translated into snow, it will bury almost anything and can keep skiers tent-bound for days on end. Plan ahead!

Mount Murray Area (Map 58/A6)

Found near Barkerville, Mount Murray is a popular backcountry skiing area for experienced skiers. The Cariboo Ski Touring Club operates huts in the area, and access is via the Jubilee Creek or Yellowhawk Trails. The Jubilee Trail is a moderately easy, 9.5 km (5.9 mi) trail that follows an old logging road, climbing 668 metres (2,190 ft) to Mount Murray. From the peak, you can return the way you came or connect with the Yellowhawk Trail for an alternative route back. The Yellowhawk Trail travels through forests and visits the alpine peaks of Mount Murray, Mount Greenbury and Mount Waverley. The 8.4 km (5.3 mi) round trip has an elevation gain of 605 metres (1,985 ft). Both these trails are relatively well signed en route. Also be wary of avalanche conditions in the alpine areas.

In addition, there is an 8 km (5 mi) unmaintained trail on the Bowron Lake Road, 6 km from Barkerville. The gentle grade makes this trail a lot easier to explore than the mountain trails.

Mount Timothy Ski Hill Area (Map 18/D1)

Mount Timothy is an undiscovered gem with deep dry powder snow, a well-equipped lodge and modern chairlifts with over 35 runs for every skill level. Located northeast of Lac La Hache, the mountain receives a healthy amount of powder in an average season. Cross-country skiers will also find 24 km (14.9 mi) of well-maintained trails in the area. Visit their website at www.skitimothy.com for more details.

Mount Waddington Area (Map 12/E7)

Home to (and named after) BC's largest mountain, this area is popular with hardcore ski tourists and ski mountaineers. Trips can range from four days to the challenging month-long venture along the entire divide from the Homathko to the Klinakline Rivers. Possible destinations include Nirvana Pass, Razor Creek, Franklin Glacier, Tellot

Glacier and the Whitemantle Range. There are a number of outfitters to get skiers into the area but it is advised that only experienced skiers with advanced intermediate skill levels and overnight winter camping experience head here.

Puntzi Lake Ski Trails (Map 26/C5)

Located about three and a half hours west of Williams Lake on Highway 20 is Puntzi Lake. This area has plenty of cross-country ski trails and excellent terrain for snowmobiling. In the winter the lake freezes allowing for skating or ice fishing. There is a 2.6 km (1.6 mi) groomed ski track and many other trails to explore whether snowshoeing or snowmobiling.

South Chilcotin Mountains Park (Maps 3, 4)

The sprawling network of over 200 km (125 mi) of trails turns into a backcountry ski/snowshoe paradise in winter. None of the trails are groomed, but snowmobilers follow a few of the trails, including the Gun Creek and Warner Pass Trails. This makes breaking snow a lot easier on skis. The other major creek valleys (Tyaughton and Relay) are also easier to ski as they gently climb towards the mountains. Taylor Basin is a popular destination since there is a cabin at the pass.

Red Coach Trails (Map 18/D4)

Part of the elaborate trail system around 100 Mile House, this system is found at the Red Coach Inn at the north end of town near First Street. The Inn offers 11 km (7 mi) of trails groomed for cross-country ski, but the more ambitious can sample more of the 150 km (93 mi) network around 100 Mile House.

Tatla Lake Trails (Map 13/E1–25/E7)

A series of loop trails that total about 30 km (18 mi) in length are found between Tatla Lake and Martin Lake. Look for trailhead signs 1.5 km off the highway on Graham Road. The longest trail, the Race Route Circuit, stretches 17.2 km (10.5 mi), while the Tatla Lake Annual Ski Challenge features an 11.5 km (7 mi) loop and a 6 km (3.7 mi) children's challenge loop. Snowshoeing and summer exploration are possible.

Ten Mile Lake (Map 56/F7)

Located just north of Quesnel on Highway 97, Ten Mile Lake Provincial park offers 10 km (6 mi) of ungroomed but well-travelled cross-country ski trails. There are also snowshoeing opportunities and, since the lake freezes over, ice skating and ice fishing too. The road into the park is ploughed to the first parking lot.

> *To maximize comfort, be sure to dress in layers so that you can peel off or add clothing as needed.*

Troll Mountain Ski Resort (Map 57/D7)

Located 44 km east of Quesnel en route to Barkerville, Troll Mountain is a good-sized ski area that caters to families. There are four surface lifts and 520 metres (1,700 ft) of vertical terrain to explore. Most runs are for intermediate skiers but there are lots of opportunities for beginners as well. The mountain offers two terrain parks with one kilometre of jumps and box rails plus lots and lots of trails for cross-country skiing and snowshoeing. In total there are 34 named runs. Visit the resort's website at www.trollresort.com.

Tweedsmuir Park (Map 37/G6–38/A7)

Volunteers from the Tweedsmuir Ski Club maintain a circuit of 30 km (18.6 mi) of trails around 'The Hill' on Highway 20, which is approximately 40 km west of Anahim Lake. Known as the Heckman Pass Cross-Country Ski Trails, they are often ready by mid-November and lead through the woods and open meadows. At the Rainbow Range trailhead, there are another 15 km of set cross-country trails. Although there is no charge to use these trails, locals are asked to join the ski club and a donation box is available at the eastern trailhead for visitors. Visit the ski club website at www.tweedsmuirskiclub.com for trail maps and more.

Adding to the fun is a small downhill ski area. Serviced by a tow rope, it is located approximately 3 km from the parking lot at the Rainbow Range. The Tweedsmuir Ski Club operates a cabin close to the downhill ski area that can be reserved by calling (250) 982-2231. Free winter camping is also permitted in the Rainbow Range parking lot.

THE CARIBOO
BRITISH COLUMBIA

Cariboo – Geoff Moore

Clear Lake – Thomas Drasdauskis

Barkerville – Thomas Drasdauskis

The Cariboo plateau stretches between the Fraser River in the west and the Cariboo Mountains in the east. Steeped in BC's history, the region once served as the heart of the gold rush in the 1860s. Gold seekers from far and wide traveled to the Cariboo in search of the land's treasures, resulting in a stream of towns cropping up across the plateau. The North Cariboo was once the most densely settled and powerful district in BC's interior. Today, ghost towns whisper of the Cariboo's rich past, and the National Historic Site of Barkerville brings history alive.

Across the Cariboo, adventurers will discover wild stretches of land. In the south, grasslands roll with open meadows, lush forests of aspen and pine, cool, deep lakes and semi-arid desert. In the Central Cariboo, humid rainforests tumble into lava-formed canyons, and traveling north, you can visit the major goldfields that first put this part of BC on the map. The Northern Secwepemc First Nations inhabit the region with deep roots, and even today the pioneer spirit of the Cariboo is alive and thriving.

Check out the BC Cowboy Hall of Fame, and the famous annual Williams Lake Stampede, held in the Cariboo's largest community. To further sample the frontier flavour, visit one of the area's famous cattle and guest ranches. The adventure is yours

to take here, with a vast network of hiking, biking and walking trails, opportunities for snowshoeing, cross-country skiing and snowmobiling in the winter, and exciting geocaches, fishing lakes and wildlife viewing hot spots. The grasslands of the

SUPER, NATURAL BRITISH COLUMBIA ✦ CANADA

Cariboo are home to the endangered American badger, and throughout the land you will hear the enchanting call of the loon.

Mighty rivers rush throughout the Cariboo, with the Fraser and Quesnel meeting in the town

of Quesnel. Cast a line into their waters for an unforgettable fishing experience, or hike the banks of the Fraser in Lillooet. Try mountain biking the epic trails in Williams Lake, or hit the multi-use trails of Wells for a variety of expeditions. Trace the footsteps of the gold rush pioneers as you follow the Cariboo Wagon Road, with pioneer cabins and historic roadhouses to visit like the Hat Creek Ranch, 108 Mile Ranch, Cottonwood House and the famous sites of Barkerville.

With sweeping mountain landscapes untouched by man, rolling forest floors that are ripe for exploration, and a wealth of historical highlights waiting to be stumbled upon, the Cariboo region is one of BC's most exciting adventure playgrounds.

EXPLORE THE CARIBOO
Highways 97, 26, 24, 99 and the Trans Canada take you through the Cariboo.

WELCOME
TO
Lillooet
GUARANTEED RUGGED

The town of Lillooet appears about 240 km (150 mi) up the British Columbia Railway line from Vancouver. Carved into the rugged, rocky and mountainous terrain of the South Chilcotin, Lillooet graces the shores of the Fraser River and bursts with opportunities for outdoor adventure. Once a gold rush era town, the community now bustles with activity. With a number of restaurants, bed and breakfasts, campsites and other lodging options, Lillooet opens a welcoming door to visitors.

The culture here pulses with appreciation for the great outdoors. Over a hundred geocaches lie hidden within the landscape. Every July, the Lillooet Apricot Tsaqwen Festival celebrates local culture with live music and delicious local eats. Experience the St'át'imc First Nations culture with a Xwísten Experience Tour, and appreciate the ancient customs of the region's first inhabitants. You will find Lillooet's Museum and Visitor Centre housed in an old Anglican church.

Stroll along the Jade Walk on Main Street and behold the beautiful jade sculptures. Follow the tracks of the Rocky Mountaineer and ride the Kaoham rail along the shores of Seton Lake. Dip your feet into the majestic Fraser River as you comb the rocks, or hit the trails and discover a world of mountain biking, hiking and snowmobiling opportunities. Rivers and lakes gleam with boating spots, and Lillooet's trademark steep mountains create an ice climber's delight during winter months.

When the snow falls, embrace the outdoors with heli-skiing and snowmobiling. In warmer months, indulge in a round of golf at the Lillooet Sheep Pasture Golf Course. Kick back and savour a taste at the Fort Berens Estate Winery, where vineyards sprawl across a sagebrush-covered bench at the foot of the mountains in the Fraser Canyon. The sandy soil of Lillooet lends itself to premium grapes.

From scenic road trips winding along the Fraser, to music-filled parks in the heart of the community, to rugged backcountry expeditions, there is something for everyone in Lillooet!

> **The culture here pulses with appreciation for the great outdoors.**

TO LEARN MORE, CONTACT

Lillooet Visitor Centre
790 Main Street, Lillooet, BC V0K 1V0
Ph: 250-256-4308
Email: lillmuseum@cablelan.net
www.lillooetbc.ca

 From top to bottom: Pavilion Lake – Brad Kasselman; Pavilion Lake – Brad Kasselman; Gun Lake Trails - Brad Kasselman; Tyaughton Lake Trails – Brad Kasselman.

WELCOME TO South Cariboo

YEAR-ROUND ADVENTURE

With the mighty Fraser River slicing through the middle of this rolling plateau, the South Cariboo stretches with breathtaking landscapes. This is a region with thousands of years of First Nations history, followed by the booming expansion of the gold rush era, with fur traders and ranchers settling in to call the South Cariboo home. Cowboy culture reigns supreme; across the region's rolling grasslands, horses trot along well-developed trails, and guest ranches offer day trips to visitors of all skill levels.

You will find a number of accommodations in South Cariboo. Follow the stagecoach path of historic travelers as you drive along Highway 97. Along the way, discover historic roadhouses approximately every 21 km (13 mi). Some have developed into villages and towns, while others have withered away. A BC Heritage Site, the Hat Creek Ranch is one of the Cariboo's largest remaining roadhouses; it appears on the hills 11 km (7 mi) north of Cache Creek, at the junction with Highway 99.

As you explore South Cariboo you will encounter a diverse selection of wildlife. Anglers revel in the boast-worthy fishing along Highway 24, where hundreds of lakes teem with rainbow trout, lake trout and kokanee. Whether you browse a museum in Clinton, behold log structures in 100 Mile House, canoe the waterways of Canim Lake or settle into a cozy lodge in Lac la Hache, your explorations of South Cariboo are sure to transport you to the days of the Wild West.

> **As you explore South Cariboo you will encounter a diverse selection of wildlife.**

COMMUNITIES

100 Mile House

The main service centre for smaller communities in the region, 100 Mile House holds the title as "Handcrafted Log Home Capital of North America." Here you can visit the 108 Mile Ranch Historic Site, which boasts the largest log barn of its kind left in Canada. Take the whole family to Centennial Park, where you can go for an easy 1.5 km (0.9 mi) stroll to picturesque Bridge Creek Falls. Jaunt through the 100 Mile Marsh Wildlife Sanctuary, where you will find a variety of bird species, or visit the world's tallest pair of cross-country skis, located in the visitor centre of this Nordic skiing haven.

100 Mile House is big enough to offer every service you may require, but small enough to offer a friendly, welcome and relaxed atmosphere. To rest your head, you will find quaint B&Bs to hotels and motels that will be sure to suit your liking, as well as a municipal campground and RV sites. In any season you'll find 100 Mile House the right place to be.

From top to bottom: 100 Mile House Visitor Centre - Chris Harris; Green Lake - Chris Harris; Bridge Creek - Chris Harris; 100 Mile House - Chris Harris.

THE FISHING HIGHWAY
OUTDOOR PARADISE

24 B.C.

WATERFALLS GALORE

RECREATIONAL OPPORTUNITIES **YEAR ROUND**

WINTER ADVENTURE **MT. TIMOTHY**

Clinton

This unique town has its roots in cattle ranching, soap-soda and Epsom salt distribution, and sawmilling. Today, Clinton offers local heritage buildings, a museum, antique shops and guest ranches. Wilderness enthusiasts delight in the geographical attractions of Clinton. The "Grand Canyon of the North," created by glacial melt cutting into lava flows, appears in the backcountry west of town along the Fraser River. Visitors can go horseback riding, pan for gold and cross-country ski.

Lone Butte

This peaceful village appears at the west end of Highway 24, aka the famous Fishing Highway. It makes a great place to stay for touring the hundreds of abundant fishing lakes along the Fishing Highway and the guest ranches along the way. Angle for rainbow trout, lake trout and kokanee in the Interlakes, challenge yourself to a hike up the volcano plug that gives the village its name, go horseback riding on scenic trails, or simply relax in the splendid wilderness of Lone Butte.

Canim Lake

Canim Lake is one of the largest lakes in the Cariboo, at 37 km (23 mi) long. It lies nestled amidst rolling forests, meadows and mountains, with a sprawling pebble beach along the shore and a number of resorts. This is an outdoor lover's playground, with opportunities for hiking, horseback riding, canoeing, boating, fishing, snowmobiling, skiing and snowshoeing. Marvel at the sights of the volcanic cones near Spanish Creek and the ancient pictographs and pit houses at Deception Creek.

Lac La Hache

This charming town rests along the popular Lac la Hache, where anglers, power boaters and water skiers flock for waterway adventures. Steeped in the history of the Secwepemc and Chilcotin First Nations, the lake was once named Kumatakwa, Queen of the Waters. In the winter, the frozen lake makes an excellent ice fishing spot. Head up Mount Timothy for skiing and snowboarding, or simply enjoy the sunny winter days of Lac la Hache. Along the 19 km (12 mi) lake shoreline, visitors will find a vast selection of fishing resorts, ranches and vacation homes.

 MAP

TO LEARN MORE, CONTACT

100 Mile House Visitor Centre
155 Airport Road, 100 Mile House, BC V0K 2E0
Ph: 250-395-5353
Email: southcaribootourism@dist100milehouse.bc.ca
southcaribootourism.ca

 From top to bottom: Clinton - Chris Harris; Flat Lake - Birgit Bienek; Canim Falls - Birgit Bienek; Mt. Timothy - Chris Harris.

WELCOME TO Williams Lake
HUB CITY OF THE CARIBOO

Situated at the junction of Highways 97 and 20, one of the Cariboo Chilcotin's primary crossroads since the early 1900s, Williams Lake is the Hub City of the Cariboo. At 11,200 city residents and nearly 30,000 people in the total service area, Williams Lake is the largest community in the region and the centre of it all.

Hailed as a "mountain biking mecca" with some of BC's top wilderness biking, the region offers three distinct riding areas: Westsyde Ridge, Desous Mountain and Fox Mountain. Try your hand at everything from double track beginner runs to challenging cross-country tracks and thrilling downhill rides.

For a more leisurely outdoor pursuit, sample one of Williams Lake's three golf courses. Or get moving on the popular River Valley Trail, a 12 km (7.5 mi) gravel trek that travels from downtown to the mighty Fraser River. Boasting useful amenities along the way, the River Valley Trail makes a great option for walking, running, mountain biking or horseback riding.

Wildlife enthusiasts will revel in the variety of creatures that inhabit the landscapes of Williams Lake. A nature sanctuary on Scout Island houses a wide array of birds and small animals. Here you will also find trails and a beach, a nature house, picnic grounds and a boat launch. In the heart of downtown, Kiwanis Park offers fields, tennis courts, a spray park and adventure playground, picnic areas and more, to help you enjoy the outdoors without even leaving the city!

History buffs will appreciate the rich First Nations history of Williams Lake. Named after Chief William, the region once served as a meeting place for the Secwepemc First Nation. Downtown you will discover beautiful galleries showcasing local and First Nations art. A two-storey log building, with ample RV parking, houses the Tourism Discovery Centre. The famous Williams Lake Stampede held every July breathes life into the city's Wild West culture. And be sure to visit the Museum of the Cariboo Chilcotin, home to the BC Cowboy Hall of Fame.

A must-see stop along your journey through the Cariboo, Williams Lake is waiting for you!

> **" Hailed as a 'mountain biking mecca' with some of BC's top wilderness biking. "**

MAP 29

TO LEARN MORE, CONTACT
Williams Lake Visitor Centre
1660 South Broadway, Williams Lake, BC V2G 2V8
Ph: 250-392-5025 Toll Free: 1-877-967-5253
Email: visitors@telus.net
www.tourismwilliamslake.com

 From top to bottom: Williams Lake - City of Williams Lake; Fraser River - City of Williams Lake; Fox Mountain Trails - John Wellburn; Springhouse - City of Williams Lake.

WELCOME
TO
Quesnel
GOLD PAN CITY

Known as the Gold Pan City, Quesnel sits at the confluence of the Fraser and Quesnel Rivers. It is the main urban centre of the North Cariboo, situated between Prince George and Williams Lake along the main route to Northern BC and the Yukon. With a long history steeped in the Chentsit'hala Carrier First Nation, the town was once a hub for gold seekers, explorers and settlers. Today, Quesnel continues to attract those in pursuit of adventure.

Visitors will discover a haven for urban green spaces in the Gold Pan City. Alex Fraser Park, the Petunia Mile and the Heritage Rose Garden offer city dwellers a taste of the region's beautiful wilderness, and personal walking guides are available to help uncover Quesnel's outdoor treasures. For the more adventurous, a world of mountain biking, camping, fishing, snowmobiling and hiking opportunities flourish around Quesnel. The scenic, 5 km (3 mi) Riverfront Trail System is a lovely loop that was built in 1990. Kilometre 0 sits at the confluence of the city's two great rivers, in Ceal Tingley Park.

At the town's north entrance you will be greeted by a 5.5 m (18 ft) high gold pan, a nod to Quesnel's rich history. Stop by the Visitor Centre and step into history with the Quesnel and District Museum and Archives, which contains North America's most significant collections of Chinese artifacts. Find your way to 30 different heritage sites in and around Quesnel, including the original 1862 Hudson's Bay Company Trading Post. Soak up the cowboy culture of this Cariboo town at the Quesnel Rodeo, BC's largest amateur rodeo. Held during the Billy Barker Days festival, the rodeo is accompanied by family-friendly shows, concerts and parades.

The city of Quesnel offers a number of amenities to visitors, including restaurants, a variety of accommodations and guided tours. For the backcountry adventurer, wilderness camping spots crop up throughout Quesnel's sweeping landscape. From Quesnel's living history to its unbeatable outdoor adventure, the Gold Pan City is a definite must-see!

> **... Quesnel continues to attract those in pursuit of adventure.**

MAP 42

TO LEARN MORE, CONTACT

Quesnel Visitor Centre
703 Carson Ave, Quesnel, BC V2J 2B6
Ph: 250-992-8716
Email: qvisitor@quesnelbc.com
www.tourismquesnel.com

From top to bottom: Pinnacles Provincial Park - Quesnel Tourism; Riverfront Trail - Quesnel Tourism; Bouchie Lake - Quesnel Tourism; Comet Creek Falls - Patty Morgan.

WELCOME TO Wells

MORE THAN JUST GOLD

The charming town of Wells lies cradled in the foothills of the Cariboo Mountains near the end of Highway 26. The community of 236 year-round residents is known for its art scene, historic gold tours and exciting outdoor recreation opportunities, including a vast network of multi-use trails. In Wells, visitors will discover hundreds of kilometres of scenic trails for everything from hiking and mountain biking in summer, to cross-country skiing and snowmobiling in winter.

Built as a company town for Fred Wells' Gold Quartz Mine during the 1930s, Wells once served as a major centre of northern BC. This small mountain town boasted of riches, and even today people continue to try to 'strike it rich' on the nearby creeks. Take your pick from a variety of accommodations, ranging from cozy bed and breakfasts, motels and RV parks, to hotels and swanky lakefront cabins. Visit the restored heritage buildings of Wells, such as the Wells Hotel and Sunset Theatre.

The Island Mountain Arts Society arts school serves as a centre for local creatives, and every summer the ArtsWells Festival of All Things Art draws visitors from far and wide to enjoy a weekend of music, performance and visual arts. 8 km (5 mi) east of Wells you will encounter historic Barkerville, one of western Canada's most famous tourist attractions. Travel back through time as you step into the living history of this preserved heritage town, once a booming centre during BC's gold rush era.

When it's time to get outside, hit the trails on the popular 7 Summits Bike and Hike Trek, or paddle the Bowron Chain of Lakes. During winter, you can cross-country ski through the Mount Murray Area. Be sure to try dog sledding along the network of sledder trails that overlap with the Trans Canada Snowmobile Trail, for a unique northern experience. Hiking opportunities range from easy city trails to nearby backcountry expeditions – the choice is yours for adventure in Wells!

" ... visitors will discover hundreds of kilometres of scenic trails for everything from hiking and mountain biking in summer, to cross-country skiing and snowmobiling in winter "

MAP57

TO LEARN MORE, CONTACT

Wells Visitor Centre
11900 Hwy 26, Wells, BC V0K 2R0
Ph: 250-994-2323
Email: info@wellsbarkervilletrails.com
www.wells.ca

 From top to bottom: Wells Outskirts - Thomas Drasdauskis; Two Sisters Mountain - Thomas Drasdauskis; Mt. Agnes - Rodney Ricketts; Wells-Barkerville Winter Connector - Thomas Drasdauskis.

WELCOME TO Barkerville

BC'S LIVING GOLD RUSH TOWN

When Billy Barker struck gold in a Cariboo creek in 1862, little did he know that a hundred years later, one of Canada's most significant historic sites would flourish in his name. Declared a National Historic Site of Canada in 1924 and a BC Heritage Site in 1958, Barkerville has been a cherished attraction for nearly a century. The cluster of buildings along a mountain creek was once the biggest boom town of the Cariboo Gold Rush. Today, Barkerville is an exciting living history site full of things to do.

Located just 8 km (5 mi) east of Wells, Barkerville offers all the amenities you need: merchants, restaurants, bed and breakfasts and facilities. Enter the town as you are greeted by interpreters dressed as historical characters. These colourful characters line the streets of Barkerville, going about their business in authentic gold rush era buildings that are perfectly preserved.

The historic town contains 135 restored buildings, a bonafide Chinatown from the 1800s, an authentic Cornish waterwheel and a photo studio. Attractions include live theatre, cemetery tours and worship services in Barkerville's beautiful preserved Anglican church, led by an historical interpreter of Reverend Reynard.

Spanning the region from Barkerville to nearby Wells and Richfield, hundreds of kilometres of multi-use trails weave through diverse landscapes. Hike the historic 1870s Cariboo Waggon Road between Stanley and Barkerville, a route that was once considered the "eighth wonder of the world". The 17 km (10.5 mi) Cornish Mountain Loop also makes for an invigorating trek. Every August, mountain bikers flock to the epic 50 km (31 mi) Barkerville Boneshaker route – a network that can be explored year-round by a variety of outdoor enthusiasts. For more heart-racing bike tracks, check out the 45 km (28 mi) Sugar Creek loop and the scenic 62 km (39 mi) Atan-Chisel Lake Loop.

Barkerville offers an experience unlike any other. Just park the car and leave the modern world behind as you pursue wild adventures and gold!

> **Declared a National Historic Site of Canada in 1924 and a BC Heritage Site in 1958, Barkerville has been a cherished attraction for nearly a century.**

TO LEARN MORE, CONTACT

Barkerville Historic Town
14301 Hwy 26, Barkerville Hwy, Barkerville, BC V0K 1B0
Ph: 250-994-3332
Email: barkerville@barkerville.ca
www.barkerville.ca

MAP 58

 From top to bottom: Barkerville - Thomas Drasdauskis; Barkerville - Thomas Drasdauskis; Barkerville - Thomas Drasdauskis; Barkerville - Chris Sharpe.

WELCOME TO
Likely

THE CARIBOO'S WILDERNESS HAVEN

Likely is a small, rural community nestled in the foothills of the Cariboo Mountains. The town sits at the junction of Quesnel River and the 100 km (62 mi) long Quesnel Lake, the deepest fjord lake in North America and part of the only inland temperate rainforest in the world. Best known as a part of BC's historic Gold Rush Trail, Likely was once called Quesnelle Dam, after the dam built in 1898 to mine the river. In 1923, the town's name was changed to honour a well-known prospector at the time, John "Plato" Likely.

The community celebrates the rich outdoor opportunities that exist in and around Likely. Here you will meet laidback folks, eager to share all that there is to do and see. Begin your adventures in Cedar Point Provincial Park, where past mining ventures have left a network of old trails to be explored. The park houses the Cedar City Mining Museum, where a visitor centre offers a wealth of information for tourists.

Hikers won't want to miss the Cameron Ridge Trail, a gorgeous 14 km (8.7 mi) trek that overlooks the watershed of the Penfold Valley. The easy trail climbs along the Cameron Ridge to the Cariboo Mountains lookout, delivering breathtaking views of Quesnel Lake. Around Gavin Lake, a network of trails lead through picturesque forest landscapes, and north of town, Ghost Lake provides pristine locations for camping, fishing and viewing majestic waterfalls.

For a taste of history, take a self-guided tour of the ghost town of Quesnel Forks. Once one of the most populated regions of mainland BC, today Quesnel Forks whispers of days gone by, with historic buildings, aged cottonwood trees and an old cemetery. Low mobility trails take you along the Cariboo River and through the heritage village, and Quesnel and Cariboo rivers offer world class kayaking. While in Likely, be sure to visit the epic Quesnel Lake, with enough bays, islands, lookout points and fishing spots for a lifetime of exploration.

From paddling, boating, fishing and hunting, to craft fairs, berry picking, birdwatching and road touring, there's always Likely something to do!

> ❝ Hikers won't want to miss the Cameron Ridge Trail, a gorgeous 14 km (8.7 mi) trek that overlooks the watershed of the Penfold Valley. ❞

MAP

TO LEARN MORE, CONTACT
Likely Community Chamber of Commerce
6281 Rosette Lake Road, Likely, BC V0L 1N0
Ph: 250-790-2342
Email: likelycommunity@gmail.com
www.likely-bc.ca

 From top to bottom: Quesnel River - Cathie Wright; Quesnel Forks - Cathie Wright; Mitchell River - Terry Borkowski; Mitchell River - Terry Borkowski.

THE CHILCOTIN
BRITISH COLUMBIA

Chilcotin – Geoff Moore

Chilcotin – Geoff Moore

Chilcotin – Thomas Drasdauskis

The Chilcotin region of BC stretches westward from the Cariboo plateau. Named for the Tsilhqot'in First Nation, the moniker means "people of the red ochre river." The vast area crosses a wide plateau with mountainous terrain west of the Fraser River. The pristine wilderness of BC reigns supreme in the Chilcotin, with few roads, little industry and small sprinklings of human settlements, mostly Tsilhqot'in and Dakelh First Nations.

Backcountry travelers delight in all that there is to be explored in the Chilcotin. Most of the region is accessible via Highway 20, aka the Freedom Road. The original highway that first opened up the central coast, the Freedom Road takes you through grassy plateaus, sweeping meadows, deep canyons and towering mountain peaks, including Mount Waddington, BC's highest peak at 4,016 m (13,176 ft) tall.

Wild creatures roam throughout the area in abundance, with free range cattle, moose and bears appearing along the road, and hundreds of species gracing the untouched forests. Encounter Canada's largest population of bighorn sheep, rare white pelicans, trumpeter swans, lynx, wolves, mountain caribou and hundreds of wild horses.

There is no shortage of outdoor recreation adventures in the Chilcotin. Enjoy aerial sightseeing over the impressive Homathko ice field, south of

Tatlayoko Lake, or go heli-skiing down the epic slopes of the South Chilcotin Mountains. Lose yourself in the vast wilderness of Ts'yl-os and Tweedsmuir Provincial Parks, or rush along the Chilcotin River for one of the most challenging whitewater runs on the

SUPER, NATURAL BRITISH COLUMBIA ♦CANADA

continent. Thrill-seekers can tackle the White Mile of the Chilko River – the longest continuous stretch of class 3-plus whitewater in North America.

Charter float planes will transport you into remote and scenic lakes in the West Chilcotin. Indulge in some of BC's best fly fishing on the

Blackwater River, or hike the Charlotte Alplands area around stunning Charlotte Lake. Surrounded by a mystical mountain backdrop, the lake will leave you speechless.

The culture of the Chilcotin is unmistakably cowboy. Saddle up and immerse yourself in the Wild West at one of the region's numerous working ranches. Many ranches offer pack trips and trail rides, and a number of riding trails wind throughout the landscape. In addition to tourism, ranching is the Chilcotin's primary cachet.

From the hush of the region's astounding wilderness, to First Nations history and the cowboy way of life, the Chilcotin is truly a place to get away from it all!

EXPLORE CHILCOTIN
Travel HW 20 from Anahim Lake to Riske Creek. Explore the plateau and the Chilcotin range.

WELCOME TO
Bridge River
VALLEY
GATEWAY TO THE SOUTH CHILCOTINS

The Bridge River Valley is a sweeping, mountainous region of the Chilcotin where 360° of wilderness await families and friends of all ages and abilities. Boosted to fame in the 1920s for its abundance of riches during the gold rush, the Valley is dotted with old gold mines amidst glistening lakes, majestic peaks and meadows filled with wildflowers. Home to several welcoming communities, the Bridge River Valley provides a launching point for a world of outdoor recreation and fun for all ages. For those seeking an escape from city living, the Bridge River Valley is only a few short hours from Vancouver with year-round access along scenic Highway 40 from Lillooet (105 km/65 mi). In May, the Hurley Forest Service Road opens and provides a short-cut for those travelling from the Lower Mainland/Vancouver area. For current road conditions, visit www.isurvivedthehurley.com.

An elaborate trail network sprawls throughout the Valley, with opportunities for hiking, biking, horseback riding, cross-country skiing and wildlife viewing. Quads, ATV's and dual sport enthusiasts can access numerous mining and forest service roads. The Bridge River Valley serves as a winter base for snowmobilers and skiers wishing to access the massive powder snowfields in the backcountry and on the Ice Cap. TLH Heliskiing operates from Tyax Lodge on Tyaughton Lake and offers dedicated helicopters to private groups of skiers.

Major trail systems exist around the communities of Gold Bridge, Bralorne, Tyaughton Lake, Gun Lake and Marshall Lake as well as in the bountiful wilderness of Big Creek Park and South Chilcotin Park. For the best trail experience, hire a local guide through Chilcotin Holidays, Tyax Adventures, Bralorne Adventure Lodge, Backcountry Snowcats or contact the Bridge River Valley Community Association directly to hook up with a local expert.

Anglers enjoy the area's deep lakes and rushing streams teeming with rainbow trout, brook trout, kokanee, Dolly Varden and whitefish. Local angling guides will show you the best spots. Wildlife abounds in both the valley and high alpine including mule deer, grizzly bears, wolves, moose, bighorn sheep and mountain goats. Please respect these creatures and their habitats by keeping a respectful distance and adhering to any non-motorized or closed access zones.

Boating, kayaking, standup paddleboarding or just lazing by the lake are all enjoyed on Gun Lake, Tyaughton Lake and Marshall Lake – bring your own gear or stay at a lodge or chalet and borrow their equipment.

Camping enthusiasts will find full service camping at Tyax Lodge, Chilcotin Holidays and in Gold Bridge and Gun Lake. Accommodation ranging from luxury lodges, guest ranches, B&B's and lakefront cabins are available. Detailed accommodation listings and contact information are available on www.bridgerivervalley.ca.

History buffs will marvel at the living stories carved into the Bridge River Valley. This area has been the home of the St'at'im'c people since time immemorial. A number of ghost towns and abandoned mining sites haunt the landscape and are often home to geocaching 'treasures'. For a more formal look at the past, check out the Haylmore Heritage Site in Gold Bridge where you can pan for gold or book a heritage tour that includes a miner's breakfast and interpretive walk along the river. The Haylmore Heritage Site is open from May to September from Thursday-Sunday and is also home to the Visitor Information Booth and Rockwall Gallery featuring the work of the Valley's many artisans and crafters.

Check out the 'Valley Vibe' on www.bridgerivervalley.ca for an up to date listing of the week's events in the Valley.

From top to bottom: Gold Bridge - Michelle Nortje; Camel Pass - Michelle Nortje; Mud Lake Trails - BRVCA; South Chilcotin Mountains Provincial Park - Mary Benson.

GOLD MINES:
THERE'S GOLD
IN THEM THAR HILLS!

SINGLE TRACK TRAILS

EXPLORE THE OUTDOORS

I SURVIVED THE HURLEY
- HURLEY RIVER RD.
- PERBERTON
- GOLDBRIDGE

COMMUNITIES

Gold Bridge

Thanks to the success of the neighbouring Bralorne Pioneer Mine, the community of Gold Bridge flourished in the 1920s. Now home to a small community of residents, it offers accommodation, groceries/hardware/BC liquor store, tire repair and fuel to visitors against a stunning backdrop of mountain peaks and rushing rivers. Outdoor enthusiasts come to the rugged mountain landscapes of Gold Bridge to pursue breathtaking glacial snowmobiling, rock hounding and sensational heli-skiing. There's even a 9-hole golf course! You can also explore ghost towns and abandoned mine sites in the area or join the fun at the annual Summerfest held each August long weekend.

Bralorne

This small community hosts a population of 60. Resting at 1,021 m (3,350 ft) at the base of Mount Ferguson, which stretches up to 2,594 m (8,510 ft), this is the highest community of the Valley. Summer hiking and mountain biking experiences are world-class. The winter season sees plenty of opportunities for sledding with hundreds of old mining trails and roads that turn into fun multi-use routes in the summer. For a taste of history, check out the Bralorne museum, church, Community Hall and abandoned mine sites and ghost towns. Don't forget to enjoy a cold beverage at the local pub in town and share stories with the locals!

Tyaughton Lake

The gorgeous Tyaughton Lake area encompasses a region at the foot of the South Chilcotin Mountains. This is a backcountry adventurer's dream, with vast hiking and biking trail networks taking you to Spruce Lake, Cinnabar Ridge, Taylor Basin, Mud Lakes and the Shulaps Range. The surrounding areas provide ample opportunity for fishing, boating, swimming, horseback riding, snowmobiling, ice skating, snowshoeing, cross-country skiing and heli-skiing. There are a number of resorts, backcountry outfitters and guided tours available. Wilderness Training Programs are also available.

Gun Lake

Gun Lake is a sparkling body of water that rests at the base of Mount Penrose, a 2,627 m (8,618 ft) peak. The lake and its surrounding region create a wealth of outdoor recreation opportunities. A series of trails begin at the scenic lake's north end and continue across to the Plateau Ponds. Gun Lake is popular for boating and angling and can be enjoyed from a number of overnight accommodation options. Winter visitors can join the fun of the annual Winterfest activities.

Marshall Lake

Marshall Lake is remote and completely unplugged – a true escape with great horseback riding, hiking and quad/dual sport trails. Please check maps and respect non-motorized zones.

MAP

TO LEARN MORE, CONTACT

Bridge River Valley Community Association
104 Haylmore Ave, Gold Bridge, BC V0K 1P0
Ph: 250-238-2534
Email: bridgerivervalley@gmail.com
www.bridgerivervalley.ca | Facebook: SouthChilcotin.ca

From top to bottom: Gun Creek Meadows - Michelle Nortje; Hurley road - Michelle Nortje; Tyaughton Lake - Michelle Nortje; Lone Goat mountains - Michelle Nortje.

WELCOME
TO
West Chilcotin

TIMELESS. INTIMATE. BEAUTIFUL.

Follow us into a land of Adventure. The spectacular Chilcotin Plateau is Cowboy Country! The West Chilcotin is steeped in the history of the Tsilhqot'in First Nation, a Northern Athabascan people, as well as the settler tradition of ranching, guiding and outfitting, and trapping.

Sprawling from Chilco Lake in the east to Heckman Pass in the west, the region contains true BC wilderness of epic proportions, like Tweedsmuir Park, one of the largest wilderness provincial parks in British Columbia. Visit the rugged Coast Mountain Range that includes Mount Waddington, the highest mountain entirely inside BC's borders and a popular destination for heli-skiing and mountaineering, or Hunlen Falls, the third highest free falling waterfall in Canada.

Ride the painted flanks of the Rainbow Mountains, noted for their excellent snow for snowmobiling and cross-country skiing or go flightseeing in a floatplane over wild, majestic peaks, like Monarch Mountain and the huge Monarch Icefield it shoulders. Go trailriding on a multi-day pack trip into the Itcha Ilgatchuz Ranges, the smooth and worn cones of old shield volcanoes that protect the grasslands, meadows, lodgepole pine forests and endless lakes of the plateau. In this country, the cattle roam, with moose, deer and caribou throughout the summer until round up in the fall, when they are still gathered up the old fashioned way: from the back of a horse.

Whether hiking, horseback riding or ATVing, experience fabulous high mountain lakes, wildflower-carpeted meadows, rolling alpine and ancient volcanic rock. Kayak or canoe our numerous lakes or try your hand at fishing for our hard fighting native rainbow trout. We have endless hiking trails, from moderate ones at lower elevations to more strenuous ones up into the alpine, where small glacial lakes sit like aqua colored jewels at the foot of mountains. Better yet, simply just relax and enjoy the quiet.

> " ... the region contains true BC wilderness of epic proportions. "

COMMUNITIES

Anahim Lake

Anahim Lake provides access to the vast Tweedsmuir Provincial Park South, where visitors can immerse themselves in true wilderness. Located 135 km (84 mi) east of Bella Coola, the region is packed with opportunities for fishing, hunting, hiking and fly-in expeditions. The annual stampede is another local favourite.

Nimpo Lake

Nimpo Lake is a go-to spot for rainbow trout anglers, as well as an attractive location for hiking, wildlife viewing, birdwatching, snowshoeing, cross-country skiing and snowmobiling. Known as "the float plane capital of BC," the region boasts a number of aerial sightseeing tours and fishing fly-ins.

 From top to bottom: Rainbow Mountains - Heidy Lenz; Anahim Lake - ResortsBC.com; Nimpo Lake – ResortsBC.com; Trumpeter Mountain - ResortsBC.com.

T R U E WILDERNESS: NATURAL WONDERS

MT. WADDINGTON 4,019 M (13,186 FT)

WORLD FAMOUS: DEAN RIVER

TRAIL RIDING: BREATHTAKING SIGHTS

1,313 FEET: HUNLEN FALLS

Charlotte Lake

This gorgeous 16 km (10 mi) long lake is a jumping-off point for hiking and mountain biking in the surrounding alpine or ATV with a guide on specified trails. Cast a line into its waters for trophy rainbow trout, or explore the trails on horseback. Local guides are available to help you make the most out of your experience.

Kleena Kleene

Kleena Kleene makes a great destination for backcountry adventurers. Try canoeing and fishing in Big Stick Lake, Clearwater Lake or One Eye Lake, or book a guide to take you to moose, bear, mountain goat and wolves. This is an incredible area for accessing high alpine by hiking, ATVing or snowmobiling.

Tatla Lake

Tatla Lake is well known for its miles of groomed cross-country ski trails in winter and its top flight rainbow trout and kokanee fishing and hiking in summer. This is a very active community with a solid volunteer base that loves to put on festivals and events throughout the year, so check out the local calendar.

Bluff/Sapeye Lake

This region is an angler's heaven, with endless fishing lakes, including Horn, Sapeye, Bluff, Middle and Twist, as well as Mosley Creek. In addition to scenic fishing, visitors can go mountaineering, heli-hiking, heli-kayaking, heli-biking, hiking, skiing, mountain biking, horseback riding and wildlife viewing!

Tatlayoko/Chilko

The stunning Tatlayoko Valley encompasses an aquamarine lake bordered by mountain ranges. Visitors can hike, kayak, camp, mountaineer and view wildlife here, with trails cutting into the mountains and through sprawling ice fields. Chilko Lake is the highest and largest freshwater lake in the world, situated just 65 km (40 mi) from Tatla Lake.

Chilanko/Puntzi

Puntzi Lake is ripe with outdoor adventures. Here you will find biking and hiking trails, canoeing and kayaking routes, and great opportunities for fishing and hiking. Anglers pursue kokanee and rainbow trout, and birdwatchers marvel at the American white pelican and trumpeter swan.

MAP

TO LEARN MORE, CONTACT
West Chilcotin Tourism Association
Box 3375 Anahim Lake, BC BC V0L 1R0
Ph: 250-742-3233
Email: info@visitthewestchilcotin.com
www.visitthewestchilcotin.com

From top to bottom: Mt. Waddington - Damian Cromwell; Dean River - John Blackwell; Itcha Ilgatchuz Provincial Park- Miriam Schilling; Hunlen Falls - Lora Vaughan.

THE COAST
BRITISH COLUMBIA

Chilcotin Coast - Geoff Moore

Gurr Lake Trail - Ximena de la Macorra

Chilcotin Coast - Resort BC

The misty coastline of the Chilcotin region of BC casts a dreamy spell over those who explore its lands. With the thriving Pacific Ocean lapping the shore, filled with killer whales, porpoises, humpback whales, seals, sea lions and seabirds, the humid coast hums with life. Within its lush forests, a variety of wild creatures roam, including black-tailed deer, wolves and bears – most notably, the mystical white Spirit Bear, or Kermode. From massive ice fields to succulent rainforests, the Chilcotin Coast is a place of beauty.

Outdoor adventurers come to the coast to pursue a variety of activities. There are endless opportunities here for fishing, hiking, biking, canoeing, kayaking and wildlife viewing. In Tweedsmuir Provincial Park, a vast network of wilderness trails allows users to hike, horseback ride or even go heli-skiing in winter. The Turner Lake Chain offers an unforgettable canoeing experience, and camping spots are aplenty. View the marvelous and colourful Rainbow Range, or hike the historic Alexander Mackenzie grease trail.

In 1793 Alexander Mackenzie paddled into the Dean Channel and so became the first person to cross North America to the Pacific. To this day, his achievement is inscribed on a rock that reads, "Alex Mackenzie, from Canada, by land, 22nd July, 1793." Before his arrival, the Chilcotin Coast was long inhabited by First Nations people. Throughout

the Bella Coola valley you will encounter Nuxalk carvings, masks and paintings.

Anglers cherish the lake and ocean treasures of the region. Along the Rivers Inlet and Knight Inlet reside some of the world's largest chinook. You can

SUPER, NATURAL BRITISH COLUMBIA ♦ CANADA

ply the waters for coho up to 9 kg (20 lbs), halibut to an astounding 91 kg (200 lbs), ling cod reaching 27 kg (60 lbs), and good numbers of steelhead, pink, chum and sockeye. For more world-class fishing, plunge into the waters of Hakai Pass, Milbanke Sound and Shearwater.

With the help of guided tours, visitors can experience the privilege of touring Princess Royal Island, a wild land that is accessible only by boat or air. Kayakers and boaters can get up close and personal with the great grizzly bear, and in the Fiordland Conservancy, explorers can travel through deep, glacially gouged fjords encased by towering sheer granite cliffs.

One of the Chilcotin Coast's main attractions, the Great Bear Rainforest encompasses 3,000,000 hectares (7,413,160 ac), the largest remaining tract of unspoiled temperate rainforest in the world. With so many natural wonders, the Coast invites you to the outdoor adventure of a lifetime!

EXPLORE THE CHILCOTIN COAST
From the centre of Bella Coola at the end of Highway 20, travel west to the coast islands.

WELCOME TO
Bella Coola

GATEWAY TO THE GREAT BEAR RAINFOREST

Few places in the world combine authentic wilderness with comfort and remoteness with accessibility the way the Bella Coola Valley does. The glacier-carved valley of the Bella Coola River winds its way through the mountains to the sea at the head of one of British Columbia's longest fjords, about 450 km (270 mi) northwest of Vancouver.

All who approach the Bella Coola Valley via Highway 20 for the first time experience the driving adventure of a lifetime. At the sub-alpine Heckman Pass (at the top of The Hill), the moist influence of the Pacific is evident, as Highway 20 begins its spectacular descent toward the sea on one of North America's steepest numbered highways. Surrounded by snow-capped mountains, waterfalls, glacial rivers and lush rainforests, you'll find beauty in every direction. Side trips from Highway 20 lead you up into the alpine.

Visit Clayton Falls and take a short walking trail to view gorgeous hard granite formations worn by water, where salmon gather during major spawning runs. East of town lies Snootli Creek Park, where picturesque nature trails wind throughout the ancient cedar groves. Walk the tidal flats and wooded trails of the estuary and the Bella Coola Government Wharf, where you can stroll the waterfront and see the old cannery sites and an array of fishing and pleasure boats.

A number of recreational sites line the valley, as well as campgrounds, small hotels and motels, family-run inns, woodsy cabins and cottages, and B&B's. Anglers will find a lifetime of fishing opportunities in Bella Coola. Throughout the valley's river system are abundant cutthroat trout, rainbow trout, Rocky Mountain whitefish, Dolly Varden and all Pacific salmon species, including chinook and Coho. Be bear aware and cougar aware; here, both abound.

For the ultimate backroad adventure, travel Highway 20 to Bella Coola: BC's only road access to the Central Coast and the heart of the Great Bear Rainforest.

The Valley community of 1,900 or so includes the descendants of the Norwegian-speaking settlers that arrived in 1894, along with a large First Nations community. For a taste of the culture, check out the many art galleries and gift shops featuring works of world-renowned Nuxalk artists and other local painters, sculptors and craftspeople. An absolute must for cultural visitors is the short hike to the petroglyphs at Thorsen Creek. Here you'll discover, hidden in the lush moss and ferns beneath a forest canopy, rock carvings believed to be at least 3,500 years old.

> **For the ultimate backroad adventure, travel Highway 20 to Bella Coola: BC's only road access to the Central Coast and the heart of the Great Bear Rainforest.**

MAP 22

TO LEARN MORE, CONTACT
Bella Coola Valley Tourism/Visitor Info Booth
450 MacKenzie St, Bella Coola, BC V0T 1C0
Ph: 250-982-0092
Email: info@bellacoola.ca
bellacoola.ca

From top to bottom: Gurr Lake Trail - Ximena de la Macorra; Bella Coola River - Michael Wigle; Fyles Glacier - Michael Wigle; Clayton Falls Park - Michael Wigle.

Index
Cariboo Chilcotin Coast BC

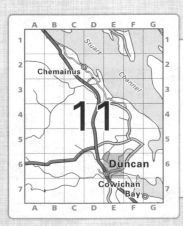

The **Map Index** listings consist of: listing name, page number/coordinates. In the example found on the left, Duncan is found on page 11/E6.

For the **Adventure Index**, the listing also consists of the Reference Page number, where the description of the listing is found. In the example below, the Stuart Channel listing description is found on page 89.

Stuart Channel............11/B1-G4;**89** ➞ Reference Page

Name   **Map Page/Coordinate**

The grid lines found in the example are used for illustration purposes only. The blue grid lines found on the maps refer to UTM coordinates.

Adventure Index

Backroad Adventures

Fishing Adventures

DAM ALONG THE CARIBOO RIVER, BC

SALMON FISHING ALONG THE FRASER RIVER IN THE CARIBOO REGION, BC

BIGHORN SHEEP NEAR THE CHILCOTIN RIVER, BC

Paddling Adventures

Hunting Adventures

Park Adventures

Recsite Adventures

CANIM FALLS IN WELLS GRAY PROVINCIAL PARK, BC

HECKMAN PASS AKA 'THE HILL' NEAR BELLA COOLA (RAINBOW RANGE), BC

Trail Adventures

CHILCOTIN BRIDGE OVER THE FRASER RIVER, BC

MALE SHARP-TAILED GROUSE AT KEITHLEY CREEK, BC

RIVER NEAR NECHAKO CANYON, BC

Map Index

WILD FLOWERS NEAR QUESNEL LAKE, BC

VIEW OF TALTA LAKE NEAR THE CHILCOTIN HIGHWAY, BC

British Columbia / Alberta Distance Chart

	Brooks	Calgary	Campbell River	Camrose	Castlegar	Cold Lake	Courtenay	Cranbrook	Dawson Creek	Drayton Valley	Drumheller	Edmonton	Edson	Fort McLeod	Fort McMurray	Fort Nelson	Fort St. John	Grand Prairie	High Level	Hinton	Hope	Jasper	Kamloops	Kelowna	Lake Louise	Lethbridge	Lloydminster	Medicine Hat	Merritt	Nanaimo	Nelson	Osoyoos	Penticton	Ponoka	Port Alberni	Prince George	Prince Rupert	Red Deer	Revelstoke	Rocky Mtn. House	Salmon Arm	Seattle (Wash.)	Slave Lake	Stettler	Taber	Terrace	Vancouver	Vegreville	Vernon	Victoria	Wainwright	Wetaskawin	Whistler	Whitecourt	Whitehorse	Williams Lake	Yellowknife
Banff	312	128	1004	381	504	695	958	275	962	367	263	401	452	292	840	1422	1035	682	1104	364	697	287	492	474	55	342	626	419	579	855	496	602	542	304	933	661	1385	253	282	259	384	956	652	338	394	1238	847	504	428	885	532	340	967	502	2300	779	1897
Brooks		185	1317	321	817	543	1271	588	1070	471	139	418	612	213	823	1530	1143	874	1154	673	1010	596	805	787	363	162	463	110	892	1168	809	915	855	339	1246	974	1698	302	595	381	697	1269	669	237	110	1551	1160	353	741	1198	368	363	1280	595	2508	1092	1956
Calgary			1132	274	632	588	1086	403	885	306	138	294	447	165	733	1345	958	720	1029	489	825	412	620	602	180	216	519	293	707	983	624	730	670	197	1061	789	1513	145	410	198	512	1084	545	230	267	1366	975	397	556	1013	425	233	1095	441	2323	907	1771
Campbell River				1398	773	1621	46	1002	1346	1441	1285	1312	1133	1305	1766	1751	1339	1485	1976	1046	312	951	512	552	965	1356	1604	1420	428	153	814	553	552	1320	148	940	238	1293	722	1128	620	366	1429	1370	1408	385	172	1432	598	266	1572	1356	253	1236	1637	702	2632
Camrose					906	326	1360	677	687	180	182	97	296	439	521	1147	760	553	832	384	1099	463	894	870	433	453	245	429	981	1257	898	1004	944	77	1335	834	1558	129	684	202	786	1358	348	85	412	1640	1226	136	830	1287	151	41	1369	274	2125	1001	1590
Castlegar						1221	727	229	1377	871	770	927	956	491	1344	1795	1434	1186	1608	780	466	700	453	297	475	542	1151	710	422	624	41	220	280	808	702	975	1699	757	245	763	345	647	1156	842	594	1552	616	1008	338	654	1036	844	736	1006	2614	737	2398
Cold Lake							1560	992	884	431	496	294	488	737	440	1344	957	690	859	576	1299	656	1094	1191	746	686	225	598	1181	1457	1213	1319	1259	398	1535	1031	1755	442	999	513	1101	1558	374	399	634	1608	1449	229	1145	1487	225	362	1569	428	2322	1198	1545
Courtenay								956	1300	1419	1246	1266	1275	1283	1842	1714	1353	1685	2176	1188	266	905	466	506	926	1334	1645	1399	382	107	768	507	506	1298	102	894	284	1247	676	1089	574	320	1571	1348	1386	431	126	1508	552	220	1533	1334	207	1378	1683	656	2531
Cranbrook									1181	642	541	698	727	262	1115	1641	1254	957	1432	584	695	504	606	526	330	313	922	481	651	853	221	449	509	725	931	880	1604	673	396	534	498	757	927	633	365	1457	845	803	509	883	828	636	965	777	2519	893	2169
Dawson Creek										541	869	590	509	1011	879	460	73	127	580	459	1040	677	931	1091	755	1062	828	1109	959	1197	1378	1161	1113	681	1275	406	1130	713	1132	709	1039	1298	445	764	1092	983	1184	683	1048	1227	790	646	1304	406	1438	644	1305
Drayton Valley											331	139	141	471	576	1001	614	414	737	229	1119	309	904	913	357	521	388	578	946	1292	863	969	909	151	1370	676	1400	172	649	108	751	1495	328	234	561	1253	1269	243	795	1338	331	142	1379	135	1979	1146	1423
Drumheller												279	472	292	703	1329	942	735	1014	560	963	547	862	740	315	282	416	247	845	1136	762	868	808	200	1214	927	1651	165	548	244	650	1339	530	97	230	1504	1113	307	694	1182	321	223	1337	456	2307	1045	1700
Edmonton													199	459	439	1050	663	456	735	287	1005	366	800	897	452	509	251	526	887	1163	919	1025	965	104	1241	737	1461	148	705	220	807	1264	251	182	509	1314	1155	105	851	1193	207	68	1275	177	2028	904	1493
Edson														612	629	509	582	382	705	88	811	167	945	769	398	662	446	719	693	984	868	892	837	292	1062	543	1267	313	622	249	714	1187	296	375	702	1120	961	300	723	1030	406	261	1420	103	1947	710	1692
Fort McLeod															898	1508	1121	884	1194	654	983	576	892	777	345	51	656	219	909	1156	483	711	771	362	1234	1462	2186	311	729	363	883	1359	710	395	101	1528	1133	547	823	1202	562	398	1367	605	2449	1070	1936
Fort McMurray																1339	952	752	920	716	1444	796	1438	1336	891	948	587	931	1326	1617	1358	1464	1404	543	1695	1176	1900	587	1144	658	1246	1820	436	605	914	1753	1594	492	1290	1663	587	507	1913	533	2317	1343	1684
Fort Nelson																	387	587	1040	1217	1454	1137	1345	1505	1370	1559	1301	1569	1373	1611	1799	1575	1527	1141	1689	820	1513	1198	1555	1109	1453	1712	905	1224	1552	1366	1598	1143	1462	1641	1250	1106	1718	866	978	1058	935
Fort St. John																		200	653	830	1093	750	964	1144	983	1172	914	1182	1012	1250	1438	1214	1166	754	1328	459	1183	811	1194	722	1092	1351	518	837	1165	1306	1237	756	1101	1280	863	719	1357	479	1365	697	1378
Grand Prairie																			453	332	1163	397	1175	1179	628	935	701	982	923	1336	1098	1122	1067	554	1414	533	1257	586	852	522	944	1539	318	637	965	1110	1313	556	953	1382	663	519	1650	279	1565	771	1178
High Level																				785	1654	850	1627	1670	1080	1244	980	1261	1376	1827	1600	1578	1530	839	1905	986	1710	883	1386	845	1488	2030	489	917	1244	1663	1804	835	1532	1873	942	803	2102	602	2018	1224	686
Hinton																					724	80	519	682	313	703	533	780	606	882	781	805	750	391	960	456	1180	401	535	337	627	983	384	502	502	1033	874	388	636	912	493	349	994	191	2095	623	1780
Hope																						644	205	245	643	1034	1282	1098	121	163	507	246	245	998	241	634	1358	947	415	806	313	259	1107	1048	1086	1211	150	1110	291	188	1250	1034	270	914	2273	396	2256
Jasper																							439	602	233	626	613	703	526	802	701	725	670	455	880	376	1100	413	455	332	547	903	464	507	678	953	794	468	556	832	573	429	914	271	2015	543	1591
Kamloops																								163	547	834	1118	911	87	363	454	286	231	796	441	525	1249	745	210	751	108	464	1144	830	886	1102	355	996	117	393	1024	832	475	994	2164	287	2058
Kelowna																									420	828	1139	893	132	403	338	128	68	792	481	685	1409	741	192	583	106	504	1065	842	880	1262	391	1002	46	433	1027	828	515	872	2324	447	2225
Lake Louise																										394	678	471	527	816	476	550	490	355	894	609	1333	304	227	256	332	1019	685	405	447	1186	793	556	376	862	583	537	1022	492	2193	727	1945
Lethbridge																											605	168	960	1207	534	762	822	412	1285	1513	2237	360	780	413	934	1410	760	379	52	1579	1184	496	874	1253	511	594	1309	656	2500	1121	2000
Lloydminster																												480	1226	1455	1143	1249	1189	322	1533	988	1712	374	929	447	1031	1658	496	318	553	1565	1432	148	1075	1501	106	330	1593	422	2266	1155	1746
Medicine Hat																													1132	1279	702	930	990	447	1349	1079	1803	409	701	488	803	1474	777	334	116	1656	1248	461	847	1317	377	611	1386	703	2547	1198	2058
Merritt																														279	463	202	154	883	357	553	1277	832	297	838	195	380	990	933	1012	1130	271	992	178	309	1111	1065	391	797	2192	315	2145
Nanaimo																															665	404	403	1171	82	791	391	1120	573	979	471	217	1280	1221	1259	538	23	1283	449	113	1423	1207	104	1087	1790	553	2475
Nelson																																261	321	800	743	979	1703	749	246	755	346	688	1165	850	586	1556	657	1024	339	695	1028	982	777	972	2618	741	2390
Osoyoos																																	60	906	482	755	1479	855	320	861	234	440	1254	956	814	1332	396	1130	174	434	1134	1088	516	996	2394	517	2618
Penticton																																		846	481	707	1431	795	260	801	174	500	1194	896	874	1284	395	1070	114	433	1074	1028	515	941	2346	469	2306
Ponoka																																			1249	831	1555	51	586	125	688	1374	355	152	464	1408	1148	208	732	1217	228	189	1271	276	2119	998	1597
Port Alberni																																				869	386	1198	651	666	549	295	1358	1299	1337	533	101	1361	527	195	1501	1285	182	1165	1785	631	2506
Prince George																																					724	789	735	708	633	892	840	883	1565	577	778	842	642	821	944	805	896	647	1639	238	1623
Prince Rupert																																						1513	1459	1137	1357	1616	1712	1643	2289	147	1502	1566	1366	504	1668	1529	1622	1371	1399	962	2357
Red Deer																																							535	81	637	1323	399	101	393	1366	1097	252	681	1166	279	233	1220	307	2151	1032	1628
Revelstoke																																								541	102	674	934	620	676	1312	565	810	146	603	814	768	685	726	2374	497	2179
Rocky Mtn. House																																									643	1182	436	175	465	1285	956	323	687	1025	353	304	1226	243	2087	1038	1709
Salmon Arm																																										572	1036	742	986	1210	463	912	60	501	916	870	583	818	2272	395	2281
Seattle (Wash.)																																											1483	1424	1462	1469	226	1486	550	247	1626	1410	349	1290	2531	654	2631
Slave Lake																																												432	760	1417	1257	351	1080	1326	458	166	1619	193	1883	1007	1496
Stettler																																													347	1460	1198	209	766	1267	224	266	1305	359	2202	1050	1729
Taber																																														2142	1236	444	926	1305	459	594	1361	686	2530	1173	2052
Terrace																																															1355	1419	1219	651	1521	1382	1475	1224	1252	815	2200
Vancouver																																																1260	441	69	1400	1184	123	1064	2417	540	2405
Vegreville																																																	956	1329	130	171	1471	277	2121	1009	1598
Vernon																																																		479	950	914	561	827	2281	404	2175
Victoria																																																			1469	1253	192	1133	1903	583	2595
Wainwright																																																				192	1499	384	2228	1204	1700
Wetaskawin																																																					1307	240	2084	1140	1561
Whistler																																																						1469	2537	660	2529
Whitecourt																																																							1844	667	1316
Whitehorse																																																								1877	2685
Williams Lake																																																									1861

How to use this Distance Chart

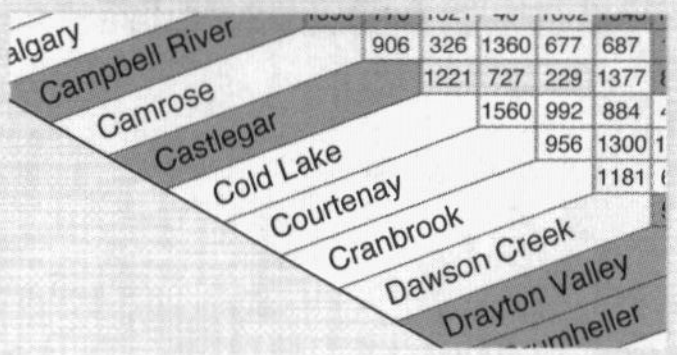

The distance from Camrose to Dawson Creek is 687 Kilometres

Speed Conversion Chart

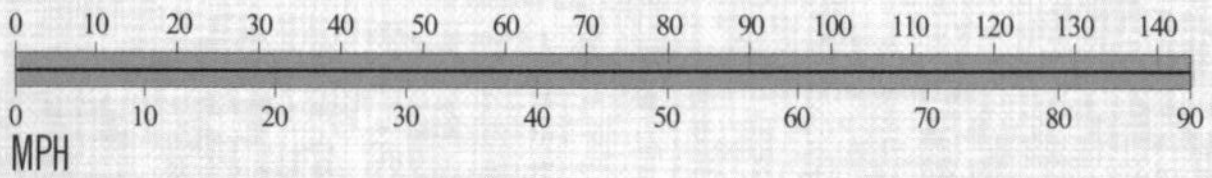

1 Kilometre = 0.621 Mile

1 Mile = 1.6 Kilometres

ADVERTISER LIST

INSIDE COVER

FRONT SOUTH CARIBOO
TOURISM
100 Mile House, B.C.
877-511-5353
www.southcaribootourism.ca

148 ATVBC
1-866-766-7823
www.atvbc.ca

64 BARNEY'S LAKESIDE
RESORT
Puntzi Lake, B.C.
250-481-1100

IV BC FOREST
SAFETY COUNCIL
1-877-741-1060
www.bcforestsafe.org

114 BC PARKS
www.bcparks.com

65 BIG RIVER COUNTRY
TOURISM
www.bigrivercountry.ca

61 CAMPING & RVING
BC COALITION
www.rvcampingbc.com

64 CARIBOO COUNTRY
INN & RANCH
250-620-3434
www.cariboocountryinn.com

62 CHAUNIGAN LAKE LODGE
Nemaiah Valley, BC
250-394-7077
www.chaunigan.com

66 CHILCOTIN GUNS
Williams Lake, BC
250-392-6800

62 CHILCOTIN HOLIDAYS
Gold Bridge, BC
250-238-2274
www.chilcotinholidays.com

66 DELUXE WALL TENTS
Sidney, B.C.
250-704-2534
www.deluxewalltents.com

74 DONEX PHARMACY
100 Mile House, BC
250-395-4004

64 EAGAN LAKE RESORT
Bridge Lake, BC
250-593-4343
www.eaganlake.com

64 ELYSIA RESORT
Quesnel Lake, BC
250-243-2433
www.elysiaresort.com

64 ESCOTT BAY RESORT
Anahim Lake, BC
250-742-3233
www.escottbay.com

66 EXTER SPORTING GOODS
100 Mile House, BC
250-395-4626

64 FAWN LAKE RESORT
Lone Butte, BC
250-593-4654
www.fawnlakeresort.com

65 FISHING HIGHWAY
LAKES MARKETS
Bridge Lake, BC
250-590-2242
250-593-4616

65 FRANK'S
SUPERMARKET
Quesnel, BC
250-747-2092

70 GOLD COUNTRY
Cache Creek, BC
1-877-453-9467
www.exploregoldcountry.com

63 HI-HIUM LAKE
FISHING RESORT
Cache Creek, BC
250-459-2306
www.hihiumlake.ca

67 HORSE COUNCIL BC
800-345-8055
www.hcbc.ca

66 HORSEFLY HARDWARE
Horsefly, BC
250-620-3338

66 JACK O CLUBS
GENERAL STORE
Barkerville, BC
250-994-3242

63 KOKANEE BAY FISHING
RESORT
Chilanko Forks, BC
250-481-1130
kokaneebayfishingresort.ca

62 LITTLEFORT FLY
& TACKLE
Little Fort, BC
250-677-4366
www.littlefort.com

100 LONE BUTTE
SPORTING GOODS
Lone Butte, BC
250-395-2217
www.lbsportinggoods.com

64 LOON BAY RESORT
Sheridan Lake, BC
250-593-4431
www.loonbayresort.com

64 NIMPO LAKE RESORT
Nimpo Lake, BC
250-742-3239
www.nimpolakeresort.com

122 RECREATION SITES
& TRAILS BC
www.sitesandtrailsbc.ca

63 SHERIDAN LAKE RESORT
Sheridan Lake, BC
250-593-4611
www.sheridanlakeresort.com

63 SHERIDAN PARK RESORT
Lone Butte, B.C.
250-593-4663
www.sheridanlake.com

65 SURPLUS HERBY'S
Williams Lake, B.C.
1-800-661-5188
www.surplusherbys.com

X VALHALLA PURE
Smithers, B.C.
250-847-0200
www.valhallasmithers.com
www.vpo.ca

66 WILLIS HARPER
HARDWARE
Quesnel, BC
250-992-2135

66 XWISTEN EXPERIENCE
TOURS
Lillooet, BC
250-256-7844
www.xwisten.ca

IMPORTANT NUMBERS

Avalanche Conditions .... www.avalanche.ca
.... 1-800-667-1105
BC Ferries .... www.bcferries.com
.... 1-888-223-3779
Highways Report................................www.drivebc.ca
.... 1-800-550-4997
Tourism BC .... www.hellobc.com
.... 1-800-435-5622
Updates................... www.backroadmapbooks.com
Weather Conditions............. www.weatheroffice.ec.gc.ca
Wildfire Information Line.................... 1-888-336-7378
To Report Forest Fires (Emergency Only)1-800-663-5555
.... *5555 (cellular phones)

B.C. FOREST SERVICES

Ministry of Forests ....www.gov.bc.ca/for
Northern Interior Forest Region ...... www.for.gov.bc.ca/rsi
.... 250-565-6100
Southern Interior Forest Region ....
.... http://www.for.gov.bc.ca/rsi
.... 250-828-4131

Fish and Wildlife

BC Fishing Regs ..www.env.gov.bc.ca/fw/fish/regulations
BC Hunting Regulations ....
..............www.env.gov.bc.ca/fw/wildlife/hunting/regulations
BC Wildlife Federation......................... www.bcwf.bc.ca
Freshwater Fisheries Society of BC .... www.gofishbc.com
Observe, Record and Report .... www.RAPP.bc.ca
.... 1-877-952-7277 or *7277
Salmon and Steelhead Regulations ....
.... www.pac.dfo-mpo.gc.ca

PARKS & RECREATION SITES

BC Parks...www.bcparks.ca
BC Recreation Sites & Trails.......www.sitesandtrailsbc.ca
Park Reservations................... www.discovercamping.ca
.... 1-800-689-9025

CLUBS & ASSOCIATIONS

ATV BC ....www.atvbc.ca
BC Fishing Resorts & Outfitters Assoc...... www.bcfroa.ca
BC Lodging & Campground Assoc. ....
.... www.travel-british-columbia.com
BC Snowmobile Federation .... www.bcsf.org
Camping & RV BC Coalition......... www.rvcampingbc.com
Canoe Kayak BC .... www.canoekayakbc.ca
Horse Council BC................................www.hcbc.ca
Trails BC ....www.trailsbc.ca

WILD & FREE

Photo Contest
Win up to $10,000
in cash & prizes

For complete contest rules & Details

visit BackroadMapbooks.com/contests

#BRMBphoto

f / backroadmapbooks

▸ @backroadmapbook

g+ /+Backroadmapbooks

◻ / backroadmapbooks

Backroad Mapbooks

For a complete list of our products

 Backroad Mapbooks

 GPS Maps

 Fishing Maps

 BRMB Navigator

 Waterproof Maps

 TOPO Maps

 Digital Maps

BRMB
backroadmapbooks.com

visit us at backroadmapbooks.com